Freedom's war

MANCHESTER
UNIVERSITY PRESS

Freedom's war

The US crusade
against the Soviet Union
1945–56

SCOTT LUCAS

SHEFFIELD HALLAM UNIVERSITY
LEARNING CENTRE
WITHDRAWN FROM STOCK

MANCHESTER UNIVERSITY PRESS

Copyright © Scott Lucas 1999

The right of Scott Lucas to be identified as the author of this work has been asserted by him
in accordance with the Copyright, Designs and Patents Act 1988.

Published by Manchester University Press
Oxford Road, Manchester M13 9NR, UK
http://www.man.ac.uk/mup

British Library Cataloguing-in-Publication Data
A catalogue record for this book is available from the British Library

ISBN 0 7190 5694 2 *hardback*

First published 1999
06 05 04 03 02 01 00 99   10 9 8 7 6 5 4 3 2 1

SHEFFIELD HALLAM UNIVERSITY
DA
327.73047
LU
COLLEGIATE CRESCENT

Typeset in Sabon with Syntax
by Best-set Typesetter Ltd., Hong Kong
Printed in Great Britain
by Bookcraft (Bath) Ltd, Midsomer Norton

To Helen

Contents

Acknowledgements

During the seven years I have worked on this project, I have benefited from the advice of many colleagues in Britain and the United States on a wide range of topics. I thank all of them for putting up with my twists and turns as I tried to come to grips with questions I had never foreseen when I started the research. For academic support, I am especially grateful to two professors at the University of Birmingham for the faith they showed in an enthusiastic if naïve staff member: John Grenville of the Department of Modern History and Richard Simmons of the Department of American and Canadian Studies. For financial support, I thank the Charles Warren Center at Harvard University for a year's fellowship which set the direction for this project and the British Academy and the University of Birmingham for backing of further research in the United States. Most importantly, for emotional support in the final stages, I thank (among others) Adrian, Liam, Maria, Al, Francesca, Aengus, Solange, Graeme, and the Laville, Lucas, and Abrahams clans. Hugh Wilford kindly looked over parts of the manuscript at the last minute to give me important feedback. I dedicate the book, as a small token of feeling, to Helen Laville. When I was ready to stop, she kept me going. If there is any value in this work, it is due as much to her spirit as to my ability. And to Ryan, who has brought unlimited happiness, I offer this (once he moves beyond *Thomas the Tank Engine* and *Mr Funny*) as a small contribution to my own history.

Abbreviations

ACCF	American Committee for Cultural Freedom
ACLPR, AmComLib	American Committee for the Liberation of the Peoples of Russia
ACUE	American Committee for a United Europe
AFL–CIO	American Federation of Labor and Congress of Industrial Organizations
CARE	Cooperative for American Relief
CCF	Congress for Cultural Freedom
CFA	Committee for Free Asia
CIA	Central Intelligence Agency (1947–present)
CPD	Committee on the Present Danger
ECA	Economic Cooperation Adminstration (1948–52)
ERP	European Recovery Program
FBI	Federal Bureau of Investigation
FEC	Free Europe Committee
FFRF	Friends of Fighters for Russian Freedom
MIT	Massachusetts Institute of Technology
MSA	Mutual Security Administration
NAACP	National Association for the Advancement of Colored People
NATO	North Atlantic Treaty Organization
NCASP	National Committee for the Arts, Sciences and Professions
NCFE	National Committee for a Free Europe
NSA	National Student Association
NSC	National Security Council (1947–present)
OCB	Operations Coordinating Board (1953–61)
OPC	Office of Policy Coordination (1948–52)
OSS	Office of Strategic Services (1942–45)
OWI	Office of War Information
POCC	Psychological Operations Coordinating Committee

PPS	State Department Policy Planning Staff (1947–present)
PSB	Psychological Strategy Board (1951–53)
PWB	Psychological Warfare Board
RFE	Radio Free Europe
RIAS	Radio in the American Sector
SPG	Special Procedures Group
USIA	United States Information Agency (1953–present)
UVO	Organization of Ukrainian Nationalists
WIN	Wolnosc i Niepodlenosc (Freedom and Independence)

INTRODUCTION

"History" and the American way

Several years ago, I set out to research and write a history of official US propaganda in the Cold War. My conception was that "propaganda" had a significant but supporting role in US foreign policy, reinforcing the more tangible instruments of diplomacy, economic activity, and military strength. I would not challenge the main currents in US diplomatic history, merely make a small contribution to them.

I reconsidered not only because of what I perceived in the 1940s and 1950s but because of what I saw in the present day. In 1989 it was the early-morning announcement of Press Secretary Marlon Fitzwater, shaking me from jet-lagged stupor, that US troops had entered Panama to liberate the country from the grip of the military dictatorship of the drug-dealing Manuel Noriega. Two years later, at the end of my Christmas holiday, it was the live coverage of the first US bombardment of Baghdad, with CNN's John Holliman breathless over its beauty, comparing it to fireworks on 4 July. (The following evening, the mood was less glorious as I watched the black comedy of a panicked CNN correspondent in gas mask in his office in Israel, waiting for the retaliation of Iraq's Scud missiles; the poor man never appeared on-screen again.) And two years after that, it was the klieg-lit charge of the first US forces on to Somali beaches to restore democracy in that now forgotten country.

The paranoia that my transatlantic crossings were somehow the catalysts for wars and interventions was intense but short-lived; the conclusion that, although the Cold War was stumbling towards US victory, the United States was pronouncing sentence upon new enemies to be vanquished was longer-lasting. So was my perception that, whatever the diplomatic, economic, or strategic dimensions of these conflicts, the US Government, through its statements to the public, was also waging a cultural battle to establish that the US "way of life" was superior to that of its opponents. At the heart of this battle was the promotion of US guardianship of "freedom" and "democracy".

The United States, just like the Soviet system with which it contended for so long, has an "ideology". It may not be as rigidly presented as Marxism–Leninism, Maoism, Islamic fundamentalism, or earlier foes like National Socialism; however, it still serves to justify and, to some extent, to

organize political, economic, and cultural activity. However calculated the
geopolitical strategy, however base the pursuit of profit and economic control,
US foreign policy has to be perceived as "right", at home and abroad.

It was this conception that led me to a different approach to "History". I
believe the Cold War was presented, first and foremost, as a clash of cultures
and ideologies. The opening passages of NSC 68, the US blueprint of 1950
for a global offensive against Soviet Communism, starkly defined the conflict:

> The idea of freedom is the most contagious idea in history, more contagious than
> the idea of submission to authority. For the breadth of freedom cannot be tolerated
> in a society which has come under the domination of an individual or group of indi-
> viduals with a will to absolute power. Where the despot holds absolute power – the
> absolute power of the absolutely powerful will – all other wills must be subjugated
> in an act of willing submission, a degradation willed by the individual upon himself
> under the compulsion of a perverted faith.[1]

I do not think that this presentation of US ideology has been simply a "screen"
for geopolitical and economic objectives. Desert Shield may have begun as an
operation to protect Middle Eastern oil supplies but Desert Storm was
whipped up by the sentiment that Kuwait had to be "liberated" from Iraqi
oppression and that Saddam Hussein was a menace to the "Free World". The
Cold War may have had its prologue in debates over the status of Germany,
the destination of Iranian oil, and the future of the Straits of the Dardanelles,
but it turned global only when the Truman Doctrine declared the universal
responsibility of the United States "to support free peoples who are resisting
attempting subjugation by armed minorities or by outside pressures".[2]

Nor do I believe that the Government imposed this conception upon an
unwilling or passive public, leading them into a half-century of conflict with
the Communist bloc. The battle against Soviet Communism was not the exclusive domain, as most histories portray, of politicians, diplomats, and generals.
It was waged at the front by covert operators and, more significantly, by
private groups working with them. The most prominent organization was the
National Committee for Free Europe, with a radio system reaching millions,
a university, research centers, and tons of pamphlets and balloons to carry
them into forbidden territory, but it was only one of many. The American
Committee for the Liberation of the Peoples of Russia, the Committee for Free
Asia, the International Rescue Committee, Harvard's Russian Research Center,
MIT's Center for International Studies, American Friends of Russian Freedom,
and many others played their part in the offensive.

A State–private network had been established. The CIA might be providing most of the finance but the impetus was coming from individuals with no
Government position, individuals with their own interests in ensuring the
triumph of freedom. This private involvement is even more striking when one
discovers that the bulk of operations were not concerned with political agita-

tion and paramilitary operations in Eastern Europe but with cultural and social activity elsewhere. By 1953 thousands of dedicated Americans, wittingly or unwittingly, would be involved in labor unions, student groups, women's organizations, professional bodies, academic institutions, and other bodies supported by the Government to safeguard the Free World.

Once one acknowledges this network, the notion of an "ideological" foreign policy is reinforced, for it was the nature of American ideology that demanded a private facade. "Freedom" meant that the US Government, unlike its evil Soviet counterpart, did not direct labor activity or academic research or journalistic endeavors; it was all the product of individuals freely making their own decisions and pursuing their own objectives. The illusion of a spontaneous effort independent of the State would be initiated in 1948, when the State Department's Llewellyn Thompson, considering the formation of the National Committee for Free Europe, established that it would be a "serious error" for the State to sponsor such efforts overtly. It was highlighted by the call of a 1953 presidential committee for "far greater effort . . . to utilize private American organizations for the advancement of US objectives".[3]

I am not seeking, through the emphasis on this projection of "freedom", to argue that ideology was dominant in the development of US foreign policy. Instead it interacted with other considerations to define the American approach. Doing so, it led to both policy and operations that cannot be explained on geopolitical, economic, or military grounds. In particular the rhetorical quest for universal freedom was translated into the pursuit of the "liberation" of Eastern Europe (and, to a degree, China) from Communism. The policy may have been muddled and beset by indecision – the ideological goal confronted other "practical" considerations dictating a more cautious approach – but, between 1948 and 1956, it was sustained by the evolving State–private network.

I hope that this conception of the Cold War will stimulate new considerations of the conflict. I do not aspire to judge US foreign policy as "right" or "wrong", labelling Presidents and advisors as "wise men" or "foolish men".[4] I have strong opinions on the matter, hints of which will no doubt emerge in my narrative, but I believe an objective answer to the question to be impossible. My challenge instead is to the mainstream of US diplomatic history which, through academic sleight-of-hand, has set itself up as the arbiter of the issue.

For many US historians, it wasn't enough to claim diplomatic and economic victory. Moral supremacy had to be claimed by closing off the historical tale, by establishing that "we" had been right all along. Through the facade of "national security", these historians have attempted to reduce the Cold War to a struggle in which the United States pragmatically defended itself and the Free World against the Soviet menace. A US ideology is given token acknowledgement but then is set aside; to address it would undermine the national security thesis, which holds that the real threat comes from the expansionism of Soviet ideology.[5]

In the national security school, there is little place for actors outside the elite of Presidents, diplomats, and generals. The notion of the Cold War as cultural conflict may be implicit in the historians' own statement but it is rarely identified explicitly. Thus the move of the US Government to implement foreign policy through the mechanism of "psychological strategy" to win the hearts and minds of people at home and abroad is never appreciated. Both the CIA's covert operations to influence overseas opinion and the development of the State–private network are blissfully ignored.

As a result there are glaring gaps, even in the national security school's chosen ground of study. US efforts at "liberation" may be cited but they are quickly pushed aside or misinterpreted. The Hungarian revolution of 1956 does get a look-in but one searches in vain for references to the US intervention in Poland and the Baltic States, to the American role in the East German uprising of 1953, or to the protracted operations to undermine the Czech and Hungarian Governments between 1952 and 1954.

This selective treatment is far from surprising. The promotion of national security in 1990s historiography fits neatly into the ideological pattern of the 1950s. It is a pattern which ironically denies the existence of a US ideology (apart from McCarthyite or Communist extremists), for ideology was an evil associated with the excesses of Nazi Germany, Fascist Italy, and the Soviet Union. The 1997 declamation of John Gaddis, one of the gatekeepers of national security, *We Now Know*, is a historian's reprise of the triumph of democracy found in Daniel Bell's *The End of Ideology* in the 1950s and in Francis Fukuyama's *The End of History and the Last Man* in the 1980s. Our side is realistic, pragmatic, and benevolent; their side, because of the nature of the system and/or the evil or insanity of its leaders, is irrational, power-hungry, and inhumane.[6]

There have been many histories of the Cold War. There will no doubt be many more, if only because of the current obsession with uncovering unpublished material in the archives of former members of the Communist bloc. Stacks of documents, however, will not complete the tale. It is not necessarily a case of "we have met the enemy and he is us", but it is one of a total conflict in which the involvement of Government agencies and private groups must be redefined. Both in the pervasiveness of a US ideology which reduced the clash to one of freedom vs. tyranny and the pervasiveness of a State–private network which rewarded participation and punished dissent, the Cold War reshaped not only US foreign policy but also the culture that helped produce that policy.

For US ideology, mobilized to fight the Cold War, did not retreat into silence with the end of the conflict. The State–private network, while damaged by Vietnam and revelations in 1967 of CIA involvement, is still in existence, embodied both in high-profile initiatives like the National Endowment for

Democracy of the 1980s and in the day-to-day operations of pressure groups, think tanks, and research projects. The rationale of American superiority is invoked for the New World Order and for whatever crisis – from the recurrent showdowns with Iraq to the quest for Middle Eastern peace to the ongoing battle with Castro's Cuba – that demands its presence. As President Bill Clinton, publicly calling for the overthrow of the Government of Iraq, stated on 15 November 1998: "In the century we are leaving America has often made the difference between tyranny and freedom, between chaos and community, between fear and hope."[7]

Notes

1 State Department/Department of Defense report, 7 April 1950, US DDRS, Retrospective 71D
2 The doctrine, and material relating to it, can be found in the Truman Presidential Library's web project http://www.whistlestop.org/study_collections/large/doctrine.html
3 E. P. Thompson, *Beyond the Cold War* (London, 1982); Lay memorandum, 1 October 1953, US DDRS, 1990 2796
4 See the conclusion to Melvyn Leffler, *A Preponderance of Power: National Security, the Truman Administration, and the Cold War* (Stanford, CA, 1992)
5 Perhaps the most surreal moment in the quest to close off the historical debate came in 1994 when Gaddis clashed with Bruce Cumings, who had waged a spirited attack upon Gaddis and the neo-orthodoxy of the national security consensus in an article in *Diplomatic History*. At the opening plenary of the conference of the Society for Historians of American Foreign Relations, Gaddis challenged Cumings's criticism, using theorists such as Friedrich Nietzsche and Martin Heidegger, of the language of "post-revisionism" in work such as Arthur Schlesinger's with the memorable declaration, "I'd rather hang out with Schlesinger and his buddies than Heidegger and his buddies!" The reduction of the discussion to a comparison between "American" values and those of National Socialism reinforced my notion of the power of ideology not only in the Cold War but in historians' approaches towards the era. (Plenary session at the annual conference of the Society for Historians of American Foreign Relations, Waltham, Massachusetts, June 1994)
6 John Louis Gaddis, *We Now Know: Rethinking Cold War History* (Oxford, 1997). See the forthcoming critique by Scott Lucas, "Appealing the Verdict of Cold War 'History'," *Over Here: Reviews in American Studies*, 1999
7 A copy of Clinton's address is at the website http://www.pub.whitehouse.gov

1

The turning point

In the days before 12 March 1947, Washington had been abuzz with rumors about the speech that President Harry Truman would make to a joint session of Congress that evening. Despite the supposed secrecy of US deliberations, it was widely known that the British embassy had notified the State Department that Britain could no longer provide economic and military aid to Greece and Turkey. The choice for the Americans was stark: let the two countries, vital to the security of the Mediterranean, face internal and external pressures on their own or fill the financial breach.

It was soon clear that the issue was not whether the United States would take up the provision of aid. Given the perception of the strategic necessity of Greece and Turkey in the Western containment of Soviet Communism, there was no alternative. The question was whether the President would go even further. The *New York Times*, intoning that the "course of history [was] held in [the] balance", reported, "[Truman] is expected to contend that the overthrow of freely elected governments by disruptive attacks from within or without any country may foment civil wars which could grow into international conflicts tending to involve the United States."[1]

Truman's wife Bess, "dressed in black with a brown fur neckpiece,... looked solemn and watched the President intently throughout his talk".[2] In the tense atmosphere, Truman spoke slowly and deliberately. The *Washington Post* noted, "He was asking America to be Atlas, offering to lead his country in that tremendous role, yet his flat voice carried no significance of his fateful recommendation."[3] It gradually became clear, however, that Truman's request for aid of $300 million for Greece and $100 million for Turkey was only the prelude to a story of suspense and horror, of entire countries and peoples on the verge of enslavement from a vague but ever-present evil. Only 18 months after the end of World War II, America again had to don the mantle of savior of the Free World:

At the present moment in world history nearly every nation must choose between alternative ways of life. The choice is too often not a free one.

One way of life is based upon the will of the majority, and is distinguished by free institutions, representative government, free elections, guarantees of individual liberty, freedom of speech and religion and freedom from political oppression.

The second way of life is based upon the will of a minority forcibly imposed upon the majority. It relies upon terror and oppression, a controlled press and radio, fixed elections, and the suppression of personal freedoms.

I believe it must be the policy of the United States to support free peoples who are resisting attempted subjugation by armed minorities or by outside pressures.[4]

In less than 20 minutes, Truman had established the Cold War not as a clash of military forces or a struggle for economic supremacy but as a contest of values. The Soviet ideology of Marxism–Leninism, never specifically identified but lurking behind Truman's warnings of coercion and political infiltration, was to be confronted by an American ideology, less systematic in its development but dedicated to the defense of "freedom" and "democracy". To promote this ideology, the United States could no longer rely upon an objective presentation of its people and institutions. Instead, every aspect of American life from religion to sport to the wonders of consumerism had to become a beacon to the world while Soviet counterparts were exposed as the perversions of a system which impoverished and enslaved its citizens.

Why had the President chosen this moment to issue the call to arms? After all, tension between the United States and the Soviet Union did not suddenly emerge in 1947. Washington and Moscow might have joined forces from 1941 to 1945 against the common enemy of Nazi Germany but disputes over the post-war settlement emerged long before the conquest of Berlin. Greece and Turkey had been among the potential points of conflict. Civil war had broken out in Greece in 1944 and the question of Soviet passage from the Black Sea to the Mediterranean through Turkey's Dardanelles Straits had been disputed throughout 1945 and 1946.

The simple answer is that Truman's sweeping rhetoric was designed to win over a Congress skeptical of large-scale disbursement of foreign aid. The Republican Party, which had won a majority in both the House of Representatives and the Senate in 1946, was balanced between isolationists and internationalists; there were also conservative Democrats who objected to additional expenditure, particularly when emphasis had been placed on demobilization and a reduced military budget. Truman also had to contend with Congressmen who objected to the United States bypassing the United Nations and those who opposed any showdown with the Soviet Union.

The nettle was grasped on 27 February during a briefing of Democratic and Republican Congressional leaders by Secretary of State George Marshall. Marshall fared badly, as he "most unusually, flubbed his opening statement".[5] When the skeptical Congressmen asked if the United States was merely "pulling British chestnuts out of the fire", Marshall's deputy, Dean Acheson, asked his boss, "Is this a private fight or can anyone get into it?"[6] He saved the day with a far different approach, telling the legislators:

We had arrived at a situation unparalleled since ancient times. Not since Rome and Carthage had there been such a polarization of power on this earth. Moreover the two great powers were divided by an unbridgeable ideological chasm. For us, democracy and individual liberty were basic; for them, dictatorship and absolute conformity.

In an early version of the domino theory, he insisted, "Like apples in a barrel infected one by rotten one, the corruption of Greece would infect Iran and all to the east. It would also carry infection to Africa through Asia Minor and Egypt, and to Europe through Italy and France."[7] His casting of the situation as the ultimate battle of ideologies so impressed the Republican leader in the Senate, Arthur Vandenberg, that he advised Truman "to make a personal appearance before Congress and scare hell out of the country".[8]

Truman's speech changed accordingly under the supervision of the President's special counsel Clark Clifford, who later claimed that the original State Department draft "was too weak. It didn't do the job." What had sounded like an "investment prospectus" became an alert to the US public, as the Communist threat was elevated to a global menace.[9] Building upon inside information, the *New York Times* summarized:

> Now our sheltered existence is over, and face to face with the realities of the world we discover that it takes more than the will of one nation to abolish power politics and that as long as power politics prevails the positions evacuated by one Power will not remain power vacuums but are likely to be taken over by another Power. . . . The epoch of isolation and occasional intervention is ended.[10]

Clifford noted, "There may have been some instances in which I perhaps wanted to go farther than the State Department wanted to go," but any concerns were met with the rationale that the Senate's approval would not be won "without the emphasis on the Communist danger".[11] Only George Elsey, a speechwriter and aide to Truman, warned of the radical effect of a "global" statement: "The public is not prepared. . . . An 'All-out speech' will have a divisive effect effect if delivered soon." Elsey also noted that the speech would sabotage any hope of a negotiated settlement with the Soviets, since its delivery as the Moscow Conference of Foreign Ministers opened could "destroy that Conference which gives promise of producing an acceptable Treaty of Peace for Austria, if not for Germany".[12]

Elsey's doubts came far too late to have any effect, and he helped Clifford proceed with "the opening gun in a campaign to bring people up to [the] realization that the war isn't over by any means".[13] If much of Truman's speech mirrored Marshall's review of the situation, the centerpiece was the call to resist the Communists at any time at any place in the world. The President concluded, "We shall not realize our objectives, however, unless we are willing to help free peoples to maintain their free institutions and their national

integrity against aggressive movements that seek to impose upon them totalitarian regimes."[14]

Yet it is hard to conceive of the construction of the Truman Doctrine merely
as a reaction to the domestic political situation, as historians such as John
Gaddis have maintained. The question of Congressional approval was a
significant catalyst, but it was not the creator of the ideological vision in the
doctrine. Clark Clifford summarized, "[President Truman] saw it just as clearly
as you can see black and white. There were good men and there proved to be
bad men, and by God, he was going to see to it that the men in the white hats
prevailed and the men in the black hats did not prevail."[15]

The global conception came from other quarters as well. As the Truman
Doctrine was being prepared, the Secretaries of State, War, and Navy agreed
that Greece and Turkey were "only part of a critical world situation confronting [the United States] today in many democratic countries" and must be
treated "as a whole". Five days before the speech, Truman told the Cabinet
that Greece was only the beginning of an intervention which required the
"greatest selling job ever facing a President".[16] Secretary of the Navy James
Forrestal summarized, "We should have to recognize [this] as a fundamental
struggle between our kind of society and the Russians."[17]

Having portrayed the situation so dramatically, the Truman Administration
could not just withdraw the challenge after passage of the aid package. The
United States was now committed to safeguarding a "Free World" with whatever economic, diplomatic, and military steps might be necessary. There was
also an unspoken but pressing question. Since it had declared its mission to
help free peoples to maintain their free institutions, shouldn't Washington
pursue that mission in Eastern Europe as well as Western Europe, in China as
well as Japan? Louis Halle, a State Department official, later wrote, "The
immediate danger was in Europe, not in the Pacific or South Asia or Africa.
It was the situation in Europe that called for containment. Nevertheless . . .
taken literally, [the Truman Doctrine] covered the whole globe. . . . So taken,
it imposed an unlimited commitment on the United States, a commitment that
might extend it far beyond its resources."[18]

Notes

1 Harold Hinton, "Plea to Congress," *New York Times*, 11 March 1947
2 "Mrs. Truman Was There, Too," *PM*, 13 March 1947
3 "President's Delivery," *Washington Post*, 13 March 1947
4 Joseph Jones, *The Fifteen Weeks* (New York, 1955), 141–2; Vandenberg quoted in Lynn Boyd
  Hinds and Otto Windt, *The Cold War as Rhetoric: The Beginnings, 1945–1950* (New York,
  1991), 139; Harry Truman, *Memoirs: Year of Decisions* (Garden City, NY, 1956), 105. See
  also Truman Library, Oral History Collection, Clark Clifford oral history, 23 March 1971
5 Dean Acheson, *Present at the Creation* (New York, 1969), 219

6 Quoted in Howard Jones, *A New Kind of War* (New York, 1989), 42

7 Acheson, *Present at the Creation*, 219

8 Arthur H. Vandenberg (ed.), *The Private Papers of Senator Vandenberg* (Boston, MA, 1952), 338–9

9 Jones, *The Fifteen Weeks*, 141–2; Clark Clifford oral history, 19 April 1971, HST, Oral History Collection

10 "Mr. Truman Goes to Congress," *New York Times*, 12 March 1947

11 Quoted in Daniel Yergin, *Shattered Peace: The Origins of the Cold War and the National Security State* (Boston, MA, 1977), 282

12 Clark Clifford oral history, 19 April 1971, HST, Oral History Collection; Elsey to Clifford, 8 March 1947, HST, Elsey Papers, Box 17, 12 March "Truman Doctrine Speech"

13 Clifford quoted in Elsey note, 9 March 1947, HST, Elsey Papers, Box 17, 12 March "Truman Doctrine Speech"

14 Quoted in the syndicated column by Barnet Nover, "It's Up to Us," in HST, Elsey Papers, Box 17, 12 March "Truman Doctrine Speech"

15 Clark Clifford oral history, 19 April 1971, HST, Oral History Collection

16 Quoted in Jones, *The Fifteen Weeks*, 38 and 43

17 Quoted in Walter Millis (ed.), *The Forrestal Diaries* (London, 1952), 248

18 Louis Halle, *The Cold War as History* (London, 1967), 159–60

2

Reviving propaganda

"Propaganda" is not a term that sits easily within the history of American foreign policy. After all, it was only in the crisis atmosphere of entry into World War I that the US Government established an agency under the innocuous name Committee for Public Information, and that organization was quickly disbanded with the return of peace. Instead of being credited with any contribution towards the defeat of the Central Powers, propaganda was vilified as a devious technique of the Allies. Books like *Propaganda for War: The Campaign against American Neutrality*[1] explained how British exploitation of events like the sinking of the *Lusitania*, the alleged bayoneting of Belgian babies, and the execution of Nurse Edith Cavell had dragged a reluctant United States into the European conflict. Visions of His Majesty's diplomats conspiring with arms manufacturers to take the lives of innocuous American volunteers dominated the political landscape of the 1930s.

It took World War II to restore propaganda as an acceptable practice. Once again, the public was conditioned to the illusion of the US Government as helpful provider of news. Nelson Rockefeller was appointed to supervise "Commercial and Cultural Relations among the Latin American Republics" while William Donovan became Franklin Roosevelt's Coordinator of Information. Eventually, as Donovan expanded more and more into the covert collection and dissemination of information, the connection between propaganda and secret activity was acknowledged. Donovan led the Office of Strategic Services (OSS), responsible for covert propaganda, while CBS newsman Elmer Davis headed the Office of War Information (OWI) for overt output. Meanwhile, the Army, Navy, and Joint Chiefs of Staff all created psychological warfare committees.

After this shaky start, the concept took hold. The OWI was constantly besieged by a Congress skeptical of its usefulness and hindered by the uncooperative State and War Departments, but the OSS operated with less interference. By 1945, more than 30,000 personnel were directly involved in psychological operations. Even the State Department, traditionally resistant to propaganda and psychological operations, acknowledged, "This Department regards this work as important and, indeed, at the present time, indispensable to the most effective conduct of American foreign affairs."[2]

As in 1918, the end of hostilities brought an end to such praise. The OSS was sabotaged by agencies like the Federal Bureau of Investigation, which would brook no rivals on its intelligence turf, and the extroverted Donovan's propensity for making Washington enemies was no great help. Advisors warned Truman that Donovan's scheme, with "all the earmarks of a Gestapo system", would cause "serious harm to citizens, business interests, and national interests of the United States".[3] The President responded by ordering in September 1945 that the OSS be wound up. The OWI, with even fewer defenders, had no chance.

While the OSS scrambled to place a "cadre of the best secret operations people . . . in secret intelligence positions",[4] the remnants of the information services, notably the Voice of America radio system, were adopted by the State Department, which created an Assistant Secretary of State for Public Affairs to supervise the operations. The first holder of the office was William Benton, member of a prominent Connecticut family, founder and chairman of Benton and Bowles advertising agency, and later a US Senator. There were special cases where the propaganda effort was sustained. For example, in occupied Germany and Austria, the American program of de-Nazification gradually turned into a campaign against Soviet rivals. The resurrected press, operating under the supervision of American military authorities, and a US-operated radio system warned of the growing Communist menace.[5]

Yet, if these services had escaped death, they were still close to comatose. Conservative Congressmen, with the memory of an Office of War Information allied with New Deal politics, applied the budgetary squeeze and cut appropriations by more than 50 percent by mid-1947. Representatives alleged that Voice of America broadcasts did "more harm than good" because "propaganda that ostensibly [was] intended to build new respect for the US [was] being used instead to criticize private enterprise, to express partisan opinions, and to distort the picture of life in the US". A State Department-sponsored art exhibition was labelled "as foreign to the American way as is the Moscow Radio", an Illinois Congressman concluding, "When the taxpayers' money is used to buy pictures painted by Communist artists, we not only distribute their propaganda, we also put money in their pockets and thereby enable them to influence their efforts to make America Red Communist."[6] In the State Department, the number of personnel for "information" was reduced from about 13,000 in August 1945 to 3,100 at the end of the year, and the budget was slashed 80 percent from its wartime peak. Benton cogently noted, "Notably in our overseas activities, but domestically as well, we continue to operate in terms of pennies in contrast to the dollars we spend for the more orthodox forms of national defense."[7]

The situation was worsened by the hostility of many within the State Department to "propaganda". Detailed reports on the information program, with everything from Disney films like *Private Pluto* to broadcasts by American schoolchildren to their French counterparts,[8] could not hide the cold welcome offered by diplomats. Embassies maintained only a limited news service and treated the "information staff as journalists". News agencies, often seeing Government information programs as unwelcome competition, refused to distribute material to US embassies, and the items they provided were not necessarily productive.[9] A traveling committee of the American Society of Newspapers Editors reported:

> One of the chief complaints we found from diplomatic and information staffs abroad was that our own news services – Associated Press, United Press, and International News Service – were sending out items which they thought would be used and displayed, in an effort to build up their services, without regard to whether the people of foreign countries were getting a picture of America and its news. Too often it is race riots, murders, Hollywood loves, divorces and so on which contribute to a distorted picture of America.[10]

The Voice of America spearheaded the American effort, but its work was carefully circumscribed. Secretary of State James Byrnes told President Truman, "The Department's proposals will constitute a modest program compared to war-time standards. We shall not seek to compete with private agencies of communication, nor shall we try to outdo the efforts of foreign governments in this field." Byrnes continued by asserting that the Voice of America was limited to an "objective" presentation, eschewing any comment on the American relationship with Moscow. "We would defeat our objectives in this program if we were to engage in special propagandist pleading. Our promise is, and will be, solely to supply the facts on which foreign peoples can arrive at a rational and accurate judgement."[11]

Even as the information services struggled to find a place in peacetime, conflict between the United States and the Soviet Union was brewing. At the Yalta Conference of February 1945, US President Franklin Roosevelt and Soviet leader Joseph Stalin, along with British Prime Minister Winston Churchill, had appeared to reach general agreement on a number of issues. Questions such as the future of Germany and the composition of Eastern European governments continued to provoke discord, however, and the Potsdam Conference of July failed to resolve the problems. When Byrnes moved toward compromise with the Soviets at the end of the year, Truman summoned him aboard the presidential yacht *Williamsburg* to chastise him and warn, "I'm tired of babying the Soviets."[12]

Hundreds of authors have debated who should bear the responsibility for the breakdown of cooperation, but the casting of blame on either side obscures the possibility that each saw its actions primarily as defense against the threat from the other. The American strategy to secure the US zone in Germany and to integrate it with a revived Western Europe was arguably motivated by fear of Soviet expansion throughout Eastern Europe; conversely, Moscow's support of one-party rule on its borders could be seen as the quest for a zone secure, politically and economically, from renewed aggression from the West.

The "true" Soviet motive in 1945–46 is tangential to a study of US action; the significant point is that, rightly or wrongly, US officials increasingly viewed Moscow through a long-term ideological prism. Soviet maneuvers were attributed not only to immediate geopolitical considerations but to a fixed world view based on Marxism–Leninism, a "state philosophy . . . in terms of historical and dialectical materialism".[13] Since one of the chief tenets of that ideology, in US eyes, was the quest for international Communism, the inevitable conclusion was that the Soviets were acting to obtain ordained goals. Any consideration that the Soviets might be reacting to a perceived US offensive was precluded.

Thus in February 1946 the pattern of a "total" Cold War began to emerge. Within weeks of Truman's dressing-down of Secretary of State Byrnes, Stalin – whether deliberately or inadvertently is disputed by historians – gave the Americans the pretext for a showdown. In an "election" speech on 9 February, in the unlikely setting of the Bolshoi Ballet House, Stalin announced a revival of the Five Year Plans of the 1930s. The goal would be to treble production, not only for the use of the military but also for the provision of consumer goods, an increased standard of living, and scientific development. The Soviet leader put his call in the context of a "historical" analysis in which he described World War II "as the result of the development of economic and political stresses on the basis of monopolistic capitalism". Victory had "proved a triumph for our Communistic order", despite criticisms from "France, Britain, and America" as well as Germany that the Red Army was unworthy, "that [Soviet] public order is a risky experiment doomed to fail, that it is a house of cards, [and] that it is imposed upon the people by the Cheka".

It is difficult, reading the speech, however, to see it as a Soviet call to arms against Britain and the United States. Stalin never criticized the policies of the Western powers and even his vision of World War II noted "the anti-Fascist coalition of the Soviet Union, the United States, Great Britain, and other freedom-loving nations which played the deciding part in smashing the armed forces of the Axis states". Most of the address was devoted to the question of economic development within the Soviet Union, an approach that could be viewed as rational in Moscow, given the cessation of Lend-Lease aid and the breakdown of loan negotiations with the US.[14]

American officials were not prepared to take such a charitable view. George Kennan, the *chargé d'affaires* at the US embassy, noted the "straight Marxist interpretation of World Wars I and II as products of crises inherent in monopoly capitalism" and assessed, "Most of the speeches [of Stalin and the Soviet Politburo] refer to the enormous 'international authority' currently enjoyed by USSR but at the same time give little or no indication that Soviet leaders place any reliance on the future of international collaboration."[15] At the State Department, H. Freeman Matthews described the speech as "the Communist and fellow-traveller Bible throughout the world", while Paul Nitze dramatically called it a "delayed declaration of war against the United States".[16]

When a concerned State Department asked for detailed evaluations of the future course of Soviet foreign policy, responses varied. The department's own intelligence unit viewed Moscow's line as pragmatic. It noted that "the contour of Soviet thinking will continue to be Marxist, with reversion to a more anti-capitalist emphasis than that of the war years" but added that "sufficient leeway will exist in both the industrial and the ideological program to accommodate the Soviet Union to continued collaboration with other Great Powers if that collaboration offers the best methods of realizing Soviet objectives".[17] This view was overshadowed, however, by the dire warnings of George Kennan.

Bedridden with cold, fever, sinusitis, and toothache, Kennan was revived by his opportunity to lift the veil from the eyes of his naive superiors, "to go back to Page 1 and tell them things I thought they'd forgotten". He composed an 8,000 word diagesis, "neatly divided, like an 18th-century Protestant sermon, into five separate parts".[18] Kennan preached that there was no possibility, in current circumstances, of cooperation with a Soviet leadership driven by Marxist-Leninist ideology, internal conditions, and a "traditional and instinctive Russian sense of inferiority". This was "a political force committed fanatically to the belief that with the US there can be no permanent *modus vivendi*, that it is desirable and necessary that the internal harmony of our society be disrupted, our traditional way of life be destroyed, the international authority of our state be broken, if Soviet power is to be secure". The threat was not that of military force but of subversion within "free" nations:

> This political force has complete power of disposition over energies of one of the world's greatest peoples and resources of the world's richest national territory, and is borne along by deep and powerful currents of Russian nationalism. In addition, it has an elaborate and far-flung apparatus for exertion of its influence in other countries, an apparatus of amazing flexibility and versatility, managed by people whose experience and skill in underground methods are ... without parallel in modern history.[19]

At the time, and in many historical accounts, the Long Telegram was treated as a reasoned assessment of Soviet intentions and motivations. In fact, as Kennan later admitted, the cable was an emotive tract to incite US action. It was "like one of those primers put out by alarmed congressional committees

or by the Daughters of the American Revolution, designed to arouse the citizenry to the dangers of the Communist conspiracy".[20] Kennan's mirage of
"realism" proved effective, however. While the analysis did not immediately
become gospel in Government circles, it was disseminated widely among
officials in Washington and at foreign posts. James Forrestal, the hard-line
Secretary of the Navy, had hundreds of copies made, sending them not only
throughout his department but "all over town".[21]

More importantly, the assessment coincided with a series of events forcing
a decision on America's future line with Moscow. On 5 March, Winston
Churchill, now out of office as Prime Minister but still for many the wartime
savior of the Free World, spoke at a small college, Fulton, in Westminster, Missouri. Before an audience that included President Truman, who introduced him
as "a great Englishman but he's half American", Churchill proclaimed, "From
Stettin in the Baltic to Trieste in the Adriatic, an iron curtain has descended
across the continent." The Soviet desire for "infinite expansion" could be
checked only by "the fraternal association of the English-speaking peoples",
for "except in the British Commonwealth and the US, where Communism is
in its infancy, the Communist parties and fifth columns constituted a growing
challenge and peril to Christian civilisation".[22]

With US policy in transition, reaction to the Fulton speech was not one of
unanimous approval. Whatever Truman's private sentiments, he insisted that
"he did not know what the former Prime Minister was going to say". Arthur
Krock, the veteran analyst of Washington politics, reported that the "timing
and content of [the] speech have defenders and critics among officials, with
the latter in majority".[23] The editors of the New York Times were not prepared to rule out an accommodation with the Soviets. "There is hope that
Russia is beginning to realize [the] consequences of her course and is beginning to adjust her policies accordingly."[24]

There was also division within the Administration, a debate that emerged
on 19 March at a dinner of the American Society for Russian Relief honor-
ing Averell Harriman, recently returned from duty as the US ambassador to
Moscow. A thousand leaders of business, industry, and the professions
attended, "a great many – both men and women ... looking like serious
thinkers, with occasional spots of rather surprising relief in the form of blonde
babes in fancy hats". Harriman bluntly stated, "I do not feel that I can in fairness join in asking the support of the American people for Russian relief unless
I make clear that I recognize the serious political differences that have arisen
between our two governments and that on these political differences I stand
squarely back of the American position." In contrast, Henry Wallace, Vice-
President under Franklin Roosevelt and now Secretary of Commerce, "vehe-
mently" contended "that even if Russia were wrong on every count, the United
States had nothing to gain in stirring up trouble between the two nations at
this point". He believed that the Soviets were motivated by fear rather than

malice. "The Soviet Union knows what the leading capitalist nations, especially Great Britain, tried to do [to] it from 1919 to 1921. They know what certain of the military in capitalist nations are thinking and saying today." A reporter at the dinner observed that Harriman's "reception by the audience throughout was warm" but Wallace, with "the best job of speech making I have heard do, . . . had the audience with him all the time".[25]

For most American policymakers, the refusal of the Soviets to withdraw their troops from northern Iran in March 1946 threatened any hope of peaceful post-war competition. Kennan intervened from Moscow to warn that any attempt to assuage Soviet suspicions would be "the most insidious and dangerous single error which Americans can make in their thinking" because "a hostile international environment is the breath of life for [the] prevailing internal system in this country. . . . That this agitation has created a psychosis which permeates and determines behavior of entire Soviet ruling caste is clear." The *Times* listed the territories annexed by Moscow since 1939 and asked, "Where does the search for security end and where does expansion begin?"[26]

A showdown over Iran was averted, however, when Moscow relented under American and British pressure at the United Nations in late March, and US policy retreated from a conception of global conflict towards a well defined doctrine of "containment". Hanson Baldwin, the *New York Times's* military correspondent, was one conduit for those who favored a firm distinction between those areas that were of vital interest to the United States and those that were not:

> Northern Iran, Manchuria, and Korea are scarcely of vital importance to the United States. . . . By arrangement, *coup*, infiltration or bare military force, Russia is going to have a dominant voice in these areas, and we are not going to fight her to prevent it, and probably could not successfully do so – in these parts of the world – even if we wanted to.
>
> But we must make it amply clear to Russia and to the world that the basic strategic reason for which we fought the last war was to prevent the domination of all of Western Europe by any power (Germany) and to prevent the domination of all of Eastern Asia by any one power (Japan).[27]

Yet what happened if the Soviets did not accept the elements in the US concept of containment – for example, a Germany tied into an American-led economic system? In such a case, Kennan's explanation of Soviet ideology became instrumental – Moscow's opposition was due not to limited geopolitical concerns but to its quest for world domination. Constantine Brown of the *Washington Star* highlighted the comparison that would soon become common currency: "Many of our political leaders who look at the present situation realistically drew a parallel between the Nazi and the Soviet totalitarianism and they find a striking similarity."[28] Driving the point home, State Department officials leaked captured German documents which were "said to reveal [the] Soviet aim to hold [the] Persian Gulf", giving Washington "exact pictures of the aims and desires that lie behind the current Soviet troop movements and diplomatic pressures".[29]

For example, in late April, Secretary of State Byrnes proposed a 25-year treaty, agreed by Britain, France, the Soviet Union, and the United States, for German and Japanese demilitarization. Anne O'Hare McCormick of the *New York Times* placed the proposal in its context of containment. "The disintegration of Europe is the greatest single cause of anxiety to the makers of our foreign policy.... Mr. Byrnes' proposal is the product of this anxiety. It is advanced as an alternative to the division of Europe, for it is already clear that partition is a prescription for ruin and perpetual conflict."[30] When the Soviets responded that they favored Byrnes's suggestion in principle but wanted to carry out previous agreements not only for German disarmament but also for German reparations to the Soviet Union, their motive was seen as no less than the spectre of international Communism. McCormick's colleague James Reston summarized, "The thesis that is rapidly gaining ground in the capital is ... [that] the Soviet Union is using its economic, political, and military power to support Communist elements all over Europe. This is true not only in the Soviet security belt ... but also westward into France ... and into Austria."[31]

Reston was on the mark. In mid-May, the State Department issued its most significant policy statement since the end of World War II. In Churchillian language, the department intoned:

> Within the past few months, Soviet influence or control has expanded to many areas – Eastern Europe from Stettin to Trieste and Albania, Northern Iran, Manchuria, Northern Korea and the Kuriles. It is not entirely clear whether these are the limits of Soviet ambitions, based in large part on Soviet estimates of USSR's alleged security requirements, or whether, as unfortunately seems more likely, the Soviets have embarked on a policy of aggrandizement which will be contained only by the limitations of Soviet power or eventually by armed resistance on the part of other major powers in areas where they feel their vital interests to be endangered.
>
> ... It is vitally important, therefore, that the United States maintain a military establishment adequate to defend the security of the United States and protect our interests elsewhere in the world.

This, however, was just a restatement of the geopolitical position. Where the report broke new ground, as with Reston's analysis, was its assessment of the conflict's basis. The main threat of Soviet ideology was not through military deployment or diplomatic maneuver but through propaganda, subversion, and manipulation of the "private" exchange of ideas:

> [The Soviets] have evolved many methods of disguised penetration and control. The first and most obvious method is through the establishment of puppet government in countries where the Soviet Government is in a position to exert strong military pressure if necessary.... Less obvious are the maneuvers of Communist parties in

countries beyond the range of Soviet military power. Here the tactics are to take advantage of the freedoms of the democratic process to carry out "smear" campaigns against all opposition including the non-Communist Left; to effect coalitions or party "fronts" which probably will eventually gain control of the Government and give Communists positions in key ministries and veto powers over vital national policies. Another method is to use various Soviet-controlled groups having international ramifications to exert influence in favor of Moscow policies or at least prevent any government from taking positive action frowned upon by the Soviet Government. These groups include front organizations such as the World Federation of Trade Unions, the All Slav Committee, the Orthodox Church, various "anti-Fascist" Committees with headquarters in Moscow and of course the Soviet-controlled parliamentary parties.[32]

Throughout the summer, the lurid menace of Soviet tyranny was "exposed" by the press. The *New York Times's* Brooks Atkinson returned from his post as Moscow correspondent to write a series of articles that paralleled the conclusions of US intelligence agencies. He supported the projection that "Socialist World Soviet Aim" with a description of the "group paranoia" of the Soviet leadership who "regard[ed] themselves as custodians of the future of the world" and "a bloodless, old-fashioned, petit-bourgeois culture that is colorless and conventional".[33] Other stories in the *Times* told of German scientists working for the Soviets "on nuclear research" and the production of tanks and bombers and of Soviet plans for "a 'mighty navy' for [the] Pacific, Far North, and Baltic".[34] Albania had "become a puppet state of Russia" living "under a Red Terror . . . where private enterprise has been thoroughly smashed, the clergy are being annihilated, individual freedom does not exist and militarism is rampant".[35] Moscow was even "pouring thousands of words of radio-transmitted press material into South America . . . to conduct a tremendous campaign against the United States and Great Britain through the continent-wide chain of Communist newspapers in the New World".[36]

The threat was also within. In July 1946, *Life* magazine devoted eight pages to a diatribe by Arthur Schlesinger, Jr., Pulitzer Prize-winning historian and prominent New Deal liberal, against "The U.S. Communist Party: Small but Tightly Disciplined, It Strives with Fanatic Zeal to Promote the Aims of Russia". Years before the rise of Joe McCarthy, Schlesinger was shrilly warning, "With history breathing down their necks, Communists are working overtime to expand party influence, open and covert, in the labor movement, among Negroes, among veterans, among unorganized liberals." He described how "a small clique in New York", under instructions from Moscow, was carrying out subversion through "secret members" and misguided "fellow-travelers" and concluded with an intriguing analogy:

> The [Communist] appeal is essentially the appeal of a religious sect – small, persecuted, dedicated, stubbornly convinced that it alone knows the path to salvation. To understand the Communists, you must think of them in terms, not of a normal political party, but in terms of the Jesuits, the Mormons or Jehovah's Witnesses.[37]

In the atmosphere of fear, the *New York Times* was on the lookout for new perils. An editorial warned in late July, "In line with her policy of military, political, economic, and ideological expansion which has already brought half of Europe and northern China under her sway and reaches out for control of all Germany, Russia now appears to be starting a similar offensive for the capture of Japan."[38]

Of course, any Soviet protest that the real aggressor resided in Washington was part of this devious offensive. Allegations of US and British "imperialistic domination" were deceitful propaganda. Refusal of US offers of "international control" of nuclear weapons was not really Soviet fear of a continued US monopoly of the atom bomb but an "amazing" rejection of proposals by a "United States that is going out of its way to make offers beyond its long-established traditions".[39] Even the Turkish elections took their place in this portrayal of US valor versus Soviet intrigue "because they represent[ed] a choice of the Western form of democracy on the part of a Russian border state. The Turks have experienced something like the Soviet brand of democracy for twenty-five years and they have had enough of it."[40]

Some commentators like Constantine Brown of the *Washington Star* were prepared for an all-out assault on the Soviet bloc. Claiming the world was "in an undeclared state of war", Brown argued:

> The masses [in the Soviet satellites] are hankering for the freedom that had been promised them in the Atlantic Charter. And while they do not have the means to stage large-scale uprisings, they are oganizing themselves into bands which live in the fastness of the mountains, in marshes, and in the woods.... Their motto, inscribed on their armbands, is "Liberty or Death".[41]

Others were not ready, less than a year after the end of World War II, to give up all hope of cooperation. In late July, the joint decision of the United States and the Soviet Union to open sessions of the Paris Peace Conference to the public and to publish the draft peace treaties was welcomed by the *Times* as "a double victory for world opinion and the Wilsonian principle of open covenants openly arrived at". Its European correspondent C. L. Sulzberger acknowledged "that both the United States and Russia . . . have individual and contrasting attitudes of ideology, justice, economic access, individual security and geographic necessity" but contended, "As far apart as they are, they know that they must get on together."[42]

Yet almost all agreed that, if the Soviets would not negotiate, the United States must establish a Western system free from the Communist menace. The *Times* praised "clever United States intervention" in French elections which "helped the more moderate Popular Republican Movement" to victory over the Communist Party. After noting that the borders in Eastern Europe had "been determined, not according to the principles of the Atlantic Charter and the wishes of the populations concerned, but according to the exclusive interests of Russia, who takes what she wants for herself", the *Times* turned to the central question. "The impending negotiations for unification of our occupation zone in Germany with other zones is an example which should be followed by others. We hope that Russia will see her way clear to cooperate, but there is no reason why the Western Powers should permit their action to be paralyzed if she does not cooperate."[43]

Such a position gave the White House the freedom to "get tough" with Moscow and implement the tenets of the State Department's policy statement of May 1946. In July, Truman asked his special counsel, Clark Clifford, for a list of agreements broken by Moscow. When Clifford asked George Elsey, another Truman assistant, to prepare the list, Elsey replied that the focus was too narrow. "There were far more fundamental issues involved. . . . The nature of these issues didn't seem to be clearly understood in large parts of the executive branch (witness the fiasco of [Secretary of Commerce] Henry Wallace)."[44] The two men accordingly agreed to collect the views of key agencies on Soviet aims.

The response was almost unanimous. Dean Acheson, the Under-secretary of State, warned that military strength had to be maintained to defend US interests. Secretary of War Robert Patterson endorsed the assessment, adding that the Administration had to combat Communist infiltration of the United States.[45] The Central Intelligence Group, in a report written by a single staffer drawing upon Kennan's cables and Army intelligence reports, noted that the Soviets "anticipated an inevitable conflict with the capitalist world". The CIG believed Moscow would move gradually to secure its position in Eastern Europe and to "extend its predominant influence to include all of Germany and Austria",[46] but Admiral William Leahy, the Chairman of the Joint Chiefs of Staff, left no room for doubt about the total nature of the conflict:

> A fundamental [tenet] of Soviet policy, which has world domination as its objective, is that the peaceful coexistence of Communist and capitalist states is, in the long run, impossible. . . . The Soviet Government is concentrating on the buildup of its war potential and is using every means, short of war, to bring satellite nations under complete domination, to acquire control of strategic areas, to cause disintegration of the resistance capability of the capitalistic nations, and to achieve their ultimate isolation.[47]

Clifford and Elsey helped the process along with annotations like "a truly terrifying confirmation . . . about the extent to which leaders of the Communist Party dominate every phase of the life and thinking of the Russian people", and Truman made his own contribution in a series of comments noted by his advisors, "Now is time to take stand on Russia – Tired of our being pushed around – Here a little, there a little, they are chiseling from us – Paris conference [of Foreign Ministers] will bust [and] be a failure if Russia want too much because we are not going to back down."[48]

On 24 September, Clifford and Elsey, having had their drafts revised by Kennan and Leahy, presented the conclusions to the President. They warned that Moscow sought "to prepare for the ultimate conflict by increasing Soviet power as rapidly as possibly and by weakening all nations who may be considered hostile." Not only were the Soviets violating agreements over Germany, Austria, the Balkans, Iran, and Korea, they were "actively directing subversive movements and espionage within the U.S.". Clifford and Elsey then outlined the appropriate response:

> The U.S. should maintain military forces powerful enough to restrain the Soviet Union and to confine the Soviet influence in its present area. All nations not now within the Soviet sphere should be given generous economic assistance and political support in their opposition to the Soviet penetration.
> If necessary, "the U.S. must be prepared to wage atomic and biological warfare".[49]

According to Elsey, Truman was so shaken by the report that he called at 7.00 a.m. on the day after its delivery. He asked for all ten copies, locking them in his office. The President asserted, "If this got out, it would blow the roof off of the White House, it would blow the roof off the Kremlin. We'd have the most serious situation on our hands that has yet occurred in my administration."[50]

As with Kennan's Long Telegram, however, a crisis could be found to elevate the vision of conflict into reality. This time it was Turkey. In August, Moscow pressed the Turks to revise the Montreux Convention and allow shared fortification in the Dardanelles Straits passing through Turkey. Britain and the United States had accepted such a revision at Potsdam a year earlier, but the Soviet renewal of the claim, as well as continued unrest in Greece and the downing of US transport planes by Yugoslavia, led the Truman Administration into a series of get-tough measures. Armed fighter-bombers would fly over Venezia Giulia, the corridor disputed between Italy and Yugoslavia. The United States would firmly oppose a Soviet presence in the straits, placing a large-scale naval presence in the Mediterranean. To symbolize US resolve, the USS *Missouri* carried the body of the Turkish ambassador in Washington, who had conveniently just died, to Ankara.[51]

In the end, the episode amounted to little, with the Soviets not pursuing their request, but Truman and his advisors were now committed to a showdown. The President argued, "We might as well find out whether the Russians were bent on world conquest now, as in five or ten years."[52] Days before the completion of the Clifford–Elsey report, James Reston was again used to publicize the Administration's thoughts. Through the journalist, Acheson emphasized the strong US line on Soviet access through the Straits of the Dardanelles, reassertion of the US position in Korea, and support for British trusteeships in Africa. Reston concluded, "Mr. Acheson is well aware of the fact that the

Russians would prefer to have us preach and run as we did after the first World War . . . but the official view here seems to be that the dangers of intervention are less than the dangers of non-intervention, since the latter policy was tried before without noticeable success."[53]

In Europe, the United States decided to press ahead with the political and economic revival of Germany, even if it forced a split with the Soviets. In a speech hailed by newsreels as "the controversial address that may decide the fate of Europe . . . widely interpreted as marking the end of America's appeasement of Russia", Secretary of State Byrnes declared in Stuttgart, "The American people want to return the government of Germany to the people of Germany. The American people want to help the German people to win their way back to an honorable place among the free and peace-loving nations of the world." Although Byrnes insisted, "It is not in the interest of the German people or in the interest of world peace that Germany should become a pawn or partner in a military struggle for power between East and West," his indication that the United States would seek modifications of the agreements of 1945, including the border settlement that had given part of eastern Germany to Poland, raised suspicions. Fifty years later, the former Polish leader Wojciech Jaruzelski would comment, "It was a shocking statement. . . . It was one of the most important things that strengthened our ties with the Soviet Union."[54]

The Clifford–Elsey report, underpinned by events, was drawing battle lines at home as well. The hardening of US policy had inevitably put the position of Henry Wallace, the former Vice-President who was still in the Cabinet, in jeopardy. In July, Wallace had critiqued the move towards confrontation in a 5,000 word letter to the President. It was a submission that would help launch the Clifford–Elsey review that would seal his fate. Clifford believed, "Wallace is paving the way for an eventual break – and a wide-open break – with Truman on the subject of U.S. policy toward Russia."[55]

The final confrontation came in mid-September when Wallace spoke at Madison Square Garden warning against a "tough" policy. Wallace, criticising "some Soviet policies" and calling for "peaceful competition", was far from advocating appeasement of the enemy – his main attack was upon the foundation of US foreign policy upon an Anglo-American alliance – but the crisis lay in newspaper reports that Truman supported him or even that the Secretary of Commerce was promoting a "Truman policy". Within days, editorials were insisting that the President had to repudiate Wallace or forfeit cooperation with the Republican-led Congress and even his own Secretary of State:

> In America we had a historic and happy status, a prolonged period of cooperation
> between our two parties in the field of foreign relations. It had endured through the
> war, and for fourteen into peace. . . . Republican leaders . . . will still practice unity
> with Democratic leaders officially responsible, specifically Secretary of State Byrnes.

But Mr Byrnes is compromised in his authority to speak even for the Democratic President.[56]

The situation was exacerbated when Wallace's July letter to Truman was leaked to columnist Drew Pearson and Byrnes threatened to resign.

On 20 September, four days before he received the Clifford–Elsey report, Truman dismissed Wallace from the Cabinet. Free from the lone voice for conciliation, Truman was now clear about the menace, within and without, in his diary:

> Wallace is a pacifist 100 percent. He wants us to disband our armed forces, give Russia our atomic secrets and trust a bunch of adventurers in the Kremlin Politburo. I do not understand a dreamer like that. The German-American Bund under Fritz Kuhn was not half so dangerous. The Reds, phonies, and the parlor pinks seem to be banded together and are becoming a national danger. I am afraid they are a sabotage front for Uncle Joe Stalin.[57]

In the move from cooperation to confrontation, the information services were retrieved from obscurity. In February 1946 Elmer Davis, the former head of the Office of War Information, declared:

> The competition in information, whether you call it propaganda or not, is already going on; the only question is whether the United States is going to take part in that competition, or whether we are condemned to sit by in silence and let foreign nations take their opinions of us from other national agencies which are concerned with advancing the policies and interests of their own countries, and not those of the United States.[58]

Three months later, the State Department policy statement on relations with the Soviet Union took up Davis's challenge. "We must make the record available to the American people and to the world. Our case is based on tolerance, generosity, justice, and a desire for freedom and a better life for men everywhere. . . . Ours is a strong case, but only by proclaiming it and implementing it can we win for it the support it deserves."[59]

Key businessmen and media representatives supported a renewed effort. The Committee for United States Information Abroad, chaired by Ralph McGill, the editor of the *Atlanta Constitution*, and including a cross-section of publishers, university leaders, advertisers, and businessmen, published an open letter, "Explaining America", in newspapers across the country. Cartoons depicted a gagged Uncle Sam unable to spread "Good Will" and "Information" through the Voice of America.[60] A group of radio executives, including Frank Stanton, President of the Columbia Broadcasting System, and David Sarnoff, Chairman of the Radio Corporation of America, supported the expansion of State Department broadcasting,[61] and Philip Reed, the Chairman of General Electric, summarized the challenge to a conference of industrialists:

We have failed to recognize that we must advertise and sell the American economic system as well as the products of that system. It is our job to explain and sell the rightness of private competitive enterprise both at home and abroad. If we don't, we shall be in very real danger of losing it.[62]

Intellectuals reasoned that the United States was only responding to the Soviets' malicious use of propaganda. Columbia University's George Counts reported that a "USSR textbook of war [World War II] glorifies role of Reds but ignores Allies", with Joseph Stalin mentioned 47 times in 63 paragraphs as "the one reliable authority on any question".[63] Arthur Koestler argued that the situation required "psychological disarmament", with "free access of foreign newspapers, periodicals, books and films to the USSR".[64]

The *New York Times* captured the changing attitude. After its initial hopes for the Paris Peace Conference in summer 1946, the paper had been horrified by "misrepresentation and abuse casting aspersions upon our role in the war and impugning our motives and our aims". These "calumnies [were] launched exclusively by Russia and her puppets" using "the smear as a regular political strategy". The *Times* reminded its readers, "We still have both power and a tremendous reservoir of good-will in the world, due to the fact that in the long run the principles we stand for are also the best hope of most nations which look to us to rise up in their defense," but it added ominously:

> This [Soviet propaganda] campaign has now reached such proportions and such a degree of intensity that the American and British Governments will soon have to take notice of it and prepare measures to meet it. These measures cannot consist of counter-propaganda of the same type, but they can embrace the greatest possible publicity for the facts in each case that arises. But the published facts will do little good unless they reach the shut-in Russian people. And that poses a problem the solution of which will demand both energy and ingenuity on the part of all Government agencies concerned.[65]

The State Department took a major step towards a more assertive stance in February 1947 when it initiated propaganda within the Soviet Union through the magazine *Amerika* and Russian-language broadcasts on the Voice of America. The activity was spurred by the US ambassador in Moscow, Walter Bedell Smith, who warned,

> In an attempt to be objective, we have actually given a false impression. . . . We should, whenever giving unfavourable news, place it in perspective for Russian listeners by explaining concisely [the] background, causes, and corrective action being taken. . . . Our aim should be to emphasize what we as a great democratic people are doing to solve these problems.

Bedell Smith suggested that commentary should be supplemented by music like "Tavern in the Town" and "three or four tunes at top of Hit Parade" ("modern symphonic music and lugubrious oboe solos are definitely out") and by radio drama. For example, a program could show "a young veteran and wife finishing a university course.... They could buy a car, plan trips, discuss the cost of living in relation to their income, talk about sports or movies or new books, participate in election campaign, etc."[66]

However, for all these changes in US diplomatic and information strategy, this was not yet a global conception of the conflict with Moscow. Once he moved from the broad ideological sweep of the Long Telegram to recommendations for US policy, Kennan identified key points for containment such as Western Europe and Japan. There was no reason for the United States to intervene in areas which did not meet the geopolitical, military, or economic criteria of "vital interest". Instead situations could be evaluated on a case-by-case basis. Kennan, seconded to the National War College in 1946–47, held that assistance for Greece might be necessary to prevent Western Europe reeling from the shock of a Communist success but that direct aid to Turkey was not necessary.[67]

It was then that Harry Truman made his speech of 12 March 1947 to the US Congress.

Notes

1 H. C. Peterson, *Propaganda for War: The Campaign against American Neutrality, 1914–1917* (Norman, OK, 1938)

2 Lilly memorandum, "Development of American Psychological Operations, 1945–1951," 19 December 1951, HST, Staff Memoranda and Office Files, PSB Files, Box 15, 091.412 The Field and Role of Psychological Strategy in Cold War Planning

3 Park to Truman, undated [1945], US DDRS, 1993 1229

4 Also see Miles Copeland, *The Real Spy World* (London, 1978), 41

5 See, for example, Jessica Gienow, "Bringing Faith to the Pagans: The Awkward Invention of U.S. Journalism and other Cultural Values in Post-war Germany, 1945–1948," paper presented before the Society of Historians of American Foreign Relations, 26 June 1994

6 Testimony cited in Hulten to Player, 22 August 1950, HST, Elsey Papers, Box 65, Foreign Relations – Voice of America

7 Benton to Marshall, 3 September 1947, HST, Sargeant Papers, Box 20

8 See HST, Hulten Papers, Box 8, Department of State Information Programs, 1946. The specific examples are from the 1946 reports of the US embassies in India and France

9 Robert Pirsein, *The Voice of America* (New York, 1979), 117–18

10 Address by Elmer Davis to Chicago Rotary Club, 26 February 1946, HST, Hulten Papers, Box 8, Department of State Information Programs. See also Benton to McLean, 16 January 1946, Records of the National Council of Negro Women, Series 5, Box 36, Folder 4

11 Byrnes to Truman, 31 December 1945, HST, Hulten Papers, Box 8, Department of State Information Programs

12 Harry Truman, *Memoirs: Year of Decisions* (Garden City, NY, 1956), 551–2

13 See Walter Millis (ed.), *The Forrestal Diaries* (New York, 1951), 248, regarding the distribution in early 1946 of a study, commissioned by Secretary of the Navy Forrestal, on Soviet ideology

14 *The Times* (London), 11 February 1946; *Manchester Guardian*, 11 February 1946. Vladimir Yerofeyev, an official in the Soviet Foreign Ministry, recently commented, "Stalin didn't say anything new or different in that speech. He said what he always believed, that with imperi-

alism and capitalism war was inevitable." (BBC Television, *The Cold War*, Part 2, 27 September 1998)

15 Moscow to State Department, Cable 408, 12 February 1946, HST, Elsey Papers, Box 63, Foreign Relations – Russia, Folder 1

16 Quoted in Daniel Yergin, *Shattered Peace: The Origins of the Cold War and the National Security State* (Boston, MA, 1977), 167; Paul Nitze interview in BBC Television, *The Cold War*, Part 2, 26 September 1998

17 "Analysis of Stalin's Address," 21 February 1946, HST, Elsey Papers, Box 63, Foreign Relations – Russia, Folder 2B

18 The first casualty of Kennan's enthusiasm was Martha Mautner, who was the code clerk on the night of the Long Telegram's despatch. She recounted that she had a "heavy date" that evening at a dance at another embassy but "about 6:30 or 7 George comes walking in with this six-part cable that he wants to send out. And I took a look and said, 'It's nice but let's not send it out. Let's send it tomorrow.' . . . He said, 'Washington wants it. They're going to get it. You stay here and do it.'" (BBC Television, *The Cold War*, Part 2, 26 September 1998)

19 George Kennan, *Memoirs, 1925–1950* (Boston, MA, 1967), 293 and 557; George Kennan interview in BBC Television, *The Cold War*, Part 2, 26 September 1998

20 Kennan, *Memoirs*, 294–5

21 Yergin, *Shattered Peace*, 171

22 Film of Fulton speech, BBC Television, *The Cold War*, Part 2, 26 September 1998

23 Arthur Krock, "Washington Splits over Churchill," *New York Times*, 13 March 1946

24 "Russia's Policies," *New York Times*, 11 March 1946

25 Alexander Feinberg, "Contrasting View on Russian Moves," *New York Times*, 20 March 1946; Jackson Papers, Box 48, Phillips to Larsen, 20 March 1946, Ha Miscellaneous

26 Moscow to State Department, Cable 878, 20 March 1946, HST, Elsey Papers, Box 64; "What does Russia Want?", *New York Times*, 15 March 1946

27 Hanson Baldwin, "A Realistic Policy is Required," *New York Times*, 27 March 1946

28 Constantine Brown, "Russian Attitude Keeps Enduring Peace Remote," *Washington Star*, March 1946

29 L. S. B. Shapiro, "Papers Hitler Left Said to Reveal Soviet Aim to Hold Persian Gulf," *New York Times*, 19 March 1946

30 Anne O'Hare McCormick, "Abroad: Mr. Byrnes Challenges the Peacemakers," *New York Times*, 1 May 1946

31 James Reston, "Soviet Bar to U.S. Alliance Supports 'Two Worlds' Idea," *New York Times*, 6 May 1946

32 State Department Policy and Information Statement, "Union of Soviet Socialist Republics," 15 May 1946, HST, Clifford Papers, Box 15, Russia (1 of 8)

33 Brooks Atkinson, "Socialist World Soviet Aim, Times Moscow Writer Says," and "Soviet Seen Wanting Peace Despite its Air of Challenge," *New York Times*, 7–9 July 1946

34 "Arms, Atom Work in Soviet Zone is Reported in Detail at Berlin," *New York Times*, 13 July 1946; Drew Middleton, "Soviet Planning a 'Mighty Navy' For Pacific, Far North and Baltic," *New York Times*, 24 July 1946 (HST, Elsey Papers, Box 63, Foreign Relations – Russia 1946 (Folder 2B))

35 Camille M. Cianfarra, "Soviet Sets up Coastal Guns and Equips Albanian Army," *New York Times*, 29 July 1946

36 Frank L. Kluckhohn, "Soviet Lashes U.S. in South America," *New York Times*, 20 July 1946

37 Arthur Schlesinger, Jr, "The U.S. Communist Party," *Life*, July 1946, 84–91

38 "Russia in Japan," *New York Times*, 22 July 1946

39 Frank L. Kluckhohn, "Soviet Lashes U.S. in South America," *New York Times*, 20 July 1946; "Bikini and 57th Street," *New York Times*, 25 July 1946; "The Snag in Atom Control," *New York Times*, August 1946

40 "Turkey Turns West," *New York Times*, 25 July 1946
41 Constantine Brown, "This Changing World," *Washington Star*, 21 August 1946; "World Tension of Today Compared to that of 1939," *Washington Star*, 18 August 1946
42 "The Peace Treaties," *New York Times*, 31 July 1946; C. L. Sulzberger, "America and Russia: Opposite Poles at Paris," *New York Times*, 11 August 1946
43 C. L. Sulzberger, "War Speculation Held Unjustified," *New York Times*, 21 August 1946; "The Peace Treaties," *New York Times*, 31 July 1946; "Mr. Byrnes' Report," *New York Times* (undated), in HST, Elsey Papers, Box 65, Foreign Relations – Truman Doctrine
44 George Elsey interview, 10 February 1964, HST, Oral History Collection. Elsey reiterated this in the 1998 documentary *The Cold War* but, on this occasion, omitted the reference to the domestic problems involving Henry Wallace. On "the fiasco" of Wallace, see pages 23–4 above
45 Acheson and Patterson views cited in Patterson to Truman, 27 July 1946, HST, Elsey Papers, Box 63, Foreign Relations – Russia, Folder 2A
46 Arthur Darling, *The Central Intelligence Agency* (University Park, PA, 1990), 130–1; Central Intelligence Group, "Soviet Foreign and Military Policy," 23 July 1946, US DDRS, 1991 183
47 Leahy to Truman, 26 July 1946, HST, Clifford Papers, Box 15, Russia (3 of 8)
48 Elsey to Clifford, 27 August 1946, HST, Elsey Papers, Box 63, Foreign Relations – Russia 1946 (Folder 2A)
49 The report is reprinted in Arthur Krock, *Memoirs* (New York, 1968), 419, and cited in Clark Clifford interview, 23 March 1971, HST, Oral History Collection
50 Clark Clifford oral history, 18 March 1972, HST, Oral History Collection
51 Dean Acheson, *Present at the Creation* (New York, 1969) 195–6; Millis (ed.), *Forrestal Diaries*, 192–3; George Elsey interview, BBC Television, *The Cold War*, 26 September 1998
52 Quoted in Yergin, *Shattered Peace*, 235
53 James Reston, "U.S. Must Wage Long Fight for Peace, Acheson Holds," *New York Times*, 3 September 1946
54 Paramount newsreel of Byrnes speech and Wojciech Jaruzelski oral history, BBC Television, *The Cold War*, Part 2, 26 September 1998
55 Quoted in Yergin, *Shattered Peace*, 250
56 *New York Herald-Tribune*, 18 September 1946
57 Quoted in Yergin, *Shattered Peace*, 253–4
58 Elmer Davis address to Chicago Rotary Club, 26 February 1946, HST, Hulten Papers, Box 8, Department of State Information Program
59 State Department Policy and Information Statement, "Union of Soviet Socialist Republics," 15 May 1946, HST, Clifford Papers, Box 15, Russia (1 of 8)
60 "Explaining America," *New York Herald-Tribune*, 20 May 1946; cartoons in HST, Hulten Papers, Box 8, Department of State Information Programs 1946, Newspaper Clippings and Press Releases
61 "U.S. Broadcast of News Backed by Radio Heads," *New York Herald-Tribune*, 19 May 1946
62 Reed to Benton, 3 October 1946, HST, Hulten Papers, Box 15, Voice of America 1946–47. The *Saturday Review of Literature*, eagerly published the summary of the "distinguished American editor, historian, and publicist" Herbert Agar: "If the future is to be brighter, we must find new ways to allow our neighbors to know us. People can always get along with each other better than governments, if people are given a chance to understand." (Herbert Agar, "They Want to Know," *Saturday Review of Literature,* in HST, Hulten Papers, Box 8, Department of State Information Programs 1946, Newspaper Clippings and Press Releases)
63 George Counts, "USSR Textbook of War Glorifies Role of Reds but Ignores Allies," *Sunday Star* (Washington, DC), 25 August 1946

64 Arthur Koestler, "Challenge to Russia: Lift the Iron Curtain!" *New York Times Magazine*, 10 March 1946, 45

65 "America under Attack," *New York Times*, 16 August 1946; "Russian Propaganda," *New York Times*, 6 August 1946

66 Moscow to State Department, Cable 563, 27 February 1947, and Cable 598, 1 March 1947, *Foreign Relations of the United States*, 1947, Volume IV, 537–8 and 541

67 Kennan, *Memoirs, 1925–1950*, 316–18

3

Debating the call to arms

The applause in the Capitol chamber for Truman's declaration indicated that the President had won over many Congressional skeptics for the moment, and most press reaction was favorable. Editorial cartoons showed Uncle Sam waving "Aid to Greece" to slay vultures labelled "Threat to a Brave People" and "World Spread of Communism" and the US dollar carrying a rifle with bayonet on "Mediterranean patrol". The *Portland Oregonian* declared, "We are drawn into the European political war because it is impossible for us to retire within our own continent."[1] The *New York Times* best enunciated the official line, comparing Truman's speech with Franklin Roosevelt's 1937 call for the "quarantine" of aggressors:

> In presenting this situation to the American people, President Truman has put in official words what has been apparent to any observer of the international scene for many months. But the fact that he did so, and the manner in which he did so, make his address an event of the first magnitude. For this is nothing less than a warning to Russia to desist from the physical aggression and the diplomatic attrition that have characterized her policy ever since the war and to abide by the Charter of the United Nations as the only safe basis of a tolerable peace.
>
> We believe that there can be no doubt that the American people stand behind this warning. Whether it is heeded will depend not only on Russia, but also on the speed and the degree of unanimity with which Congress endorses the President's recommendations. The "quarantine" speech of President Roosevelt failed of its purpose because it was not followed by action, and the consequences are now history.[2]

An army of *Times* correspondents lent support. Anne O'Hare McCormick explained that Truman, "the man who a few months ago was rated timid, uncertain, and overpowered by events and responsibilities too big for him", was now being seen by Europe "for the first time as a looming figure on the international stage".[3] Felix Belair predicted that "Mr. Truman's message will take its place beside the Monroe Doctrine in the niche of history once reserved for the Atlantic Charter"[4] while James Reston persisted with the warning, "The Soviet state, center of a world movement bent on creating a Communist federation, has risen to challenge not only the independence of weak sovereign states but to defy the very essence of our belief in individual liberty."[5]

Not all, however, took Truman's rhetoric for gospel. From the left, the *Nation* and the *New Republic* blasted the "immoral and dangerous" proposals.[6] The New York daily *PM*, after sneering, "Things are back to normal. We have an international crisis again. Say, wasn't the past month dull?" noted, "Obviously [Truman's] definition of a 'free' government is a non-Communist one. How else could the oppressive monarchical police-state of Greece and the streamlined fascist state of Turkey be called 'free'?"[7] Some on the conservative side of the Democratic Party echoed the charge. Senator Richard Russell of Georgia snapped, "I want to help Greece but I have many misgivings about helping King George and propping up his decadent form of government."[8]

Of course, attacks came from defenders of US "isolationism" such as Senator Robert Taft of Ohio and the *Chicago Tribune*, which called the speech "a complete confession of the bankruptcy of American policy as formulated by Mr. Roosevelt and pursued by [President Truman] himself".[9] Critics of British foreign policy chimed in with the allegation that the United States was pulling London's chestnuts out of the fire. Even Eleanor Roosevelt asked, "Why must this country accept Great Britain's military responsibilities?" and suggested that "Secretary Marshall . . . have a talk with Mr. Stalin very soon" to prevent a US–Soviet conflict in Greece.[10]

The most telling objection came not from those who opposed aid to Greece and Turkey but from those who questioned how it was being provided. The President's message of the US mission confronted a belief, born out of the Allied struggle in World War II and the statement of aims in the 1941 Atlantic Charter, that peace and security had to be maintained by the United Nations. That method had been ruled out by the Administration because, in the words of Clark Clifford, "it could have taken months before anything was done".[11] Freda Kirchwey of the *Nation* argued, "The President's brusque dismissal of the United Nations as an agency through which relief and rehabilitation could be brought to Greece was alone sufficient to expose the political nature of his program,"[12] and Senator Claude Pepper of Florida insisted, "The time has come when the U.N. must succeed or be discredited."[13]

Observers far less hostile to the President shared the concern. While George Elsey still argued, "Putting [the issue] into the U.N. would have been totally fruitless. . . . We would have in effect been watching from the sidelines as Greece and Turkey slipped behind the Iron Curtain," he also reflected, "The apparent failure of the administration to consider the United Nations . . . was very costly."[14] On the eve of the speech, the *Washington Post* had cautioned, "While waiting for our downfall, [the Russians] want to bypass the United Nations and divide the world between Russia and America. This would be a fatal policy for us to pursue. We must resist aggression, but our destiny also calls upon us to stand firmly for the international principles to which we sub-

scribed in the charter of the United Nations."[15] Arthur Vandenberg, the Senate
majority leader who would ultimately be instrumental in obtaining the passage
of aid for Greece and Turkey, wrote privately that the Administration made
"a colossal blunder in ignoring the United Nations".[16]

Henry Wallace, now leading the new political group Progressive Citizens
of America, emphasized the issue by arguing on radio and in national
advertisements:

> President Truman's proposals divide the world into two camps and head the country
> toward war.
> American dollars and American men should not be pledged to the support of
> kings and empires.
> The full power of the U.S. should be behind the United Nations.
> Our confidence should be placed only in world partnership creating peace for all
> peoples.[17]

The *Washington News* called the statement "a new Wallacian low in hypocrisy
and misrepresentation in its all-out support of the Moscow party line",[18] but
the *New York Times* was shaken enough to move from the doctrine towards
an economic program "with full emphasis on public action, private action and
as much action as possible, as soon as possible, by the United Nations".[19]
Detailed opinion polls carried out by Elmo Roper in April 1947 confirmed
that the "largest single objection" to Truman's proposals was their unilateral
nature.[20]

The Administration launched its counter-attack by releasing a document
stating that the United Nations was already involved with the Greek situation
through a commission investigating border violations and other matters. The
United States "would look to the United Nations to solve any problems which
it is equipped to handle, but we must not expect the United Nations to be
something which it is not or to assume responsibilities now beyond its
scope".[21] The US delegate to the United Nations, Warren Austin, followed
with a speech arguing that, since Greece could "not qualify as a good credit
risk for bank loans" through the United Nations, the United States had to fill
the vacuum "as one member of a U.N. team".[22] Truman's reference to military aid for Greece and Turkey was downplayed, if mentioned at all.[23]

This was still not enough to ensure Congressional passage of assistance by
31 March, the target set by Truman. Even if the internationalists had been
accommodated, the challenge of the "China first" lobby, as well as of those
concerned about the cost of any additional US commitment, remained. The
influential columnist Drew Pearson reported on 19 March that 44 of the 51
Republican Senators attended a briefing by Arthur Vandenberg on the situation. Only two of the 44 "pledged all-out support" for the President. One
group questioned why Truman should be intervening in the Middle East while
blocking unconditional aid to Chiang Kai-shek against the Chinese Commu-

nists. "A large bloc" still asked, "Where will the money come from to aid Greece and Turkey – later Korea, Palestine, India, and perhaps other countries in the battle to stop communism? There'll be no end of it, they fear, and they see their hopes of budget balancing gone glimmering."[24]

In the turmoil, there were even appearances that the Administration was not unified behind its effort. Secretary of State Acheson told Truman's close advisor, Clark Clifford, that "President should not and could not 'talk up' United Nations in his forthcoming speech [on Jefferson Day on 5 April] ... U.N. had been greatly 'over-played' and 'over-sold'." Hearing this, George Elsey "blew [his] top" and said, "President could not in the world take a course of ignoring U.N. or announcing it was a 'dead duck' – he has to continue to profess faith in its ultimate success or it really will be dead for all time." Clifford agreed with Elsey that no changes should be made to the speech.[25]

The Administration was saved by key allies in Congress. Vandenberg, whether from concern for the legislation or for self-promotion, introduced a series of amendments explaining the United Nations could "not now ... furnish to Greece and Turkey the financial and economic assistance which is immediately required"; however, the US aid would be withdrawn if subsequent UN action met Greek and Turkish needs. Senator Thomas Connally tried to defuse the issue of aid to China with soft questions to Acheson: "This is not a pattern out of a tailor's shop to fit everybody in the world and every nation in the world, because the conditions in no two nations are identical, is that true?"[26]

In the end, the Congressional vote for aid to Greece and Turkey was the clearest bipartisan mandate given to the President since 1939. The Senate passed the measure 67-23 and the House adopted it 287-107. By 22 May 1947, when the Greek–Turkish Aid Bill became law, the Truman Administration was embarking on the next stage of its global crusade.

Notes

1 "Fear of Russians is Dominant Note," *New York Times*, 23 March 1947
2 "Warning to Russia," *New York Times*, 13 March 1947
3 Anne O'Hare McCormick, "The Emergence of President Truman as a World Leader," *New York Times*, 15 March 1947
4 Felix Belair Jr, "Truman Assumes Lead in Fight on Communism," *New York Times*, 16 March 1947
5 James Reston, "The Big Question: What Will Our World Role Be?", *New York Times*, 16 March 1947
6 Freda Kirchwey, "Manifest Destiny, 1947," *The Nation*, 22 March 1947, 317–19; "The Truman Doctrine," *New Republic*, 24 March 1947
7 "Greece and the Shadow of War ...," *PM*, 13 March 1947
8 Willard Shelton, "Congress Divided on Military Aid," *PM*, 13 March 1947

9 Louther S. Horne, "Chicago: Opinion is Sharply Divided over our New Policy," *New York Times*, 23 March 1947

10 Eleanor Roosevelt, "I Cannot Accept Parts of President Truman's Speech," *Washington Daily News*, 15 March 1947

11 Clark Clifford interview, 19 April 1971, HST, Oral History Collection

12 Kirchwey, "Manifest Destiny, 1947"

13 Shelton, "Congress Divided on Military Aid"

14 George Elsey interview, 10 February 1964, and Clark Clifford interview, 23 March 1971, HST, Oral History Collection

15 "Awaiting the President," *Washington Post*, 12 March 1947

16 Arthur H. Vandenberg (ed.), *The Private Papers of Senator Vandenberg* (Boston, MA, 1952), 345. See also Walter Millis (ed.), *The Forrestal Diaries* (New York, 1951), 252–3

17 Progressive Citizens of America advertisement, "Henry Wallace Answers President Truman" in HST, Elsey Papers, Box 17, 12 March "Truman Doctrine Speech"

18 "Anything to Distort and Deceive," *Washington News*, 22 March 1947

19 *New York Times*, 23 March 1947 in HST, Elsey Papers, Box 64, Foreign Relations – Russia

20 Public Opinion Survey of Reactions to President Truman's Proposals Regarding Greece and Turkey, HST, White House Confidential File, Files 3–4

21 "U.N. Role in Greece Explained by U.S.," *New York Times*, 24 March 1947

22 "Mr. Austin to the Council," *New York Times*, 29 March 1947

23 See Richard Freeland, *The Truman Doctrine and the Origins of McCarthyism* (New York, 1972), 104–9

24 Drew Pearson, "The Washington Merry-Go-Round," *Washington Post*, 19 March 1947

25 Elsey notes, 3 April 1947, HST, Elsey Papers, Box 17, 5 April "Jefferson Day Speech"

26 Quoted in Dean Acheson, *Present at the Creation* (New York, 1969), 224–5

4

Securing the West

The Truman Doctrine had been put into practice but, given its portrayal of the worldwide contest, the passage of aid for Greece and Turkey could be only a limited if essential victory. With its message that any country threatened by subversion or aggression would receive American assistance, the Administration faced the prospect of numbers of States, within Europe and without, asking for help. The choice seemed obvious: either accept the open-ended commitment and the challenge of winning Congressional acceptance for it or retreat from "containment" of the Soviet threat.

Even as the doctrine was being proclaimed, James Reston of the *New York Times* was reporting that the sentiment of Truman's advisors was that "what is needed in the economic field to do the job right is not two isolated loans but a kind of peacetime lend-lease act that would enable the President to 'defend America by aiding the Allies' ". Reston concluded with a flourish from Britain's nineteenth-century policy in the Mediterranean: "We may again go into a difficult situation with too little and lay ourselves open to the charge that Lord Derby made against Disraeli's policy: that he merely 'muddled and muddled' until Britain's 'menaces are disregarded, its magniloquent language is ridiculed and its remonstrances are treated with contemptuous indifference' ".[1]

As usual, Reston's material was based on inside information, notably from Under-secretary of State Acheson. A week before the Truman Doctrine was issued, the State–War–Navy Coordinating Committee had been directed to examine an aid program to Europe. On the same day, Will Clayton, Assistant Secretary of State for Economic Affairs, wrote an influential memorandum which called for an emergency fund of $5 billion and a series of speeches by Truman and Secretary of State Marshall to "shock" the US public into support of the initiative.

Planning moved at an extraordinary pace. On 29 April, Marshall created a Policy Planning Staff (PPS) to design the program. On the same day, he delivered a national radio broadcast on the deadlocked talks with the Soviet Union at the Moscow Conference of Foreign Ministers, concluding, "The recovery of Europe has been far slower than had been expected. Disintegrating forces are becoming evident. The patient is sinking while the doctors deliberate. . . . Whatever action is possible . . . must be taken without delay."[2] Ten days later, Acheson previewed that action in a speech at the unusual venue of Delta State Teachers' College in Cleveland, Mississippi. He profiled "a state of utter exhaustion and economic dislocation" in Europe and Asia and concluded with a purple passage setting out not just an economic initiative but also an ideological program to establish the superiority of US values in the battle against Soviet Communism:

> Not only do human beings and nations exist in narrow economic margins, but also human dignity, human freedom, and democratic institutions.
>   It is one of the principal aims of our foreign policy today to use our economic and financial resources to widen these margins. It is necessary if we are to preserve our own freedoms and our democratic institutions. It is necessary for our national security. And it is our duty and privilege as human beings.[3]

This moral dimension emerged during the Policy Planning Staff's discussion on inclusion of Eastern European countries and the Soviet Union. To deny these countries the opportunity offered to Western Europe would expose the American presentation of a humanitarian offer to all as a sham; to allow participation risked Soviet obstruction. The PPS's solution was to invite the countries to participate in pan-European discussions as a sign of American belief in the universal appeal of its offer and "to tear off the veil . . . which forces the Russians to reveal the crude and ugly outlines of their hold" over the satellites.[4] Truman's assistant George Elsey summarized, "There was never any thought that the Soviets would actually join the Marshall Plan but it was a desirable step to persuade the world that we really were being altruistic."[5] Now it was the Kremlin that must make the difficult decision. Participation by any of the Eastern European countries would open up the Soviet buffer zone to a US-led economic system; Moscow's veto on that participation would expose its "domination" of countries that were supposedly free.

The initiative was supported by a barrage of publicity to keep the Soviets on the defensive. Within days of the PPS discussions, Kennan's Long Telegram was leaked to the press. Columnists Joseph and Stuart Alsop gave a full description of the document and the US strategy:

> Meet Soviet aggression and pressure with firm resistance, yet continue to extend the hand of friendship and avoid indulgence in threats. Meanwhile promote political and economic stability in the non-Soviet world. Put food in men's bellies and coal in their stoves. Strengthen the democracies, whether socialist or capitalist, by all economic and political means. Try, in short, to bring about a situation in which the rulers of the Kremlin, inspecting the world even through their distorting glasses, must admit the error of their previous analysis. When that time comes, they must formulate a new analysis and new policy.[6]

US News and World Reports studied "The Development of Russian Policy" to hint at the intent of the Marshall Plan:

> From now until the next meeting of the Council of Foreign Ministers in November at London, Russia will watch intently developments in the U.S. and in Europe. If the course of events tends to confirm Russia's expectations of a crisis in America and collapse in Europe, Russia will make no concessions at London. The cleavage between East and West then would be more clear cut than ever.
>
> If, on the other hand, the U.S. remains prosperous at home, and succeeds in leading Western Europe toward recovery, Russia may be expected to make concessions toward peace settlements.[7]

The planning culminated in Marshall's address to a commencement audience at Harvard University on 5 June. The Secretary of State carefully emphasized the positive dimension of his plan, stating, "Our policy is directed not against any country or doctrine but against hunger, poverty, desperation, and chaos." Without mentioning Moscow, he put the onus on the Soviets to accept US conditions. "Any government that is willing to assist in the task of recovery will find full cooperation, I am sure, on the part of the United States Government. Any government which maneuvers to block the recovery of other countries cannot expect help from us."[8]

East European and Soviet delegations did attend the first planning sessions of the European nations at Paris, but the PPS had correctly gauged Moscow's reaction. In the middle of the talks, Soviet intelligence from London revealed the US calculations. Vladimir Yerofeyev of the Soviet Foreign Ministry confirmed more than 50 years later, "This information confirmed that America didn't really want us to participate in it. They just made this demonstrative gesture in order not to scare away those already dealing with them."[9] The Soviets soon left the conference table and pressed countries like Poland, Czechoslovakia, and Hungary to renounce their initial acceptance of the plan. The walkout was a victory for the United States, with vindication through comments like that of the *Washington Star*:

> The first thing for the American people to do is to recognize that the parting of the ways has been reached, that there is no longer any tenable hope of working with Russia and that the only alternative is to face the bleak prospect of reorganizing as much of the world as we can without Russia. . . . The long-impending open clash between East and West has begun. It will be a hard and costly struggle for us. But we must strive to understand its implications; to comprehend the fact that defeat in this contest means the loss of all the things which we have held to be worthwhile in life.[10]

While this condemnation of the Soviets was a necessary part of the US strategy, the real challenge was to sell the Marshall Plan at home and abroad. As early as 28 May, a week before Marshall's speech at Harvard, Under-secretary of State Acheson had asked his officials for the machinery for "intensive public education on the Marshall Plan".[11] The US embassy in Moscow warned that it was essential to counteract an anti-American campaign which "repeated falsehoods and half-truths more often and louder than others so that many people believed them".[12] The problem was that the State Department was ill prepared for an information offensive. The Assistant Secretary of State for Public Affairs, William Benton, complained to Under-secretary of State Robert Lovett about the "sharp criticism from the public – both from political and other leaders and from press – saying that the government is not supplying the necessary information to obtain understanding of the European economy crisis".[13] Even after the issuance of the Truman Doctrine, the State Department remained aloof from any provision of information beyond a "full and fair picture" of American life.[14] "A substantial element" in the department had

> not wholly accepted (1) that there could be such a thing as aggressive, factual, and accurate propaganda distinct from the destruction, deceit, and purposeful confusion associated with the Nazi and Soviet kind; (2) that legitimate propaganda should be used, not only to reveal or "explain" U.S. moves in the field of foreign policy . . . but actually to help implement policy; or (3) that the Department of State could, without being accused of dictating a "party line", justifiably enunciate information policy which would provide a homogenous and consistent pattern throughout U.S. government information operations.[15]

The solution to the problem would be a watershed in the promotion of US ideology in the Cold War. For the first time outside war, the State's mission would be carried out through a network of "private" individuals, most linked by previous Government service and membership in influential New York associations. The opportunity for the Marshall Plan came through the Council on Foreign Relations, which had launched a study group in February 1947 on "Foreign Policy and Public Opinion". Chaired by Lester Markel of the *New York Times*, the panel included other representatives from the *Times*, the *New York Herald-Tribune*, and *Newsweek*, publishers, and leading academics. Many on the panel, such as Alger Hiss, had served in the Government; others, like Edward Barrett, a future Assistant Secretary of State for Public Affairs, would soon be working in the Executive Branch.[16]

After the announcement of the Marshall Plan, Theodore Repplier, the President of the Advertising Council, wrote Truman's Staff Assistant, John Steelman, to promise the council's support. He spoke of "a general vague realization that we are involved in an ideological war" but added, "The concern will need to penetrate very deep if we are to have the radical measures that would seem to be called for."[17] Benton's office drew up plans for a propaganda organization with Ira Mosher, President of the National Association of Manufacturers, and members like Thomas Watson of IBM, H. J. Heinz III, and John Winant, former US ambassador to London, but nothing came of the proposal.[18]

The solution came in early October when Clark Eichelberger, Director of the American Association for the United Nations, and Hiss, a former State Department official and the President of the Carnegie Endowment for International Peace, approached former Secretary of War Robert Patterson about an executive committee to promote the plan. Patterson in turn contacted Lovett and Secretary of Commerce Averell Harriman, both of whom assured him that the Government would welcome the initiative.[19]

So on 30 October 1947 a small group gathered at the Harvard Club in New York City to launch the Citizens' Committee to Defend the Marshall Plan. Henry Stimson, former Secretary of State and then Secretary of War under Roosevelt and Truman, agreed to serve as a figurehead chairman, and Patterson was named to lead the executive committee. A cross-section of the US elite was represented by other members, including Acheson, Allen Dulles, who had been a leading official in the wartime intelligence service, bankers Winthrop Aldrich and Frank Altschul, Philip Reed of the General Electric Corporation, the public relations guru Herbert Bayard Swope, and trade unionists James Carey and David Dubinsky.[20]

At the end of the year the committee, supported by $145,000 in contributions, launched a multi-media campaign. Its policy statement on 27 December stressed "effective aid is prompt aid . . . based on mutual respect and recovery".[21] Advertisements in leading newspapers urged readers to back the new US mission, although one ad to "Stop Stalin Now!" was never published because it was too blatantly anti-Soviet with its argument, "Weakness will foster Stalin's drive, abetted by his fifth columns everywhere, to establish the Russian brand of totalitarianism throughout the world."[22] The *Washington Post* published a special supplement on the plan and the *New York Times Sunday Magazine* printed Hiss's arguments for European recovery.[23] Booklets like *The Marshall Plan is Up to You* and *Who is the Man against the Marshall Plan?* used cartoons and simple explanations, such as "It's not being a sucker to help put out a fire in your neighbor's house so your own house won't burn down."[24] Committee members were given free time on national radio to state their case,[25] and Allen Dulles prepared a book in January 1948 describing the situation in Europe since 1945, the history of the Marshall Plan, and the European reaction. He concluded, "The Marshall Plan is not merely a philanthropic program. It is an attempt, in one vitally important area of the world, to protect free institutions, because we feel that in the world today we cannot live safely if these institutions disappear elsewhere."[26]

Speeches to influential groups were carefully designed for maximum publicity. Acheson was featured in a debate on *America's Town Hall Meeting of the Air* on "What Should We Do for Europe Now?", and his talks from Spokane to Minneapolis to San Francisco received headlines like "Europe Must Bow to Reds if Aid is Withheld" in the national press.[27] A conference in March was addressed by Secretary of State Marshall and chaired by Hiss, soon to achieve lasting fame for other reasons. Through Under-secretary of State Lovett, the committee also responded to the call of Senator Vandenberg, the majority leader, for testimony from "four or five top-level business executives". Eventually 26 members spoke before Senate and House committees.[28]

It is still open to question how far the committee succeeded in winning the approval of the general public. As late as March 1948, an extensive survey found only 45 percent of the public supported the Marshall Plan.[29] However, the committee was influential with key centers of opinion. The press and radio responded favorably, and most Congressmen were impressed with the committee's presentation. The campaign may not have been the primary catalyst for the plan's final passage in April 1948 – the worsening international situation, with the Communist *coup* in Czechoslovakia and the threat of a Soviet blockade of West Berlin probably settled matters – but it had helped mobilize pro-Administration forces at a critical juncture.

The Committee to Defend the Marshall Plan was only part of the new State–private effort, for even 100 percent domestic support would have been fruitless if European populations were not convinced of the benefits of the Marshall Plan. The apparent lure of free goods and commodities was balanced by the fear that the Americans were using the plan to control the economies of other countries. With the State Department's reluctance to conduct propaganda, the Economic Cooperation Administration (ECA), created to supervise the planning and allocation of Marshall aid, took up the challenge. The ECA disseminated pro-American news to local media, planted material with the Voice of America, and organized publicity for the effort through the advertising agency J. Walter Thompson.[30] Its staff proclaimed the merits of the plan on NBC Radio's *Report from Europe*, and the "Answer Man" handled audience questions "to give Europeans the American outlook".[31] Deals were negotiated to establish US magazines in Germany, Ireland, Norway, and the Netherlands, and key publications like the "Made in France" issue of *Fortune* magazine were placed "in the hands of some strategically-placed people in Europe". The *International Herald-Tribune* was eager to lend a hand to the ECA's campaign, especially after it received $15 million in assistance.[32]

Other covert schemes were necessary since, as an internal review of US propaganda noted, "signs of any American connection would immediately injure nationalistic sensitivities and destroy the movement before it really started". Material was regularly fed to radio stations in Belgium, France, Italy, the Netherlands, and Britain. Funds were channeled to labor unions, and Italian businessmen and heads of local Chambers of Commerce were "organized into an Italian National Committee to support the Marshall Plan", publishing material and preparing radio programmes with ECA material and assistance.[33]

By and large, the program was a success. By 1951, the 135 documentaries distributed by the ECA had been seen by 54 million Europeans. Each week, newsreels were watched by 30 million. Others could learn about the

Marshall Plan from millions of pamphlets such as "Qu'est que c'est le Plan Marshall?" and posters, including those carried by a "Train of Europe" making its way across the Continent. More than 90 percent of the non-Communist press was considered favorable to the plan, as US Labor Information Officers reported:

> Marshall Plan propaganda is ubiquitous. Hardly a day goes by without a good blurb in the papers, and even shop windows are loaded with subtle US propaganda. Marshall Plan literature is distributed by the bale. In all, one feels that the workers have been exposed to our propaganda and have absorbed a certain amount of it – the anti-Communist angle, for instance.[34]

Communist counter-propaganda was reduced, according to the US press, to ditties like "ERP [European Recovery Program] comes down to one thing only: Half a case of Coca-Cola."[35]

The ECA also performed another valuable service. Even after the issuance of the Truman Doctrine, Congress was slashing the budget requests of the information services by more than 50 percent. Congressmen like John Taber of New York, chairman of the House Appropriations Committee, alleged, "Propaganda that ostensibly is intended to build new respect for the United States is being used instead to criticize private enterprise, to express partisan opinions, and to distort the picture of life in the U.S." One representative even saw Moscow's evil influence, "When the taxpayers' money is used to buy pictures painted by Communist artists, we not only distribute their propaganda. We also put money in their pockets and thereby enable them to influence their efforts to make America Red Communist."[36] So when four Senators and 11 Representatives travelled to Europe to see the situation first-hand, the ECA seized the opportunity, not only to emphasize the virtues of the Marshall Plan but also to point to the necessity of a general information program about the United States. The Congressmen were "intentionally made aware of the extent of European ignorance regarding America, its purposes and objectives. The important role played by Communist propaganda in perpetuating these misconceptions was made clear."[37]

The delegation was convinced. Representative Karl Mundt, the co-chairman of a Congressional committee "studying propaganda, politics, and economics in Europe", told the Associated Press, "In the battle of ideologies, the blows are being struck with increasing strength and violence on each side, and something has got to give." The committee had concluded "that the United States information program . . . was inadequate in Europe's battle of ideas".[38] In January, within weeks of the delegation's return to Washington, Congress had passed the Smith–Mundt Act. The Act authorized the Secretary of State "to provide for the preparation, and dissemination abroad, of information about the U.S., its people, and its policies, through press, publications, radio, motion pictures, and other information media, and through information centers and instructors abroad".[39] The ECA pressed home its success by ensuring that more than 200 Congressmen on trips overseas could "see for themselves the unbelievably distorted picture of this country that the combination of foreign newsprint shortage, foreign publishing apathy, and organized anti-American propaganda has produced".[40]

The significance of "propaganda" in promoting US ideology and foreign policy was accentuated because the machinery to implement that policy was being radically overhauled even as the Marshall Plan was winning acceptance. The three military services were unified within the Department of Defense, and the National Security Act created the Central Intelligence Agency and instituted the National Security Council for decision-making. The public campaign for the use of the machinery was led by Kennan, who wrote in the influential journal *Foreign Affairs* in July 1947 on "The Sources of Soviet Conduct". According to Kennan, "The Soviet pressure aginst the free institutions of the Western world [posed] a test of the overall worth of the U.S. as a nation among nations." It was imperative for the United States to demonstrate that it had "the spiritual vitality capable of holding its own among the major ideological currents of the time".[41]

The article was published under the sobriquet "Mr. X", but the press soon learned the author's identity from Government sources. All major newspapers picked up the story, and magazines devoted several pages to descriptions of Kennan and his plans. The *Washington Post*'s Ernest Lindley best summarized the message for the public:

> In the calculable future . . . the U.S. cannot afford to relax. It must remain strong in every way and must employ its strength alertly and fearlessly.
>
> This may seem a dark analysis to those who still cling to the hope that stable peace can be worked out with the Kremlin – that the Russians, although hard bargainers, will stick to the agreements which they make. But, among close observers of the events of the last few years, there are not many left with those illusions.
>
> However, X. displays no pessimism about the ultimate result if the United States retains the strength, determination, and wisdom to wage a long struggle – if, as he says, the American public pull themselves together and accept "the responsibilities of moral and political leadership that history plainly intended them to bear".[42]

The role of the United Nations, the issue that had plagued the Truman Administration in March, was no longer a question. Columnist Marquis Childs reviewed the quarrel in the Security Council over the report of a UN commission on Greece and profiled one of the commission's members, newspaperman Mark Ethridge. Childs explained, "Here is a fair-minded man, of liberal-progressive thought, who became convinced of the reality of the Soviet plot. Unlike a certain type of liberal, who would prefer not to be troubled by facts, Ethridge had both the ability and the courage to examine the truth in all its tragic meaning." The conclusion was that "the United Nations was not an instrument for the relief of Greece. Recent events have demonstrated that unmistakably."[43]

Instead the question was what action the US Government, on its own or with selected allies, would take while awaiting the passage of the Marshall Plan. Any chance of American–Soviet cooperation was buried at the ill-tempered Moscow Conference of Foreign Ministers in December 1947. *US News and World Reports*, in a lengthy portrait of Secretary of State Marshall drawn from State Department sources, reported, "The time had arrived, he concluded [at Moscow], for a break with Russia, the abandonment, temporarily, of all efforts to settle Europe's affairs by agreement; for strong, independent action by the United States and her diplomatic allies. Russia, the conclusion was, will agree to nothing that she is not forced to accept."[44] With few exceptions, other publications agreed. Drew Middleton, who was the Moscow correspondent of the *New York Times* until he was refused entry into the Soviet Union in May 1947, revised history to portray the inevitable showdown, "Post-war cooperation between the East and West was doomed from the start. The Communist state could not cooperate in peace, as it had been forced to do in war, and remain true to Communist principles. The only question that arose after [the] Potsdam [conference of 1945] was when the break should be made."[45]

The immediate areas of concern were France and Italy, two of the linchpins of Western European recovery. Secretary of the Navy Forrestal had asked his colleagues in June 1947 how the United States would respond if confronted "with a Russian *démarche* accompanied by simultaneous *coups* in France and Italy".[46] The CIA's first special evaluations for the National Security Council (NSC) assessed that, while the Soviet Union was "unlikely to resort to open military aggression", it was "deliberately conducting political, economic, and psychological warfare" in such countries.[47] Communist-led trade unions were instigating general strikes and Communist parties were trying to build support for victory in general elections in the spring of 1948. If either country came under Communist rule, whether through military operations or the ballot box, the Marshall Plan might be doomed.[48] At the first meeting of the NSC, Undersecretary of State Robert Lovett verged on the melodramatic: "Our failure to act would mean the negation of any effort we had made in Turkey and Greece. . . . The whole position in the Middle East would be threatened. . . . Iran and Iraq and Saudi Arabia would have to reassess their position *vis-à-vis* Russia."[49]

In its first policy paper, the NSC concluded that, if the Communists won the Italian elections, the United States would consider support for military activity to undermine the new Government. The optimal situation, however, was to prevent the Communist accession to power. This would be sought through "all available economic, political, and, if necessary, military means to ensure that Italy remained a friendly, independent, democratic, and anti-Communist state", including "a vigorous propaganda campaign designed to show US support for and interest in Italy and its future". The United States would have to intervene in the country's internal affairs while maintaining the fiction that it was respecting Italy's right to free elections.[50]

Kennan pressed home the NSC's decision by writing to Lovett, "This country did not fight the war in Italy to see the Italian people again subjected to the totalitarian rule of a foreign country."[51] Indeed, he went further than the council by arguing that even the appearance of supporting freedom of choice might have to be abandoned, since the outlawing of the Communist Party was "preferable to a [Communist] bloodless election victory".[52] Secretary of State Marshall, far from opposing covert action, was "very concerned about the lack of financial resources in this Government to do things quickly, particularly when it is desirable that the actions not be documented. . . . There [was] an urgent necessity for concealed funds which should probably come from the CIA."[53] Most importantly, as Director of Central Intelligence Roscoe Hillenkoetter hesitated, Secretary of Defense Forrestal, responding to Kennan's call for a "guerrilla warfare corps" trained by the US military to "fight fire with fire", pressed for large-scale covert expenditure to defeat the Communists.[54]

Two significant conclusions followed. First, no campaign could rest on economic incentives or political pressure alone; electors had to be persuaded, through propaganda, that Communism was ideologically inferior to a "democratic" system. The situation required no less than a comprehensive plan for "psychological" activity. Second, the US ideology of "freedom" meant any campaign had to rely upon the public–private network such as the one developed to sell the Marshall Plan. While criticising the State "propaganda" of the Soviet Union, the US Government would limit its overt involvement to the "information" provided by the Voice of America. Most of the plans would be implemented through private groups and the covert channels of the CIA, financed by the diversion of $10 million from the US Government's "Exchange Stabilization Fund".[55]

In March 1948, a month before the Italian elections, the National Security Council confirmed the "private" approach in a revised document, NSC 1/3. Among its provisions were the channeling of campaign funds "from unvouchered and private sources" to non-Communist parties in Italy. Friendly Italians would be assisted in the establishment of clandestine radio stations, and a private letter-writing campaign by Italian-Americans would be supported by the US Government. The American message exploited positive initiatives, including Congressional passage of the Marshall Plan, the transfer of 29 US merchant ships to the Italian Government, American support for the return of Trieste to Italian jurisdiction, and $4.3 million to Italian prisoners of war who worked during captivity in the United States, as well as the not-so-positive consequences of a Communist victory, such as the cut-off of American aid and the refusal of immigration visas to the United States to any suspected Communist.[56] The playwright Arthur Miller, touring Italy during the campaign, recounted, "The Italian Communist Party might be the largest in Europe, but it was quietly advising people to vote for the Christian

Democrats in the upcoming election lest America cut off its food shipments and the country starve, the Russians having nothing to send in the event of a Red electoral victory."[57] With programs like a one-hour show from Hollywood for the orphans of Italian pilots, the Voice of America contrasted "the unequivocal assurances of the effective U.S. support for the free nations of Western Europe" with the reminder "that all previous working agreements or political compromises with Communists had always resulted in disaster and eventual Communist domination". Eleanor Roosevelt, boxer Rocky Graziano, actor Walter Pidgeon, and entertainers like Bing Crosby, Frank Sinatra, and Dinah Shore broadcast their commitment to Italian democracy. The message was also seen through newsreels and feature films – Greta Garbo's *Ninotchka* was said to have been particularly effective.

The common man was included through the "letters to Italy" campaign begun in Toledo, Ohio, propelled by an Italian-American newspaper editor in New York, and publicized by nationally syndicated columnist Drew Pearson.[58] Pearson also informed Italian readers "that they could not expect financial gifts or presents from American relatives" if the Communists won the elections. Amidst "the beginning of quite a friendship" between the Government and Cardinal Spellman of New York,[59] the National Catholic Welfare Council ensured that Italian priests and clergymen promoted the letter-writing campaign from the pulpit.[60] A typical form letter, one of 10 million that would be sent during the campaign, read:

> It is Easter Sunday and the bells ring joyously forth. In this country where people of every race and creed live together we would like to celebrate this Holy Day singing hymns for the peace and prosperity of the people.
>
> We are thinking especially of our beautiful and dear Italy, which after so much suffering, we finally want to see rebuilt and free from all tyranny and injustice. . . . Therefore it shouldn't surprise you if we ask, if we implore you not to throw our beautiful Italy into the arms of that cruel despot Communism.

Another more ominous message warned, "By voting for the Communists on April 18, you make yourselves slaves of Russia, which looks for the destruction of Religion, the Fatherland and the Family. . . . The Pope would probably be constrained to leave Rome, and the Holy City – beacon of the whole world – would be reduced to a heap of ruins."[61] Pius XII told a crowd of 350,000, as planes overhead scattered leaflets for the Christian Democrats, "The great hour of Christian conscience has struck! There can be no room . . . for pusillanimity or for the irresoluteness of those who believe they can serve two masters."[62] He backed up his words by excommunicating Communists.

Covert funding found a receptive Italian audience. Allen Dulles, the former spymaster working as a lawyer in New York, collected funds to provide free newsprint for cooperative newspapers.[63] The ECA pushed through a grant to build a printing plant in Rome, an effort which later had unexpected results when the plant began the publication of Communist tracts.[64] The CIA funneled money to the ruling Christian Democratic Party, a contribution which would reach an average of $3 million per year, and US corporations and labor unions were "persuaded" to make secret contributions to the non-Communist, moderate left Social Democratic Party.[65] One law firm alone sought $1 million from businessmen like Thomas Watson of IBM and labor leaders like David Dubinsky of the International Ladies Garment Workers Union.[66] In the most curious operation, private US firms, with or without support from within the Government, clandestinely transported arms into northern Italy, an initiative which provoked the concern of Director of Central Intelligence Hillenkoetter.[67]

US efforts in France focused on the development of an anti-Communist labor movement. Officials recognized that "America could not formally and openly interfere in the French labor question. Pressure might be put on the French Government but the US could not formally influence the labor leaders of France."[68] So, from autumn 1947, the State Department and CIA funded the efforts of Irving Brown, an American labor organizer, to split the Communist-led Confédération Générale du Travail and to promote the leading anti-Communist union, Force Ouvrière. Funds for other anti-Communist organizations came from American businesses, the CIA, and the US embassy, which provided at least $100,000 in early 1948.[69] In addition, the new Secretary of Defense, James Forrestal, arranged with New York bankers to send funds "to bribe French labor leaders to stop the strikes".[70] Special efforts were made to control docks, with the CIA allegedly using the American Federation of Labor to set up a front organization, the Mediterranean Port Committee.[71]

As with the activities of the Committee for the Marshall Plan, it is impossible to measure the effect of the campaign to save France and Italy. It could be argued that, irrespective of the US involvement, the Communists were never likely in the polarized political atmosphere of 1948 to gain a dominant plurality, let alone a majority, of the vote. A later evaluation claimed, however, that US programs "aided materially – perhaps decisively" the anti-Communist majority with "moderate" parties winning 65 percent of the vote. The Christian Democrats, who led the non-Communist coalition and received the largest share of "private" US support, increased their share from 37 percent to 49 percent.[72]

What was important was that the Truman Administration believed it had secured a major victory in the Cold War.[73] The contacts in France and Italy, as well as the broader campaign for European recovery, were maintained, with continued payments to trade unions and political parties. When Truman publicly claimed in 1963, "For some time I have been disturbed by the way the CIA has been diverted from its only assignment. It has become an operational and at times a policymaking arm of government," the CIA Director, John

McCone, sent two emissaries to remind Truman that he had been responsible for the change because of operations such as those in Italy. Truman supposedly recanted, "You're right and I would do it again today."[74]

Spurred by the French and Italian cases, the Government now treated "information" programs as an essential part of the American defense of the Free World. Wary of direct military involvement in the Greek civil war, the NSC instead sanctioned "actively combatting Communist propaganda in Greece by an effective US information program and by all other practical measures, including the use of unvouchered funds", and even countries like Norway and Denmark became the targets of "an aggressive combatting of communist propaganda by a vitalized, highly selective and intensified US information program".[75] Considering the matter in December 1947, the NSC acknowledged propaganda as a vital part of Cold War strategy, since "the USSR [was] conducting an intensive propaganda campaign directed primarily against the U.S. and is employing coordinated psychological, political, and economic measures designed to undermine non-Communist elements in all countries".[76]

The outcome was the first comprehensive mandate for Government "psychological strategy". This went beyond the traditional definition of propaganda as the provision of information. Instead it encompassed any initiative which might affect the position of a foreign regime. The State Department was charged with the responsibility to counter the Soviets "with sharpened contrast between US policies and way of life and those of the Soviet Union and its satellite regimes, in terms of human value". An Interdepartmental Coordinating Staff, with representatives from the State Department, the CIA, and the military services, was established to consider "a worldwide system of communications completely under government control", "timely guidance concerning subjects to be stressed or omitted from speeches" by Government officials and, for the first time, coordination with the "private" American media, "particularly columnists and radio commentators".[77]

Even more important was a secret annex, NSC 4-A, which sanctioned a covert psychological offensive under the oversight of the CIA. Secretary of State Marshall, while not questioning the need for secret operations, "was greatly concerned that the Secretary of State should not be identified with them".[78] So the impetus came from Secretary of Defense Forrestal, who asked Director of the CIA Hillenkoetter if the Agency could pursue programmes similar to those carried out in France. The CIA's legal counsel, Lawrence Houston, noted that the initiative was technically illegal, since "these activities were only related in a very general sense to intelligence affecting the national security as provided in [the 1947 National Security] Act"; however, he noted that the Agency had the capability if "given appropriate policy directives by the National Security Council and ... provided with funds for the purpose by Congress".[79]

Hillenkoetter was far from enthusiastic, since he perceived that "it was going to be practically impossible for the strategists to tell him *what* they wished him to do without insisting also upon telling him *how* he should do it";[80] however, there were others in the CIA who were more than ready for covert operations. Ever since the end of World War II, rump elements of the disbanded Office of Strategic Services had pursued their own plans in Eastern Europe, and those *ad hoc* progams continued in the new CIA. In autumn 1947, "two young and exuberant army officers attached to CIA as carry-overs from the Office of Strategic Services made contact almost openly with anti-communist and opposition leaders in Rumania, urged formation of anti-communist group, and recorded their efforts, names of conspirators, and even minutes of 'secret' meetings". The officers fled the country quickly but their incriminating notes ensured the arrest of their agents. "Loose work" also led to the round-up of agents in Hungary and Denmark.[81] Now, with the backing of NSC 4-A, the CIA could exercise formal control, establishing a Special Procedures Group (SPG) to broadcast from "black" radio stations and drop propaganda by balloon into Eastern Europe.[82]

The ideology of freedom, the broad notion of "propaganda", and the new Government machinery were converging to move foreign policy beyond "containment", particularly with pressure from US diplomats in Eastern Europe for an aggressive campaign. US ambassador Walter Bedell Smith warned from Moscow, "We have . . . been too preoccupied in the past with feeding the stomachs of people while the Soviets have concentrated on feeding their minds," while the US ambassador in Poland argued that information services "should either be discounted completely or expanded many times", since operations were "so limited as to appear almost ridiculous" when compared with Soviet output.[83] If the Truman Doctrine promised freedom and the Marshall Plan promoted economic progress for all, not just those living in non-Communist areas, shouldn't the United States pursue that dream within the Soviet bloc? Even George Kennan wrote of action "to promote tendencies which must eventually find their outlet in either the breakup or the gradual mellowing of Soviet power".[84]

The new Assistant Secretary of State for Public Affairs, George Allen, set out the harder line in an article for the journal *This Week*. Commenting on the case of two Soviet pilots who had defected to the United States after hearing Voice of America broadcasts, Allen announced that the old mission of a "full and fair picture" of the United States had been eclipsed:

> The State Department's Office of International Information has stopped dueling and started slugging, not with name-calling or vilification but with cold, hard facts. With vigorous new American techniques we are establishing the Voice of America as the Voice of Truth to a world-wide audience that has been confused, disturbed and betrayed by destructive propaganda from other sources. . . .

In this battle for men's minds, the Soviet Union itself is more important to us than any one country. No people are more jealously guarded or harder to reach, no other state has such absolute control over the information its citizens are permitted to receive.[85]

When an interdepartmental committee on psychological warfare noted, "Certain British criticisms have recently been made that we were too 'aggressive' and that we should merely strive to build up a large audience in peacetime by factual presentation," not a single member "seemed to be too sympathetic".[86]

The US offensive was about to begin.

Notes

1 James Reston, "Implications of Greek Aid Worry Truman's Advisers," *New York Times*, 12 March 1947
2 Quoted in Louis Halle, *The Cold War as History* (London, 1967), 127
3 Quoted in Dean Acheson, *Present at the Creation* (New York, 1969), 229
4 PPS-38, "US Objectives with Respect to Russia," *The State Department Policy Planning Staff Papers*: Volume 2, *1948* (New York, 1983), 385–6
5 George Elsey oral history, BBC Television, *The Cold War*, Part 3, 3 October 1998
6 Joseph and Stewart Alsop, "The Kennan Dispatch," *Washington Post*, 23 May 1947
7 "The Development of Russian Policy," *US News and World Reports*, 3 June 1947
8 Quoted in Acheson, *Present at the Creation*, 233
9 Vladimir Yerofeyev and Yuri Modin interviews, BBC Television, *The Cold War*, Part 3, 3 October 1998
10 "Russia Chooses Chaos," *Washington Star*, 3 July 1947
11 Michael Wala, "Selling the Marshall Plan at Home: The Committee for the Marshall Plan to Aid European Recovery," *Diplomatic History*, summer 1986, 249
12 Moscow to State Department, Cable 2094, 10 June 1947, FRUS, 1947, Volume IV, 567–9
13 Michael Wala, "Introduction," in Allen Dulles, *The Marshall Plan* (Oxford, 1993), xii
14 See the comments by William Benton to Laird Bell of the Chicago Council of Foreign Relations in Wala, "Selling the Marshall Plan," 248
15 Annual Report of the Interdepartmental Coordinating Staff, 1947, US DDRS, 1991 1448
16 See C. D. Jackson, "Food for Thought", undated [1948] in DDE, C. D. Jackson Papers, Box 37, Council on Foreign Relations
17 Robert Griffith, "The Selling of America: The Advertising Council and American Politics, 1942–1960," *Business History Review*, autumn 1983, 396
18 Wala, "Selling the Marshall Plan," 249–50
19 Wala, "Selling the Marshall Plan," 251–2
20 Circular memorandum, 28 October 1947, and press release, 9 December 1947, HST, Acheson Papers, Box 3, Committee for the Marshall Plan (Folder 1)
21 Press release, 22 December 1947, and Grew to Acheson, 31 December 1947, HST, Acheson Papers, Box 3, Committee for the Marshall Plan (Folder 1)
22 HST, Acheson Papers, Box 3, Committee for the Marshall Plan 1947–1948
23 "Report on the Activities of the Committee for the Marshall Plan to Aid European Recovery," 5 April 1948, HST, Acheson Papers, Box 3, Committee for the Marshall Plan 1947–1948

24 "The Marshall Plan is Up to You," and "Who is the Man against the Marshall Plan?", HST, Acheson Papers, Box 3, Committee for the Marshall Plan 1947–1948

25 "Report on the Activities of the Committee for the Marshall Plan to Aid European Recovery," 5 April 1948, HST, Acheson Papers, Box 3, Committee for the Marshall Plan 1947–1948

26 See Dulles, *The Marshall Plan*

27 Summary of America's Town Hall Meeting of the Air, 14 October 1947, HST, Acheson Papers, Box 4, Marshall Plan; "Acheson Says Europe Must Bow to Reds if Aid is Withheld," *Washington Star*, Acheson Papers, Box 4, Marshall Plan; Acheson, *Present at the Creation*, 240

28 Wala in Dulles, *The Marshall Plan*, xv; Wala, "Selling the Marshall Plan," 258–9. See HST, Acheson Papers, Box 3, Committee for the Marshall Plan 1947–1948

29 Wala, "Selling the Marshall Plan," 264

30 Lilly memorandum, "Development of American Psychological Operations," US DDRS, 1991 2302

31 NBC Radio program, "Report from Europe," 28 August 1948, USNA, Lot 53 D 47, Box 9, Records Relating to International Information Activities, 1938–1953, General Records; Player to Barrett, 14 September 1950, USNA, Department of State, Lot 53 D 47, Records Relating to International Information Activities, 1938–1953, Box 17, Miscellaneous

32 Korns to Sherman, 26 September 1951, HST, Staff Memoranda and Office Files, PSB Files, Box 1, 040 ECA; Jackson to Allen, 11 September 1949, DDE, Jackson Papers, Box 3, Time Inc., AA–AL Miscellaneous; Harriman to Luce, 24 January 1950, DDE, Jackson Papers, Box 48, HA Miscellaneous; Lilly memorandum, "Development of American Psychological Operations," US DDRS, 1990 567; Jacques Ellul, *Propaganda: The Formation of Men's Attitudes* (New York, 1973), 69–70

33 Lilly memorandum, "Development of American Psychological Operations," US DDRS, 1990 567

34 Korns to Sherman, 26 September 1951, HST, Staff Memoranda and Office Files, PSB Files, Box 1, 040 ECA; Anthony Carew, "Labour and the Marshall Plan," in Charles Maier (ed.), *The Cold War in Europe* (New York, 1991), 316–17

35 *Time*, 10 October 1949

36 "USIE Fight for Survival 1947" in Hulten to Player, 22 August 1950, HST, Elsey Papers, Box 65, Foreign Relations – Voice of America

37 Lilly memorandum, "Development of American Psychological Operations," US DDRS, 1991 2302

38 Associated Press, "Europe 'Slugging it Out' on Ideology, Says Mundt," *New York Times*, 6 October 1947

39 U.S. Information and Educational Exchange Act, January 1948, Public Law 402, 80th Congress, 2nd Session, 62 Stat. 6

40 C. D. Jackson, "Food for Thought," undated [1948], DDE, Jackson Papers, Box 37, Council on Foreign Relations

41 Mr. X [George Kennan], "The Sources of Soviet Conduct," *Foreign Affairs*, July 1947, 566–82. See the analysis of the article in Anders Stephanson, *Kennan and the Art of Foreign Policy* (Cambridge, MA, 1989), 73–9

42 Ernest Lindley, "The Article by 'X': Containment of Russia," *Washington Post*, 11 July 1947. See also "Stop-Russia Policy for U.S.," *US News and World Reports*, 25 July 1947, and "Messrs Bohlen and Kennan, Authors of Firm Policy to Russia," *US News and World Reports*, 8 August 1947

43 Marquis Childs, "U.N. and Greece," *Washington Post*, 22 July 1947

44 "Mr. Marshall's Advance from Worry to Decision over Russia," *US News and World Reports*, 2 January 1948

45 Drew Middleton, "Time, and Not War, is Goal of Soviets," *New York Times*, 8 February 1948

46 Walter Millis (ed.), *The Forrestal Diaries* (New York, 1951), 274

47 CIA 1, "Review of the World Situation as it Relates to the Security of the US," 26 September 1947, *Minutes*, Reel 1; CIA Special Evaluation 2, 7 November 1947, US DDRS, 1988 2415

48 CIA 3, "Review of the World Situation as it Relates to the Security of the US," 17 December 1947, *Minutes*, Reel 1

49 Quoted in Forrestal diary, 26 September 1947, in Millis (ed.), *The Forrestal Diaries*, 309–10

50 NSC 1/1, 14 November 1947, *Minutes*, Reel 2; Kennan to Lovett, 1 December 1947, USNA, State Department Lot Files, Lot 64 D 563, Records of the Policy Planning Staff, 1947–1953, Box 18, Italy

51 Kennan to Lovett, 1 December 1947, USNA, Department of State, Policy Planning Staff, Country and Area Files, Box 18, Italy

52 Cited in Stephanson, *Kennan and the Art of Foreign Policy*, 97

53 Seventh NSC meeting, 11 March 1948, USNA, Records of the National Security Council, Offical Meeting Minutes 1–40

54 Jacob Heilbrun, *New Republic*, 5 October 1992, cited in Alex Constantine, *Virtual Government: CIA Mind Control Operations in America* (Venice, CA, 1997), 27; William Corson, *The Armies of Ignorance: The Rise of the American Intelligence Empire* (New York, 1977), 295

55 Corson, *The Armies of Ignorance*, 298–300; Christopher Simpson, *Blowback: America's Recruitment of Nazis and its Effects on the Cold War* (New York, 1988), 89–94

56 NSC 1/3, 8 March 1948, USNA, Department of State, Policy Planning Staff, Country and Area Files, Box 18, Italy

57 Arthur Miller, *Timebends: A Life* (London, 1987), 162

58 James Miller, *The United States and Italy, 1940–1950: The Politics and Diplomacy of Stabilization* (Chapel Hill, NC, 1986), 49–51; Davis to Johnson, 25 July 1951, US DDRS, 1991 3538; Simpson, *Blowback*, 89–94; Lilly memorandum, "Development of American Psychological Operations," US DDRS, 1990 567; M. J. and Elizabeth Marvick, "U.S. Propaganda Efforts and the 1948 Italian Elections," in William Daugherty and Morris Janowitz (eds), *A Psychological Warfare Casebook* (Baltimore, MD, 1958), 322–4

59 Hillenkoetter oral history, 2 December 1952, USNA, Records of the CIA, History Source Collection of the CIA Historical Staff, Box 12, HS/HB 800B, Interviews H–J

60 Lilly memorandum, "Development of American Psychological Operations," US DDRS, 1990 567

61 Marvick in Daugherty and Janowitz (eds), *A Psychological Warfare Casebook*, 323

62 *Time*, 5 April 1948

63 Burton Hersh, *The Old Boys: The American Elite and the Origins of the CIA* (New York, 1992), 231–2

64 Dalcher memorandum, 7 February 1951, USNA, State Department Decimal File, 511.00/2-751

65 FRUS, 1947, III, 721. See Robert Borosage and John Marks (eds.), *The CIA File* (New York, 1976), 23

66 Robert Filippelli, "Luigi Antonini, the Italian-American Labor Council, and Cold-War Politics in Italy," *Labour History*, winter 1992, 117

67 Hillenkoetter to President and others, 12 April 1948, US DDRS, 1992 1218

68 Lilly memorandum, "Development of American Psychological Operations," US DDRS, 1992 2959

69 Irwin Wall, *The U.S. and the Making of Postwar France, 1945–1954* (Cambridge, UK, 1991), 101–12; Roger Faligot and Pascal Krop, *La Piscine* (London, 1989), 84–7; "Psychological Operations Plan Incident to Reduction of Communist Power in France – Annex A," 1 November 1951, US DDRS, 1991 1585

70 Lilly memorandum, "Psychological Operations, 1945–1951," 4 February 1952, HST, Staff Memoranda and Office Files, PSB Files, Box 15, 091.412, The Field and Role of Psychological Strategy in Cold War Planning

71 Wall, *The U.S. and the Making of Postwar France*, 108

72 PSB D-29, "An Evaluation of the Psychological Effect of US National Effort in Italy," 26 February 1953, US DDRS, 1989 3538

73 See, for example, the oral history of the CIA's Mark Wyatt in BBC Television, *The Cold War*, Part 3, 3 October 1998

74 Wayne Jackson, CIA Historical Review Program, *Allen Welsh Dulles as Director of Central Intelligence*, Volume III, USNA, Military Branch

75 NSC 5/2, 12 February 1948, *Documents*, Reel 2, Greece; NSC 28/1, 2 September 1948, *Documents*, Reel 2, Scandinavia

76 Lay memorandum, "The Foreign Information Program and Psychological Warfare Planning," 15 March 1955, US DDRS, 1977 306A; Souers memorandum, 2 June 1948, US DDRS, 1978 56C

77 State Department circular, 8 December 1947, FRUS, 1947, IV, 630–2; Meetings of the Interdepartmental Consultative Group on Psychological Warfare, March 1948, US DDRS, 1980 63 B–C; Annual Report of the Interdepartmental Coordinating Staff to Allen, 31 December 1948, US DDRS, 1991 1448

78 James Lay oral history, 17 December 1952, USNA, Records of the CIA, History Source Collection of the CIA Historical Staff, Box 12, HS/HB 800C, Interviews K–R

79 Lay memorandum, "The Foreign Information Program and Psychological Warfare Planning," 15 March 1955, US DDRS, 1977 306A; Lilly memorandum, "Psychological Operations, 1945–1951," 4 February 1952, HST, Staff Memoranda and Office Files, PSB Files, Box 15, 091.412, The Field and Role of Psychological Strategy in Cold War Planning; Wayne Jackson, CIA Historical Review Program, *Allen Welsh Dulles as Director of Central Intelligence*, Volume III, USNA, Military Archives; Mark Wyatt oral history, BBC Television, *The Cold War*, Part 3, 3 October 1998

80 Arthur Darling, *The Central Intelligence Agency: An Instrument of Government, to 1950* (University Park, PA, 1990), 250

81 Hanson Baldwin, "Errors in Collecting Data Held Exceeded by Evaluation Weaknesses," *New York Times*, 23 July 1948

82 Simpson, *Blowback*, 96–7; Sig Mickelson, *America's Other Voices: The Story of Radio Free Europe and Radio Liberty* (New York, 1983), 13–14; John Ranelagh, *The Agency: The Rise and Decline of the CIA* (New York, 1987), 114

83 Bedell Smith quoted in John Whitton and Arthur Larson, *Propaganda: Towards Disarmament in the War of Words* (Dobbs Ferry, NY, 1964), 47; Warsaw to State Department, Cable 1873, 15 November 1947, FRUS 1947, IV, 458

84 Kennan, "The Sources of Soviet Conduct"

85 A copy of the article is in HST, Sergeant Papers, Box 4, Deputy Assistant Secretary for Public Affairs, State Department 1947–1950

86 Meeting of the SANACC Subcommitee on Psychological Warfare, 8 July 1948, USNA, Records of the CIA, History Source Collection of the CIA Historical Staff, Box 23, HS/HC 291, SANACC Subcomm, Psychological Warfare

5

On to the attack

On 17 March 1948, just over a year after the presentation of the Truman Doctrine, the President was again addressing a joint session of the Congress. Truman was dressed for St Patrick's Day, his light gray suit set off by a green tie and pocket handkerchief. As he walked to the podium down an aisle strewn with green carnations to match the one in his lapel, he received prolonged applause from Democrats, Republicans, and the standing-room-only specta-tors' galleries. In contrast to the jovial setting, the atmosphere was tense. A grim-faced Truman warned "in sober and somber language" that the global threat envisaged in 1947 was now a reality which required an emergency response. A year earlier, Truman had at least refrained from mentioning the Soviet Union by name, but he now spared no rhetoric:

> The Soviet Union and its agents have destroyed the independence and democratic character of a whole series of nations in Eastern and Central Europe. It is this ruth-less course of action, and the clear design to extend it to the remaining free nations of Europe, that have brought about the critical situation in Europe today.
>
> The tragic death of the Republic of Czechoslovakia has sent a shock throughout the civilized world. New pressure is being brought to bear on Finland, to the hazard of the entire Scandinavian Peninsula. Greece is under direct military attack. . . . In Italy, a determined and aggressive effort is being made by a Communist minority to take control of that country.

Truman called for a quick and firm response: final passage of the Marshall Plan by Congress, support for the Western Union defense pact, to be signed by five European powers on the following day, universal military training, and temporary revival of the draft.

Not all of the proposals would receive Congressional support. The Marshall Plan was already on its way to completion, and the call for US support of the Western Union, led by Britain and France, was warmly greeted by Truman's fellow Democrats and a few Republicans. The Republicans were less receptive to universal military training and the draft, as were the public. One Boston clerk warned, "If they institute the draft, I'm going into the swamps."

Yet the importance of the President's call once more went beyond any specific proposal. To obtain bipartisan support for his general policy, Truman appealed for all Americans to "join hands, wholeheartedly and without reservation, in our efforts to preserve peace in the world". The reaction in Congress was overwhelming: "The Democratic-led response all but drowned out his last line: 'With God's help we shall succeed.' As he finished and again as he walked out of the chamber, both sides came to their feet applauding and there were a couple of rebel yells."

The ideological call to arms had been renewed. Truman explained that, facing the Soviet campaign to destroy "the remaining free nations of Europe, . . . the time [had] come when the free men and women of the world must face the threat to their liberty squarely and courageously". Even those Republicans who objected to the draft or universal military training praised Truman's "purpose to oppose" Communism, explaining that they stood "ready to do whatever is necessary for the defense of the country". When Senator Glen Taylor, the vice-presidential running mate of Henry Wallace, criticized Truman, Republican Senator Leverett Saltonstall replied that "the President spoke as a 'United States citizen' but he was not sure whom Taylor was speaking for", and Democratic Senator Spessard Holland announced his dissociation from Taylor's "over-friendly expressions toward Russia".[1]

Truman had more to do on this day. It was not enough to prepare Americans to fight the overseas threat; they also had to stop the Communist menace at home. So as soon as he finished his Congressional address, Truman flew to New York for a white-tie dinner with the Society of the Friendly Sons of St Patrick. The Catholic Archbishop of New York, Cardinal Spellman, "as American as an apple dumpling", warmed up the guests with the declaration, "We are permitting Soviet Russia to continue her policy of persecution and slaughter, dooming our neighbor-nations and ourselves to reap a rotted harvest of appeasement," and the prayer "As we stand at the crossroads of civilization – a civilization threatened with crucifixion by Communism – I beg Thee Almighty God that Thou, Who from out of confusion and disorder fashioned beauty and design, will once again come to the world's salvation, and give unto man the grace and will to choose Thy side, O God!"

Truman, with an "evident fervor and sincerity" that gave his speech "much more effectiveness" than previous addresses, reiterated his call to "join our strength with the strength of other free men the world over who believe as we do in liberty and justice and the dignity of men". This time the invocation of freedom followed a moment of high drama when Truman decided to depart from his prepared text and confront the challenge by labeling Henry Wallace, the former Vice-President who was now the presidential candidate of the Progressive Party, as an agent of Communism:

> I do not want and I will not accept the political support of Henry Wallace and his Communists. If joining them or permitting them to join me is the price of victory, I recommend defeat.

> These are days of high prices for everything, but any price for Wallace and his Communists is too much for me to pay. I'll not buy it.

The *New York Times* reported that, throughout this declaration, "a burst of cheers filled the emerald-decked ballroom and for a moment the President had to halt while the tumult continued".[2]

Undoubtedly the timing of Truman's St Patrick's Day mission had been motivated in part by domestic politics. The President had been lagging in opinion polls with estimates that Wallace's upstart candidacy could attract up to 8 million votes, about 15 percent of the electorate. In a special Congressional election in February, the Progressive-backed candidate, Leo Isaacson, easily defeated three challengers. So when news that the Communists had seized power in Czechoslovakia reached the United States, the President's special counsel, Clark Clifford, saw an opportunity. He proposed to Truman, on holiday in Key West, Florida, that the President speak to a joint session of Congress. Truman had "to demonstrate his leadership which country needs and want. Pres's prestige in foreign matters low now (Palestine, China) – [Republican Senator Arthur] Vandenberg and [Secretary of State George] Marshall get all credit on Marshall Plan."[3] George Elsey, who had already been preparing a St Patrick's Day address by Truman on the "problem of getting along with Russia", took up the challenge to show that "only leadership and timely action by the U.S. can prevent World War III".[4]

Yet, as with the Truman Doctrine, the domestic challenge did not create the trends in US foreign policy; it only highlighted them. First, Truman's speeches were needed to bolster "containment", portraying a defensive response to an emergency caused by Soviet aggression. Communist parties had consolidated their position in Eastern Europe and were still threatening electoral victory in France and Italy. Cooperation between the Soviets and the other three powers in Germany had irreparably broken down after the Moscow Council of Foreign Ministers in December 1947. Greece was still embroiled in civil war. A voluminous report by a Congressional subcommittee on "the strategy and tactics of world communism" summarized the dangers:

(1) The Communists have one goal – world revolution.
(2) They assume the revolution will be violent.
(3) They are incapable of accepting the idea that peace can endure from now on, and they expect one more catastrophic war.
(4) The Soviet Union is regarded as the main force of the revolution. . . .
(10) The division of Europe and Asia between the victors of World War II is to be settled by power politics and not by negotiation.[5]

Fear of the expanding Communist menace was crystalized in late February 1948 by the news that the Communist Party in Czechoslovakia had removed its coalition partners from government. The drama escalated when Jan Masaryk, Foreign Minister and son of the first President of Czechoslovakia, fell from an office window to his death, and rumors spread that Soviet pressure would turn neighboring Finland into a puppet State. The *Washington Evening Star* intoned, "A ruthless and vaultingly ambitous tyranny – the tyranny of Red totalitarianism – is on the march. If it is allowed to keep marching, not many years from now, there will be a titanic death struggle between it and what is left of the earth's free nations, meaning chiefly our own."[6] Scattered commentators such as the columnist Walter Lippmann questioned the US commitment to global containment,[7] but they were drowned out. The *New York Times*, urged on by the Administration, again invoked the ghost of the 1930s and the recent history of Soviet treachery to argue against immediate negotiation with Moscow. "If any chance now remains to halt Russian expansion, and reach an agreement with that country that will be more than a scrap of power, the European Recovery Program holds this hope. To abandon or seriously impair this program in favor of a new policy of appeasement would be not only one more tragic folly but the suicide of the Western World."[8]

Government reaction to the Czech *coup* was more symbol than substance, since US officials like Kennan had long anticipated that the Communists would "probably have to clamp down in Czechoslovakia".[9] A CIA assessment concluded that the *coup* did "not reflect any sudden increase in Soviet capabilities or any change in current Soviet policies or tactics".[10] The "crisis" coincided, however, with the assessment of General Lucius Clay, the US military commander in Berlin, that he "felt a subtle change" in the Soviet position and feared war would occur with "dramatic suddenness". The message, sent on 5 March, struck a chord with an Administration seeking Congressional passage of the Marshall Plan and military commanders who were looking for increased budgets as well as for preparations to meet Moscow head-on. The Joint Chiefs of Staff prepared an emergency war plan to confront a Soviet invasion of Western Europe and the Middle East while Secretary of the Army Kenneth Royall dramatically asked how long it would take to move atomic bombs to the Mediterranean and insisted, "We have no troops for Alaska and Greenland now to seize airbases there if the Soviets invade. If we got into trouble, we would lose all our troops in Japan and Europe."[11]

The war scare passed but Western Europe, led by Britain's search for a "third force", had already forged a defense system with the formation of the Brussels Pact by Britain, France, and the Benelux countries. Truman's speech, occurring on the same day as the signature of the pact, served as a public signal of US support for the initiative, as did Administration-inspired commentaries like that of Joseph and Stuart Alsop, "The United States will participate [in Western European defense]. The alternative is too clear and too grim to permit any other outcome."[12]

Indeed, while the attack on Wallace would become increasingly important in both the presidential campaign and the search for Communist subversives inside and outside Government, it was Truman's support of containment through the call to defend freedom abroad that captured press attention. Several newspapers cited his declaration, "We must be prepared to pay the price of peace or assuredly we shall pay the price of war," a paraphrase of George Washington's call in 1793 for a strong military establishment. A more important historical parallel was drawn between the Soviet menace and that of the 1930s. The *New York Times* explained:

> The ominous parallelism between Stalin's and Hitler's course makes it all the more essential to learn from the lessons of the past and to attempt to stem the tide of aggression before it engulfs us all. . . .
>
> We are confronted with the age-old conflict between freedom and tyranny. In that conflict the United States bears a special responsibility for leadership, because it is the only champion of freedom able today to stand up against tyranny.[13]

The *Washington Post* added, "To arm ourselves with and use the techniques of defense in this cold war upon which Moscow has embarked in the subjugation of the west and to ready ourselves for an emergency – this is the presidential summons which can be ignored only at the national peril,"[14] and the *Washington Daily News* amplified, "Soviet aggression has engulfed eastern Europe. Western Europe is next. If that happens, America's defense line is gone."[15] Western Europe's reception of the message was described in loving detail, from the London *Daily Telegraph*'s assertion that the message "may well rank among the greatest pronouncements in history" to the belief of "high French officials" that Congressional approval of Truman's proposals "would leave no room for misunderstanding, either in the East or West, that the United States means business about stopping communism". Of immediate importance was the "extremely deep impression" made in Italy, about to go to the polls, where the speech "was received with elation in the anti-Communist camp and with gloom by the extreme Left Wing parties".[16]

This aspect of Truman's speeches is now enshrined in History; what is left out is that the President had a second objective which went well beyond "containment". Even before the Czech *coup*, the Policy Planning Staff was considering "specific projects in the field of covert operations; where they should be fit into the structure of this Government, and how the Department of State should exercise direction and cooperation".[17] One example was the training and employing of refugees from the Soviet bloc in psychological operations, initially proposed by George Kennan in October 1947, because "we are ill-equipped to engage in the political and psychological conflict with the Soviet world".[18] The PPS then laid the foundation for a general offensive in an extraordinary report of March 1948. Labelled NSC 7, it jettisoned practical assessment of Czechoslovakia and other cases such as Germany for moral invocations. After repeating the litany that "the ultimate objective of Soviet-directed world communism is the domination of the world" with "aggressive pressure from without and militant revolutionary subversion from within", it established an ominous parallel to depict the ultimate threat:

> Today Stalin has come close to achieving what Hitler attempted in vain. The Soviet world extends from the Elbe River and the Adriatic Sea on the west to Manchuria on the east and embraces one-fifth of the land surface of the world. . . . The USSR has engaged the US in a struggle for power, or "cold war", in which our national security is at stake and from which we cannot withdraw short of eventual national suicide.

Kennan, who had spelled out "containment" only two years earlier, now believed that the strategy was insufficient:

> A defensive policy cannot be considered an effectual means of checking the momentum of communist expansion and inducing the Kremlin to relinquish its aggressive designs. . . . It leaves the initiative to the Kremlin, enabling it to strike at the time and place most suitable to its purpose and to effect tactical withdrawals and diversions. It permits the Kremlin to hold what it has already gained and leaves its power potential intact.

What else could be done? The Policy Planning Staff answered directly. "As an alternative to a defensive policy, the U.S. has open to it the organization of a world-wide counter-offensive against Soviet-directed world communism . . . aimed at mobilizing and strengthening our own and anti-Communist forces in the non-Soviet world and at undermining the strength of the Communist forces in the Soviet world." Economic, diplomatic, and military planning would be part of "a vigorous and effective ideological program" at home and abroad to vanquish Communism. Containment, with Western Europe "as an anti-communist association of states" defended by Washington's military strength and "overwhelming US superiority in atomic weapons", would be linked to "a coordinated program to support underground resistance movements in countries behind the Iron Curtain, including the USSR" and "a substantial emergency fund to combat Soviet-directed world Communism". The report even offered a prescription for "internal security": "a firm and coordinated program (to include legislation if necessary) designed to suppress the communist menace in the US in order to safeguard the US against the disruptive and dangerous subversive activities of communism".[19]

Truman eagerly took up the report's depiction of the final battle between good and evil. He labelled the Soviet Union "a Frankenstein dictatorship . . . worse than any of the others", including Hitler's Germany. In his diary, he confided:

> We cannot sit idly by and see totalitarianism spread to the whole of Europe. . . . We must meet the challenge if civilization is to survive. We represent the moral God-fearing peoples of the world. We must save the world from Atheism and totalitarianism. Only our strength will save the world.[20]

Similarly, a report by the National Security Council on internal security, fore-shadowing the rhetoric of McCarthyism, seized upon the struggle for hearts and minds at home:

> From [the] contrast of Communist and democratic ideas, the general outlines of the conflict of the ideological can be seen. . . . The Communists begin their attack with ideas and intend to finish it with guns if necessary. With ideas they spread their poisonous germs in every phase of American life either openly or by subtleties and indirection. These ideas seep into American politics, American economics, American educational institutions, American neighborhoods, and American homes.[21]

The US desire to take the fight to the Soviets was reinforced by a curious incident which linked foreign policy with the tensions of the presidential cam-paign. Henry Wallace, the Progressive Party's candidate, had made a series of statements criticizing Truman's policy of confrontation and calling for nego-tiations between Washington and Moscow. In early May, Stalin intervened with an open letter to Wallace accepting talks. This was followed by discus-sions between Stalin and US ambassador Bedell Smith.

Instead of pursuing the possibility of a thaw, however, the Truman Admin-istration regarded Stalin's approach as an insidious maneuver to influence the election and damage the American position abroad, especially in Western Europe. The US embassy in Moscow assessed, "This incident is first serious attack in what will no doubt prove to be long psychological warfare offensive designed to undermine growing resistance to Soviet expansionism both in Europe and America." The United States had to "hold firm and act posi-tively".[22] Officials "deplored the ability of the Russians to capitalize on the ignorance of the American public" and worried that "the President was getting forced into the position of apparently basing his actions on the expectation of war, whereas his aims were toward precisely the opposite objective". Secretary of Defense Forrestal summarized, "We must have a resolute and firm atittude behind which we can advance on a solid front and not on a jagged and spasmodic line."[23]

The Policy Planning Staff accordingly called for "The Inauguration of Organized Political Warfare", defined as "the employment of all the means at a nation's command, short of war, to achieve its national objectives". Kennan's officials established:

> This Government has, of course, in part consciously, and in part unconsciously, been conducting political warfare. Aggressive Soviet political warfare has drawn us overtly, first to the Truman Doctrine, next to ERP [the European Recovery Plan], then to sponsorship of Western Union. [*Deleted passage on covert activities*.] This was all political warfare and should be recognized as such.

To the PPS, the conclusion was evident: "The time is now fully ripe for the creation of a covert political warfare operations directorate within the Government."[24] Even Charles Bohlen, the prototypical State Department diplomat, acknowledged in a speech at the University of Arizona, "Propaganda means playing fast and loose with the truth as a means of confusing and not enlightening public opinion."[25]

As the report traveled through Government machinery, Kennan grew more and more agitated. By late May, he was warning Under-secretary of State Robert Lovett that further delay risked the loss of secret Congressional funding: "If it is not done now, it will mean that this Government has given up hope of conducting effective political warfare activities for the duration of this administration."[26] He was spurred by his belief that the CIA's existing *ad hoc* unit for covert activity, the Special Procedures Group, was operating "too freely". Hillenkoetter, who had little interest in covert activities apart from keeping them out of Kennan's domain, had appointed a Thomas Cassady, whom he knew from wartime activities in Vichy France, to head the Special Procedures Group and "develop his ideas on sabotage and subversive practices". Kennan and the State Department's opposition, however, limited the SPG "to a few persons in Washington . . . and Germany". SPG projects for radio transmissions and balloon drops, including distribution of "candy bars, soaps, and Mickey Mouse watches", were delayed. Allegedly "Kennan did not wish to hurt Russian feelings"; more likely, it was because the Policy Planning Staff was already "engaged in black propaganda against the Soviet Union and its satellites". Cassady was eventually forced to leave the CIA.[27]

The bureaucratic wrangling ensured that the PPS faced stiff opposition to its proposal for political warfare. Hillenkoetter countered with the suggestion that the CIA conduct covert operations with the assistance of a State Department liaison,[28] a conclusion reinforced by a special committee reviewing the CIA. Led by the ubiquitous Allen Dulles, who had just finished assisting the CIA with the anti-Communist effort in Italy, the committee recommended that covert action be developed within the CIA's Office of Special Operations to avoid duplication of effort.[29]

Kennan stood his ground. When the National Security Council suggested placing responsibility for political warfare within the CIA, he snapped that any program must be under the State Department's "intimate direction and control".[30] The NSC compromised by establishing an agency which was within neither the CIA nor the State Department. The Office of Special Projects, supervised by the Secretaries of State and Defence, would be responsible for operations

> conducted or sponsored by this Government against hostile foreign states or groups or in support of friendly foreign states or groups but which are so planned and executed that any U.S. Government responsibility for them is not evident to unauthorized persons and that, if uncovered, the U.S. Government can plausibly disclaim any responsibility for them. Specifically, such operations shall include any covert activities related to: propaganda; economic warfare; preventive direct action, including sabotage, anti-sabotage, demolition, and evacuation measures; subversion

against hostile states, including assistance to underground resistance movements, guerrillas and refugee liberation groups, and support of indigenous anti-Communist elements in threatened countries of the Free World.

The head of the Office of Special Projects would be appointed by the Secretary of State and would report to the Director of Central Intelligence. Review and evaluation would take place at weekly meetings of "senior consultants" from the CIA, State Department, and Department of Defense.[31]

Kennan was concerned that the arrangement made "too sharp a distinction between operations and planning" and was "too remote from the conduct of foreign policy" but accepted it as the best short-term solution. He then strengthened his position through the appointment of the director of the Office of Special Projects. Kennan's shortlist included Matthew Correa, who had served with Allen Dulles on the committee reviewing the CIA, Irving Brown, the labor leader who had assisted the CIA with its operations in France, and Kennan's assistant, John Paton Davies, but Kennan finally settled upon Frank Wisner, a veteran of the Office of Strategic Services, "on the recommendations of people who know him" and, perhaps, on the strength of his social contact with Wisner at the "Sunday Night Suppers" in Georgetown that brought together Washington's elite.[32]

Wisner was a colorful choice. A native of Mississippi, he had attended Princeton, earned a law degree at the University of Virginia, and joined a leading corporate law firm in New York. During his service with the OSS, he served as Allen Dulles's deputy in Germany but his principal work was in South-eastern Europe. Further opportunity came in 1947 when he was offered a post in the State Department with responsibility for the Balkans. His contacts with émigrés, furthered in summer 1947 by his tour of displaced persons camps in Germany, would be the perfect preparation for the covert pursuit of liberation.[33]

Kennan and Wisner soon established an effective link between the Policy Planning Staff and the Office of Special Projects.[34] Arrangements were consolidated in August by a "memorandum of conversation and understanding" signed by Kennan, Wisner, Hillenkoetter, and other representatives of the military and National Security Council. The Office of Special Projects, now renamed the Office of Policy Coordination (OPC), would be "a major political operation" with "the greatest flexibility and freedom from the regulations and administrative standards governing ordinary operations".[35] Robert Joyce, Kennan's liaison with the new organisation, was so keen on covert operations that he was "more CIA than the CIA" in the words of one OPC official.[36]

Thus, even before the breakdown in US–USSR relations culminated in the Soviet blockade of access to West Berlin in June, Washington had launched its covert offensive. Secretary of State George Marshall, long resistant to the

revival of propaganda and psychological operations, told US ambassadors that
the ultimate objective in Eastern Europe was the establishment of the Balkan
States "as democratic independent members [of the] family of nations".[37] In
South Korea, US ambassador Arthur Bunce tied American aid to "a whole
series of necessary reforms which [would] so appeal to the North Koreans that
their army [would] revolt, kill all the nasty Communists, and create a lovely
liberal democracy to the everlasting credit of the USA!"[38]

US plans were given a powerful boost by Yugoslavia's split with the Soviet
Union in June 1948. The Policy Planning Staff agreed that "Titoism as a disintegrating force in the Kremlin monolith should be stimulated and encouraged by all devices of propaganda".[39] The US ambassador to Yugoslavia,
Cavendish Cannon, gleefully told the US delegation to an international conference on the status of the river Danube, "I'm trying to break up the Soviet
bloc."[40] Formal policy, adopted by the NSC in the autumn, was slightly more
cautious, "Care should be taken . . . not to present Tito and his regime as anything other than what it is, i.e. a ruthless Communist police-state dictatorship.
Tito deserves and is receiving support from the West only because he is resisting the efforts of the Kremlin to destroy the independence of the Yugoslav
state." At the same time, it was imperative that the United States "disseminate in all areas, and particularly in Soviet-dominated areas, developments
relating to the Moscow–Belgrade controversy . . . [documenting] discrepancies
between Soviet myth and reality regarding peace, equality of nations, and
defense from imperialism, emphasizing concern for Yugoslav national independence, and strengthening Yugoslav resolve to defend independence and
sovereignty".[41]

The Policy Planning Staff, responding to the call of Secretary of Defense
Forrestal, was already considering "US defense arrangements in the light of
Soviet policies".[42] Now Kennan went much, much further. In a lengthy document completed in August, the PPS defined "US objectives with respect to
Russia". On the surface, the policy proclaimed that it was not seeking "to
bring about the overthrow of the Soviet Government", merely to reduce
Moscow's power and influence and to pressure the Soviet regime to abandon
its current policies; however, its tenor pointed to a more substantial effort to
undermine the Soviet bloc. Since it was "quite clear that the present leaders
of the Soviet Union can themselves never be brought to view [peaceful coex-
istence] . . . as intrinsically sound and desirable", the United States could "state
publicly that it is our objective to bring to the Russian people and government, by every means at our disposal, a more enlightened concept of international relations". More importantly, once the PPS looked beyond the Soviet
Union to the satellites, it moved from "letting the chips fall where they may
in terms of internal development" to the explicit recommendation: "The aim
of US policy in time of peace is to place the greatest possible strain on the
structure of relationships by which Soviet domination of this area is main-

tained." This could "be done by skillful use of economic power, by direct or indirect informational activity, . . . and by building up the hope and vigor of western Europe".[43]

The PPS was not only advocating the gradual retraction of Soviet power by sustained economic and political strength outside Eastern Europe, a sort of "containment plus"; with its vision of a battle against an intransigent, ideologically driven Soviet leadership, it was opening up the possibility of a more aggressive strategy. NSC 20/4, approved by the National Security Council in November 1948, restated the aim of "gradual retraction of undue Russian power and influence from the present perimeter areas around traditional Russian boundaries and the emergence of the satellite countries as entities independent of the USSR". The recommendation for "the greatest possible strain" on the Soviet bloc had been strengthened to "the maximum strain on the Soviet structure of power and particularly on the relationship between Moscow and the satellite countries".[44]

From Moscow, US ambassador Walter Bedell Smith outlined the ideological challenge, "It is extremely important for the democracies, and especially the United States, never to lose sight of the fundamental fact that we are engaged in a constant, continuing, grueling struggle for freedom and the American way of life that may extend over a period of many years."[45] In Washington, Frederick Oechsner, the State Department's representative on the interdepartmental committee discussing "information activities" insisted:

> The Services are disturbed at the lack of progress (I think it would be accurate to say "lack of State initiative") in carrying out the "intensification of foreign information measures" called for by NSC-4. A more aggressive line toward the Soviets is desired, putting Soviet totalitarianism on the defensive rather than being on the defensive ourselves. . . . State has here a clear responsibility to go over to a more positive information policy on a broad front."[46]

Once again, it was Kennan who put the mission in practical terms. He explained in a long letter to the new Secretary of State, Dean Acheson, "I am really not interested in carrying on in government service unless I can feel that we have at least a sporting chance of coping with our problem – that we are not just bravely paddling the antiquated raft of U.S. foreign policy upstream, at a speed of 3 miles an hour, against a current which is making 4." The ideological fight had to be taken to the Soviets:

> We must accept propaganda as a major weapon of policy, tactical as well as strategic, and begin to conduct it on modern and realistic lines.
>   This means a change in subjective attitude at the top of the Department. No important step should be decided without a simultaneous determination of the nature of its propagandistic development.[47]

Kennan told his staff that, with the objective to save Western Europe from Communism "achieved to a large extent. . . . Our objective now must be to obtain the retraction of Soviet power from Eastern Europe. If we can do this, war should not be necessary." The Staff's task was to study the Soviet satellites, separately and collectively, "to determine what are the weak spots on which to hammer relentlessly".[48] Reviewing the proposals of the Office of Policy Coordination for 1949–50, he wrote Frank Wisner, "In my opinion, this presentation contains the minimum of what is required from the foreign policy standpoint in the way of covert operations during the coming year. There may be one or two instances in which we will have to ask you to add to the list of functions set forth in this representation."[49]

The linkage of psychological strategy and covert action was confirmed at a PPS meeting on 1 April 1949. The meeting, reiterating the emphasis on Titoism as a disintegrating force, called for US information services to make "the peoples of the satellite countries quite certain that the U.S. stands for basic human freedoms and dignities and is with them in their struggle against communist domination and Russian imperialism". Eastern Europeans would be constantly reminded that "their respective cultures are being destroyed by a small minority of foreigners or native quislings who are working in the interests of the Soviet Union". This propaganda would underpin the "assistance and, wherever possible, support . . . given to elements within the captured countries which represent a weakness in the political control within the Russian orbit".[50]

Thus the United States had a multi-faceted offensive working at different levels. One dimension came through propaganda disseminated through Government money to journals like *Der Monat*, with "a definite impact on its intended German audience" to cause "worry and unhappiness to the Communist Party in Germany, and *Problems of Communism*.[51] State Department information officers in summer 1949 were authorized "to point out Soviet Union ties and point an accusing finger at the Soviets", and the Voice of America's programming, "posited on a peacetime basis until 1949, . . . underwent a slow change" with the tone "becoming more aggressive . . . and efforts made to put the USSR on the defensive". US authorities in Germany focused upon "charges of slavery, kidnapping, and the use of forced labor in the uranium mines" by the Soviets[52] while the Economic Cooperation Administration expanded its activities in Western Europe to include covert programmes, especially among "labor and progressive groups".[53] US ambassadors to Soviet bloc countries, meeting in October 1949, unanimously endorsed the strategy of "stressing particularly . . . independence from Kremlin domination that Yugoslavia has attained and . . . the exploitation of the satellite countries by the Soviet Union".[54]

The covert services made a unique contribution to the "information" offensive, with the Office of Policy Coordination developing plans through its Psychological Warfare Workshop. It was the workshop that first promoted funding for George Orwell's *Animal Farm* to be made into a feature film – the head of the workshop even arranged for Mrs Orwell to meet Clark Gable. A cruder idea, legendary in CIA folklore, was the proposal that extra-large condoms be dropped into the Soviet Union. The condoms would be labeled "Made in the USA: Medium".[55]

The recruitment of personnel for operations spearheaded by the Policy Planning Staff emphasized the use of refugees and defectors from the Soviet bloc. In 1947 the State–Army–Navy Coordinating Committee called for the identification of "political figures among [Eastern European] refugees . . . [as] the potential nucleus of possible Freedom Committees encouraging resistance movements in the Soviet World . . . [and] providing contacts with an underground";[56] the PPS turned this into a plan in March 1948 to "increase defections among the elite of the Soviet World and to utilize refugees from the Soviet World in the national interests of the U.S.", even considering the establishment of an American Foreign Legion.[57] Kennan and John Paton Davies of the PPS worked with Charles Thayer of the Voice of America, Llewellyn Thompson of the State Department's Office of European Affairs, and Wisner on Operation Bloodstone for the support of "anti-Communist elements . . . which [had] shown extreme fortitude in the face of [the] Communist menace and [support of] 'know-how' to counter Communist propaganda and . . . techniques to obtain control of mass movements". The network would be financed by $5 million from the military budget, "bootlegged" through the State Department for "secret disbursement".[58]

The system was further refined in late 1948 as Charles Thayer sought technical advice for broadcasting into the Soviet bloc and Kennan thought of a Eurasian Institute to consider East European problems. Authorization was sought for 250 refugees to enter the United States each year without the hindrance of immigration checks and clearances – one historian has estimated at least 200 who were brought in had Nazi connections[59] – and the State Department and Office of Policy Coordination were supporting a number of "national committees", such as the Council of Free Czechoslvakia and the Hungarian National Committee.[60] Discreet financing of the network continued via an unexpected source: the 5 percent of funds under the Marshall Plan reserved for the discretionary use of the United States in Europe. The amount, which came to about $200 million per year, was allocated by Richard Bissell; conveniently, Bissell's assistant, Frank Lindsay, had just moved to the Office of Policy Coordination.[61] An aide to Wisner recalled, "We couldn't spend it all. I remember once meeting with Wisner and the comptroller. My God, I said, how can we spend that? There were no limits and nobody had to account for it. It was amazing."[62]

The most dramatic use of the émigrés was in the paramilitary operations supported by the Office of Policy Coordination. From September 1949 the OPC, using US aircraft stripped of all markings, sent hundreds of personnel, supplies, dollars, and gold into the Baltic States, the Ukraine, Czechoslovakia,

Yugoslavia, and Rumania.[63] CIA officer Harry Rositzke recalled, "These cross-border operations involved enormous resources of technical and documenta-tion support, hundreds of training officers, thousands of safe houses, and, above all, hundreds of courageous men who preferred to fight the Russians or the Communists rather than linger in the DP [displaced persons] camps or emigrate to Brazil."[64] The scale of operations, and the accompanying delusions of grandeur, were exemplified when John Bross joined the Eastern European division of the OPC in 1951. Asked by a staffer on the Polish desk how many guerrillas were ready for development in the event of war, Bross flippantly replied, "37,000." The colleague readily accepted the estimate as realistic.[65]

Operations against the Ukraine combined the training of émigrés with support for the partisan movement the Organization of Ukrainian National-ists (UVO) and the Russian émigré group the National Labor Alliance (NTS). In the Baltic States, the US operations backed a war by partisans against Soviet troops, a conflict at its height between 1946 and 1949. The OPC developed operations with the intelligence network of Reinhard Gehlen, a German officer who began working with US authorities in 1946, and Britain's MI6 to recruit, organize, and infiltrate agents.[66]

The primary target was the small country of Albania on the Adriatic Sea, with the CIA persisting in the belief that 90 percent of the population opposed the Communist regime of Enver Hoxha and Wisner looking for "a clinical experiment to see whether larger rollback operations would be feasible else-where".[67] Britain also wanted to intervene, but it was strapped for funds; as a Foreign Office official noted, "Church mice don't make wars."[68] So in March 1949, a British delegation came to Washington for three days of talks about the Albanian situation with Robert Joyce, the PPS's liaison with the Office of Policy Coordination, and Wisner. According to Wisner's assistant, Frank Lindsay, the State Department was looking "to relieve the [Communist] pres-sure on Greece by stirring up a little trouble" in neighboring Albania, but the PPS discussions a few weeks later went even further. The meeting decided "something very definitely might be accomplished now in the way of (a) assist-ing in the overthrow of the present pro-Kremlin regime by a pro-Tito gang or (b) assisting in the setting up of a new regime which would be anti-Communist and therefore pro-west".[69]

Further discussions between Wisner and British officials confirmed an oper-ation in which Albanian émigrés, based in Malta, would be smuggled into the country to stir up resistance while American planes in Italy were used for "pro-paganda or intelligence operations".[70] Plans were developed by Lindsay and the OPC's Paramilitary Staff, and by September even the State Department was accepting the call for action within the Soviet bloc.[71] Secretary of State Acheson and British Foreign Secretary Ernest Bevin agreed to "try to bring down" the Hoxha Government "when the occasion arises".[72] The initial

British landings in October were followed by a CIA-created Albanian force of 250 refugees which began paratroop operations the following year.[73] An American-run base of operations was established in Athens under Michael Burke, an OSS veteran who would later become the chief officer of the New York Yankees.[74]

In the long run, however, the most significant aspects of the offensive would turn upon the development of a State–private network. With the Truman Administration charging the Communists with subversion of other countries; the US Government could not afford to be accused of doing the same. The answer was to establish a "private" facade for overt activities. In particular, that facade would support the national committees of émigrés, keeping officials "informed" about developments.[75]

Kennan toyed with the idea of an "American Freedom Committee" for months until the Policy Planning Staff finally developed a proposal based on the model of the Committee to Defend the Marshall Plan.[76] In spring 1949, Kennan and Wisner presented the plan to Acheson, with Kennan arguing that "the purposes and possibilities of such a Committee, if properly organized and properly headed, are of such vital importance as to warrant the exertion of the strongest possible effort to make it effective. It is designed to become one of the principal instrumentalities for accomplishing a number of our most important policy objectives." The Secretary of State concluded that "the idea underlying this project [was] a sound one".[77]

The immediate task was to find a chairman for the organization. George Marshall was unable to accept, having "only recently agreed, at the request of the President, to undertake another important responsiblity",[78] and Henry Stimson also declined. Joseph Grew, former Under-secretary of State, took on the task, however, and the National Committee for Free Europe (NCFE) was incorporated in May 1949 with luminaries like Lucius Clay, the former American commander in Berlin, Dwight Eisenhower, and Cecil B. DeMille on the board. It was far from a coincidence that DeWitt Poole, the former OSS official responsible for the Foreign Nationalities Branch, took on the post of Executive Secretary. Poole combined experience with energy: Robert Lang, who would soon work for the NCFE, described him as a "lovely guy without being practical. All that he ever said was, 'Bob, it looks good to me. Just dream. You can't dream big enough.' "[79]

In his initial press conference, Grew announced that the NCFE would "put the voices of these exiled leaders on the air, addressed to their own peoples back in Europe, in their own languages, in the familiar tones". Such a project would circumvent the State Department's "general belief . . . that refugees should not be used except in very unusual circumstances". Grew's promise was fulfilled through Radio Free Europe, which began broadcasting in 1950 to, in the words of Assistant Secretary of State Edward Barrett, "do broadcasting of a type which the Voice of America cannot afford to do".[80]

In October 1949, the PPS's John Paton Davies reviewed the new arrangements for "Political Warfare against the USSR". He noted that "the violent Soviet reaction [of] massive jamming of our broadcasts" on the Voice of America was "sound confirmation, if any was needed, of the Kremlin's fear of its own people", but this was "the only weapon being employed to penetrate this curtain". Davies suggested two immediate operations: (1) leaflet drops by balloon over the eastern part of the Soviet Union and (2) training of "anti-Soviet elements [as] airborne and parachute guerrilla units", to be introduced "in the event of war . . . into the interior of Russia for purposes of organizing civil war".[81] The National Security Council summarized the vision in its "US Policy toward the Soviet Satellite States". "[Propaganda should] sustain the hope and morale of the democratic imperatives in these countries and at the same time to take full advantage of actual and potential cleavages among the Communists and ruling groups in order to weaken the Soviet grip and make [it] possible for the [satellites] to be drawn out of the orbit of Soviet domination." The United States "should be alert to any opportunity to further the emergence of non-communist regimes in the satellite states, providing such non-communist regimes would have a reasonable prospect of survival"; however, it could work in the short term with existing regimes, as in Yugoslavia, "to cause an increasing isolation of the confirmed Stalinists from the nationalist elements of the communist party and from popular support in the satellite states toward the end that their power will be reduced". Economic operations would be used "in conjunction with other operations, such as psychological and unconventional operations, . . . to weaken the Soviet–satellite relationship". The policy concluded, "The propensity of the revolution to devour its own, the suspicions of the Kremlin regarding its agents, and the institutions of denunciation, purge, and liquidation are grave defects in the Soviet system which have never been adequately exploited."[82]

The transition from limited geopolitical strategy to global ideological crusade was almost complete. In early 1948, the Policy Planning Staff, had struck the "realist" pose that the United States "should refrain from offering moral and ideological advice" but argued six months later, "We are entirely within our own rights, and need feel no sense of guilt, in working for the destruction of concepts inconsistent with world peace and stability and for their replacement by ones of tolerance and international collaboration." The process was completed in May 1949 with the assertion "To attempt evasion of an obvious ideological issue is (1) objectively, to yield much of the field of conflict to our adversaries and (2) subjectively, to subvert our own ideological integrity – that is, deny subconsciously heritage and philosophic concepts which are inner reasons that we are, for all our shortcomings, not only great but good, and therefore a dynamic force in the mind of the world."[83]

Kennan, of course, would take a far different line after he left Government service, condemning the "moralism" in US foreign policy. To do so, he had to ignore or downplay his role in the policy. There is no mention in his memoirs of the OPC; it was only in 1975 that he spoke about his instrumental part in covert activity; even then, he insisted, "It did not work out at all the way I had conceived it or others of my associates in the Department of State. We had thought that this might be a facility which could be used when and if an occasion arose when it might be needed. There might be years when we wouldn't have to do anything like this."[84] Privately, Kennan expressed no such regrets. Writing to the Executive Director of the Congress for Cultural Freedom, a recipient of CIA support from 1950 to 1966, he contended:

> The flap about CIA money [exposed in the press in 1967] was quite unwarranted.
> . . . I never felt the slightest pangs of conscience about it. . . . This country has no
> ministry of culture, and the CIA was obliged to do what it could to fill the gap. It
> should be praised for having done so, not criticized.[85]

So, after the fact, was Kennan forgetful or disingenuous when he denied his role in the moral crusade of the United States? The answer is irrelevant. Long before he left the Policy Planning Staff in 1950, Kennan and others had established the organization for freedom's war against the Soviet Union.

Notes

1 "Truman's Minimum," *Washington Post*, 18 March 1948; Robert Albright, "U.N. Veto Abuse, Subjugation of Free Nations Cited in Speech," *Washington Post*, 18 March 1948; Felix Belair Jr, *New York Times*, 18 March 1948; "The West Acts to Stop Soviet Russia," *New York Times*, 21 March 1948

2 Frank S. Adams, "Truman Rejects any Backing of Wallace and Communists," *New York Times*, 18 March 1948. The description of Cardinal Spellman is in *Time*, 6 January 1947, 52

3 Elsey note, undated, HST, Elsey Papers, Box 21, March 17 Foreign Policy Address to Congress

4 Elsey draft, 3 March 1948, HST, Elsey Papers, Box 21, 17 March St Patrick's Day Speech; Elsey draft, undated, HST, Elsey Papers, Box 21, 17 March Foreign Policy Address to Congress

5 Robert F. Whitney, "Revolution Sole Soviet Aim, Says House Subcommittee," *New York Times*, 1 March 1948

6 "Real, Grim and Urgent," *Washington Evening Star*, 3 March 1948

7 Lippmann argued, "The policy of containment has . . . become what it was bound to become – an ever deeper entanglement in ever more insoluble difficulties." (Walter Lippmann, "The Costs of Containment," *Washington Post*, 10 February 1948)

8 "Cooperating with Russia," *New York Times*, 3 March 1948. See also "The Truman Doctrine," *New York Times*, 12 March 1948

9 Kennan to Marshall, 5 November 1947, USNA, Policy Planning Staff, Subject Files, Box 10, General

10 CIA 3–48, 10 March 1948, *Minutes*, Reel 1

11 Quoted in Daniel Yergin, *Shattered Peace: The Origins of the Cold War and the National Security State* (Boston, MA, 1977), 351–3

12 Joseph and Stewart Alsop, "The Military Phase Begins," *Washington Post*, 5 March 1948

13 "The Call to Action," *New York Times*, 18 March 1948

14 "Truman's Minimum," *Washington Post*, 18 March 1948
15 "Act Now!", *Washington Daily News*, 18 March 1948. Surprisingly, the loudest voice of dissent, apart from Wallace's forces, came from the conservative columnist David Lawrence. He urged Truman to "ask the Russian Government to appoint a mission of outstanding citizens to come to Washington" and to send a parallel mission of US citizens to Moscow: "We owe it to the people of both countries whose sons will have to be sacrificed if we fail to prevent war." (David Lawrence, "The War Nobody Wants", *US News and World Reports*, 26 March 1948)
16 Associated Press, "West Europe Cheered by Truman Talk," *New York Times*, 18 March 1948; Drew Middleton, "Britain Welcomes Truman's Message," *New York Times*, 18 March 1948; Arnaldo Cortesi, "Truman Heartens Anti-Reds in Italy," *New York Times*, 18 March 1948
17 Policy Planning Staff report, 30 April 1948, USNA, Policy Planning Staff, Subject Files, Box 11A, Political and Psychological Warfare. All information on the three projects discussed by the PPS is still classified
18 Jacob Heilbrun, *New Republic*, 5 October 1992, cited in Alex Constantine, *Virtual Government: CIA Mind Control Operations in America* (Venice, CA, 1997), 27; PPS/22, "Utilization of Refugees from the Soviet Union in U.S. National Interest" in *The State Department Policy Planning Staff Papers*, Volume 2, 1948 (New York, 1983), 88–95; Souers memorandum, 21 April 1948, US DDRS, 1991 1532
19 NSC 7, "The Position of the U.S. with Respect to Soviet-directed World Communism," 30 March 1948, USNA, Department of State, Lot 64 D 563, Records of the Policy Planning Staff, 1947–1953, Subject File, Box 8, Communism 1947–1951
20 Truman quoted in Robert Donovan, *Tumultnous Years: The Presidency of Harry S. Truman, 1949–1953* (New York, 1982), 358
21 NSC 17, "The Internal Security of the US," 28 June 1948, *Documents*, Reel 1
22 Moscow to State Department, Cable 890, 12 May 1948, FRUS, 1948, IV, 865–6
23 Forrestal diary, 18 and 21 May 1948, in Walter Millis (ed.), *The Forrestal Diaries* (New York, 1951), 416–17
24 Policy Planning Staff report, "The Inauguration of Organized Political Warfare," 30 April 1948, USNA, Department of State, Lot 64 D 563, Records of the Policy Planning Staff, 1947–1953, Subject Files, Box 11A, Political and Psychological Warfare 1947–1950
25 Bohlen statement, 26 May 1948, cited in Meeting of SANACC Subcommittee on Psychological Warfare, 6 July 1948, USNA, Records of the CIA, History Source Collection of the CIA Historical Staff, Box 23, HS/HC 291, SANACC Subcomm, Psychological Warfare
26 Kennan to Lovett, 25 May 1948, USNA, Department of State, Lot 64 D 563, Records of the Policy Planning Staff, 1947–1953, Subject Files, Box 11A, Political and Psychological Warfare 1947–1950. See also Kennan to Marshall and Lovett, 19 May 1948, USNA, Department of State, Lot 64 D 563, Records of the Policy Planning Staff, 1947–1953, Chronological File, Box 33, Chronological 1948
27 Roscoe Hillenkoetter oral history, 2 December 1952, USNA, Records of the CIA, History Source Collection of the CIA Historical Staff, Box 12, HS/HB 800B, Interviews H–J; John Baker oral history, 1 July 1953, USNA, Records of the CIA, 12, HS/HB 800A, Interviews A–G; Cassady to Dulin, 27 April 1948, USNA, Records of the CIA, History Source Collection of the CIA Historical Staff, Box 14, HS/HC 807A–807FF
28 Hillenkoetter to Souers, 24 May 1948, USNA, Records of the CIA, History Source Collection of the CIA Historical Staff, Box 14, HS/HC 807A–807FF
29 Thomas Powers, *The Man who Kept the Secrets: Richard Helms and the CIA* (London, 1979), 38 and 59
30 Kennan to Lovett, 2 June 1948, USNA, Department of State, Lot 64 D 563, Policy Planning Staff, Subject Files, Box 11A, Political and Psychological Warfare 1947–1950

31 Souers memorandum, 15 June 1948, US DDRS, 1978 189C
32 Kennan to Lovett, 30 June 1948, USNA, Department of State, Lot D 64 D 563, Policy Planning Staff, Subject Files, Box 11A, Political and Psychological Warfare; Evan Thomas, *The Very Best Men: Four who Dared in the Early Years of the CIA* (New York, 1995), 27–8
33 Sig Mickelson, *America's Other Voices: The Story of Radio Free Europe and Radio Liberty* (New York, 1983), 15–16; Thomas, *The Very Best Men*, 17–21
34 See, for example, Sidney Souers oral history, 9 December 1952, USNA, Records of the CIA, History Source Collection of the CIA Historical Staff, Box 12, HS/HB 800D, Interviews S–Z
35 Kennan to Webb, 30 March 1950, USNA, Department of State, Lot 64 D 563, Records of the Policy Planning Staff, 1947–1953, Chronological, Box 34, Chronological 1950
36 Quoted in Thomas, *The Very Best Men*, 40
37 Cited in Beatrice Heuser, "Covert Action within British and American Concepts of Containment, 1948–1951," in Richard Aldrich (ed.), *British Intelligence, Strategy and the Cold War, 1945–1951* (London, 1992), 67–8
38 James Matray, "Truman's Plan for Victory: National Self-determination and the 38th Parallel Decision in Korea," *Journal of American History*, September 1979, 315
39 Joyce to Savage, 1 April 1949, FRUS, 1949, V, 10–13
40 John Campbell oral history, 24 June 1974, HST, Oral History Collection
41 NSC 18, 2 September 1948, *Minutes*, Reel 2
42 The study culminated in PPS-33 in June 1948. (*The State Department Policy Planning Staff Papers*: Volume II, 1948, 281–92)
43 PPS-38, "US Objectives with Respect to Russia," *The State Department Policy Planning Staff Papers*: Volume II, 1948, 372–411
44 NSC 20/4, 23 November 1948, FRUS, 1948, I, 662–9
45 Cited in Norman Graebner (ed.), *Ideas and Diplomacy: Readings in the Intellectual Tradition of American Foreign Policy* (New York, 1964), 716
46 Oechsner to Allen, 9 September 1948, USNA, Department of State, Lot 53 D 47, Records Relating to International Information Activities, General Records, Box 9, NSC-4
47 Kennan to Acheson, 3 January 1949, USNA, Department of State, Lot 64 D 563, Policy Planning Staff, Chronological File, Box 33, Chronological 1949
48 Joyce to Savage, 1 April 1949, FRUS, 1949, V, 9–10. See also John Campbell oral history, 24 June 1974, HST, Oral History Collection
49 Kennan to Wisner, 6 January 1949, USNA, Department of State, Lot 64 D 563, Policy Planning Staff, Subject Files, Box 11A, Political and Psychological Warfare 1947–1950
50 Joyce to Savage, 1 April 1949, FRUS, 1949, V, 9–10
51 "First Report and the Preliminary Recommendations of the Panel on Doctrinal Warfare," undated, US DDRS, 1992 2961
52 Twenty-fifth NSC meeting, 21 October 1948, *Minutes*, 2nd Supplement
53 Lilly memorandum, "Development of American Psychological Operations," US DDRS, 1990 567
54 US Chiefs of Mission to Satellites Conference, 24–6 October 1949, FRUS, 1949, V, 28–35
55 Thomas, *The Very Best Men*, 33
56 Burton Hersh, *The Old Boys: The American Elite and the Origins of the CIA* (New York, 1992), 225
57 Quoted in Sigmund Diamond, *Compromised Campus: The Collaboration of Universities with the Intelligence Community, 1945–1955* (New York, 1992), 103–4
58 Butler to Wisner, 9 March 1948, and subsequent memoranda, USNA, Policy Planning Staff, Chronological Files, Box 33, Chronological 1948; Hersh, *The Old Boys*, 225–6. The émigré operations made a slow start. Operation Zrelope sought 1,000 recruits but found only 17,

trained at a cost of $30,000 each at Fort Meade, Maryland. (Thomas, *The Very Best Men*, 357)

59 Hersh, *The Old Boys*, 224; John Prados, *Presidents' Secret Wars: CIA and Pentagon Covert Operations from World War II to Iranscam* (New York, 1986), 56

60 State Department to US Delegation United Nations (Paris), Guide 1297, 25 October 1948, FRUS 1948, IV, 433; State Department to Heidelberg, Cable 248, 17 December 1948, FRUS 1948, IV, 435

61 Hersh, *The Old Boys*, 235–6

62 Quoted in Thomas, *The Very Best Men*, 40–1

63 Rhodri Jeffreys-Jones, *The CIA and American Democracy* (New Haven, CT, 1989), 50; John Ranelagh, *The Agency: The Rise and Decline of the CIA* (New York, 1987), 156–7; John Campbell oral history, 24 June 1974, HST, Oral History Collection; Powers, *The Man who Kept the Secrets*, 47–8

64 Final Report of the Select Committee to Study Governmental Operations with Respect to Intelligence Activities, *Foreign and Military Intelligence*, Book I, 26 April 1976, 322

65 Powers, *The Man who Kept the Secrets*, 49

66 Prados, *Presidents' Secret Wars*, 37–44 and 50–60

67 Michael Dravis, "Storming Fortress Albania: American Covert Operations in Microcosm, 1949–1954," *Intelligence and National Security*, October 1992, 430; Hersh, *The Old Boys*, 271

68 Quoted in Thomas, *The Very Best Men*, 38

69 Hersh, *The Old Boys*, 261–2; Joyce to Savage, 1 April 1949, FRUS, 1949, V, 10–13

70 Hersh, *The Old Boys*, 263; State Department memorandum, "Albania," undated, US DDRS, 1992 649

71 Powers, *The Man who Kept the Secrets*, 53; Dravis, "Storming Fortress Albania," 431

72 Acheson–Bevin meeting, 14 September 1949, FRUS, 1949, VI, 415

73 Dravis, "Storming Fortress Albania," 432–3

74 Thomas, *The Very Best Men*, 39. See also Thomas Rees, "Blunder and Betrayal in the Balkans," *Guardian Weekend* (London), 10 October 1998

75 Thompson to Butler, 7 April 1948, USNA, Department of State, Lot 64 D 563, Records of the Policy Planning Staff, 1947–1953, Subject Files, Box 11A, Political and Psychological Warfare 1947–1950

76 Arthur Darling, *The Central Intelligence Agency: An Instrument of Government, to 1950* (University Park, PA, 1990), 274

77 Kennan to Acheson, 19 April 1949, USNA, Department of State, Lot 64 D 563, Records of the Policy Planning Staff, 1947–1953, Chronological File, Box 33, Chronological 1949

78 Kennan to Acheson, 19 April 1949, USNA, Department of State, Policy Planning Staff, Chronological File, Box 33, Chronological 1949

79 Robert Lang oral history, 31 May 1981, Hoover Institution Archives, Sig Mickelson Collection, Audiotape 29

80 Robert Holt, *Radio Free Europe* (Minneapolis, MN, 1958), 9–13; Mickelson, *America's Other Voices*, 18; Barrett memorandum, 22 March 1950, USNA, Department of State, Lot 53 D 47, Records Relating to International Information Activities, 1938–1953, Box 14, Free Nations (Europe)

81 John Paton Davies memorandum, "Political Warfare against the USSR," 19 October 1949, USNA, Department of State, Lot 64 D 563, Records of the Policy Planning Staff, 1947–1953, Box 11, Political and Psychological Warfare 1947–1950

82 NSC 58/2, 8 December 1949, Minutes, Reel 1; NSC Progress Report on NSC 58/2, 29 May 1950, US DDRS, 1992 886

83 PPS/23, "Review of Current Trends in U.S. Foreign Policy," and PPS/38, "U.S. Objectives with Respect to Russia," 384, *The State Department Policy Planning Staff Papers*, Volume II: *1948*

(New York, 1983), 122 and 384; Kennan to Acheson, 15 May 1949, *The State Department Policy Planning Staff Papers*, Volume III: *1949*, 43

84 See William Leary (ed.), *The Central Intelligence Agency: History and Documents* (University, AL, 1984), and Thomas, *The Very Best Men*, 30

85 Quoted in Diamond, *Compromised Campus*, 315

6

Declaring war for freedom

A US official surveying the world situation in autumn 1949 should have had cause for celebration. "Containment" had succeeded in Western Europe. The Communists had been excluded from the French and Italian governments. Greece was emerging from civil war. Billions of dollars of Marshall Plan aid were financing a resurgent economy. The blockade of Berlin, lifted in spring 1949, only accelerated the formation of an independent West Germany and the North Atlantic Treaty Organization.

However, any optimism was blunted by disheartening, even traumatic events elsewhere. The Soviets erased the US monopoly of the atom bomb with their first test explosion in August, and Mao Tse-Tung's forces had emerged victorious in China. The Joint Chiefs of Staff were panicked: "The U.S. may lose this war and the American way of life without firing a shot."[1] Truman again tried to steel public resolve:

> The earth is deeply divided between free and captive peoples. There is no appeal to the brotherhood of men who live in deadly fear of the concentration camp. Until the captive peoples of the world emerge from darkness, they cannot see the hand we hold out in friendship. While they are made to respond to our hand-clasp with a mailed fist, we have no choice but to stand ready in self-defense.
>
> Much as we prize peace and friendship, we prize freedom more.[2]

The "loss" of China was especially damaging, for it exposed the limits of the ideology behind the Truman Doctrine. Critics had long argued that, if the speech promised a defence of freedom against subversion in Europe, it should also make that pledge to Asian regimes like the Nationalist Chinese Government of Chiang Kai-shek. General Albert Wedemeyer summarized, "Secretary of State [Marshall] seems to have failed to appreciate the ambiguity of his policy when he recommended that $400,000,000 be given to Greece to keep the Communists out of power while continuing to deny military or economic aid to our Chinese ally unless until Chiang Kai-shek should agree to take the Communists in." Yet as late as April 1948 Truman was calling for a Chinese coalition Government which included the Communists.[3] Late in the year, the

Administration fulfilled an agreement with the Soviets under which both countries withdrew their troops from Korea.[4]

The Administration had turned away from the universal commitment to freedom because of the pragmatic assessment that the Communists were gaining the upper hand in much of China and that the Nationalist Government was riddled with corruption and inefficiency. Secretary of State George Marshall informed the National Security Council in late 1948 that 33 Chinese Nationalist divisions had surrendered without even burning their arms depots, lamenting, "We couldn't even state the facts if we wish to continue supporting Chiang Kai-shek."[5] Notes for Marshall's successor, Dean Acheson, concluded, "No amount of monetary aid with or without military advice can help so discredited and inefficient an outfit. Gimo [Chiang] has lost confidence of all groups. . . . [Aid] prolongs war which cannot be won."[6] Even after the outbreak of the Korean War, Truman insisted, "We were not going to give the Chinese 'a nickel' for any purpose whatsoever. . . . All the money we had given them is now invested in US real estate."[7]

Yet the vision of a global Communism with Peking linked to Moscow, and of the corresponding need for appropriate US action to split the two powers, was never discarded. The Administration was still concerned that "the growing military and political power of the Chinese Communists [was] making a substantial contribution to the attainment of Soviet objectives in the Far East".[8] Thus, if the National Security Council was concluding in March 1949 that it would "avoid military and political support" of any non-Communist regime unless it was "willing actively to resist communism", it was looking for that willing regime by covertly seeking "A Third Force" as an alternative to the ineffectual Chiang Kai-shek: "Our principal reliance in combatting Kremlin influence in China should . . . be on the activities of indigenous Chinese elements. Because we bear the incubus of interventionists, our official interest in and support of these elements, a vast and delicate enterprise, should not be apparent and should be implemented through appropriate clandestine channels."[9]

In April 1949, the Policy Planning Staff suggested that the Office of Policy Coordination embark on Operation Tawny Pippit, with meteorological balloons dropping thousands of leaflets to lead the population to resistance. The OPC bought Civil Air Transport, the service famed for its World War II operations under General Claire Chennault, which had been flying relief supplies into the interior of China as "the most rugged rough-and-tumble flying show in the world". The State Department embarked upon the production of pamphlets, "describing the true nature of Communist domination" and promoting US democracy, such as "Education for Freedom", "Government by the People", and "Toward World Peace and Progress".[10] High-ranking officials discussed the increased use of radio and noted the "great importance that a private undertaking be set in operation" to work with Chinese students in the

United Sates.[11] In the most ambitious (and costly) operation, Wisner sent a "pot of gold" to a Chinese Nationalist general to hold the island of Hainan off the southern coast of China; unfortunately, the Communists made a higher offer.[12]

In a detailed paper summarizing the initiatives, Kennan tied the Chinese campaign to the efforts to turn East European regimes against Moscow.[13] While overt propaganda should not concentrate on an anti-Soviet line, clandestine operations could play upon a number of themes to meet the National Security Council's goal of "exposure of Soviet imperialism and driving a wedge between the Chinese and Stalinism":

> Some of these mouthpieces will inevitably go bad on us or get off the track. That is a risk which any imaginative and aggressive covert organization must take . . . but only by intelligently taking such risks will we achieve the . . . prolific and catholic appeal necessary to produce quickly in Communist China a widespread reaction against Soviet imperialism.[14]

A week later, the State Department's International Broadcasting Division was instructed to take the stern, disinterested approach "that China [was] under the heel of a ruthless imperialism, that a semi-independent communism [was] far more desirable than one completely dominated by a foreign power", and that the United States, while far from sympathetic to Communism, might be able to do business with a Tito figure.[15]

The American approach was consolidated in a comprehensive statement of policy, NSC 48/2, in December 1949. In one sense, the document tried to distance the United States from the immediate conflict between the Chinese Communists and the discredited regime of Chiang Kai-shek, who had retreated to the island of Taiwan. Acheson stressed that any aid to Taiwan would "place [the United States] in the position of subsidizing attacks on a government [in Peking] which will soon be generally recognized" and alienate nationalist sentiment in Asia. He concluded sharply, "We had now extricated ourselves from the Chinese civil war and it was important that we would not be drawn into it again." At the same time, NSC 48/2 set out the long-term vision of the "gradual retraction and eventual elimination of the preponderant power and influence of the USSR in Asia to such a degree that the Soviet Union will not be capable of threatening from that area the security of the US or its friends". The Administration would "exploit, through appropriate political, psychological, and economic means, any rifts between the Chinese Communists and the USSR and between the Stalinists and other elements in China, while scrupulously avoiding the appearance of intervention".[16]

The outcome was a tension between the "realistic" programme of accommodation with the new China and the "ideological" impulse to overthrow Communism, or at least any pro-Soviet variant of it. On the one hand, Truman considered recognition of Mao's regime and Acheson tried to define a system of containment in Asia in a speech on 12 January 1950 to the Senate Foreign Relations Committee. On the other, the Policy Planning Staff and the CIA continued their support of anti-Communist elements, inside and outside China, who might organize successful resistance campaigns. A key State Department official argued that it might still be possible "to retain footholds in South China" as "rallying points susceptible for use in future efforts to deliver the country from Communism".[17] Kennan struck a balance between the two approaches, advising Acheson that the key to success was the use of psychological strategy. "Remember, Russians haven't attacked anyone militarily since V-J Day. Their successes, such as they have been, have been primarily in [the] minds of men. True, their communist stooges have used force, but they first had to be convinced themselves."[18]

This balance was upset in February when China and the Soviet Union signed a Pact of Friendship. The CIA analysis was doom-laden:

> The USSR, exploiting China's needs for "friendly aid", can gradually strengthen the Soviet hold on the party machine, the armed forces, the secret police, communications, and channels of information. Communist control of China, assuming Sino-Soviet cooperation, provides the base for spreading revolutionary propaganda and subversive activities, particularly guerrilla warfare, in Southeast Asia.[19]

The spectre of a monolithic Red bloc loomed just as Senator Joseph McCarthy was launching his first accusations of Communist infiltration of the US government. On 9 February, addressing the Ohio County Women's Club in Wheeling, West Virginia, the Senator from Wisconsin proclaimed, "The reason why we find ourselves in a position of impotency is not because the enemy has sent men to invade our shores but rather because of the traitorous actions of those . . . who have had all the benefits that the wealthiest nation on earth has had to offer – the finest homes, the finest college educations, and the finest jobs in Government we can give." He then declared that he had "in his hand a list" proving the large-scale penetration of the State Department by Communists. The number of spies varied, according to time and place of presentation, from 57 to 205, but it was the general message, not the specific figure, that would rock the United States.[20]

The Truman Administration had been cornered by its promise of a global crusade. Regardless of the practical considerations, any retreat would represent capitulation to the Communist enemy, so the question was no longer whether the United States would pursue an all-out offensive against Moscow but how and when. The process was set in motion on 31 January when the President asked officials to submit a comprehensive report about Moscow's acquisition of the atomic bomb.

Truman's request coincided with a significant change of leadership at the Policy Planning Staff. Kennan had left at the end of 1949 to be replaced by Paul Nitze, who was in no mood for a case-by-case assessment of the situation. Instead he started from the premise that, as Moscow was committed to a global conflict, the US response could not be limited to "containment". "What we found most disturbing was not that the Soviet Union would espouse such objectives but that it had developed a political, economic, and military structure designed specifically for their eventual realization. It followed that if the US were to deal effectively with this threat, it had no choice other than to take the lead in initiating a substantial and rapid building-up of strength in the free world . . . to support affirmative policy intended to check and roll back the Kremlin's drive for world domination."[21]

By 2 February Nitze, supported by strident intelligence assessments of Moscow's world-wide challenge reflecting "the aggressive, self-confident, even boastful Soviet attitude",[22] was telling Acheson's daily meeting of officials that the danger of war was "considerably greater" than the previous autumn. The PPS agreed that there was an "increasing number of signs of toughness on the part of the Kremlin" and noted the opinion of the Joint Chiefs of Staff that the Soviets could launch a sneak attack without any signs of mobilization. In short, Moscow had jettisoned the Marxist tenet that Communism had an "infinite time" to achieve its aims.[23] Nitze summarized the conclusions in a formal "study":

> Stalin's election speech of 1946 was an open declaration of hostility, and since that time the USSR has given every sign that it neither intends to abandon the struggle, other than on its own terms, nor pause in its prosecution. . . . This approach, on the one hand, holds out for the USSR the possibility that it can achieve success over the U.S. without ever resorting to an all-out military assault. On the other hand, it leaves open the possibility of a quick Soviet decision to resort to military action, locally or generally.[24]

At this point Kennan dramatically broke with his old office. The issue, however, was not the aim of US foreign policy. Kennan never renounced his earlier campaign to break up the Soviet bloc, and he was just as eager to rest his position upon a clear conception of the superiority of American values, warning of the mistaken "belief that we can achieve our purposes . . . without real ideological discipline".[25] Instead, Kennan's difference was with Nitze's presentation of Moscow's threat. By mid-1949, Kennan was arguing that the Soviets appeared "to have adopted a containment policy",[26] and he now asserted, "There is little justification for the impression that the 'cold war', by virtue of events outside of our control, has suddenly taken some drastic turn to our disadvantage." He urged Acheson to shed the American dependence on atomic weapons and, rather than adopting the sweeping global conception, to pursue a more limited diplomatic and economic strategy.[27]

Kennan's voice was scarcely heard as Nitze dominated the meetings of the State–Defense Policy Review Group. A survey of "Soviet Intentions and Capabilities" rested upon the assumption, "The entire power system of the USSR impels it to engage in a struggle with the US. There is consequently no prospect that the USSR will abandon the struggle of its own volition."[28] Another intelligence assessment noted, "Soviet policy is based on the belief that the establishment of World Communism is inevitable and that, provided the Soviet Union is strong enough to deter capitalist aggression, it can be achieved without the Soviet Union becoming involved in a major war with the non-Communist world."[29]

In April the Review Group submitted its report, "The Strategy of Freedom", to Truman. Formally labeled NSC 68, the document did not begin with a geopolitical assessment. Instead it spent several pages defining the apocalyptic struggle of American good and Soviet evil:

> Unwillingly our free society finds itself mortally challenged by the Soviet system. No other value system is so wholly irreconcilable with ours, so implacable in its purpose to destroy ours, so capable of turning to its own uses the most dangerous and divisive trends in our own society, no other so skilfully and powerfully evokes the elements of irrationality in human nature everywhere, and no other has the support of a great and growing center of military power.
>
> There is a basic conflict between the idea of freedom under a government of laws and the idea of slavery under the grim oligarchy of the Kremlin. . . . The birth of freedom cannot be tolerated in a society which has come under the domination of an individual or group of individuals with a will to absolute power. There the despot holds absolute power. . . . All other wills must be subjugated in an act of willing submission, a degradation willed by the individual upon himself under the compulsion of a perverted faith.

The threat was formidable, but the US had the ultimate weapon: the universal values that would triumph over the perversion of Communism, "Soviet ideas and practices run counter to the best and potentially the strongest instincts of men and deny their most fundamental aspirations. Against an adversary which effectively affirms the constructive and hopeful instincts of men and was capable of fulfilling their fundamental aspirations, the Soviet system might prove to be fatally weak."

NSC 68 had effectively linked the American rhetoric of freedom to a protracted campaign to free those within the Soviet bloc:

> The vast majority of Americans are confident that the system of values which animates our society – the principles of freedom, tolerance, the importance of the individual and the supremacy of reason over all – are valid and more vital than the ideology which is the fuel of Soviet dynamism. Translated into terms relevant to the lives of other peoples, our system of values can become perhaps a powerful appeal to millions who now seek or find in authoritarianism a refuge from anxieties, bafflement, and insecurity.[30]

In this ideological conflict, NSC 68 reiterated the objectives of its predecessor, NSC 20/4, adopted 16 months earlier. It was no longer sufficient "to reduce the power and influence of the USSR to limits which no longer constitute a threat to the peace, national independence and stability of the world family of nations". The United States also had "to place the maximum strain on the Soviet structure of power . . . to encourage . . . the emergence of satellite countries as entities independent of the USSR" and "the revival [in the Soviet Union] of the national life of groups evidencing the ability and determination to achieve and maintain national independence".[31]

More importantly, NSC 68 set out the comprehensive program to achieve those objectives. The United States would not only defend the Free World through enhancement of diplomatic, economic, and military strength. It would take the fight to the Soviets in two ways. First it would develop "overt psychological warfare calculated to encourage mass defections from Soviet allegiance and to frustrate the Kremlin design". This would be accompanied by "intensification of affirmative and timely measures and operations by covert means in the fields of economic warfare and political and psychological warfare with a view to fomenting and supporting unrest and revolt in selected strategic satellite countries".

Most historians have focused upon the "practical" recommendations of NSC 68, such as development of the hydrogen bomb, expansion of conventional military forces, and economic and military aid to US allies, while ignoring the covert and psychological dimensions of the program.[32] Ironically, however, those diplomatic, economic, and military measures were not immediately adopted by Truman. Concerned about the probable cost of the proposals, the President asked for further study of their financial impact. It was only in the autumn, in the crisis atmosphere after the outbreak of the Korean War, that the National Security Council proceeded with the package.

In contrast, the secret initiatives for the liberation of Eastern Europe did not depend upon formal approval of NSC 68's demand for "large-scale covert operations". Combined with military pressure for "stay-behind networks" and the sabotage of 2,000 Soviet airbases in wartime, the emphasis on covert action would lead to the expansion of the OPC from a staff of 302 and a budget of $4.7 million in 1949 to a staff of 2,812 and 3,142 contract personnel and a budget of $82 million, projected to rise to $200 million, within three years.

Even failure could not dampen enthusiasm. While the British were discouraged when four of the first 20 infiltrators into Albania were killed, Frank Wisner contended that a 20 percent rate of loss was normal and immediately authorized further operations. Wisner's view was shared by the new Deputy Director of Central Intelligence, Allen Dulles. Told of yet another mishap, he commented, "Well, at least we're getting good experience for the next war." A more realistic but ultimately futile opinion was that of the Reverend William Sloane Coffin, the Yale recruit who would supervise OPC parachute drops before becoming a university chaplain, anti-war activist, and model for Garry

Trudeau's Reverend Scott Sloan in *Doonesbury*: "It was all tragic, all lost, but it was war. You buried your buddies and kept fighting."[33]

In Germany, the United States now had 1,400 operatives, including psychological warfare specialists who set off stink bombs at Communist festivals and despatched glossy invitations to non-existent receptions at the embassies of Soviet bloc countries. Outside Munich, a sizable portion of the men from the Yale class of 1950 were receiving parachute training for drops behind the Iron Curtain. A case officer recalled, "The whole thing was silly. Their wives would come out in their convertibles to watch."[34]

Even more importantly, the psychological strategy appealing to "hearts and minds" at home and abroad was being implemented before NSC 68's submission to Truman. Soon after the President's request for the report on Soviet capabilities, Acheson spoke to the Advertising Council to called for an effort at "total diplomacy".[35] Francis Russell drafted an analysis of US public opinion for the PPS:

> The American people have repeatedly demonstrated that they can be depended upon to rise to any emergency, however grave, if they understand what is required of them and are convinced that extraordinary exertions and sacrifices are necessary in the national interest. This kind of response is most likely to be achieved if the people feel that they are taken fully into the confidence of the Government.[36]

Assistant Secretary of State Dean Rusk wrote Nitze as NSC 68 was being drafted, "[The] section on the underlying conflict in the realm of ideas and values is a first-class job and should be used as the basis for a nationwide statement by the Secretary of State on the elementary principles of our foreign policy."[37] The State Department accordingly insisted that the document conclude with the passage, "Because the program is unprecedented in time of peace, the effort to create and to sustain understanding and support must be vigorous, extensive, and capable of being maintained."[38]

The challenge was taken up by Edward Barrett, who had just become Assistant Secretary of State for Public Affairs. Barrett had experience in both the private and the public sectors. A veteran of both the Office of War Information and the Psychological Warfare Board (PWB) of Allied Forces Headquarters in Europe, he served as the Editorial Director of *Newsweek* from 1946 to 1950. When he was appointed by Truman, he professed his concern was "increasing public pressure, which could become dangerous, for some sort of bold action".[39]

Barrett was either disingenuous or deceitful. He realized that the problem was not that the US public would lead the government into precipitous action but that, without a vigorous propaganda effort, it would be too hesitant. CIA and State Department assessments feared a complacent and naive American people, citing "the reluctance of non-Communists. . . . to admit that the standards and aims of the USSR are different from theirs and that the Soviet program carries with it a terrifying menace to their way of life, if not their existence".[40] C. D. Jackson, the Managing Director of Time-Life Inc. and President of the National Committee for Free Europe, put the problem more colorfully:

> I am furious at the simpering crowds of fuzzy-headed, self-styled Liberals fascinated by this Russian mystery, totally oblivious of the fact that they will be the first ones stood up against a wall and shot if Communism were ever to take over in this country. And this despite the fact that the only honest thing about the Russian has been his repeated dress rehearsals, open to the public, of exactly what will be done, and how it will be done, when he takes over.[41]

The first witness before the State–Defense Policy Review Group, the atomic scientist Robert Oppenheimer, paid as much attention to the necessity for an all-out information program as he did to the virtues and vices of the hydrogen bomb, although he viewed propaganda as the path to conciliation with Moscow rather than the foundation for an anti-Soviet offensive:

> If one is honest, the most probable view of the future is that of war, exploding atomic bombs, and the end of most freedoms. The people must see this and then will they do what must be done. . . .
> The first thing . . . is to make an understandable, honest statement with no sugar-coating.[42]

Subsequent witnesses seized upon Oppenheimer's suggestion while replacing his plea for cooperation with the spectre of inevitable confrontation. Robert Lovett, the former Under-secretary of State who had supervised the "education" program for the Marshall Plan, summarised the psychological effort:

> We must realize that we are now in a mortal conflict; that we are now in a war worse than any we have ever experienced.
> We must meet the threat of international communism in the field of ideas and this means we must capitalize on our standard of living, the role of the individual, and the fact that our system is based on a freedom of choice. . . . We have the latent competence to do this job, becuase if we can sell every useless article known to man in large quantities, we should be able to sell our very fine story in larger quantities.[43]

Barrett, comprehensive in his vision, outlined both the domestic and the overseas dimensions of the psychological strategy. At home, he admitted privately that the issue was not how to restrain the public but how to mobilize them, writing to Acheson,

> However much we whip up sentiment, we are going to run into vast opposition among informed people to a huge arms race. We will be warned that we are heading toward a "garrison state". Moreover, even if we could sell the idea, I fear that the U.S. public would rapidly tire of such an effort. In the absence of real and continuing crises, a dictatorship can unquestionably out-last a democracy in a conventional armament race.

The psychological campaign would first inform the people, then frighten them into support of a US offensive:

> The first step in the campaign is obviously building up a full public awareness of the problem. This might take three months or it might require no more than ten days. My hunch is that it will be nearer ten days. We must be sure that the Government is in a position to come forward with positive steps to be taken just as soon as the atmosphere is right. . . . We should have at least the broad proposals for action well in hand before the psychological "scare campaign" is started.[44]

Abroad Barrett's hope lay in programs where the United States had a "natural superiority", including economic and technical aid, psychological initiatives, and the scientific aspects of weapons development. On 6 March, Barrett put his preliminary recommendations to Acheson. The US government would accelerate the program for better radio transmitters to overcome Soviet jamming and establish a high-level committee to study all techniques of infiltration into the Soviet Union. Within hours of receiving Barrett's memorandum, Acheson discussed it with the President, and after a further meeting three days later, Truman endorsed the programme.[45]

The new offensive inevitable reinforced efforts for liberation. In February 1950, a staff report informed the National Security Council that, "in the atmosphere of suspicion and fear" surrounding purges in the Soviet Union, "it may be open to us to widen some of the cracks which are appearing in the structure of Soviet control by psychological, economic, and other means". A subsequent analysis in the spring confirmed that "the long-term objective of the establishment of free governments in the satellite countries is supported by present propaganda operations, particularly through the Voice of America, which [would] be supplemented in the near future by radio broadcasts operated by the refugee national committees in the US". State Department propaganda directives placed emphasis "on expressing Soviet exploitation and domination of the satellite nations and on cultivating their spirit of nationalism . . . to increase confusion, suspicion, and fear among the Communist leaders and parties in these countries as well as to fortify the anti-Communist resistance of the masses of the population".[46] By May, the CIA was reporting "considerable progress . . . , particularly in Bulgaria" with "projects for operations in the other satellite countries . . . now well advanced and concrete activities . . . soon underway".[47]

The plans lacked only a high-profile catalyst. Even before the discussion of NSC 68, Administration officials were hinting at a psychological offensive. Briefing Acheson for an appearance before the Senate Foreign Relations Committee, George Kennan emphasized, "Remember, Russians haven't attacked anyone militarily since V-J Day. Their successes, such as they have been, have been primarily in the minds of men."[48] On 9 March, as Barrett's program was receiving Truman's assent, the State Department issued a press release calling for the creation of "those economic, political, social, and psychological conditions that strengthen and create confidence in the democratic way of life". They added that "business, agriculture and labor, with the press and with the radio, with all of our great national organizations . . . must agree voluntarily to concert our efforts" to show the advantages of US economic life and "the greatest attraction of all – human freedom".[49] By the end of the month, the White House's Charles Jackson was asking the Advertising Club of Washington for a full media program "to enlist the American public in the 'total diplomacy' effort. Every citizen would feel he is a soldier in the cold war – and he would be."[50]

Barrett would not be satisfied, however, unless the call came from the top. On 21 March, he prepared for Acheson a new version of the "Proposal for a Total Information Effort Abroad". Barrett insisted, "A new lead from the President . . . would give the pitch for gearing up our present information program to meet the critical situation that confronts us in the field of propaganda."[51] Two weeks later, John Hickerson, the Director of the Department's Office of European Affairs, informed Acheson that he had to spell out the new program "in simpler, clear, understandable terms that will capture the imagination of our people and make them willing to assume additional burdens which will be involved".[52]

After the Secretary of State paved the way for the launch with an address at the University of California which insisted that the United States and the Soviet Union were separated by a "moral issue of the clearest nature" and a speech contrasting "the individual's loss of identity in Soviet society and [the] importance of the individual as a basic element of strength in the US", Truman launched the Campaign of Truth on 20 April before the American Society of Newspaper Editors. Deriding the "absurd propaganda" of Moscow, Truman warned, "When men throughout the world are making their choice between Communism and democracy, the important thing is not what we know about our purposes and our actions – the important thing is what they know. . . . We cannot run the risk that nations may be lost to the cause of freedom because their people do not know the facts." Truman then made his appeal:

> We must pool our efforts with those of the other free peoples in a sustained, intensified program to promote the cause of freedom against the propaganda of slavery. We must make ourselves heard round the world in a great campaign of truth. This task is not separate and distinct from other elements of our foreign policy. It is a necessary part of all we are doing . . . as important as armed strength or economic aid.[53]

Three days later, Acheson explained to the same group that America's first action was "to demonstrate that our own faith in freedom is a burning and a fighting faith. . . . [It is] the most revolutionary and dynamic concept in human history and one which properly strikes terror into every dictator." He concluded, "The US must, with a thousand voices and with all the resources of modern science, preach this doctrine (of freedom) through the world. The world must hear what America is about, what America believes, what freedom is, what it has done for many, what it can do for all."[54]

The US Government was now publicly committed, at home and abroad, to global victory over Communism. As Barrett revoked the ban on the appearance of State Department officials on current affairs programs like *America's Forum of the Air*,[55] Truman and Acheson followed up their declarations with a series of speeches in the spring of 1950 dedicating the Free World "to the construction of strength necessary to keep peace" and "to preserve freedom and justice as inalienable rights of men".[56] Paul Hoffman, the head of the Economic Cooperation Administration, told the National Security Council that the Soviet Union "would blow up". When Truman agreed but asked for an elaboration, Hoffman declared, "The dynamics of freedom, provided we maintained our strength, could not fail to come out on top. We have no such internal worries as the tremendous slave labour problem in the USSR. In making over a hundred speeches around the country, he had felt among the people a need for hope that some day, not necessarily tomorrow, we would win."[57]

Barrett and Wisner agreed that the National Committee for Free Europe "would have to speed up its program considerably if it [was] to be of real usefulness in the near future".[58] Meanwhile, in the "first effort to do detailed long-range planning" for propaganda, Barrett's staff fleshed out the rhetoric of Truman and the National Security Council by designating four categories of target areas: (1) the "hard core" of the Soviet Union; (2) nine Soviet satellites in Eastern Europe and Asia; (3) peripheral areas susceptible to Communist take-over; and (4) peripheral areas to be aligned to the West in wartime such as Scandinavia and the Arab States.[59] They also seized upon the ideas of Wallace Carroll, a United Press veteran who worked in the Office of War Information under Barrett. Although Carroll had turned down a State Department approach in 1949 to head its psychological operations, he continued to work closely with the officials. For example, he produced an article in *Life* magazine praising the Vlasov movement which had fought for the Nazis against the Soviet regime in World War II; the material for the piece came from Wisner and the PPS's John Paton Davies and Robert Joyce.[60]

Pressed by Joyce, Nitze and Barrett hired Carroll to produce a series of reports on psychological strategy in May and June 1950. The conclusions were in line with the all-out campaign of NSC 68:

> We must supplement our picture of America with vigorous offensive action. In this period of political warfare we may be able to register a truth which is harmful to our opponents when we cannot undertake the long educational effort to implant a truth which is helpful to ourselves. . . .

Policies which are well-conceived and actions which are well-timed and well-presented will produce psychological effects in areas to which no American can now penetrate.[61]

Carroll's suggestions included exploitation of Soviet defectors, propaganda on Soviet economic "miscalculations", covert operations to counter the Stockholm Peace Petition, and a "black book" on the evils of Soviet concentration camps. He even produced a booklet, *A Program for Peace*, to guide the US delegation to the UN General Assembly.[62]

Most importantly, Carroll produced a plan for an integrated information program. He warned that the lack of planning for the Office of War Information meant it "had little or no influence on important policy actions or statements" and "mighty little influence on OWI's own overseas operations". Therefore, it was essential to have "a planning unit which [would] keep all the pipes in mind" from the President to correspondents of foreign newspapers.[63]

The proposals had an immediate impact. George Kennan, opposing NSC 68 but still concerned about US "ideological discipline", had already circulated a paper endorsing the conclusions and calling for closer liaison between the State Department and the Office of Policy Coordination.[64] As Barrett's staff enthused about Kennan's "superlative contribution",[65] the Voice of America defined its aim to roll back Soviet influence by all means short of war, including "making the captive peoples realize they still belong with us. This means weakening the will of the Red Army officers and Red officials at home and abroad. It means keeping the Soviet Bear so busy scratching its own fleas that he has little time for molesting others."[66]

The Voice portrayed the Soviet Union as "the scheming villain . . . all black and sinister" while the United States stood "up against the powers of evil with unyielding determination and fierce goal-consciousness".[67] An example of the approach came in sketches on Soviet elections in spring 1950:

Commissar. Comrades, if you think because we have devoted years to simplifying the electoral process for you, that it is only a token duty you perform – let me reassure you on that point. This year 1950 is a momentous opportunity for the people of the Soviet Union. There is a record to be surpassed. In the 1937 elections, we had a 95.4 vote in favor of the proposed candidates. In the 1946 elections – much better, much better – a 96.7 vote for the candidates. But the record still holds – and that record is 99.8!
Woman (very timid). But, comrade, isn't that voting record held by an outsider – by Hitler?
Commissar. Comrade, did I hear you correctly? (Aside) Officer, quick, get that woman's name![68]

As one staffer summarized, "[The Administration] expected us to 'make propaganda' and we made it. Anything more subtle than a bludgeon was considered 'soft' on communism."[69] The press was told of the Voice's "technical tricks" to get its message into the USSR, including "slipping its broadcasts in alongside Russian programs on a neighboring channel" and "broadcasting in International Code".[70]

The outbreak of war in Korea confirmed the US offensive. Within weeks, US officials were pondering the reunification of Korea as UN operations could "set the stage for the non-communist penetration into an area under Soviet control".[71] Secretary of State Acheson declared that Korea would be "a stage to prove what Western Democracy can do to help the underprivileged countries of the world".[72] Thus encouraged, the Voice of America became even more strident – in the words of Truman's assistant, George Elsey, "at last becoming a 'shout' "[73] – winning the praise of the American press:

> [The Voice of America] is determinedly hanging blame for the war on the North Korean Communists – and it emphasizes the label "Communists" rather than North Koreans.
>
> It attacks Communist propaganda as the same line used by Hitler in going into Poland and calls the North Korean regime "Soviet puppets".
>
> It stresses the United Nations character of the anti-Communist fight.
>
> It emphasizes the support by U.S. newspapers, labor groups and others for the war effort.
>
> It is assuring Western Europe and other parts of the Far East outside Korea that aid to these areas will continue. It does a fair job of reporting the course of actual fighting.[74]

Meanwhile, the National Security Council demanded "an intensive effort, using all information media, to turn the inevitable bitterness and resentment of the war-victimized Korean people away from the US and to direct it toward the Korean Communists, the Soviet Union and, depending on the role they play, the Chinese Communists, as the parties responsible for the destructive conflict". The campaign would "effect the reorientation of the North Korean people, cause defection of enemy troops in the field, and train North Korean personnel to participate in activities looking to unification of the country". Similarly the treatment of prisoners of war would be "directed toward their exploitation, training, and use for psychological warfare purposes" to achieve American goals.[75] About 3,000 guerrillas would eventually be infiltrated into North Korea, killing 225 of the enemy, capturing 600, and destroying five bridges and eleven buildings. Eventually most of the infiltrators were killed or captured by the Chinese or North Koreans; many of them were "doubled" and fed disinformation back to the United States.[76]

The formal adoption of NSC 68 soon followed with its injunction "for the covert support of dissident groups in satellite areas".[77] When Truman's staff assistant, Charles Murphy, affirmed that this meant "we should intensify our efforts to look for ways to wrest the initiative from the Soviets and to roll them back", Acheson agreed this was "very important and quite right".[78]

National Security Council staff considered "a national and allied policy and organizations to promote and sustain mass defection from satellite countries and from Soviet Russia itself as an indispensable starting point for successful psychological warfare".[79]

It was clear, in the context of NSC 68 and the Korean War, that "liberation" now encompassed Communist China as well as Eastern Europe. In 1950 a CIA front, Western Enterprises, had been established on Taiwan with more than 600 personnel. Working with the CIA-backed Civil Air Transport, Western Enterprises arranged for the training of 8,500 Chinese Nationalist soldiers. The troops were dropped, along with 75 million leaflets, into China to carry out sabotage and stir up resistance. Frank Wisner and his staff were lured by false reports from Hong Kong into thinking that there were 500,000 guerrillas in China. Demanding why CIA intelligence had not identified the rebel force, the OPC's Chief of Far Eastern Operations demanded, "I've got an order to roll back communism. I've got an airline, I've got a training base. Let's go!"[80] Western Enterprises and another CIA outlet, the Sea Supply Company in Thailand, even financed an entire army run by General Li Mi on the Burma–China border. In 1951, several thousands of Li Mi's troops entered Yunnan Province only to be defeated by the Chinese military. The CIA persisted, working with Li Mi to recruit 8,000 Burmese volunteers and shipping in another 1,000 crack Chinese Nationalist soldiers for another offensive.[81] The supervisor of the operation insisted, "Anti-communist Chinese spirit throughout the Far East has been given a shot of Adrenalin."[82]

Clearly, the "full and fair" presentation of the United States would no longer suffice. Instead, American values had to be promoted aggressively, with Nitze encouraging Acheson to publish the "essential data and lines of reasoning on NSC 68 . . . [since] the American people [could] always be counted on to face up to the requirements of a situation, provided they [were] given the whole story in a straightforward manner".[83] Nitze's suggestion was finally rejected, ironically, because of "considerations involving national security", although "the thinking underlying it and the logic of its argument [would] be made widely familiar".[84]

Considering the changed environment in October 1950, the Policy Planning Staff's Robert Tufts offered the clearest statement on the comprehensive nature of "psychological strategy":

> The conflict between the US and the USSR will continue until one or the other is defeated. Defeat may be brought about by the exploitation of a military victory or by peaceful means, but what is on trial is the survival power of two systems. It follows that, although the conflict may be waged with the entire armory of weapons – political, psychological, economy, and military – at the disposition of the adversaries, the process is essentially a political and psychological one, aimed at the transformation of one system or the other.[85]

Notes

1 Joint Chiefs of Staff memorandum, April 1950, US DDRS, Retrospective 263D

2 Quoted in Athan Theoharis, *Seeds of Repression: Harry S. Truman and the Origins of McCarthyism* (Chicago, 1971), 57

3 Albert Wedemeyer, *Wedemeyer Reports!* (New York, 1958), 378–9

4 NSC Notes on Korea, 2 April 1948, *Minutes*, Reel 2

5 Twenty-seventh NSC meeting, 25 November 1948, *Minutes*, 2nd Supplement

6 Notes for China Meeting, 24 February 1949, HST, Acheson Papers, Box 64

7 Memorandum of White House conference, 26 June 1950, HST, Acheson Papers, Box 65

8 NSC 22, 26 July 1948, *Documents*, Reel 1

9 NSC 34/2, 3 March 1949, *Minutes*, Reel 2

10 *Life*, 7 June 1948; Sargeant to Webb, 3 October 1949, USNA, Policy Planning Staff, Box 11A, Political and Psychological Warfare 1947–1950. See Christopher Robbins, *Air America* (New York, 1979)

11 Record of State Department meeting, "Preliminary Areas of Agreement with Respect to Ideological Campaigns in China," 6 October 1949, USNA, Department of State, Lot 53 D 47, Records Relating to International Information Activities, 1938–1953, Box 20, Southeast Asia

12 Evan Thomas, *The Very Best Men: Four who Dared in the Early Years of the CIA* (New York, 1995), 51

13 For example, the Tawny Pippit operation in China became the model for the balloon operations proposed for Eastern Europe in autumn 1949. (John Paton Davies, "Political Warfare against the USSR," 19 October 1949, USNA, Department of State, USNA, Lot 64 D 563, Records of the Policy Planning Staff, 1947–1953, Subject File, Box 11A, Political and Psychological Warfare)

14 Kennan to Rusk, 7 November 1949, USNA, Lot 64 D 563, Records of the Policy Planning Staff, 1947–1953, Subject File, Box 11A, Political and Psychological Warfare 1947–1950

15 Connors to Newton, 14 November 1949, USNA, Department of State, Lot 53 D 47, Records Relating to International Information Activities, 1938–1953, Box 27, Miscellaneous

16 NSC 48/2, 29 December 1949, *Minutes*, Reel 2; fiftieth NSC meeting, 29 December 1949, *Minutes*, 2nd Supplement, Reel 1

17 Bruce Cumings, *The Origins of the Korean War*, Volume 2: *The Roaring of the Cataract, 1947–1950* (Princeton, NJ, 1990), 166

18 Kennan to Acheson, 6 January 1950, FRUS, 1950, I, 129–30

19 CIA 2–50, 15 February 1950, *Minutes*, Reel 1

20 David Oshinsky, *A Conspiracy so Immense: The World of Joe McCarthy* (New York, 1983), 108–9

21 Paul Nitze, *From Hiroshima to Glasnost: At the Center of Decision* (New York, 1989), 95

22 CIA 2–50, 15 February 1950, *Minutes*, Reel 1

23 "Soviet Intentions and Capabilities," 27 February 1950, USNA, Department of State, Lot 64 D 563, Records of the Policy Planning Staff, Subject File, Box 12, Regaining the Psychological Initiative; Policy Planning Staff meeting, 2 February 1950, FRUS, 1950, I, 142–3

24 Nitze study, 8 February 1950, FRUS, 1950, I, 145–7

25 Draft Kennan to Acheson, 17 February 1950, FRUS, 1950, I, 160–7

26 Forty-first NSC meeting, 1 June 1949, *Minutes*, 2nd Supplement, Reel 1

27 Draft Kennan to Acheson, 17 February 1950, FRUS, 1950, I, 160–7

28 "Soviet Intentions and Capabilities," 27 February 1950, USNA, Department of State, Lot 64 D 563, Records of the Policy Planning Staff, Subject File, Box 12, Regaining the Psychological Initiative

29 "Soviet Intentions," undated [spring 1950], USNA, Department of State, Lot 64 D 563, Records of the Policy Planning Staff, Subject File, Box 23

ate Department/Department of Defense report, 7 April 1950, US DDRS, Retrospective 71D. ne State Department official who was troubled by the ideological emphasis was Charles ohlen, who wrote Nitze, "While I believe the section on a free vs. slave society to be excellent and well worth retaining as supplementary reading, I believe, for the purposes of this paper, too much attention is devoted to this section. This tends somehow to blur the sharp edge of the effectiveness of the paper by diverting attention to questions which lie more in the realm of political philosophy and which I do not believe are a subject of debate by the American Government." (Bohlen to Nitze, 5 April 1950, USNA, Department of State, Lot 64 D 563, Records of the Policy Planning Staff, 1947–1953, Box 54, NSC 68)

31 State Department/Department of Defense report, 7 April 1950, US DDRS, Retrospective 71D; NSC 68 Series, April–September 1950, *Minutes*, Reel 2

32 See, for example, Ernest May, *American Cold War Strategy: Interpreting NSC 68* (Boston, MA, 1993)

33 Thomas, *The Very Best Men*, 39 and 60; Harry Rositzke, *The CIA's Secret Operations: Espionage, Counter-espionage and Covert Action* (New York, 1977), 37

34 Thomas, *The Very Best Men*, 65

35 Cumings, *The Origins of the Korean War*, 435

36 Russell to Stone, 14 February 1950, USNA, Department of State, Lot 64 D 563, Records of the Policy Planning Staff, Subject File, Box 28, Public Affairs Section of S/P Paper

37 Rusk to Nitze, 23 February 1950, USNA, Department of State, Lot 64 D 563, Records of the Policy Planning Staff, 1947–1953, Box 54, NSC 68

38 O'Gora to Nitze, 27 September 1950, undated, USNA, Department of State, Lot 64 D 563, Records of the Policy Planning Staff, 1947–1953, Box 54, NSC 68

39 Barrett to Webb, 6 March 1950, FRUS, 1950, I, 185–7

40 "Soviet Intentions and Capabilities," 27 February 1950, USNA, Department of State, Lot 64 D 563, Records of the Policy Planning Staff, Subject File, Box 12, Regaining the Psychological Initiative

41 Jackson to McClure, 25 April 1950, DDE, C. D. Jackson Papers, Box 40

42 State-Defense Policy Review Group, 27 February 1950, FRUS, 1950, I, 168–75

43 State-Defense Policy Review Group, 16 March 1950, FRUS, 1950, I, 196–200

44 Barrett to Acheson, 25 April 1950, FRUS, 1950, I, 225–6

45 Barrett to Webb, 6 March 1950, and Barrett to Acheson, 9 March 1950, FRUS, 1950, IV, 274–5

46 Webb progress report, 3 February 1950, US DDRS, 1988 3446; Webb progress report, 29 May 1950, US DDRS, 1992 886

47 Webb to Lay, Progress Report on NSC 58/2, 26 May 1950, USNA, Department of State, Lot 63 D 351, Records Relating to State Department Participation in the OCB and the NSC, 1947–1963, NSC 58. The offensive was reinforced by developing links between the United States and European allies, especially Britain. Barrett's idea for cooperation with the British Broadcasting Corporation and services of other "free nations" on a 15-minute program entitled "The Voice of Freedom" did not come to fruition, but his trip to London produced agreement with British representatives "that the time is ripe for a psychological offensive", expanding the cooperation on individual projects such as the overthrow of the Albanian Government. Liaison was established through the designation of a British embassy officer in Washington and a US embassy officer in London to oversee "psychological interests". (Barrett to Webb, 6 March 1950, and Barrett to Acheson, 9 March 1950, FRUS, 1950, IV, 274–5)

48 Kennan to Acheson, 6 January 1950, FRUS, 1950, I, 129–30

49 State Department press release, 9 March 1950, HST, Elsey Papers, Box 64, Foreign Relations – Russia

50 Jackson address to Advertising Club of Washington, 28 March 1950, DDE, Jackson Papers, Box 51, Charles W. Jackson

51 Barrett memorandum, 21 March 1950, USNA, Department of State, Lot 53 D 47, Records Relating to International Information Activities, Box 12, Regaining the Psychological Initiative

52 Hickerson to Acheson, 5 April 1950, USNA, Department of State, Records of the Policy Planning Staff, 1947–1953, Box 54, NSC 68

53 *Time*, 27 March 1950; Thomas Sorensen, *The Word War: The Story of American Propaganda* (New York, 1968), 26; Donald Browne, *International Radio Broadcasting: The Limits of the Limitless Medium* (New York, 1982), 98; "Truth as a Weapon in Cold War," *The Times* (London), 21 April 1950. In later years, Barrett would be disingenuous, if not deceptive, on the motives for the Campaign of Truth, focusing solely upon the budgetary battle with Congress: "Once, when we wanted to get our appropriations raised greatly, and decided to dress up the program, we got the President to make a speech. Some White House speechwriter came up with a line about a psychological offensive. George Elsey [Truman's staff assistant], somebody else, and I persuaded the President to call it a 'Campaign of Truth'." (Edward Barrett interview, 9 July 1974, HST, Oral History Collection)

54 "The US in World Affairs," undated, USNA, Department of State, Records of the Policy Planning Staff, 1947–1953, Box 54, NSC 68, Folder 2; Michael Parenti, *The Anti-Communist Impulse* (New York, 1969), 150–1; "US as Soviet Target," *The Times* (London), 24 April 1950

55 Wood–Barrett luncheon, 3 May 1950, USNA, Department of State, Central Decimal File, 511.00/5-350, Box 2237

56 Weekly Information Policy Guidances #9, 1 June 1950, and #11, 15 June 1950, USNA, Department of State Decimal File, 511.00/6-1550, Box 2237

57 Fifty-sixth NSC meeting, 4 May 1950, *Minutes*, Reel 1

58 Barrett memorandum, 22 March 1950, USNA, Department of State, Lot 53 D 47, Records Relating to International Information Activities, 1938–1953, Box 14, Free Nations (Europe)

59 Barrett to Nitze, 6 May 1950, USNA, Department of State, Lot 64 D 563, Records of the Policy Planning Staff, 1947–1953, Box 54, NSC 68; Advisory Commission on Information, Sixth Report to Congress, 1952, HST, Hulten Papers, Box 13

60 Joyce to Nitze, 10 February 1950, USNA, Department of State, Lot 64 D 563, Records of the Policy Planning Staff, Subject File, Box 8, Consultants 1944–1953

61 Carroll to Barrett, 2 June 1950, USNA, Department of State, Lot 64 D 563, Records of the Policy Planning Staff, Subject File, Box 11A, Political and Psychological Warfare, 1947–1950

62 Phillips to Barrett, 23 June 1950, USNA, Department of State, Lot 53 D 47, Records Relating to International Information Activities, 1938–1953, Box 12, Miscellaneous Carroll Papers; Carroll memorandum, July 1950, USNA, Department of State, Lot 64 D 563, Records of the Policy Planning Staff, 1947–1953, Subject Files, Box 8, Consultants 1944–1953

63 Carroll to Barrett, 9 May 1950, USNA, Department of State, Lot 53 D 47, Records Relating to International Information Activities, 1938–1953, Box 12, Administration

64 Kennan to Webb, 30 March 1950, USNA, Department of State, Lot 64 D 563, Records of the Policy Planning Staff, 1947–1953, Chronological File, Box 34, Chronological 1950

65 Phillips to Barrett, 9 August 1950, USNA, Department of State, Lot 64 D 563, Records of the Policy Planning Staff, 1947–1953, Subject File, Box 11A, Political and Psychological Warfare, 1947–1950

66 Sig Mickelson, *America's Other Voices: Radio Free Europe and Radio Liberty* (New York, 1983), 53–5; Webb memorandum, 26 May 1950, US DDRS, 1992 1493; Lilly memorandum, "Development of American Psychological Operations, 1945–1951," US DDRS, 1991 2302; Browne *International Radio Broadcasting*, 99

67 Walter Hixson, *Parting the Curtain: Propaganda, Culture, and the Cold War, 1945–1961* (New York, 1997), 38

68 Quoted in Robert W. Ruth, *Baltimore Sun*, 30 April 1950

69 Hixson, *Parting the Curtain*, 38

70 *Time*, 27 March 1950. See also *Time*, 23 May 1949

71 Cumings, *The Origins of the Korean War*, 710

72 Rosemary Foot, *A Substitute for Victory: The Politics of Peacemaking at the Korean Armistice Talks* (Ithaca, NY, 1990), 25. See also William Stueck, "The March to the Yalu: The Perspective from Washington," in Bruce Cumings (ed.), *Child of Conflict: The Korean–American Relationship, 1943–1953* (Seattle, WA, 1983), 195–237

73 Elsey to Truman, 26 October 1950, HST, Elsey Papers, Box 65, Foreign Relations – Voice of America

74 Charles Lucey, "The Voice Gets Louder," *Washington News*, 13 July 1950

75 NSC 81, 1 September 1950, *Documents*, Reel 1. See also Foot, *A Substitute for Victory*, 114–18

76 Thomas, *The Very Best Men*, 53 and 360–1

77 Lilly memorandum, "Development of American Psychological Operations, 1945–1951," US DDRS, 1990 567

78 Sixty-eightieth NSC Meeting, 29 September 1950, *Minutes*, 1st Supplement

79 Watts to Nitze, 4 October 1950, USNA, Department of State, Lot 64 D 563, Records of the Policy Planning Staff, 1947–1953, Chronological File, Box 34, Chronological 1950

80 Thomas, *The Very Best Men*, 51–2

81 Ralph McGehee, *Deadly Deceits: My Twenty-five Years in the CIA* (New York, 1983), 25–6; William Corson, *The Armies of Ignorance: The Rise of the American Intelligence Empire* (New York, 1977), 320–3

82 Thomas, *The Very Best Men*, 55

83 Nitze to Acheson, 9 October 1950, USNA, Department of State, Lot 64 D 563, Records of the Policy Planning Staff, 1947–1953, Chronological File, Box 34, Chronological 1950

84 Ferguson and Schwinn to Watts, 5 January 1951, USNA, Department of State, Lot 64 D 563, Records of the Policy Planning Staff, 1947–1953, Box 54, NSC 68, Folder II

85 Tufts draft, 13 October 1950, USNA, Department of State, Lot 64 D 563, Records of the Policy Planning Staff, 1947–1953, Box 23

7

The State–private network
and liberation

Superficially one might argue that there were two Cold Wars for the United States. One Cold War was waged against the Soviet Union by the Government with diplomatic, economic, and military measures throughout the world. This was a Cold War of geopolitics, of action and reaction calculated by an official bureaucracy. The other Cold War was waged within, a battle against fellow Americans suspected of Communist betrayal or naïve fellow-traveling. This struggle was conducted not just by the Government through judicial and exec-utive measures but by "private" groups and individuals keeping their own houses in order. This was a war not for territory or profit but for a culture.

This artificial divide has been sustained, in part by a diplomatic history devoted to the study of official elites and the "national security State", in part by the equation of the anti-Communist culture with the extremism of Joseph McCarthy rather than the mainstream of the entire society. The division can easily be overcome, however, by recognition of the US ideology of freedom. In a country supposedly fighting enemy tyranny through the power of the indi-vidual, the official and the "private" were linked. Foreign policy interacted with domestic concerns, and diplomacy rested upon the mobilization of a superior "culture".

Of course World War II had fostered a State–private network in support of global involvement. Some members of pressure groups who had urged US entry in 1940–41, such as the Council for Democracy and the Committee to Defend America by Aiding the Allies, joined the Washington bureaucracy after Pearl Harbor. Others remained in the "private" sector but worked closely with Government officials.[1]

With the post-war demobilization, much of the formal network was dis-mantled; however, if patriotic folk returned to law firms, newspaper offices, or Wall Street in 1945, they were in close touch with those who stayed on in Washington. It only took the call to "freedom" in the Truman Doctrine to revive cooperation. The Committee to Defend the Marshall Plan was an important and highly successful example but, even before its inception, the quest at home for a properly educated public had led to joint ventures. In May 1947, Attorney General Tom Clark linked his "Zeal for American Democ-

racy" campaign to the establishment of the "private" American Heritage
Foundation. The foundation's major effort was the Freedom Train, which
toured more than 200 cities as "a Paul Revere [going] around behind a modern
engine" to warn of the Communist threat.

Ironically, though, the network was initially defined not by the American
fight abroad but by various battles at home. In 1948 the "liberal" movement
was irreparably split amidst Congressional investigations, fractious debates
over civil rights, economic policy, and labor relations, and an election campaign in which Truman's advisors believed victory could be achieved only by
labeling the Progressive Party and Democratic dissidents as fellow-travelers or
even worse. Clark Clifford summarized, "Every effort must be made now to
jointly and at one and the same time – although, of course, by different groups,
to dissuade [Wallace] and also identify him and isolate him in the public mind
with the Communists." The attacks would be carried out not by the Administration but by "private" representatives in the press and groups like Americans for Democratic Action.[2]

Yet it was one thing for "party" factions within the Adminstration to mobilize the network in an electoral battle, another for the Government to implement a "private" Cold War. The cultural offensive against the Soviet Union
would begin to emerge only at the Waldorf Conference on 27–9 March 1949.
Organized by the National Committee of the Arts, Sciences and Professions
(NCASP) at the Waldorf Hotel in New York, the gathering of more than 800
literary and artistic figures was billed as a discussion of intellectual freedom
in the Cold War. Anti-Communist liberals feared, however, that the conference would be a platform for Soviet propaganda following the lines of the
Communist-led World Congress of Intellectuals for Peace, held in Wroclaw,
Poland, the previous August.

Three weeks before the conference, George Allen, the Assistant Secretary
of State for Public Affairs, met the organizer of the conference, Harvard
astronomer Harlow Shapley. Shapley's explanation of his intentions was far
from persuasive, for Allen's immediate recommendation was to ban visas to
all delegates from the Soviet bloc. This was partially implemented: visas were
denied to all private individuals, as well as the Hungarian delegation because
of the expulsion of the US Minister from Budapest, but 13 "official" representatives from the Soviet Union, Czechoslovakia, and Rumania were allowed
into the country to dispel perceptions of US intransigence.[3]

Allen and another department official, John Peurifoy, soon devised a more
subtle strategy. They suggested to Secretary of State Dean Acheson that
officials "discreetly get in touch with reliable non-Communist participants in
the New York Conference to urge them to do what they can to assure objective debate and to expose Communist efforts at controlling the Conference".
Working with the anti-Communist liberals, the department would also launch

a public relations offensive to question the purposes of the conference's sponsors, link the proceedings with the Wroclaw gathering, and publicize Soviet
refusal of US efforts at cultural interchange.[4]

The department's first achievement was to ensure that they had full information on the movements of the Soviet delegation to the conference. Fred
Warner Neal, an official at New York University, had been asked by Shapley
to escort the Soviets during their stay. When Llewellyn Thompson, a Soviet
specialist in the department, met Neal on 11 March, he immediately arranged
for regular reports to be sent to him.[5]

The department then turned to the counter-propaganda campaign, promoting a new group called the Americans for Intellectual Freedom, spearheaded by philosopher and former Communist Sidney Hook and including
literary figures Dwight Macdonald and Mary McCarthy, composer Nicolas
Nabakov, and labor reporter Arnold Beichman. Through Beichman's union
contacts, the organization based itself in a three-room suite at the Waldorf and
arranged for ten phone lines.[6] AIF tried to disrupt the Waldorf proceedings
with provocative questions at panel discussions and plenary sessions and held
a counter-rally at Freedom House "in the spirit of free inquiry and honest differences of opinion – the true hallmark of a gathering of intellectuals whose
minds are not twisted into the straitjacket of the Communist party line".[7] The
members also joined picket lines of veterans, religious organisations, and
Eastern European émigrés, shouting at delegates, "Go back to Russia where
you belong."[8]

Almost all US media coverage of the conference unquestioningly followed
the Government's line. The State Department's smear campaign against
the NCASP was taken up by *Newsweek*, which labelled the organization a
"Communist front" conducting the conference as "part of the Cominform's
attempt . . . to win the minds of the world's intellectuals".[9] *Life* tarred non-
Communists who attended the conference with the headline "Red Visitors
Cause Rumpus" and a rogues' gallery of photographs including Clifford
Odets, Dorothy Parker, Langston Hughes, Arthur Miller, Norman Mailer,
Charlie Chaplin, and Albert Einstein.[10]

The Government strategy to polarize the liberal split obscured the reality
that Waldorf was far more complex than a "let's-all-love-Russia clambake",
as the United Press cast it.[11] Of course, many of the delegates were hostile
towards US foreign policy. Dmitri Shostakovich warned of "a small clique
of hate-mongers preparing global war" and urged artists to unite against the
new Fascists. Aaron Copland declared, "The present policies of the American
Government will lead inevitably into a third world war."[12] One of the featured
incidents in the press was the booing of Norman Cousins, the editor of the
Saturday Review of Literature, for his statement in the opening session that
the American people opposed a "small political group" which was loyal "not

to America but to an outside government". One delegate who reported back
to the State Department spoke of discussions "heavily packed with Communist sympathizers".[13]

The conference, however, was not a forum for the Communists. Shapley,
far from wishing to replicate the Wroclaw meeting, wanted to broaden discussion beyond narrow anti-American denunciations, and few who attended
Waldorf were members of Communist parties. Neal, the escort for the Soviet
delegation, gave a full summary to the State Department:

> There were a great number of regrettable Communists around, that is, notorious
> Communists like Howard Fast and Lillian Hellmann, and many others I read about
> in the papers, and many who, from their remarks, appeared to be pro-communist,
> but I had the impression that the conference was not actually communist-run. There
> was, for example, a great deal of criticism of the USSR and Communism voiced by
> various participants in the program. The bulk of those having to do with the con-
> ference seemed to be naive, well-meaning, and vague Wallaceites, a surprising
> number of them bewildered, unemployed, young men who gave up their positions
> (or were fired) to help Henry in the campaign.[14]

An editorial in the *Bulletin of Atomic Scientists* noted that scientists who par-
ticipated were not linked to "groups about whose political bias they had no
illusions" but had a genuine desire for the abolition of atomic weapons.[15]

For the "mainstream" US media, however, this supposed desire for peace,
if it entailed criticism of US foreign policy, was a Soviet device. *Newsweek*
recorded, " 'Peace' was a fighting word. Everyone was for it, naturally, just as
everyone was against the man-eating shark. The trouble was that it didn't
mean the same thing in Russian that it did in English."[16] Thus the State Department, through the alliance with private groups, was satisfied with its conversion of the conference from an intellectual gathering for peace into a forum
where "Communist delegates [would] defeat their own purposes".[17] For
example, the press never noted the department's role in Norman Cousins's
statement at the opening session. Cousins made the speech only after he was
persuaded of its necessity by Assistant Secretary of State George Allen, and
the department was effusive in its praise afterwards. Allen wrote Cousins,
"[The speech] helped to set the Conference in its proper light," and another
official added, "You did a first-rate job. I wish that we had had a few more
like you to get up and say the same thing."[18]

With another peace conference scheduled for Paris in April 1949, the Office
of Policy Coordination launched plans for another US counter-offensive. The
American Federation of Labor's European representative, Irving Brown, put
the OPC in contact with the leftist but anti-Communist newspaper *Franc-
tireur*, which agreed to organize an International Day of Resistance to Dictatorship and War. The OPC paid the travel costs of delegations from Germany,
Italy, and the United States, led by Hook and novelist James Farrell.

The International Day did produce criticism of Stalin, but the meeting was not pro-American enough for Hook, the OPC, or the State Department. US officials were far from amused when the gathering "was disrupted by a noisy band of anarchists". So chastened Government officials redoubled efforts for a "reliable" private effort. Opportunity came through a discussion at the International Day between Hook and Melvin Lasky. Lasky, who had edited the German publication *Der Monat* for the US military government, had been pressing for a wider initiative in Europe, complaining, "There are only a handful of us left and we can't battle on every front."[19] Now he and Hook took the idea for a permanent committee of anti-Communist intellectuals to others. One of their contacts, a former leader of the German Communist Party, Ruth Fischer, notified the Office of Policy Coordination.

The Cold War's intellectual battle lines had been established. In March 1950, as US Government officials were designing the Campaign for Truth, the World Congress of Partisans of Peace met in Stockholm. The congress, led by Communist delegations, passed a resolution calling for the prohibition of atomic weapons and the condemnation of the first government to use them as a war criminal. By the end of May, supporters of the Stockholm Petition claimed the collection of 100 million signatures in 50 countries for the Stockholm Resolution.

The Truman Administration viewed the resolution as the center of a Soviet psychological campaign which could undermine the American position in Europe and Asia. Secretary of State Acheson summarized, "[The resolution] should be recognized for what it is – a propaganda trick in the superior 'peace offensive' of the Soviet Union."[20] State Department analysts noted that Radio Moscow was devoting more than 40 percent of its commentaries to the resolution and that non-political committees were being formed to collect signatures. Members of the French Cabinet, the Supreme Court, and high clergy were reported to have signed, as were the former Italian Prime Minister Vitorio Orlando and the writer Thomas Mann.[21]

In May, as the Communists sponsored a World Youth Festival in East Berlin to promote the theme of peace, the State–private network launched its counter-attack. The State Department responded with postage stamps to "depict subjects such as freedom, personal rights and liberty, democracy in action, and so forth".[22] Counter-propaganda in West Berlin included an automobile show with eight US and six European manufacturers, a Rights of Man exhibit by UNESCO, a campaign for additional CARE packages, and events like Theater Week and Motion Picture Week. The Advertising Council, always helpful, promoted these activities and added the suggestion that West Berlin be referred to as "Free" Berlin; coincidentially, the message "F for Freedom" began appearing in both Western and Eastern Zones. The ECA sponsored a European Youth Organisation while covert activity "fostered the preparation and distribution of literature and even posters which attacked the principles of

Communism and which centered attention upon the need for European economic unity".[23]

The most significant initiative was a cultural congress for leading anti-Communist intellectuals. After months of bureaucratic wrangling, the Office of Policy Coordination had finally pushed through the Hook–Lasky initiative. The vital link was Michael Josselson, a former employee of the US occupation authority in Germany, who arranged a subsidy of $50,000. With Josselson disguising the OPC's involvement and Lasky, allegedly unwitting of the covert interest, pressing ahead, the cultural congress was organized, with philosophers such as John Dewey, Bertrand Russell, and Karl Jaspers agreeing to serve as honorary presidents. More than 100 delegates from 20 countries attended. The most prominent was Arthur Koestler, who shouted, "Friends! Freedom has seized the offensive!" as he read the Freedom Manifesto to a crowd of 15,000.[24] The foundation had been laid for the Congress for Cultural Freedom, the spearhead of the campaign to align intellectuals with the West.

The State–private network also took on another challenge: the US Congress. The information budget of the State Department, less than $25 million in 1948, was to rise up to six times with the Campaign for Truth,[25] but opposition on Capitol Hill, despite Congress's proclamation of America's "continuing friendship for the Soviet people" and demand for a public assault against Communism, came from a variety of sources. Some Congressmen resisted any increase as an extension of "big government"; Republicans associated the information services with the tenets of the New Deal; and other groups accused the programs of being riddled with incompetents. Representative John Taber of New York, the Chairman of the Appropriations Committee, told Barrett, "Some of the stuff you put out indicates to me that some of your people aren't very bright. Sometimes I think you ought to cut down the size of your program and get it going right." Money for the Campaign of Truth's center-piece, a global ring of 14 high-powered radio transmitters, was not allocated, and the expansion of information centers and personal exchanges was hindered by budget limitations.[26] Even $10 million "for the discretionary use of unconventional devices" was held up.[27]

Those drafting NSC 68 had anticipated the problem in their call for the provision of information, in "understandable terms for the average man on the street", to influential statesmen and recipients at schools, universities, and churches. These groups would then spread the message throughout the American public. By June, the State Department's Office of Public Affairs staff was proposing "a responsible committee which could develop support for specific policies, meanwhile developing wider public understanding of over-all American foreign policy". The committee of "men and women of stature, from both political parties, known nationally or having influence in the various states" would "be prepared to engage in public education activities and to support specific items of legislation where appropriate".[28]

One of the earliest products of the strategy was the formation of the Committee on the Present Danger (CPD). In March 1950 Chester Barnard, the President of the Rockefeller Foundation, had suggested to the Policy Review Group considering NSC 68 that a group of five to ten citizens "of good reputation and high integrity who have no connection with government" should be established to promote the new foreign policy.[29] The suggestion bore fruit in December 1950 when the CPD was founded by Barnard, Vannevar Bush, head of the Office of Scientific Research and Development from 1941 to 1946, Tracy Voorhees, formerly Under-secretary of the Army, and James Conant, the former US High Commissioner in Germany, who then became President of Harvard University. The founders had discussed their plans at length with Secretary of Defense George Marshall and his deputy Robert Lovett. Marshall even arranged for the CPD to receive confidential information on the military position.[30]

The CPD became a pivotal group in the campaign for NSC 68's vision of European and US rearmament. It launched a series of pamphlets and weekly radio programs on the need for an "effective" US military deterrent to Soviet aggression. A broadcast by the former director of the Office of Strategic Services, William Donovan, turned to the question of a covert offensive to undermine Moscow. Calling for "all-out employment of the nation's economic, political, and psychological weapons to regain the initiative in the Cold War", he concluded, "Stalin might be deterred by the fear that he cannot determine in advance the loyalty of his own people. For no dictator dare move if uncertain of his safety at home. Our greatest ally therefore can be the Russian people."[31] In 1952, as Dwight Eisenhower was preparing to take over the presidency, he and his closest advisors met with Conant and Voorhees to discuss how "to present to the public and to Congress a warning of the danger our country is facing at the present time from the world-wide Communist threat".[32]

The use of the "private" sphere to promote the Government's strategy to the American people went hand in hand with its other role of carrying the US offensive into the Soviet bloc. The National Committee for Free Europe had been established as a channel for émigré operations, but those operations still lacked organization. So in June 1950 the Assistant Secretary of State for Public Affairs, Edward Barrett, initiated the first systematic study of Soviet vulnerabilities in discussions with Lloyd Berkner of the Massachusetts Institute of Technology (MIT). Barrett explained to his staff, "MIT has the best collection of broad-gauged electronic people available today. . . . They are fully cleared by the Government. . . . They have done much work for the military and have their confidence, and . . . they could effectively needle the military by pointing out new approaches to the problem whenever the military think the job is hopeless."[33]

After extensive discussions and bureaucratic maneuvering, the State Department finally arranged for a study based at MIT. The initial remit for Project Troy was an examination of how to overcome Soviet jamming; inevitably, the research soon went beyond the narrow technical problem "to look at other means of perforating the Iron Curtain" and developing a concept of political warfare.[34] The panel expanded to 22 academics, including psychologists, historians, and geographers as well as electrical engineers and physicists. It concluded:

> Fear of all-out war has so far kept us from aggressive steps to halt the Russian advance. This is just the wrong attitude. A carefully-planned series of fundamental steps that erode the Russian power provides the best way of avoiding, not provoking, the last great battle of the West.
>
>   In planning these steps we must remember clearly that all international actions – wars included – are directed at the minds and emotions of men.[35]

The National Committee for a Free Europe looked to strike quickly. As C. D. Jackson, the President of NCFE, noted in a letter to Professor William Elliott of Harvard University, "Things are hotting up in the satellites, and I think hotting up in our favor – if we can move with boldness and intelligence, and above all, unorthodox, imaginative thinking."[36] The major project was Radio Free Europe (RFE), established with a pilot transmitter in Lampertheim, West Germany, in July 1950. Within the next year, transmitters with six times greater power were operating in Portugal as well as West Germany; programming was directed from RFE's headquarters in Munich and involved 1,100 employees.[37]

With Radio Free Europe receiving its guidance from State Department and CIA liaison officers, it had a "greater flexibility and freedom from official taboos" and was always able to accept "a nasty idea or two".[38] The arrangement was consolidated through the agreement that, "as . . . the Assistant Secretaries of State who were responsible for the Foreign Information Program gave up their jobs . . . [they] became members of the Board of Directors of the National Committee for Free Europe".[39] As for finance, one high-level RFE employee commented, "One thing there was never a problem about was money. . . . So much money it wasn't true."[40]

The guidelines for Radio Free Europe defined the ideology propelling the State–private effort, even as ideological motives were denied:

> The central characteristic of RFE is that it is the instrument of men who are engaged in fighting for freedom and justice. As such, it encourages resistance to every tyrant, great and small, in the countries it addresses. However, its speakers speak, not as doctrinaires or ideologues opposing other doctrinaires or ideologues but as men of

good will who seek to contribute to the elimination of old enmities and the building of an enduring democratic order.

The purpose of RFE is to contribute to the liberation of nations imprisoned behind the Iron Curtain by sustaining their morale and stimulating in them a spirit of non-cooperation with the Soviet-dominated regimes.

This campaign was carefully detailed in the organisation's policy handbook:

Speakers on RFE will deal with topic of liberation as follows:
(A) Assert that they see no possibility of an enduring peace anywhere in the world until the Moscow-dominated regimes have been overthrown and the tide of Soviet imperialism has, by one means or another, been induced to withdraw from the lands of our listeners;
(B) Assert . . . it is unquestionable that the Western powers will resist Soviet Russian aggression at any point on the globe . . . ;
(C) Quote, as evidence of Western intent that the countries of our listeners should be free, appropriating sentences from other UN resolutions, declarations by the President and the Secretary of State and by other Western statesmen; and – excluding promises of armed intervention – statements and resolutions of authoritative organizations of European exiles and representatives of Western opinion (trade union, church, and other) which express an interest in the liberation of our listeners;
(D) Take every occasion to display convincingly, by citing facts and figures, the superiority of the West over the Soviet Union in the elements that enter into military strength: resources, skills, manpower, and the spirit of initiative that dwells in free men.[41]

NCFE officials, unhindered by the diplomatic restraints of Government service, put their goals bluntly. DeWitt Poole, the former OSS official who became President of NCFE, wrote, "It is the work of gray-black propaganda to take up the individual Bolshevik rulers and the quislings and tear them apart, exposing their motivations, laying bare their private lives, pointing to their meannesses, pillorying their evil deeds, holding them up to ridicule and contumely." Frank Altschul, who directed the radio operations, added, "[We] are unhampered by the niceties of intercourse. We enter this fight with bare fists."[42]

The overseas activities of NCFE were linked to domestic campaigning through the Crusade for Freedom, established with General Lucius Clay, the former US military commander in Germany, as chairman. The initiative was launched by Dwight Eisenhower in September 1950: "We need powerful radio stations abroad, operated without Government restriction, to tell in vivid and convincing form about the decency and essential fairness of democracy. . . . The Crusade for Freedom will provide for the expansion of RFE into a network of stations. They will be given the simplest, clearest charter in the world: 'Tell the Truth'."[43]

The highlight of the crusade's first effort was the production of a Freedom Bell, modeled on the Liberty Bell of the American revolution. A laurel of peace circled the top of the bell while the words of Abraham Lincoln, "That this world under God shall have a new birth of freedom," ran along the bottom. In the middle, five figures representing the major races of the planet, stood "with arms outstretched passing from hand to hand the torch of freedom until one day it [should] light the whole world".[44]

The bell was christened with a ticker-tape parade in New York, exalted in a television address by an actor named Ronald Reagan, and carried across the United States on the Freedom Train as spectators signed Freedom Scrolls. This was followed by a dedication in West Berlin, where Communism had been successfully resisted during the blockade of 1948–49. About 400,000 people witnessed the ceremony in Schönerburger Platz and another 2 million viewed the procession of the bell from Templehof airport to the Rathaus. The plaque of dedication explained:

> "That this World, under God, shall have a new Birth of Freedom"
> So Speaks the Bell of Freedom from the Rathaus Tower to all Mankind
> Gift to the Steadfast Citizens of Berlin from their Friends, the American People
> Dedicated October 24, 1950 by Governing Mayor Ernst Reuter and General Lucius
> D. Clay in the Presence of more than 500,000 Berliners from both Parts of the City[45]

In its first two years, the Crusade for Freedom raised $3.5 million from private donations, a small but symbolic contribution to the NCFE, and collected 25 million signatures on the Freedom Scrolls "supporting the fight against Communism".[46]

The Crusade for Freedom orchestrated news coverage for maximum impact. When a new, more powerful transmitter was opened in April 1951 for broadcasts into Czechoslovakia, both the *New York Times* and *New York Herald-Tribune* ran articles with headlines like "RFE Adopts Red Tactic: Denounces Police Agents by Name".[47] The station even won the highest honor for US radio, the George Peabody Award, "for the promotion of international understanding". The citation continued, "[RFE] is striving for and we hope succeeding in educating the populace of the Communist-dominated areas in joining the fight against tyranny."[48]

Hundreds of newspapers throughout the United States supported the cause with editorials. For example, the *Liberty News* in North Carolina infomed readers:

> Every citizen can fight Communism by Supporting "Crusade for Freedom"!
> Most Americans – most citizens like those living right here in Liberty and sur-
> rounding areas – deplore Communism, but calmly shrug their shoulders with the
> words, "What can I do about it?"
> These citizens can ask the question no longer without getting an answer. A
> program has been set up so that every American can have an active part in fighting
> and crushing Communism.

The program is the "Crusade for Freedom" – its most vital weapon is Radio Free Europe and Radio Free Asia. The Crusade is fighting Communism, the "big lie", with TRUTH.[49]

Civil Air Patrols "bombed" patriotic citizens with pre-printed "Freedom-grams", to be signed and sent to NCFE for distribution behind the Iron Curtain. A typical Freedom-gram read:

Do you listen to Radio Free Europe? I hope you do, for I am one of millions of American citizens who have voluntarily contributed to building these stations, which bring truth to you who are deprived of it.

In America millions regularly pray for an understanding between our peoples. Please add your prayers to ours. Surely our common faith in God is the place where hope for freedom begins.[50]

Overseas, radio broadcasts were dramatically supplemented by balloon operations to distribute large numbers of leaflets to the "captive" peoples. An interdepartmental committee under Barrett approved the stockpiling of balloons in September 1950, and public pressure for operations, led by the columnist Drew Pearson, promoted the collaboration between Government agencies and NCFE.[51] Further prompting came from Project Troy, which foresaw balloons, as well as rivers, ocean currents, and migratory birds and animals, carrying "penicillin and sulfa drugs; cheap watches; fountain pens; playing cards; plastic chess sets; cheap cameras; flashlights and batteries; toy stereoscopic viewing devices showing colored pictures (preferably of America), [and] crystal radios".[52] A State Department request to share costs on the project was eagerly met by the CIA, which committed $300,000 to research and development. The first balloons were launched from West Germany, with Czechoslovakia as their target, in mid-August 1951.[53]

Barrett also used the National Committee for Free Europe to propel Operation Brainwave from December 1950. The project started from the premise that "a really large-scale free-world propaganda offensive can be generally effective only if the US label is taken off of it and it is internationalized". Private groups, supported by Government funds, would establish a "Legion of Freedom" across the continent of Europe. Its symbol would be a bell, distributed on stickers and leaflets "to be slapped on walls, floated downstream or ashore, or carried by toy balloon". The slogan "The Welfare of the Many vs. the Tyranny of the Few" would be supported by 10 simple points, such as "The Right to Worship as you Please". Full-time "Truth Squads" would give talks and heckle Communist speakers, care would be provided for defectors, and radio broadcasts would promote contests "with fat awards for the best editorials on 'The Cause for which we Fight'".[54]

Other NCFE projects included a Free European University in Exile in Strasbourg, France. The first group of 86 students, each receiving a scholarship of $800 per year, was drawn from 700 applications in November 1951. The

Chairman of Trustees was Adolf Berle, a former Assistant Secretary of State. Past and present NCFE presidents Joseph Grew and C. D. Jackson, Frederick Dolbeare, the NCFE's liaison with émigrés, and anti-Communist intellectuals James Burnham and Sidney Hook were also trustees.[55] A Mid-European Law Project examined the development of law in Soviet satellites since 1945 while scholarships sent 40 East European exiles to US universities.[56]

With the development of NCFE, the "private" crusade against the Soviet bloc had made a spectacular start. For the Government, it was only the beginning.

Notes

1 For the most recent work on the subject, see Andrew Johnstone, "Private Interest Groups and the Lend-Lease Debates, 1940–1941," M. Phil. dissertation, University of Birmingham, 1998

2 Quoted in Irwin Ross, *The Loneliest Campaign* (New York, 1968), 23–4. See also Richard Freeland, *The Truman Doctrine and the Origins of McCarthyism* (New York, 1972), 298–306

3 Allen to Webb, 8 March 1949, USNA, Department of State, Lot 53 D 47, Records Relating to International Information Activities, Box 27, Shapley Meeting; Humelsine and Allen memorandum, 14 March 1949, HST, Acheson Papers, Box 64

4 Mack to Allen, 18 March 1949, USNA, Department of State, Lot 53 D 47, Records Relating to International Information Activities, Box 27, Shapley Meeting

5 See Neal–Thompson meeting, 11 March 1949, USNA, Department of State, Lot 53 D 47, Records Relating to International Information Activities, Box 27, Shapley Meeting

6 Michael Warner, "The Origins of the Congress of Cultural Freedom, 1949–50," *Studies in Intelligence*, 1995, 90; Sidney Hook, *Out of Step: An Unquiet Life in the Twentieth Century* (New York, 1987), 394–5

7 *New York Times*, 23 March 1949

8 *New York Times*, 27 March 1949

9 *Newsweek*, 4 April 1949, 19–22

10 Quoted in *Hidden Hands: A Different History of Modernism*, Channel 4 Television, London, 1995

11 Quoted in Robbie Lieberman, "Communism, Peace Activism, and Civil Liberties: From the Waldorf Conference to the Peekskill Riot," *Journal of American Culture*, fall 1995, 61

12 Quoted in Warner, "The Origins of the Congress of Cultural Freedom," 90

13 Lieberman, "Communism, Peace Activism, and Civil Liberties," 60–1; Blake to Allen, 28 March 1949, USNA, Department of State, Lot 53 D 47, Records Relating to International Information Activities, Box 27, Shapley Meeting. Years later there was an intriguing postscript to Cousins's role in the conference. Attacked for being present at the "Communist-front meeting" by an official of the American Legion, "Cousins replied that he had done so at the request of the State Department in order to present the United States' anti-Communist views, had been roundly booed and hissed and had needed police escort to leave the hall." (*The Federalist*, April 1953, quoted in Jon Yoder, "The United World Federalists: Liberals for Law and Order," in Charles Chatfield (ed.), *Peace Movements in America* (New York, 1973))

14 Neal to Thompson, 12 April 1949, USNA, Department of State, Lot 53 D 47, Records Relating to International Information Activities, Box 27, Shapley Meeting

15 *Bulletin of the Atomic Scientists*, June 1950, 163–5. Later in 1949, *Time*, while claiming that Shapley had "long gazed upward with Red stars in his eyes", recounted that he had told an interviewer, "To the extent that they are prostituting their sciences . . . , the Russians will be losers. . . . We cannot condone the Soviet infringement . . . (but) perhaps in some way we can

help them discover the error and ultimate futility of their policy." Of course, the idea that Shapley might be an "independent" critic of both the Soviet Union and the United States rather than a disillusioned fellow-traveler never occurred to *Time*. (*Time*, 29 August 1949)

16 *Newsweek*, 4 April 1949

17 Humelsine and Allen memorandum, 14 March 1949, HST, Acheson Papers, Box 64

18 Cousins to Allen, 28 March 1949, Allen to Cousins, 6 April 1949, and MacKnight to Allen, 6 April 1949, USNA, Department of State, Lot 53 D 47, Records Relating to International Information Activities, Box 27, Shapley Meeting

19 Warner, "The Origins of the Congress of Cultural Freedom," 91–2; Peter Coleman, *The Liberal Conspiracy: The Congress for Cultural Freedom and the Struggle for the Mind of Postwar Europe* (New York, 1989), 7; Hugh Wilford, *The New York Intellectuals: From Vanguard to Institution* (Manchester, 1995), 196

20 State Department Press Release 743, 12 July 1950, USNA, Lot 64 D 563, Records of the Policy Planning Staff, 1947–1953, Subject Files, Box 8, Communism 1947–1951. See also the CIA assessment in CIA 5–50, 17 May 1950, *Minutes*, Reel 1

21 State Department memorandum, "Moscow's 'Signatures for Peace' Campaign," 15 June 1950, USNA, Department of State, Lot 53 D 47, Records Relating to International Information Activities, 1938–1953, Box 20, The Soviet Union and Satellites

22 Begg to Jackson, 19 April 1950, USNA, Department of State, Central Decimal File, 511.00/4-1950

23 Acheson to National Security Council (NSC 70/1), 3 May 1950, USNA, Department of State, Lot 53 D 47, Records Relating to International Information Activities, Box 16; fifty-sixth National Security meeting, 4 May 1950, *Minutes*, Reel 1; Lilly memorandum, "Development of American Psychological Operations, 1945–1951," US DDRS, 1990 567. When the World Youth Festival was staged again in 1951, the US centered the West Berlin Cultural Festival around the theme of television. One million spectators visited in two weeks and the proceedings were broadcast to East Berlin. (Mullen to Gray, 21 September 1951, HST, Staff Memoranda and Office Files, PSB Files, 040 ECA)

24 Warner, "The Origins of the Congress of Cultural Freedom," 94–5; Hook, *Out of Step*, 433–44; Coleman, *The Liberal Conspiracy*, 1 and 19–32

25 Draft Senior NSC Staff Report NSC 114 and Annex 5, 27 July 1951, US DDRS, 1980 284B–285A

26 Barrett memorandum, 27 June 1950, USNA, Department of State, Central Decimal File, 511.00/6-2,750, Box 2,237. See also Edward Barrett interview, 9 July 1974, HST, Oral History Collection

27 Draft Senior NSC Staff Report NSC 114 and Annex 5, 27 July 1951, US DDRS, 1980 284B–285A

28 Russell to Barrett, 14 June 1950, HST, Sargeant Papers, General File, Box 4, Deputy Assistant Secretary for Public Affairs, State Department, 1947–1950. The proposal was so sensitive that the Public Affairs section ensured that it was not discussed at a formal meeting; instead Acheson and Under-secretary of State James Webb were briefed orally

29 Minutes of State–Defense Policy Review Group, 10 March 1950, FRUS, 1950, I, 190–5

30 Jerry Sanders, *Peddlers of Crisis: The Committee on the Present Danger and the Politics of Containment* (Boston, MA, 1983), 66–8

31 Sanders, *Peddlers of Crisis*, 94–5

32 Norberg to Taylor, 22 December 1952, HST, Staff Memoranda and Office Files, PSB Files, Box 23, 334 CPD

33 Barrett to Hulten and Stone, 9 June 1950, USNA, Department of State, Lot 53 D 47, Records Relating to International Information Activities, 1938–1953, Box 13, Intelligence

34 Curtin to Gray, 9 October 1951, HST, Staff Memoranda and Office Files, PSB Files, Box 1, 000.1 Rand Corporation Structure

35 Report of Project Troy, Annex 1, Political Warfare, 1 February 1951, USNA, Department of State, Lot 52 D 283, Records Relating to Project Troy
36 Jackson to Elliott, 3 February 1951, DDE, Jackson Papers, Box 40, E Miscellaneous
37 See Sig Mickelson, *America's Other Voices: Radio Free Europe and Radio Liberty* (New York, 1983)
38 C. D. Jackson to Cutler, 4 March 1953, US DDRS, 1980 115D
39 Thirteenth PSB meeting, 12 June 1952, US DDRS, 1988 1770
40 Robert Lang oral history, 31 May 1981, Hoover Institution, Sig Mickelson Papers, Audiotape 29
41 'Radio Free Europe Policy Handbook,' 30 November 1951, US DDRS, 1986 1974. See also Robert Holt, *Radio Free Europe* (Minneapolis, MN, 1958), 22
42 Quoted in Mickelson, *America's Other Voices*, 40–1
43 Quoted in Nickels to Gullion, 8 April 1960, US DDRS, 1986 3110
44 Mickelson, *America's Other Voices*, 54
45 Abbott Washburn interview, 20 April 1967, HST, Oral History Collection; Photograph of plaque in DDE, Jackson Papers, Box 40, Abbott Washburn. An extract from Reagan's address for the Crusade for Freedom is in BBC Television, *The Cold War*, Part 6, 31 October 1998
46 Crusade for Freedom Fact Sheet, November 1952, HST, Hulten Papers, Box 22
47 "Radio Free Europe Adopts Red Tactic," *New York Times*, 23 May 1951, and "Czechs Charge U.S. Aids Spies and Terrorists," *New York Times*, 23 May 1951
48 Crusade for Freedom press release, 29 April 1951, Eleanor Roosevelt Library, FDR, Eleanor Roosevelt Papers, Correspondence 1945–1952, Box 3275, Crusade for Freedom
49 *Liberty News* (North Carolina), 1 December 1952
50 *Charlotte Observer*, 6 December 1952
51 Barrett to Nitze, 15 September 1950, Record of Meeting with Drew Pearson, 2 April 1951, and Wilber to Barrett, 25 June 1951, USNA, Department of State, Lot 53 D 47, Records Relating to International Information Activities, Box 15, National Psychological Strategy Board
52 Report of Project Troy, Annex 1, Political Warfare, 1 February 1951, USNA, Department of State, Lot 52 D 283, Records Relating to Project Troy
53 Stone to Harris, 30 November 1950, USNA, Department of State, Lot 53 D 47, Records Relating to International Information Activities, 1938–1953, Box 10, NSC – Miscellaneous; POC Meeting D-15a, 24 September 1951, USNA, Department of State, Lot 53 D 47, Records Relating to International Information Activities, 1938–1953, Box 23
54 Barrett to Sargeant, 2 January 1951, USNA, Department of State, Lot 53 D 47, Records Relating to International Information Activities, 1938–1953, Box 15, National Psychological Strategy Board; Barrett note, 22 December 1950, USNA, Department of State, Lot 53 D 47, Records Relating to International Information Activities, Box 15, Operation Brainwave
55 *New York Times*, 13 January 1952; Psychological Aspects of Phase A Defection Program; List of Trustees, 1952, DDE, Jackson Papers, Box 45, Free Europe University in Exile
56 Sherman to Taylor and Browne, "The Voices of America," 4 March 1952, US DDRS, 1991 1666

8

Joe Public fights the Cold War

The immediate success of the State–private network against Communist and Congressional foes now had to be translated into a complex system of organization. In 1951 John Phillips, an official in the newly established Psychological Strategy Board, laid out the new strategy:

> Use is already made of domestic public opinion in psychological operations. The reluctance to "propagandize" the domestic public is so strong, however, and the nature of psychological operations is so ill understood, that this weapon is not used to maximum extent and even the present limited use is poorly coordinated.
>
> ... [Current] activities scarcely stratch the surface of the number of statements, editorial campaigns, actions, such as boycotts, letter-writing campaigns, protest meetings, etc., which could be inspired and coordinated for psychological operations.[1]

As a start, the PSB would build a "sort of cadre of base-runners or pinch-hitters" from academia, foundations, publishing, and business to prepare material for dissemination at home and abroad.[2]

But how would the "private" facade be funded? Frank Wisner, the head of the Office of Policy Coordination, answered with a flourish, "It is essential to secure the overt cooperation of people with conspicuous access to wealth in their own right."[3] The CIA responded by establishing an International Organizations Division, headed by Tom Braden, a former journalist, English professor, and Executive Secretary of the Museum of Modern Art. Braden later explained his mission:

> We wanted to unite all those the people who were writers, who were musicians, who were artists and all the people who follow those people, people like you and me who go to concerts or visit art galleries. [We wanted] to demonstrate that the West and the US was [sic] devoted to freedom of expression and to intellectual achievement without any rigid barriers as to what you must write and what you must say and what you must do and what you must think, which was what was going on in the Soviet Union. I think we did it damn well.[4]

Overt funding was out of the question, since "the idea that Congress would have approved many of our projects was about as likely as the John Birch

Society's approving Medicare".[5] In contrast, Donald Jameson, a CIA officer who helped establish the funding network, found the private sector more than cooperative, "It's hard, I think, for people, particularly of a younger generation, to understand the degree to which the Government and its activities had the confidence of its people. It was almost nobody that I couldn't go to in those days and say I'm from the CIA and I'd like to ask you about so-and-so and at the very least get a respectful reception and a discussion."[6]

Some of the money came from established organizations. The Advertising Council was quick to offer free publicity for Government initiatives, as well as contributing between $9 million and $17 million of free advertising to the National Committee for Free Europe.[7] The Executive Director of CARE told Government contacts, "A great deal could be done, mainly under private auspices, in persuading wealthy foreign individuals to finance foundations and projects for socio-economic improvement in their own countries."[8] The CIA worked with a "prominent business association to promote a favorable image of the US in unfriendly countries and to promote citizen-to-citizen contacts".[9]

The Ford Foundation was the primary source of overt support. In 1949 it signalled its intent by announcing its search for programs to "advance human welfare ... synonomous with democratic ideals on challenge in the world today". The foundation coordinated its Intercultural Publications project with the State Department and funded the department's publishing outlet, Franklin Press.[10] Grants were also provided to establish the curriculum of the Free University of Berlin.[11]

Although Ford was formally "opposed to the support of aggressive cold war operations", Government agencies were able to link other grants to the pursuit of liberation. A notable example was the support of refugees and defectors from the Soviet bloc. Just before he left the State Department, George Kennan met with officials from the Policy Planning Staff and the Office of Policy Coordination to discuss the implementation of a "major project" led by the CIA. Within a year, more than $500,000 had been allocated by the foundation for the care and resettlement of refugees and defectors through the Fund for a Free Russia. Far from coincidentally, Kennan was the fund's first president. Other anti-Soviet projects included the finance of the Chekhov Publishing House and Columbia University's exile research project. Meanwhile, "good" Communists from Yugoslavia were rewarded by Ford grants for visits to the United States.[12]

The system was limited, however. The Ford Foundation was still wary about openly financing programs in Eastern Europe. Bernard Gladieux, the assistant to the foundation's president, explained, "Our principal purpose was not the negative one of merely fighting Communism."[13] There was also a ceiling on the foundation's resources; projects were measured in thousands, rather than millions, of dollars. A Government official summarized, "Most of the foundations have many links with the US Government; at the same time they are sensitive to political direction. However, their general orientation, together with the calibre of their administrators, make them susceptible to greater use than has been achieved."[14]

The answer for the International Organizations Division was to expand the funding of the network through "shell" foundations. Braden explained the process. "We would go to somebody in New York, who was a well-known rich person, and we would say, 'We want to set up a foundation.' We would tell him what we were trying to do and pledge him to secrecy and he would say, 'Of course, I'll do it,' and then he would publish a letterhead and his name would be on it and it would be a foundation. It was really a pretty simple device." The rules for distribution of money to recipients were straight-forward: "(1) Limit the money to amounts private organizations can credibly spend; (2) Disguise the extent of American interest; (3) Protect the integrity of the organization by not requiring it to support every aspect of official American policy".[15]

The outcome of the strategy was staggering. In 1975 a Congressional com-mittee established, from a sample of 700 grants of more than $10,000 from 164 foundations outside the "big three" (Ford, Rockefeller, and Carnegie), that 108 were "partial or complete CIA funding". More than half the grants for international activities involved the Agency.[16] A leading example of the approach was the Farfield Foundation, nominally headed by the yachtsman and philanthropist Julian Fleischmann, a director of the Metropolitan Opera in New York, a fellow of the Royal Society of Arts in London, and the backer of many Broadway productions. Michael Josselson, the CIA contact who had helped set up the Berlin Cultural Congress, served as the foundation's "Inter-national Director". In one year Farfield gave $1.5 million to grantees ranging from the American Federation of the Arts to Carleton College to writers Mary McCarthy and Boris Souvarine.[17]

The most prominent "private" ventures funded through the network were the liberation efforts modeled on the National Committee for Free Europe. The Committee for Free Asia (CFA) was organized by the State Department in spring 1951 to ensure "that Radio Free Asia will operate through local Asian stations, will broadcast the type of programs which VOA cannot under-take, and will work toward removing the U.S. label – public and private – from such broadcasts". The CFA was based in San Francisco with 120 em-ployees and maintained an office in Hong Kong. Its projects ranged from aid to the National League for Free Elections in the Philippines to creation of a Chinese bookstore in Hong Kong to employment of refugee Asian intellectuals.[18]

The American Committee for the Liberation of the Peoples of Russia (ACLPR), first designed by George Kennan and the Office of Policy Coordi-nation, was developed by the State Department through a series of meetings with private sponsors, including Harvard's William Elliott, Allan Grover, the chief of staff to *Time-Life* magnate Henry Luce, and prominent New York lawyer John F. B. Mitchell, and Soviet exiles in 1951.[19] Its 314 employees – 96 US nationals and 218 émigrés – were mandated "to aid anti-Communist émigrés from the Soviet Union to unite in a Political Center for the purpose of conducting psychological warfare against the Stalin Regime".[20] The first three directors were the Russian-born journal editor Eugene Lyons, Admiral Leslie Stevens, who had been working for the Joint Chiefs of Staff, and Admiral Alan Kirk, who resigned as US ambassador to the Soviet Union to take up the post.

ACLPR's broadcasting outlet, Radio Liberation, finally went on air in 1953. Its objective was free from the ambiguities of Government edicts: "We must make it possible for great masses of fugitives from Stalin's prison-state now living in our midst to undertake practical anti-Soviet activities. . . . An alliance between the free world and the peoples of the Soviet Union, over the heads of their masters, can bring victory in the cold war and thereby obviate the catastrophe of a hot war."[21] As a 1955 policy manual bluntly stated, "Radio Liberation's ultimate aim is stated simply as the achievement by the peoples of the USSR of a democratic order in place of the present totalitarian Communist regime."[22] Radio Liberation was soon directed by Howland Sargeant, who had just stepped down as Assistant Secretary of State for Public Affairs.[23]

Among the other private groups who advanced liberation were the Friends of Fighters for Russian Freedom, with an organizing committee consisting entirely of women. FFRF was established "to provide material and moral help to . . . courageous men and women . . . [as] a dedicated advance guard in the offensive against Stalinist tyranny". The group promoted "the American idea that carries a greater explosive potential than any hydrogen bomb; i.e., that outlaw governments which do not respect the life, liberty, and pursuit of happiness of every individual must perish from the earth".[24]

As important as these "marquee" efforts were for liberation, they were only a small part of the promotion of US ideology through the private sector. The Government's involvement in all aspects of culture was illustrated by a 1951 interdepartmental "Inventory of Cold War Operations", 144 pages long. For research alone, 105 non-governmental agencies were listed, while cooperation on operations came from the American Legion, the Lions Club, the Anti-Communist League, the US tennis team in the Davis Cup, and even the Yale Glee Club.[25]

CIA funds supported groups as diverse as the Pan-American Foundation, the World Veterans Foundation, the International Marketing Institute, the International Development Foundation, and the American Society of Anglo-French Culture. US Olympic athletes allegedly received subsidies in 1952, and other unwitting recipients included the Symphony of the Air and author William Faulkner.[26] A spiritual offensive was conducted via the Pax Romana, the International Catholic Youth Federation, and the interdenominational organisation Pro Deo, also known as the American Council for the International Promotion of Democracy under God.[27] In its most unusual operation, CIA money was funneled to the Communist *Daily Worker* because the Agency "wanted to know where our enemy was".[28]

The "intellectual" dimension of the crusade was led by the Congress for Cultural Freedom (CCF), which had emerged from the 1950 cultural congress in Berlin. Funds channeled through the American Federation of Labor launched the Executive Committee, but the chief conduit for CIA money to the CCF became the Farfield Foundation, which gave almost $1.3 million in 1962 alone. Michael Josselson, the chief CIA contact, was the CCF's Executive Director as well as Farfield's International Director.[29]

The CCF's most important ongoing role was its responsibility for the global range of "intellectual" journals. These included *Encounter* (British), *Preuves* (French), *Tempo Presente* (Italian), *Quest* (Indian), *Quadrant* (Australian), *Forum* (Austrian), *Hiwar* (Lebanese), and *Chinese Quarterly*. Irving Kristol, one of the first co-editors of *Encounter*, summarized its role succinctly:

> As a cultural-political journal, it published many fine literary essays, literary criticism, art criticism, short stories, and poetry, and in sheer bulk they probably preponderated. But there is no doubt its ideological core – its mission, as it were – was to counteract, insofar as it was possibility, the anti-American, pro-Soviet views of a large segment of the intellectual elites in the Western democracies and the English-speaking Commonwealth.[30]

The French journal *Preuves* was financed by Irving Brown, the American Federation of Labor's link with the CIA; Brown was also behind the launch of *Cuadernos* in Latin America. Arthur Koestler's *Darkness at Noon* was converted, through Agency support, into a play touring Western Europe.[31] Showpiece projects included the 1952 Paris Festival, which featured the Boston Symphony, 19 leading conductors, 63 composers,[32] the New York City Ballet, and artistic "Masterpieces of the Twentieth Century", the 1953 Hamburg Conference on "Science and Freedom", and the 1955 Milan Conference on "The Future of Freedom". In France, the CCF also established the Friends of Liberty to sponsor seminars and women's, youth, and film groups.[33]

The US "branch" of CCF, the American Committee for Cultural Freedom (ACCF), was established in 1951. Its chairmen included Hook, the educator George Counts, the novelist James Farrell, and Norman Thomas. The head of the Administrative Committee was the literary critic Diana Trilling. It was perhaps the only organization in the 1950s that could bring together Norman Cousins, John Dos Passos, George Balanchine, Jackson Pollock, McGeorge Bundy, and Arthur Schlesinger, Jr. As the ACCF's promotional literature boasted in 1953:

> Members of the Executive Committee of this nonpartisan group include an advisor to President Eisenhower, an advisor to Adlai Stevenson, and a prominent Socialist;

also, a university president and several distinguished educators; a Nobel Prize-winning scientist; editors and staff members of various national magazines and newspapers; trade-union leaders; a number of well-known writers, including a Pulitzer Prize-winning poet; and a distinguished scholar in the field of Soviet affairs.

ACCF activities included distribution of more than 50,000 books each year, a reception center for "visiting foreign intellectuals", and an "information program on Communist fronts still operating in the United States".[34]

The origins of the CIA support for the ACCF are unclear. According to Diana Trilling, at a time of grave financial crisis for the committee, Norman Thomas said he would telephone "Allen", his friend from Princeton days. A gift of $10,000 soon arrived. Whether the money was courtesy of Allen Dulles is still debated, but the CIA was soon involved through backing from the Farfield and Fleischmann foundations.[35]

Other intellectual ventures were dedicated to keeping Western Europe "free". At the forefront was the American Committee for a United Europe (ACUE), founded in 1949 by the former head of the OSS, William Donovan, to bring leading Europeans like Winston Churchill to the United States. Allen Dulles, still a private citizen, appeared as "Vice Chairman of the ACUE" on NBC's *Today* with Mrs Roosevelt from the Park Sheraton Hotel in New York, speaking about "How can World Peace be Achieved?".[36] Even more significant was Thomas Braden's service as the ACUE's Executive Director.

The ACUE became a vital conduit for CIA money to the European Movement. From 1947 to 1953, half of the European Movement's budget of £760,000 came from the Agency. The movement in turn helped created other groups like the European Youth Campaign, a response to the Communist Youth Rally of 1951 in East Berlin. The Youth Campaign would eventually receive more than £1.3 million of CIA largesse in the 1950s.[37]

The goal of a pro-US Europe was also promoted by $150,000 to the International Information Exchange[38] and by funds to Paix et Liberté, the creation of French politician Jean-Paul David.[39] Meanwhile the "Letters from America" campaign of the Common Council for American Unity, which had been so effective in the 1948 propaganda campaign in Italy, was revived with support from the Ford Foundation and Hollywood. MGM made a 10-minute film, *The Million-dollar Nickel*, "dramatically pointing out how much can be accomplished with a 5-cent postage stamp. It closed with appeals from actors and actresses destined for fame, including Leslie Caron (*Gigi*) in French, Eva Gabor (*Green Acres*) in Hungarian, and Ricardo Montalban (*Fantasy Island*) in Spanish. Recordings for the Voice of America during Letters from America Week were made by Bing Crosby, Perry Como, Bob Hope, Basil Rathbone, and many others.[40]

The development of the intellectual crusade was replicated in other sectors. The foundation for labour activity had been laid through the *ad hoc* cooperation with US organizations in the French and Italian crises of 1948 and then by the development of the non-Communist International Confederation of Free Trade Unions. Government officials agreed to "encourage US labor groups to expand their efforts in behalf of international organizations of Free Trade Unions, especially in Asia, Africa, and colonial areas".[41] The CIA furthered these links at home and overseas with the American Federation of Labor and the Congress of Industrial Organizations (AFL-CIO). Leading unionists Irving Brown, David Dubinsky, Jay Lovestone, and Walter and Victor Reuther continued to funnel money to US-sponsored activities in Europe. Brown and Dubinsky, for example, were the CIA's links for subsidies to the "socialist" newspaper *Le Populaire* and politician Leon Blum.[42] In Latin America, CIA contact Serafino Romualdi directed the Inter-American Regional Organization.[43] There was even a sustained attempt by the Government to recruit "Eyebrows" – John Lewis, the leader of the United Mine Workers – who had revealed "the most extraordinary amount of detailed, accurate, international knowledge, way beyond just labor affairs", although Lewis finally turned down the invitation to go abroad.[44]

The CIA's use of labor was extended by working with individual US trade unions to influence their international affiliates. The American Federation of State County and Municipal Employees became a channel for CIA operations with the Public Service International in London, the Retail Clerks International Association linked the Agency with the International Federation of Clerical and Technical Employees, and the Communications Workers of America were the route to influence the Post Telegraph and Telephone Workers International. The CIA even created the International Federation of Petroleum and Chemical Workers from scratch.[45]

American universities, whether from ideological commitment, the possibility of financial reward, or the familiarity of wartime links with the Government, provided valuable support for the psychological campaign. Professor Conyers Read, the President of the American Historical Association, issued the call in 1949: "Discipline is the essential prerequisite of every effective army whether it marches under the Stars and Stripes or under the Hammer and Sickle. . . . Total war, whether it be hot or cold, enlists everyone and calls upon everyone to assume his part. . . . This sounds like the advocacy of one form of social control as another. In short, it is."[46]

Even before Read's speech, the State Department was conferring with émigrés about an institute of Eastern European studies and assuring them that "plans for its realization were being developed".[47] The process was accelerated in the aftermath of NSC 68, encouraged by letters like those of Professor William Elliott of Harvard urging the use of "key figures in the ranks of journalists, top intellectual leaders, artists of various sorts, and academic figures". He assessed, "Even though one may regard Jean Sartre as a less serious philosopher than others, he has great public influence." The first step was the formation of an advisory panel "of people who would be useful as centers of influence in strategic academic sections". The list included George Kennan, who had moved from the State Department to Princeton, Gordon Gray, who would hold key posts in both the Truman and Eisenhower Administrations, and Arthur Schlesinger and McGeorge Bundy, future aides in the Kennedy Administration.[48] Ten days after Elliott's letter, Secretary of State Acheson met a number of prominent academics and labour leaders for an "exchange of views on [the] content of material exposing fallacies of communist ideology and setting forth some of the aspects of [the] democratic way of life primarily for groups abroad who are objects of Soviet propaganda".[49] Elliott quickly became a consultant for the Office of Policy Coordination and was one of the "founders" of the American Committee for the Liberation of the Peoples of Russia.[50]

In addition to Project Troy, the study by the Center of International Studies (CENIS) at the Massachusetts Institute of Technology on Soviet vulnerabilities and psychological strategy, Harvard University's Russian Research Center, founded in 1947 with a Carnegie Corporation grant, was interviewing more than 3,000 escapees and refugees on the nature of the Soviet system. The ten reports included studies of industry, social change, the "Nationalities Problem", and "Strengths and Weaknesses".[51] The center was also linked with the Munich Institute for the Study of the USSR, financed by the CIA through the American Committee for the Liberation of the Peoples of Russia.[52] An interdisciplinary study at the California Institute of Technology, Project Vista, evaluated "the full political, moral, and psychological forces of the free world" to counteract the Soviet bloc's 10:1 advantage in military manpower. A typical suggestion was that "this country should develop its own psychological warfare agents . . . by giving young men (and maybe women) with linguistic ability and some social science training experience in one or more skilled or semi-skilled occupations and then planting them in European countries to make a living".[53]

By the end of 1951, academics from Harvard, Princeton, Carnegie-Mellon, MIT, and Michigan had formed an Ad Hoc Group on Psychological Warfare for the military's Human Resources Research and Development Board.[54] The Government's newly formed Psychological Strategy Board devised its plans with the help of consultants like Walt Rostow of MIT, Henry Kissinger of Harvard, Stefan Possony of Georgetown, and Hans Speier and Philip Davidson of the Rand Corporation.[55] After the director of the Hoover Institution on War Revolution and Peace wrote "to assure [the State Department] of the full cooperation" of the institute, the institute contracted with the Air Force to study the psychological vulnerabilities of military and scientific leaders. Johns Hopkins's Operations Research Office examined psychological warfare in Korea, Yale's Institute of Human Relations consulted officials about financial support for their Area Files, and the University of Pittsburgh offered its 18 "nationality classrooms", including Russian, Yugoslav, and Romanian, to the Government.[56]

According to one source, the CIA would eventually work, directly or indirectly, with about 5,000 academics. Most, such as the dean of students at Princeton, William Lippincott, or the rowing coach at Yale, served by recruiting students as future CIA operatives and foreign agents,[57] but some took prominent positions in "private" think tanks. For example, Evron Kirkpatrick and Max Kampelman, the President and Treasurer of the American Political Science Association, also served as President and Vice-President of the CIA-funded Operations and Policy Research Inc.[58] An even more blatant example of the CIA's connection with academia was its sponsorship of one of the best known forums for discussion, William Elliott's International Summer School at Harvard. In early 1954 the White House's C. D. Jackson recorded, "[With] Mallory Browne on Bill Elliott Harvard Seminar financial requirements. Phoned Tom Braden to tell him I thought this was useful activity."[59]

Propaganda to young people was led by the CIA's support from 1950 of the National Student Association (NSA). CIA officials claimed that they were approached by students "virtually paralyzed by lack of funds . . . to propaganda in other countries the distinctly liberal but anti-totalitarian ideals which they were soon to defend at home against McCarthyism". The question of who initiated the relationship is irrelevant; both the Agency and the NSA shared the goal of promoting an anti-Communist liberalism throughout the world. They established the International Student Conference, with the NSA leading the efforts from offices in Philadelphia, "donated" by a local department store, and from an international affairs division in Cambridge, Massachusetts. Initially, the NSA was coached by a journalist in making proposals to foundations, but when these efforts were unsuccessful, the CIA stepped in and channeled its own money through "shell" charities.[60]

Leading African-Americans, already recruited for the first United Nations Conference in 1945 and for service with the Committee to Defend the Marshall Plan, were used to spread the American message to Africa and Asia, countering Soviet propaganda about racial discrimination in the United States. For example, in autumn 1950 Edith Sampson, a Chicago lawyer, became the first African-American woman to serve as a US delegate to the United Nations. Her appointment was in part to pre-empt a damning indictment by the Civil Rights Congress of American race relations, *We Charge Genocide*, in part to turn the charge of "slavery" against the Soviet Union in its extensive use of work camps. Her efforts were highlighted in numerous newspaper articles, in a *Readers Digest* profile, and in a State Department film, and her success was immediately rewarded with a State Department Leader Grant to tour Western Europe.[61] The Voice of America trumpeted other condemnations of *We Charge Genocide* from Walter White, the Executive Secretary of the National Association for the Advancement of Colored People, singer Marian Anderson, labor leader A. Philip Randolph, and boxer Joe Louis. Josephine Baker made her contribution in French.[62]

Women, far from being apolitical, increasingly became a vital part of the Government's efforts, especially in the face of the anti-American propaganda of the Women's International Democratic Federation. Anna Lord Strauss of the League of Women Voters was part of the Committee to Defend the Marshall Plan and traveled overseas for the State Department while the General Federation of Women's Clubs was used to send radio sets to women in Iran.[63] The Crusade for Freedom targeted women with special pamphlets, explaining that if they were behind the Iron Curtain, Radio Free Europe "would serve as your afternoon with friends where you keep up with the local news – only in this case it's the latest information on local Communist undercover agents and collaborators. There wouldn't be much talk of new styles – who can afford an interest in style when it takes a month's wages to buy a pair of stockings? It would be your current events discussion, your book club afternoon, your garden club lecture." US women could help the crusade by "inspiring contributions" from their local groups and serving as "volunteers for booths or door-to-door solicitation . . . , speakers for meetings and radio programs, and all other important 'jobs to be done' in a big campaign".[64]

The most sustained and unusual effort was the CIA's funding of a small group of New York women, the Committee of Correspondence, in their attempt to distribute pro-American information overseas and to organize international conferences. The Agency learned of the 1952 initiative through the freelance journalist Dorothy Bauman, a friend of Tom Braden's who had worked for the Government in World War II. Through her contacts with Braden and those of the committee's founder, Rose Parsons, with Allen Dulles, a subsidy of $25,000 suddenly materialized from "an anonymous donor". Over the next 15 years the committee would receive more than $500,000 from the Agency. Most of the money was funneled through a "shell foundation", the Dearborn Foundation, nominally operating out of the offices of a Chicago insurance company, although contributions were also channeled through a number of other conduits, including the McGregor Fund, a charity nominally established to support operations in Vigo County, Indiana.[65]

Just as every part of US society had become part of the Government's campaign, every medium was necessary to distribute freedom's message. NSC 68 had directed that "a large portion" of the mountain of anti-Soviet booklets, magazines, and news articles "was to appear under auspices other than that of the U.S. Government". The goal was to encourage understanding by "political parties, churches, armed forces, labor, students and youth, intellectuals and educators, businessmen, women, agrarian elements and key local groups . . . of the subversive, conspiratorial, fraudulent and brutal nature of Communist action and of its overriding ulterior purpose to serve Soviet Bloc intervention at the sacrifice of the welfare of the people".[66] A subsequent directive confirmed the production of "cartoon or comic book style leaflets . . . [and] pamphlets, largely pictorial" on topics like "The Farmer and his Land", "Meet some Americans", and "Fables for our Times". There were also materials for schools on "The Meaning of Freedom",[67] and 250,000 copies of a booklet on tourist behavior by the American Heritage Foundation. After Assistant Secretary of State Barrett complimented *Washington Post* publisher Phil Graham on the work of his political cartoonist, Herblock, the *Post* put a selection of the cartoons into a book and published 60,000 copies.[68] Five comic books on citizenship, distributed by US armed forces overseas, included characters like Kerry Drake, Steve Canyon, and Joe Palooka.[69]

By 1951, books "advancing themes hostile to communism and promoting national freedom" were being translated into 28 languages and "issued by sources other than the U.S. Government". Notable examples included *Animal Farm, 1984,* and *La Vie et la mort en URSS (Life and Death in the USSR)*. Books on counter-propaganda, supposedly written by the political scientist Evron Kirkpatrick, were actually penned by Government research staff; Kirkpatrick was listed as the author to "get them published and distributed overseas as a scholarly and, therefore, 'unpropagandistic' document".[70] Payments for "freelance" work went to anti-Communist stalwarts like Franz Borkenau, Sidney Hook, Arthur Koestler, Jacques Barzun, and Bertram Wolfe, as well as literary critic Lionel Trilling, political philosopher Hannah Arendt, and even the left-of-centre sociologist C. Wright Mills.[71]

Even this was inadequate, so the Government set up "front" publishers to complement the State Department-backed Franklin Publications. Arlington Press was established for Government-subsidized "private" output, and projects were developed "with various private agencies, social, commercial, and philanthropic, to provide foreign groups with books and magazines, to assist Americans traveling abroad, to provide radio facilities to underdeveloped areas, to project a balanced picture of Wall Street, to promote the exchange of persons and to develop bi-national community relationships".[72] Reviewing one book which had been developed by the Agency and had a significant reception in the United States and abroad, television commentator Eric Sevareid unwittingly came close the mark: "Our propaganda services could do worse than to flood [foreign] university towns with this volume."[73]

The CIA supported an international organisation of "free" journalists and ensured "that many overseas officers . . . [had] something more than a nodding acquaintance with a variety of American journalists", be they freelance, "stringers", or permanent staff.[74] Other ideas were generated by the State Department's interaction with publishers, editors, and writers. Joseph Pulitzer proposed an essay competition on "The Letter I would Send behind the Iron Curtain".[75] Norman Cousins, after his stand against the hecklers at the Waldorf conference, was sent on a seven-week tour of India, Pakistan, and Ceylon.[76] *Life* magazine produced pictures and color plates for the Campaign of Truth as well as for the official publications *Amerika* in the Soviet Union and *Heute* in Germany.[77] The Scripps newspaper chain made a special contribution by offering to finance balloon drops of literature behind the Iron Curtain.[78]

Complementing its backing of the Congress for Cultural Freedom's global network of journals, the CIA was subsidizing "established" journals.[79] One mystery surrounds support of *Partisan Review*, the periodical of the left established in the 1930s and still a touchstone for "intellectuals" in the Cold War. The publication was indirectly funded from the late 1950s when it received money from the ACCF, which in turn had Agency backing. More controversial is the possibility that the *Review*'s editors sought CIA money before this but were rebuffed because of worries that the journal's intellectual and political line, despite its fervent anti-Soviet position, might not accord with CIA aims.[80]

A more clearly documented and even more dramatic example of the Agency's effectiveness was its sustenance of the influential *New Leader*. Edited by Sol Levitas, an émigré who fled from the Soviet Union in 1923, the publication had brought to prominence authors like Daniel Bell and Melvin Lasky. By 1950, however, it was appealing for funds to pay off $40,000 of debts. Somehow the magazine struggled on; in 1961 Levitas's successor, William Bohn, wrote of "the journalistic miracle" by which Levitas obtained the necessary funds. Bohn could "not pretend to explain how this miracle was achieved.... We always worked in an atmosphere of carefree security. We knew that the necessary money would come from somewhere and that our checks would be forthcoming." It was not divine intervention that saved the *New Leader*, however, but the CIA's provision of money through the J. M. Kaplan Fund, endowed by the head of the Welch fruit juice empire, and the American Labor Conference for International Affairs.[81]

This sleight-of-hand had a significant effect overseas. The *New Leader* was a vital forum for the writings of British socialists opposed to Communism, notably the Labor Party leader Hugh Gaitskell, Anthony Crosland, Denis Healey, and Rita Hinden, the long-time editor of *Socialist Commentary*. This network was also a driving force in the "European Movement", the pressure group for European unity supported by the CIA-financed American Committee on United Europe. Links were further cemented by the connections of the British contingent with another CIA beneficiary, the Congress of Cultural Freedom. Crosland became a key participant in CCF seminars and Gaitskell, Healey, and Hinden all attended the 1955 CCF international conference in Milan.[82]

The Government also sought Hollywood's involvement in the struggle. As early as 1948, officials were considering "how [Economic Cooperation Administration] funds could be used to encourage the industry to export films which constructively advance the prestige of this country abroad",[83] but two years later, the State Department was seeking a global effort. Secretary of State Acheson, ECA head Paul Hoffman, and Assistant Secretary of State Barrett conferred with Eric Johnston, the President of the Motion Picture Association of America, on "mobilizing the motion picture industry in this cold war much as was done in the last war" and "dramatizing to the top stars and top creators exactly what the problem is that we face and what is needed to solve that problem".[84] Movies for the Middle East and Far East were being produced "under the imprint of principal American film companies", and the State Department was supplying others to local producers, "ostensibly as private ventures", in France and Italy. For Eastern Europe, it was "arranged with the Motion Picture Association of America to furnish each year a limited number of quality entertainment films".[85]

There was no problem of industry cooperation apart from "the reluctance of the theater owners [overseas] . . . on the ground that such showings [of anti-Communist films] can or may incite riots in the audience".[86] By 1951 the Government was working with most of the major studios. Twentieth Century Fox organized an essay competition on the impact of American movies overseas, with the winner receiving a free trip to the United States and six months' training in a motion picture theater.[87] In 1951, Government agencies considered negotiations with Frank Capra, the Oscar-winning director and maker of the "Why we Fight" series in World War II, for a new film on the new fight against Communism and helped complete the conversion of *Animal Farm* into a feature film.[88]

The Eisenhower Administration went even further in talks with film executives. The USIA's Theodore Streibert and Abbott Washburn came up with "a good and workable formula" which the President presented to studio heads at a White House stag dinner. Those attending included Cecil B. deMille, who was chief consultant to the USIA on film, Carey Wilson, the President of the Motion Picture Producers Guild, and Walt and Roy Disney.[89] The Agency subsequently "arranged with the Motion Picture Association of America to furnish each year a limited number of quality entertainment films for the personal use of chiefs of mission."[90] A typical example was MGM's *The Hoaxters*, nominated for an Academy Award, which showed "how the dictators of the world up to and including Joseph Stalin have been much like the hucksters who attempt to fool the people with 'snake oil' ".[91] In other cases, like *The POW Story*, the Government ensured input through technical advisors.[92]

The new medium of television took on a role. David Sarnoff, the Chairman of the Board of the Radio Corporation of America and the National Broadcasting Corporation, made dramatic and significant interventions during the drafting of NSC 68. His call for a high-level panel to suggest improvements for the Voice of America was turned by Assistant Secretary of State Barratt into "an all-out effort to penetrate the Iron Curtain with our ideas".[93] The State Department soon supplied material for anti-Communist programs such

as NBC's *Malice in Wonderland*, Dumont's *Our Secret Weapon*, and NBC's
The Battle Report with its slogan "Battle of Democracy against World Communism".[94] Barrett met regularly with the heads of the major networks, including Sarnoff, CBS's William Paley, ABC's Edward Noble, and the Mutual
Broadcasting System's Theodore Streibert, who would later become the head
of the US Information Agency, and encouraged Acheson to make appearances
on programs like "Mrs Roosevelt meets the Public".[95]

In 1955 Sarnoff presented the government with a 42-page "Program for a
Political Offensive against World Communism", arguing that the "best and
surest way to prevent a Hot War [was] to win the Cold War, [with] propaganda as the primary weapon". Specifically, "America's propaganda could be
proliferated overseas via television and other media sources".[96] CBS's Paley, a
veteran of World War II psychological operations, offered an example by designating Sig Mickelson, the President of CBS News and later director of Radio
Free Europe and Radio Liberty, as his liaison with the CIA.[97]

Perhaps the most striking cultural effort, however, was through the medium
of modern art, in particular the CIA's sponsorship of abstract expressionism.
Before joining the CIA, Tom Braden had been Executive Secretary of New
York's Museum of Modern Art. Julius Fleischmann and Paley were on
MOMA's International Board. The President of MOMA, John Hay Whitney,
was also supportive of the Agency, allowing his Whitney Trust to serve as a
"front" for CIA funds.[98]

The CIA's sponsorship not only challenged the Soviets; it allowed the Government to circumvent a Congress suspicious of modern art. A 1947 State
Department exhibition, "Advancing American Art", had been sabotaged, even
before it could be sent abroad, by Congressmen who believed that "ultra-
modern artists are unconsciously used as tools of the Kremlin and that some
abstract paintings were actually secret maps of strategic US fortifications".
Even President Truman offered the critique "If that's art, then I'm a Hotten-
tot. . . . Modern art was merely the vaporings of half-baked, lazy people, frustrated ham-and-egg men." In contrast, MOMA's most ambitious project, the
"Masterpieces of the Twentieth Century" exhibition at the Paris Festival in
May 1952, garnered little Congressional attention and was well received by
foreign audiences, as the State Department assured that "no US Government
funds [were] involved in exposition which [was] privately sponsored and
financed". The "Modern Art in the US" exhibition, displayed in autumn 1955
in Paris and dominated by abstract expressionists such as Willem de Kooning,
Arshil Gorky, and Jackson Pollock, received a mixed reception from critics but
also generated a great deal of pro-American publicity.[99]

With the Government now intimately involved in "culture", it is unsur-
prising that some initiatives verged on the surreal. US officials devoted much
time to the International Society for the Welfare of Cripples, aspiring to "get
into the headquarters in New York the right kind of person who could exert

influence".[100] The State Department gave "most serious consideration" to the proposed donation by Ohio manufacturers of toy balloons to carry propaganda, although an offer by the Bowman Gum Company of Philadelphia to drop chewing gum, with anti-Communist cards rather than baseball cards, had to be turned down because "use of any edible substance in connection with balloon activities would open the possibility of counter-measures mixing poison-bearing balloons with harmless ones".[101] The Vice-President of the Souvenir Lead Pencil Company, who had offered to distribute pencils abroad, was referred to the National Committee for Free Europe and the American Red Cross while proposals by private groups to give away used sporting equipment overseas were rejected because of problems with storage and transport.[102]

Suggestions which crossed the line of feasibility came from the New Day of Father Divine Movement, who advised that a ball of dust would envelop the earth on 21 September 1952, and a "Count Berni Vici" who offered the production of the motion picture The Communist Cancer, to be shown on a Stagemobile screen, illustrating "the cure of the patient with an injection of Dr. Freedom's and Dr. Democracy's healthful anti-biotic".[103] However, advice from a photographer to learn about extra-sensory perception, as he knew "one person who is being driven almost to the point of insanity by the continued reception of the magnetic drivel", was not too bizarre for the CIA, although they warned "that the current sociological conditions within police states such as the USSR would prevent the possibility of utilizing" psychiatric warfare.[104] The agency conducted experiments with a "Mr Brown" in Istanbul, successfully sending messages by telepathy to "Mrs Brown" in Richmond, Virginia.[105]

Within a few years, the State–private network had mobilized the entire spectrum of US society to fight the Cold War. By doing so, it met the challenge of a New York Times editorial of December 1950:

> We in the US do not usually think of culture as playing any part in the propaganda war. And yet when Russians are represented in European festivals and the US is not, the loss is ours. We can be proud of a vibrant and flourishing culture. But because of our foolish disregard of the immense important of the "cultural offensive" we have, as Assistant Secretary Barrett said the other day, lost many an intellectual battle throughout the civilized world without a struggle.[106]

Notes

1 Phillips to Gray, 26 July 1951, US DDRS, US 1991 2282
2 Norberg to Sherman, 20 February 1952, US DDRS, 1991 543; PSB Staff Meeting, 7 February 1952, US DDRS, 1992 1117; Gange memorandum, "Use of Private Brains," undated, and subsequent memoranda, US DDRS, US 1991 3584
3 Thomas Powers, The Man who Kept the Secrets: Richard Helms and the CIA (London, 1979), 38
4 Tom Braden interview, in Hidden Hands: A Different History of Modernism, Channel 4 Television, London, 1995. Braden initially joined the CIA in October 1950 to supervise

the Agency's work with labor. He soon proposed an expansion of his role through the formation of the IOD and won his case after overcoming internal opposition. (Thomas Braden oral history, 1983, Hoover Institution, Sig Mickelson Collection, Audiotape 56)

5 Thomas Braden, "I'm Glad the CIA is Immoral," *Saturday Evening Post*, 20 May 1967
6 Donald Jameson interview in *Hidden Hands: A Different History of Modernism*, Channel 4 Television, London, 1995
7 Wilson to Jackson, 5 April 1961, DDE, Jackson Papers, Box 44, Free Europe 1961; Sig Mickelson, *America's Other Voices: Radio Free Europe and Radio Liberty* (New York, 1983), 55–6
8 Irwin to Browne, 29 April 1952, US DDRS, 1988 3546
9 Final Report of the Select Committee to Study Governmental Operations with Respect to Intelligence Activities (Church Committee), *Foreign and Military Intelligence*, Book I, 26 April 1976, 183
10 Francis X. Sutton, "The Ford Foundation: The Early Years," *Daedalus*, winter 1987, 48–9 and 56–60; Kathleen D. McCarthy, "From Cold War to Cultural Development: The International Cultural Activities of the Ford Foundation, 1950–1980," *Daedalus*, winter 1987, 96–8
11 Gladieux to Schroeder, 19 December 1951, HST, Staff Memoranda and Office Files, PSB Files, Box 4, 080 Ford Foundation
12 PSB Draft Program for Soviet Orbit Escapees, 11 December 1951, US DDRS, US 1990 3560; OCB Action Items, 2 November 1953, US DDRS, 1991 2971; *New York Times*, "Project for Assisting Soviet Exiles Faces a Revision and Curtailment," 1 December 1951
13 Gladieux to Schroeder, 19 December 1951, HST, Staff Memoranda and Office Files, PSB Files, Box 4, 080 Ford Foundation
14 Korns to Sherman, 4 June 1952, US DDRS, 1990 1545
15 *Newark Star-Ledger*, 30 March 1967; Tom Braden interview in *Hidden Hands: A Different History of Modernism*, Channel 4 Television, London, 1995
16 Church Committee, *Foreign and Military Intelligence*, Book I, 182
17 *Hidden Hands: A Different History of Modernism*, Channel 4 Television, London, 1995; 990-A Tax Form for Farfield Foundation, 1962, NSA, Project Vista File
18 Sherman to Taylor and Browne, "The Voices of America," US DDRS, 1991 1666
19 Frank Lindsay oral history, 1 February 1983, Hoover Institution, Sig Mickelson Collection, Audiotape 56. John F. B. Mitchell is not to be confused with the John Mitchell who later achieved notoriety as Attorney General in the Nixon Administration. The forerunner of the ACLPR, at least for intelligence and analysis, was the Institute for the Study of the USSR, established in Munich in 1950 by the Office of Policy Coordination.
20 Sherman to Taylor and Browne, "The Voices of America," US DDRS, 1991 1666; Jackson Committee report, 30 June 1953, US DDRS, 1997 2351
21 Jackson to Miller, 28 March 1952, DDE, Jackson Papers, Box 24, America Miscellaneous
22 Radio Liberation Policy Manual, undated [1955], HST, Sargeant Papers, Box 11, Radio Liberty, General 1956
23 W. G. to Blum, undated, and "U.S. Political Warfare vs. the USSR," 5 January 1953, US DDRS, 1991 752; Scott in William Daugherty and Morris Janowitz (eds), *A Psychological Warfare Casebook* (Baltimore, MD, 1958), 155; Mickelson, *America's Other Voices*, 59–61
24 Friends of Fighters for Russian Freedom brochure, undated, and "Liberation – A Policy for Peace," *Bulletin of American Friends of Russian Freedom*, November 1952, DDE, Jackson Papers, Box 24, America Miscellaneous
25 Davis memorandum, 11 October 1951, HST, Staff Memoranda and Office Files, PSB Files, Box 34, Inventory of Resources Presently Available; "Inventory of Resources Presently Available for Psychological Operations Planning," 5 January 1952, US DDRS, 1992 1113

26 Progress Report on NSC 5516, "US Policy toward Japan," 29 March 1995, US DDRS, 1987 2888. In July 1953 the State Department and CIA discussed covert assistance to the New York City Ballet to send it to Moscow, but the proposal was not approved. (Schwinn to Smith, 29 July 1953, USNA, Department of State, PSB Working File, 1951–1953, Box 4, PSB D-23; Morgan memorandum, 29 July 1953, USNA, Department of State, PSB Working File, 1951–1953, Box 7, Informal PSB Meetings)

27 Jackson to Dulles, 10 December 1956, DDE, Jackson Papers, Box 40; Philip Agee, *Inside the Company: CIA Diary* (Harmondsworth, 1975), 73

28 Miles Copeland, *The Real Spy World* (London, 1978), 221; "The Front Page," *Washington Post*, 2 November 1975

29 *Hidden Hands: A Different History of Modernism*, Channel 4 Television, London, 1995; 990-A Tax Form for Farfield Foundation, 1962, NSA, Project Vista File; Pierre Gremion, *Intelligence de l'anti-communisme: le Congrés pour la liberté de la culture à Paris* (Paris, 1995), 448

30 Irving Kristol, "Why I am Still Fighting my Cold War," *The Times* (London), 9 April 1993

31 Rhodri Jeffreys-Jones, *The CIA and American Democracy* (New Haven, CT, 1989), 87; Gremion, *Intelligence de l'anti-communisme*, 78 and 146; MacKnight to Hulten, 26 February 1951, USNA, Department of State, Lot 53 D 47, Records Relating to International Information Activities, Box 55, MacKnight

32 The composers included Bartok, Britten, Copland, Mahler, Rachmaninov, Schoenberg, and Shostakovich.

33 Frank Costigliola, *France and the United States: The Cold Alliance since World War II* (New York, 1992), 89; Gremion, *Intelligence de l'anti-communisme*, 81–2. See Peter Coleman, *The Liberal Conspiracy: The Congress for Cultural Freedom and the Struggle for the Mind of Post-war Europe* (New York, 1989).

34 American Committee for Cultural Freedom brochure, "These Pages Provide Answers to Three Questions," DDE, Jackson Papers, Box 24, America Miscellaneous

35 Sidney Hook, *Out of Step: An Unquiet Life in the Twentieth Century* (New York, 1987), 425–6; Hugh Wilford, *The New York Intellectuals: From Vanguard to Institution* (Manchester, 1995), 131–2

36 "Today with Mrs Roosevelt," March–April 1950, FDR, Eleanor Roosevelt Papers, Speech and Article File, Box 3055

37 Philip Agee and Louis Wolf (eds), *Dirty Work: The CIA in Western Europe* (New York, 1983), 201–3; Richard Aldrich, "OSS, CIA and European Unity: The American Committee on United Europe, 1948–60," *Diplomacy and Statecraft*, March 1997, 184–227

38 See file in DDE, Jackson Papers, Box 33, Hans Cohrssen

39 The material on the funding of Paix et Liberté is so sensitive that almost all of it is classified, but references can be found in Gruenther to Gray, 16 July 1951, HST, Staff Memoranda and Office Files, PSB Files, Box 23, 334 HICOG Communication with General Gruenther; Jackson daily logs, 29 September and 16 November 1953, DDE, Jackson Papers, Box 56, Log 1953 (2); Kirkpatrick to Phillips, 26 June 1953, DDE, Jackson Papers, Box 4, K

40 Stone to Gray, 29 November 1951, HST, Staff Memoranda and Office Files, Box 4, 080 Recommendations of the Review Group to PSB; LENAP meeting, 19 November 1952, HST, Staff Memoranda and Office Files, PSB Files Box 23, 334 LENAP; Gedalead to Streibert, undated [1953], HST, Hulten Papers, Box 14, Department of State Information Programs 1953, General

41 Humelsine memorandum, 1 June 1949, USNA, Department of State, Lot 64 D 563, Records of the Policy Planning Staff 1947–1953, Subject Files, Box 10, Labor

42 See Braden, "I'm Glad the CIA is Immoral"

43 Agee, *Inside the Company*, 76

44 Jackson to Eisenhower, 25 June 1953, and Lewis to Jackson, 14 October 1953, DDE, Jackson Records, Box 4, L

45 Agee, *Inside the Company*, 76

46 Quoted in Noam Chomsky, *The Culture of Terrorism* (London, 1988), 2–3. Another historian, Yale's Samuel Flagg Bemis, asserted to the State Department's Francis Russell that foreign nationals at American universities, working for their native country, were "trying to form US public opinion". He helpfully suggested that the department publicise information collected about these suspect academics. Bemis's proposal was rejected, since it "would probably result in a storm of criticism" and "undoubtedly have a bad effect overseas". (Bemis to Russell, 29 November 1950, USNA, Department of State, Central Decimal File, 511.00/11-2950, Box 2239; Johnstone to Russell, 8 December 1950, USNA, Department of State, Central Decimal File, 511.00/12-850, Box 2239). The CIA was assisted by professors like Yale's Norman Holmes Pearson, a former operative, who recommended that each university ensure its staff forwarded the names of promising students to the Agency. (Sigmund Diamond, *Compromised Campus: The Collaboration of Universities with the Intelligence Community, 1945–1955* (New York, 1992), 53)

47 Stevens memorandum, FRUS 1948, IV, 404–6

48 Elliott to Barrett, 13 November 1950, and Elliott to Lanigan, 5 December 1950, USNA, Department of State, Office of the Assistant Secretary of State for Public Affairs, Office of Public Affairs, Subject Files 1945–1952, Box 2

49 Acheson to Commager *et al.*, 15 December 1950, USNA, Department of State, Central Decimal File, 511.00/12-1550, Box 2239

50 Diamond, *Compromised Campus*, 145; Mickelson, *America's Other Voices*, 61–2

51 Watts to Staff, 30 March 1953, USNA, Department of State, Lot 64 D 563, Records of the Policy Planning Staff, 1947–1953, Chronological File, Box 35, Chronological, January–December 1952; Laura Nader, "The Phantom Factor," in Noam Chomsky *et al.*, *The Cold War and the University* (New York, 1997), 112

52 Diamond, *Compromised Campus*, 94–102

53 Abstract of Project VISTA report, undated, PSB Files, Box 1, 014.3 Social Science Research, Loomis Report; Watson to Gray, 19 November 1951, US DDRS, 1991 1119

54 Committee on Human Resources Research and Development Board, 18 December 1951, HST, Staff Memoranda and Office Files, PSB Files, Box 1, 014.3 Social Science Research, Loomis Report

55 Allen to PSB Members, 29 July 1952, USNA, Department of State, Lot 62 D 333, PSB Working File, Box 3, PSB D-21

56 HUMRRO memorandum, 13 May 1952, US DDRS, 1988 3547; fifteenth PSB meeting, 11 September 1952, US DDRS, 1988 1779; Rothwell to Foster Dulles, 10 February 1953, USNA, Department of State, Central Decimal File, 511.00/2-1053, Box 2246; Stone to Norberg, 24 February 1950, USNA, Department of State, Lot 53 D 47, Records Relating to International Information Activities, Box 14, Intelligence; Pray to Kirk, 23 January 1952, HST, Staff Memoranda and Office Files, PSB Files, Box 4, 080 Recommendations of the Review Group to PSB

57 William Corson, *The Armies of Ignorance: The Rise of the American Intelligence Empire* (New York, 1977), 309–11; Robin Winks, *Cloak and Gown: Scholars in the Secret War, 1939–1961* (New York, 1987), 52–5

58 Marshall Windmiller, "The New American Mandarins," in Theodore Roszak (ed.), *The Dissenting Academy*, (Harmondsworth, 1969), 113

59 Jackson daily log, 10 March 1954, DDE, Jackson Papers, Box 56, Log 1954

60 CIA memorandum, "American Students in Post-war International Affairs," undated, US DDRS, 1994 1781; CIA memorandum, undated, US DDRS, 1992 12

61 See Helen Laville and Scott Lucas, "Edith Sampson, the NAACP, and African American Identity," *Diplomatic History*, fall 1996, 565–90.

62 Kohler to Devine, 17 November 1951, US DDRS, 1991 3015

63 See material in USNA, Department of State, Lot 53 D 47, Records Relating to International Information Activities, Box 55.

64 Crusade for Freedom brochure, undated [1951], DDE, Jackson Papers

65 Helen Laville, "The Committee of Correspondence: CIA Support for Women's Groups, 1952–1967," *Intelligence and National Security*, January 1997, 104–21; Committee of Correspondence Papers, Sophia Smith Collection, Smith College, Northampton, Massachusetts; Lena Phillips and Eleanor Coit Papers, Schlesinger Library, Radcliffe College, Cambridge, Massachusetts

66 Draft Senior NSC Staff Report NSC 114 and Annex 5, 27 July 1951, US DDRS, 1980 284B–285A; OCB memorandum, 5 April 1956, US DDRS, 1991 2172

67 Circular Airgram, "Proposed Publication Program," 7 October 1950, USNA, Department of State, Central Decimal File, 511.00/10-750, Box 2237

68 Barrett to Humelsine, 1 August 1951, USNA, Department of State, Lot 53 D 47, Records Relating to International Information Activities, Box 55, Public Affairs, Assistant Secretary (P Area)

69 Sherman to Taylor and Browne, "The Voices of America," 4 March 1952, US DDRS, 1991 1666

70 Barrett to Taber, 19 July 1951, USNA, Department of State, Central Decimal File, 511.00/7-1950, Box 2242. Kirkpatrick's wife Jeanne would also combine academic and Government service, publishing the 1964 work *Strategy of Deception* and writing on the differences between authoritarianism (which could be supported by the United States) and totalitarianism (which could not) before becoming the US representative to the UN in the Reagan Administration

71 Barrett to Taber, 19 July 1951, USNA, Department of State, Central Decimal File, 511.00/7-1950, Box 2242

72 Draft Senior NSC Staff Report NSC 114 and Annex 5, 27 July 1951, US DDRS, 1980 284B–285A; Kirk to PSB Members, 27 October 1952, US DDRS, US 1991 3556

73 Church Committee, *Foreign and Military Intelligence*, Book I, 193–4

74 CIA memorandum to Associate Deputy Director of Operations, 3 October 1973, US DDRS, 1980 9C; Assistant Deputy Director of Operations to Director of Central Intelligence, 8 May 1974, US DDRS, 1980 10B

75 Church Committee, *Foreign and Military Intelligence*, Book I, 183; State Department meeting with Grant and Deuel, 13 October 1950, USNA, Department of State, Central Decimal File, 511.00/10-1350, Box 2238

76 State Department to New Delhi, Cable 766, 21 November 1950, USNA, Department of State, Central Decimal File, 511.00/11-2150, Box 2239

77 Barrett to Baker, 19 December 1950, USNA, Department of State, Central Decimal File, 511.00/12-1950, Box 2239

78 PSB staff meetings, 14 April 1952 and 9 May 1952, HST, Staff Memoranda and Office Files, PSB Files, Box 27, 337 Staff Meetings

79 Of course, there were still problems with the "independence" of editors and essayists. For example, Michael Josselson, the Executive Secretary of the Congress for Cultural Freedom and a CIA agent, was unable to place an "analysis" of Eisenhower's "Atoms for Peace" speech with *Preuves* – three French scientists declined the invitation and David Lilienthal, the former Chairman of the Atomic Energy Commission, turned down an appeal by the American Committtee for Cultural Freedom. (Josselson to "Larry", undated, DDE, Jackson Records, Box 5, P)

80 Wolfe to Lasky, 22 January 1973, Hoover Institution, Bertram Wolfe papers. (I am grateful to Hugh Wilford for this reference.)

81 Richard Fletcher, "How CIA Money Took the Teeth out of British Socialism," in Agee and Wolf (eds), *Dirty Work*, 191–2 and 199. For a description of the anti-Communist content of the *New Leader*, see Andre Liebich, "Mensheviks Wage the Cold War," *Journal of Contemporary History*, 1995.

82 Fletcher, "How CIA Money Took the Teeth out of British Socialism," 188–200

83 Edwards to Macy, 20 May 1948, USNA, Department of State, Lot 53 D 47, Records Relating to International Information Activities, Box 20

84 Memorandum of conversation with Johnston, 26 April 1950, HST, Acheson Papers, Box 65

85 Draft Senior NSC Staff Report NSC 114 and Annex 5, 27 July 1951, US DDRS, 1980 284B–285A; Kirk to PSB Members, 27 October 1952, US DDRS, US 1991 3556

86 Sherman to Norberg, 3 October 1952, HST, Staff Memoranda and Office Files, PSB Files, Box 11, 091.4 Europe

87 Begg to Miller, 1 June 1951, USNA, Department of State, Central Decimal File, 511.00/6-151, Box 2241

88 Sherman to Gray, 7 September 1951, US DDRS, US 1991 1115; Gray–Lovett meeting, 5 October 1951, HST, Staff Memoranda and Office Files, PSB Files, Box 24, PSB Staff Coordination and Liaison with the White House, File 2; Hirsh to Barnes, 23 January 1952, HST, Staff Memoranda and Office Files, PSB Files, Box 3, 062.2 Proposal to Make a Series of Films. The epitome of Government links with Hollywood was the work of the actress Myrna Loy. In 1950 Howland Sargeant of the State Department's Public Affairs staff reported, "Miss Myrna Loy has been here for the past week . . . doing more things than you can shake a stick at. Myrna appeared before the Executive Committee of the National Commission (on Information) and I understand made a very eloquent and persuasive presentation which will result in further developing our work with the Hollywood Committee and the Hollywood people. She is certainly a charming person." Several years later, Howland Sargeant and Myrna Loy were married. (Sargeant to Allen, 4 February 1950, HST, Sargeant Papers, Box 4, Deputy Assistant Secretary for Public Affairs, State Department 1947–1950)

89 Jackson daily log, 14 January 1954, DDE, Jackson Papers, Box 56, Log 1954. At the time, DeMille was developing *The Ten Commandments* to teach some Cold War lessons. The souvenir program for the movie explained, "In the relationship between Moses and Rameses, we have the clash between two great opposing forces which have confronted each other throughout human history and which still . . . are engaged in mortal combat for the future of mankind.

 "On the one hand there is the Pharaoh Rameses – worshipped as a god – the massive machinery of oppression at his command, his people chattels, and his will their only law.

 "Opposing him stands Moses, armed only with a staff – and the unquenchable fire of freedom under God." (Quoted in Sumiko Higashi, "Anti-modernism as Historical Representation in a Consumer Culture: Cecil B. DeMille's *The Ten Commandments*, 1923, 1956, 1993," in Vivian Sobchack (ed.), *The Persistence of History: Cinema, TV, and the Historical Event* (New York, 1996), 101–2. See also Alan Nadel, *Containment Culture* (Durham, NC, 1995), 93)

90 "Part 6 – The USIA Program," 11 August 1955, US DDRS, 1991 2022

91 Hanes to Ryan, 8 April 1953, DDE, John Foster Dulles Papers, Special Assistants Chronological Series, Box 2, Chronological – O'Connor and Hanes, 1–31 April 1953 (6)

92 Meeting of POW Working Group, 8 December 1953, US DDRS, 1992 2860

93 Truman to Acheson, 1 March 1950, and Barrett to Acheson, 2 March 1950, FRUS, 1950, IV, 271–2

94 Barrett to Belding, 28 November 1950, USNA, Department of State, Central Decimal File, 511.00/11-2850, Box 2238; Seamans to Wilber, 3 December 1951, USNA, Department

of State, Lot 53 D 47, Records Relating to International Information Activities, Box 17, Miscellaneous

95 Barrett Roundtable with Broadcasting Executives, 26 January 1951, USNA, Department of State, Central Decimal File, 511.00/1-2651, Box 2239; "Mrs Roosevelt Meets the Public," 1 October 1950, FDR, Eleanor Roosevelt Papers, Speech and Article File, Box 3055

96 Shawn Parry-Giles, " 'Camouflaged' Propaganda: The Truman and Eisenhower Administrations' Covert Manipulation of News," *Western Journal of Communication*, April 1996, 146, cited in Alex Constantine, *Virtual Government: CIA Mind Control Operations in America* (Venice, CA, 1997), 50–1

97 Carl Bernstein, "The CIA and the Media," *Rolling Stone*, 20 October 1977

98 *Hidden Hands: A Different History of Modernism*, Channel 4 Television, London, 1995

99 *Time*, 29 August 1949; *Hidden Hands: A Different History of Modernism*, Channel 4 Television, 1995; State Department Circular 912, 2 May 1952, USNA, Department of State, Central Decimal File, 511.00/5-252, Box 2244

100 Browne to Allen, 5 May 1952, HST, Staff Memoranda and Office Files, PSB Files, Box 4, 080 International Society for the Welfare of Cripples

101 Devine memorandum, 29 May 1951, USNA, Department of State, Central Decimal File, 511.00/5-2951, Box 2241; Barry to Barrett, 6 March 1950, USNA, Department of State, Lot 53 D 47, Records Relating to International Information Activities, Box 18, Liaison with National Security Resources Board

102 Stewart to Thorpe, 27 October 1950, USNA, Department of State, Central Decimal File, 511.00/10-2750, Box 2238; State Department memorandum, "Presentation of American Sports Equipment Abroad," 23 May 1952, USNA, Department of State, Central Decimal File, 511.00/5-2352, Box 2245

103 Wright to Gray, 10 June 1951, Johnson to Mundt, 16 September 1952, HST, Staff Memoranda and Office Files, PSB Files, Box 34, Inventory of Resources Presently Available; Vici memorandum, "The Communist Cancer," 2 August 1951, USNA, Department of State, Central Decimal File, 511.00/8-251, Box 2242

104 Sprinkel to PSB, 26 July 1952, HST, Staff Memoranda and Office Files, PSB Files, Box 34, Inventory of Resources Presently Available

105 Miles Copeland, *The Game Player: Confessions of the CIA's Original Political Operative* (New York, 1989), 121

106 *New York Times*, "Export of Culture," 4 December 1947

9

The strange tale of the Psychological Strategy Board

By early 1951, the State–private network had turned the Campaign of Truth into a global crusade. US projects covered 93 countries, targeting "urban and rural workers, youth, the professional and governing classes and intellectuals, with emphasis among the latter on journalists and teachers".[1] The Voice of America had increased broadcasting from 30 hours per day in 24 languages to 61 hours per day in 45 languages. Printing capacity was raised to 60 million booklets and leaflets, 6 million magazines, 40 million posters, and 32 million words in press releases. The number of information centers increased from 105 to 128, exchanges of persons expanded from 3,000 to 3,900, and documentaries were made in 32 languages to be shown by 145 mobile units. Congressional opposition had been overcome to the mysterious category of "the appropriation of [$10 million] for discretionary use of unconventional devices for affecting popular attitudes".[2] MIT's Lloyd Berkner, the director of Project Troy on Soviet vulnerabilities, effused to Secretary of State Acheson, "It is possible to organize an aggressive political war of sufficient effectiveness to bring the Soviet Union to its knees in a relatively short time without resorting to widespread military action. Furthermore, it appears that this can be done without serious danger of precipitating total military action."[3]

The increase in effort brought problems of organisation, however. The speedy mobilisation of "information programs" and the adoption of liberation in 1948 through a series of National Security Council documents – NSC 4 and 4-A, NSC 10/2, and NSC 20/4 – had led to a patchwork of responsibilities and tension between overt and covert activities. The State Department, the CIA, the Office of Policy Coordination, the military, and the White House each had a share of the psychological offensive without having overall control. Throughout 1950 there were protracted deliberations on coordination of a psychological organisation in wartime,[4] but this did little to solve the problem of operations in peacetime or even during a period of "limited" war. When Edward Barrett took over as Assistant Secretary of State for Public Affairs in 1950, his plans for a total effort at home and abroad included "gearing the information machinery in such a way that it could fire all its guns in the form of campaigns, on important themes, carefully selected in advance". Unfortunately officials had "been so overwhelmed by the press of day-to-day work that nothing precise or tangible [had] resulted".[5] The academics of Project Troy concluded, "There must be some *single authority* concerned with political warfare exclusively, with the capacity to design a comprehensive program and the power to obtain execution of this program through the effective action of all the agencies and departments that are now engaged in waging political warfare."[6]

The Korean War exposed the problems of coordination. Operation Rattrap, in which Army psychological warfare units and State Department information officers supported South Korean propaganda, was developed, and other leaflets stressed the basics of the Free World to North Korean troops: "The United Nations gives you ready-made cigarettes. ENJOY LIFE and plenty of cigarettes away from war by coming over to the UN side. Escape. Save your life."[7] The Air Force concluded that, while the average cost of killing an enemy soldier by air action was $4,500, the cost of winning his allegiance through psychological warfare was only $750.[8] For all the promise of individual actions, however, a military survey team concisely evaluated the state of plans: "None exist for that twilight zone such as has existed in Korea."[9]

The problem was compounded by both military success and military disaster. In the aftermath of the US landing at Inchon in September, which not only relieved the pressure on South Korea but suddenly raised the prospect of victory in the North, the US Government was uncertain about publicising the goal of Korean reunification,[10] although privately it instructed General Douglas MacArthur, the commander of UN forces, "to prepare the way for the unification of a free and independent Korea . . . an intensive re-education and re-orientation program".[11] In the political vacuum, MacArthur seized the initiative by pressing further into North Korea and launching air attacks against China, but the Chinese reacted by pouring their own troops across the border, throwing UN forces back into South Korea. At a tense press conference in late November, President Truman was so shaken that he left open the prospect of using the atomic bomb, but he quickly retracted the possibility in the face of a worried public and an emergency visit by British Prime Minister Clement Attlee.

Once again Edward Barrett stepped into the void. He warned Undersecretary of State James Webb, "From where we sit, the Administration seems in danger of erring very badly in the direction of 'Let's wait and see' and 'Let's not do anything until we are absolutely sure of it'." In the short term, Truman had to make a clear statement before a joint session of Congress. Secretary of State Acheson agreed. He recommended to the National Security Council that the United States prepare for the possibility of total war with a sustained psychological campaign at home and abroad, including a declaration of unlimited national emergency. The President issued the call on 16 December.[12]

Barrett's search for coordination was reinforced by the concerns of the new Director of the CIA, General Walter Bedell Smith, over the rapid expansion of the Office of Policy Coordination. Smith was far from enamored of his colleagues in covert action. Reports reached him of the staff of the OPC's Psychological Warfare Workshop passing time by shooting at balloons in their office with BB guns. Frustrated, Smith told one workshop staffer, "If you send me one more project with goddamned balloons, I'll throw you out of here." Informed of another OPC operative committed to a mental hospital for bestiality, the General exclaimed, "Can't I get people who don't hire people who bugger cows?"[13]

The CIA director began by ordering the firing of 50 personnel and then moved to establish direct control. Pursuing plans to merge the CIA and OPC, Smith asked for "more specific guidance from the National Security Council in order the define the project scope and pace of covert operations".[14] Specific questions to be clarified included:

1 Should Office of Policy Coordination emphasize covert activities in support of cold war or in support of preparation for hot war?
2 How should Office of Policy Coordination resolve the differing military and political concepts relating to the build-up, maintenance, and use of resistance groups?
3 Should activities, such as paramilitary, be changed from covert to overt?[15]

White House officials not only accepted Smith's view but pressed even harder for a renewed US offensive against Moscow. Concerned that MacArthur, dismissed by Truman from command in Korea, had returned to a hero's reception, the President's chief assistant, Charles Murphy, and his staff argued for a "more precise expression of our objectives in relation to the Soviet Union". Specifically, they suggested that the State Department should stop balking at an aggressive strategy, noting that the White House had "sought to express our policy as being intended to achieve the overthrow of the Soviet regime, and the liberation of the satellite states, but [had] withdrawn these efforts following strong representations from [the State Department] that this would be untimely and unsound".[16]

Under the label of "psychological operations", both the Department of Defense and the CIA advocated an independent board to coordinate all Cold War activity. The State Department resisted, however, contending that such a body would undermine its policy.[17] After months of inconclusive negotiations, a hybrid proposal finally emerged. The Psychological Strategy Board (PSB) would be autonomous, but its formal membership would consist of the Director for Central Intelligence, the Under-secretary of State, and the Deputy Secretary of Defense. Support would come from a director, appointed by the President, and a staff which would plan operations to fulfill the objectives of the National Security Council, coordinate their implementation, and evaluate the results. On 4 April, Truman signed the order creating the board.[18]

As an agency coordinating rather than implementing policy, the PSB had a limited number of staff. There were between 50 and 75 officials at any one time, 25 of whom were "permanent", with the rest seconded from other departments. Offices were on Jackson Place, just around the corner from the White House and near the National Security Council area in the Old Executive Office Building. Space was limited; this, however, was a minor problem compared with the building's lack of air conditioners to contend with the swampy heat of Washington.[19]

To direct the agency, the White House selected Gordon Gray, who had been Secretary of the Army and a special assistant to Truman before becoming President of the University of North Carolina. In 1949 Frank Wisner, who had worked with Gray in a New York law firm, and other key officials had pressed for Gray to replace Admiral Roscoe Hillenkoetter as head of the CIA, but the proposal never reached Truman.[20] The choice of Gray was popular, criticized only by African-Americans because of Gray's proposal that the University of North Carolina establish segregated facilities for students pursuing doctoral degrees.[21] The immediate problem was Gray's insistence that he retain some role at the university, limiting his presence in Washington. Even the broadcast journalist Ed Murrow took note, writing to Assistant Secretary of State Edward Barrett, "I know Gordon Gray very well, but I cannot believe that this is not a job that requires more than part time."[22]

Beyond this was the fundamental question which would plague the PSB throughout its short existence. In the formal invitation to Gray, Truman wrote, "It is hardly an exaggeration to say that the possibility of averting a third World War may depend upon our strength and effectiveness of our efforts in the field of psychological warfare."[23] So was "psychological strategy" limited, leaving the board to do little more than devise "information" for the operations of other agencies? Or was the PSB's role to equate psychological strategy with Cold War strategy, coordinating diplomatic, economic, and military planning?

President Truman's order left the question open, charging the PSB with "the formulation and promulgation, as guidance to the departments and agencies responsible for psychological operations, of overall national psychological objectives, policies, and programs, and for the coordination and evaluation of the national psychological effort".[24] The State Department maintained that the PSB was only a support group for diplomatic, economic, and military initiatives, but the CIA was campaigning for a broad definition, with the PSB coordinating action on immediate crises such as Korea and Iran, reviewing covert operations, and clarifying US policy toward emigres from Eastern Europe and the Soviet Union.[25]

Not surprisingly, the PSB's staff agreed with the CIA. Most of their suggestions for "appropriate" duties are so sensitive that they are still classified; however, those that are known reveal their broad aspirations: "establishment

of Free Russia, Poland, Lithuania, etc., units under NATO or US aegis";
"control or seizure of industries to keep key outputs away from the Soviet
Union"; "gold manipulation". They even ventured to suggest that Dr Ralph
Bunche, the winner of the 1949 Nobel Peace Prize for his mediation of the
Arab–Israeli conflict, be appointed US ambassador to the Soviet Union.[26]
Gordon Gray supported his officials, contending that Truman had intended
psychological operations as

> a cover name to describe those activities of the U.S. in peace and in war through
> which all elements of national power are systematically brought to bear on other
> nations for the attainment of U.S. foreign policy objectives. . . . The purpose of cre-
> ating the PSB was not to act as planner or coordinator with respect to any one
> major effort, but to act as planner and coordinator with respect to all.[27]

The issue inevitably produced friction with the State Department. After a
meeting in late July with the PSB's staff, Charles Marshall of the State Department noted that the PSB believed, "(1) Its job will be to run the Cold War.
The Cold War means the frustration of the Kremlin design. (2) It will get up
the master plan to defeat the Kremlin." Marshall urged his boss, Paul Nitze,
to meet with Assistant Secretary Barrett and then solicit the Under-secretary
of State to press for a "workable" definition of psychological strategy.[28] On a
personal level, Nitze told Gray, "Look, you just forget about policy, that's not
your business; we'll make the policy and then you can put it on your damn
radios."[29]

To avert conflict, Gray decided "that a precise definition [of psychological
operations] was unnecessary, since . . . he had no intention of barging
unwanted into the jurisdictions of other agencies"; however, he instructed his
staff to prepare a list of plans in four categories ranging from "crisis problems" to long-term projects, informing them, "It is my conviction that virtually no major decision or action of the government in the foreign field is
without the deepest psychological considerations."[30] Gray's assistant, Robert
Cutler, summarized the process as "the creation of a nerve-center for initiating, receiving, coordinating, and evaluating psychological impulses. This
concept is more that of a command post than an information center."[31] Speaking to the American Legion, Cutler was even more expansive: "We come to
the new concept in [the] US Government of a unified Cold War strategy – positive over-all psychological plans utilizing all the vast potential of the US in a
unified effort [and] striking at the chinks in the [Soviet] monolith".[32] He
notified the PSB staff, "This task is what in other times might have been called
a 'holy Crusade'."[33]

In its early months, the PSB's position was bolstered by the White House's
growing sense of final confrontation with the Soviet bloc. NSC 114/2, the
August 1951 revision of NSC 68, stated:

Since April 1950 the USSR has been engaging in a deliberate and systematic campaign to prepare the Russian people psychologically for possible war with the U.S.
A similar campaign is being carried out in the European satellites and China. . . .
Fifteen months ago, 1954 was regarded as the time of maximum danger. It now
appears that we are already in a period of acute danger which will continue until
the U.S. and its allies achieve an adequate position of strength.[34]

US policy in Eastern Europe would seek "independent, non-totalitarian, and
non-Communist governments willing to accommodate themselves to and to
participate in the Free World Community".[35] The US Foreign Information and
Educational Exchange would "maintain hope of ultimate liberation and
identification with the free world among peoples behind the Iron Curtain", as
the Voice of America had already "contributed materially to maintain the
popular unwillingness to accept the Sovietization of the satellite nations".[36] In
Asia, the United States would increase South Korean and Japanese strength
and use covert operations for "the achievement of US objectives vis-a-vis Communist China and Korea".[37] Unification of Korea was still "a political objective", even if the chances of obtaining the goal were "not very substantial";[38]
meanwhile the United States aspired to "detach China as an effective ally of
the USSR and support the development of an independent China which has
renounced aggression".[39] The Administration reiterated its policy to "foster
and support anti-communist Chinese elements both outside and within China
with a view to developing and expanding resistance in China to the Peiping
regime's control, especially in South China".[40]

Yet the National Security Council had doubts as to whether "liberation"
was possible. Intelligence assessments conceded that Soviet control of the bloc
was "virtually complete", with old parties and opposition groups "decapitated
and pulverized" by the Kremlin. Discontent would "persist and perhaps
increase" but "the subservience of the Satellites [would] be guaranteed by
present Soviet authority, the power of Soviet advisors and missions in the
Satellite governments, Soviet economic and military controls, the rigorous
training and education programs, and calculated use of terror to create the
sense of isolation, helplessness, and physical and moral fear".[41] Even NSC
114/2 accepted that there had been "no fundamental change in the
Soviet–satellite relationship".[42]

The PSB's plan was to establish its authority by turning pessimism into
hope, building on the NSC's command to establish the "Plan for a Psychological Offensive (USSR)" and to make "tactical use of Titoism".[43] Asked by
the National Security Council "whether there was really any practical chance
of a fall-out among the Communist military leaders which would result in
fissions and the emergence of a new leadership in Communist China", CIA
Director Bedell Smith reflected the PSB's wish for a firm, sustained commitment from policy-makers, "It is always possible . . . to start a fire but the fire

can't be kept going unless fuel is provided. What was needed in China was the provision of a stable rallying point which must either be the present Nationalist forces or some other dissident group."[44]

Opportunity for the PSB appeared to come in October 1951 when the National Security Council met Bedell Smith's demands for clear authority for the scope and pace of CIA programs. The document NSC 10/5, a revision of the 1948 blueprint for covert action, reconfirmed the goal of "placing the maximum strain on the Soviet structure of power, including the relationship between the USSR, its satellites, and Communist China, and when and where appropriate in the light of US and Soviet capabilities and the risk of war, contribute to the retraction and reduction of Soviet power and influence to limits which no longer constitute a threat to US security". It then went further than previous guidelines with the command to "develop underground resistance and facilitate covert and guerrilla operations in strategic areas to the maximum practicable extent".[45] The Soviet Union and Communist China were identified as specific targets of covert action, with a still-classified passage indicating that specific offensive operations were sanctioned against Peking.[46]

Consultants advising Gray took up the challenge and eagerly offered grand strategies. General Wallace Carroll, who had helped Barrett establish the Campaign of Truth the previous year, now called for three or four major operations, "largely offensive in character". For example, Operation 1 would liberate East Germany while Operation 2 restrained the Kremlin from recourse to war and Operation 3 implemented "wedge-driving . . . between the Soviet Union and Red China". He concluded, "Now is the time to fire the rocket."[47] The Ford Foundation's William Kennedy decorated his memorandum with slogans like REMEMBER THE AIRLIFT: REMEMBER KOREA! to publicize "a tradition of violent and dramatic reaction to Soviet aggression, in keeping with the world's concept of us as a young and vital nation endowed with the spiritual qualities necessary for world leadership", POISON THE TENTACLES! to spread Titoism among Communists outside the Soviet Union, and PROMOTE THE VLASOV LEGEND! to encourage a Free Russia movement. General Vlasov, he explained, "should be on Broadway, in Hollywood, and in many of our magazines and newspapers". Kennedy did not ponder whether Vlasov, who had fought with the Germans against the Soviet regime in World War II, might be a tarnished hero.[48]

Palmer Putnam, the executive secretary for the consultants, brought the suggestions together in a five-year plan. In the near future, the West would ensure "deterrents" to Soviet expansion were "in full swing". After driving Soviet forces from certain areas through a series of intermediate operations, still classified in American documents, the United States would aid risings in Eastern Europe and throughout the Soviet Union. Putnam labeled the plan "a high-hearted crusade – gay, dashing, gleaming, even hilarious – a crusade to let people everywhere choose how they wish to be governed", culminating with the "collapse of the World Communist Movement" through uprisings supported by UN resolutions and the bombing of Soviet railroads and communications.[49]

By November the consultants had agreed a global strategy. In Asia the pursuit of a unified Korea was simply the first step in breaking up Communist China, "US power interests require continuation of the present hostilities in Korea, either on an active or standby basis until such time as the Japanese can be infiltrated on to the Asian land base. This concept requires control of a resurgent, re-armed Japan with a major drive towards the Manchurian complex." Meanwhile the United States would work with Western Europe, including a regenerated West Germany, to ensure "the breakup of the USSR into separate national component states so that, in effect, the emissaries of the Grand Dukes of Moscovy are sent back to Moscow".[50]

The PSB's permanent staff were more measured in their approach. While one of the first three interdepartmental panels, Panel B, conducted an inventory of American agencies and policies to exploit Soviet vulnerabilities, the other two panels addressed immediate issues rather than optimal strategy. For example, Panel A reviewed American psychological action if the negotiations to end the Korean War were successful (Operation Affiliate) or if the negotiations broke down (Operation Broadbrim).[51] Panel A's deliberations included advice on leaflets to the enemy – by the end of 1951, 14 million per week were being dropped in North Korea – as the PSB also considered dropping propaganda into China.[52] There was also the onerous task of downplaying certain aspects of the war. It was agreed, for example, "to ignore Soviet attempts to make [a] propaganda issue of napalm" used by US forces. This was an "absolutely legitimate weapon; however, we derive no benefit from publicity regarding its use".[53]

Beyond Panel A, the PSB staff was always seeking a broader strategy for the "reorientation" of North Korea. Its "sister" body, the State Department-led Psychologial Operations Coordinating Committee (POCC) for overt operations, had broached the possibility of taking prisoners of war to Japan "to produce a group of people favorable to our political aims" and "exploiting" Chinese prisoners for propaganda.[54] The PSB staff focused these plans on the issue of "repatriation", recognising that even if Korea ended in a military stalemate, the United States would win victory in the global battle for hearts and minds. The key was to identify those North Korean and Chinese prisoners who might wish to remain in the Free World rather than return to their homes at the end of the war. By insisting on the non-repatriation of these men, the United States could portray their wish, given access to "information", to exercise freedom against tyranny.[55]

The PSB's intervention swung the bureaucratic balance. Previously the State Department had replied to military proposals to refuse repatriation with the warning, "While the psychological warfare advantages of the proposed policy are recognized, it is difficult to see how such a policy could be carried out without conflict with the provisions of the 1949 Geneva Prisoner of War Convention."[56] However, when the writer Bertram Wolfe told the PSB's Charles Norberg that the "PoW exchange issue in Korea . . . would have great impact in our total program combating Communism", Norberg replied that the scheme was being "given most serious consideration in Washington".[57] Over the next 18 months, the project was developed by both the PSB and the POCC, including "suggested actions for an aggressive UN propaganda offensive about North Korean and Chinese PoWs who do not wish repatriation" and a proposal that Truman solicit the views of religious leaders and moral philosophers at home and abroad.[58]

It could easily be argued that the insistence on non-repatriation, the sticking point in armistice negotiations, prolonged the war for more than a year and cost thousands of lives. Having established the psychological offensive, however, the United States could not retreat. In January 1952, a meeting of the PSB staff with Assistant Secretary of State Barrett and Frank Wisner, the head of the Office of Policy Coordination, produced the unanimous conclusion that the United States must maintain the "basic moral principle of political freedom . . . to give way . . . would undermine the whole basis of psychological warfare since neither soldiers or civilians would defect" from the Communist bloc.[59] The position was reiterated a year later.[60]

The discussions on Korea have an intriguing postscript. US officials knew that Soviet personnel, not only technicians but also ground "advisors" and pilots, were involved in the conflict. American PoWs confirmed that they had seen uniformed Soviets flying MiG fighters only 200–300 yards from their barracks.[61] The Administration decided, however, that any psychological advantage from exposing the Soviet presence was outweighed by the prospect of direct confrontation between Washington and Moscow. US information officers were advised that, while they should show the Soviets had "instigated" the North Korean aggression and trained North Korean forces in "rear areas", there should be no statements that Soviet personnel were participating in aerial or ground combat.[62]

The third interdepartmental panel, Panel C, returned to the original catalyst for American psychological operations, the "massive popular support which continue[d] to be given the Communists" in French and Italian elections.[63] In April 1950 the National Security Council had reaffirmed that the United States should "continue to make full use of its political and economic resources, and such use of its military power as it may agree to be necessary . . . to assist in preventing Italy from falling under the domination of the USSR either through external attack or through Communist movements within Italy".[64] Even after a reduction in support for the Communists in 1951, State Department officials warned of Communist exploitation of "great poverty and unemployment" and their successful posturing as a "peace party".[65] They concluded passionately:

> We can no longer afford to "hope" that somehow or other the Communist problem in Italy and France will be solved. The French and Italian Governments must come up with a plan and program and we must ask what they have in mind. This is not a question of interfering in *their* affairs. What is involved here is *our* responsibility to Congress and our people, and *our* ability to carry out our present policies with full confidence of success.[66]

Within weeks of its creation, Panel C had devised a comprehensive anti-Communist assault. The French Government would reorganize its internal security system, outlawing international Communist organizations and fronts, banning their publications, prohibiting demonstrations by the French Communist Party, and "eliminating Communists and fellow-travellers from posts of responsibility in the government and from sensitive jobs in private life". It would also "revise electoral laws to discriminate against Communists", "amend rules of parliamentary immunity so as to eliminate this protection for Communists", "deport foreign Communists", withhold newsprint from Communist and Communist-front presses, and "preclude Communists from administering and benefiting from social welfare benefits". Strict measures would curb the Confédération Générale du Travail and Communist-dominated unions, while American officials would "develop existing media . . . to propagandize the French concerning the real nature of the Stalinist myth and to convince them of the right, strength, and sincerity of our cause", direct aid and contracts to non-Communist unions, assist private groups advocating French participation in NATO and a united Europe, and spread "scandals concerning leaders of CP [Communist Party]". All this was supported by at least $2 million in CIA funds.[67]

While full implementation of the program was hindered by the reluctance of the French Government to act quickly, general progress was made throughout 1952. The Pinay Government maneuvered Communists out of positions in the French press, industry, and government agencies like the Social Security Administration and the Atomic Energy Commission. The American Federation of Labor's Irving Brown, supported by the CIA and working with non-Communist trade unionists, helped reduce blockages of shipping by Communist workers and broke the Communist hold on the *concierge* system.[68] Dramatic steps, such as the cancellation of tours by dancers from Moscow and operas from Leningrad and bombings of French Communist headquarters and newspapers, would follow.[69]

The program for Italy was similar, with the United States seeking to "instill in Italy's democratic leaders a determination to take a forthright stand against the Italian Communist Party". Electoral law was revised "to allow for the possibility of anti-Communist majorities in the next election". The Italian Government would treat "Italian Communists as Communists rather than Italians through legislative and administrative harassment, suppression, and control" and take "progressive steps to remove Communists from administrative positions in government ministries, in schools and in unions". Meanwhile, the United States would engage "in aggressive propaganda, including an information program, coordinated with that of the Italian Government, and having the appearance of being of Italian, rather than U.S. inspiration".[70] The Americans tried to unify non-Communist labor unions, developed a touring exhibition of life behind the Iron Curtain, planted articles in the Italian media on the success of the Italian Government and the dangers of Communism, and, in preparation for the spring 1953 national elections, revived the "Letters from America" campaign of 1948.[71] The program would be expanded throughout the 1950s, with the CIA station chief in Rome, William Colby, funneling "several million dollars" to US allies; a version of it was still operational in 1962.[72]

Panel C set an example for other national and regional plans. A German Plan was completed in September 1952 with similar measures, and Japanese, Southeast Asian, and Middle Eastern Plans followed in early 1953. The Japanese Plan emphasized "arrangements, preferably thorugh private auspices, to confront Japanese intellectuals with outstanding American and European liberals and intellectuals, including those who formerly espoused communist doctrine and renounced it, and refugees from Iron Curtain countries, including China". It also called for "covert support . . . to the organization of militant anti-communist student and faculty groups thorughout Japan" and "covert measures to extend material assistance to the anti-communist labor press of Japan".[73] The Middle Eastern Plan tried to bolster an anti-Communist system through psychological operations "to ensure that the 'American Way of Life' theme is appropriately tailored to the needs and capacities of the area", "to ensure that propaganda emphasis is focused on concrete actions rather than on abstract principles of Western political democracy", and "to publicize Point 4 programs [for technical and economic aid] primarily on a localized basis revolving around the theme of personal advantage to a given group or community".[74]

In addition, other agencies took up planning for regions not immediately covered by the PSB. Thomas Mann of the State Department analyzed Latin America for the White House and made specific suggestions, such as an increase in "tailor-made" material for the region and specific countries, covert counter-propaganda against the Peronist campaign from Argentina, "a covert campaign to create an awareness of the danger . . . which the Soviet Union represents", and increased efforts to convince Latin America that the United States treated its economic and social aspirations fairly. To oversee the programme, Mann recommended a two-man unit in the American Division "to prepare papers, fully documented with the facts and statistics available in the various departments of government in Washington, which present our point of view concerning concrete, specific issues". These would be "offered to friendly newspapers in the area as background material to be used in articles and editorials of their own".[75]

The careful attention of the PSB staff to country and regional plans which could be placed within the framework of containment did not mean that they had turned their backs on liberation. Panel B's study of Soviet vulnerabilities and the consultants' hopes of a grand offensive were developed through Operation Cancellation, with contingency plans for propaganda and agitation within the Soviet Union in the event of Stalin's death or fall from power. Told in October 1951 of the results of Project Troy at MIT's Center for International Studies (CENIS), Gray noted that it "appeared to be very closely related to the problems of the PSB".[76] The academics accordingly considered US reactions to Stalin's death, ranging from a restrained position to an aggressive strategy which might encourage distrust by claiming certain leaders were "trying to make deals with enemies of Bolshevism", "throwing covert support to an individual" either to ensure his success or for the "kiss-of-death treatment", "spreading accounts of upheavals through the land", "encouraging military leaders to take control", or "encouraging the peasants to destroy the collectives". One consultant, Professor John Morrison of the University of Maryland, proposed a rumor campaign with tales "of high Party officials fleeing abroad to live on funds previously deposited in foreign banks" and "murders of collective farm directors and seizure of Machine Tractor stations by kolkhozniks".[77]

Other plans also pointed to liberation. The German Plan not only sought "to facilitate the integration of West Germany into Western Europe" but also "to contribute to making East Germany a strategic liability to the Soviet Union" and, ultimately, "to support the unification of East Germany with a West Germany which is a reliable member of the Western community". Contact with the population of the Soviet Zone and East Berlin would be maintained "to stiffen their spirit of resistance to Soviet Communist rule" and to promote integration with the West. East Germans would be encouraged to engage in "work slowdowns, faulty workmanship, misrouting of shipments, . . . [and] passive non-compliance with Communist government and political regulations and arrangements".[78] Particular attention was paid to stimulating defections by East German youth "without encouraging general defection".[79]

The German Plan also was "to convince Soviet-orbit peoples that the weakening of Soviet power in East Germany is a necessary prerequisite for their own liberation". Likewise, the Yugoslav Plan considered "the extent to which [that] country [could] be used as a springboard for propaganda to the Iron Curtain countries" and the isolation of Albania. It also considered possible successors to Tito, insisting "that pro-democracy forces and influences within

Yugoslavia are promoted". Measures including the showing of training films to Yugoslav troops, the promotion of King Peter, and the display of stickers such as "US–Yugoslavia Friendship" on military supplies sent to Belgrade.[80] There was "A Plan for Exploitation of Dissidence in the Soviet Bloc: USSR Armed Forces" and a special program "for the discreet encouragement and assistance of the non-Soviet Orthodox Church to prevent Soviet penetration and to increase the prestige and influence of the Orthodox Church within the Soviet atmosphere".[81]

In late 1951, the PSB took up the touchstone of liberation, the issue of refugees and defectors from the Soviet bloc. Although the Policy Planning Staff and the CIA had developed plans over the last three years, there were persistent problems with implementation. It was difficult to distinguish an ordinary refugee from a "defector", defined as an escapee from the Soviet bloc "of special interest to the US Government (a) because they are able to add valuable new or confirmatory information to exist US knowledge of the Soviet world, (b) because they are of operational value to a US agency, or (c) because their defection can be exploited in the psychological field".[82] For those defectors who could be identified, Congressional restrictions were a further obstacle.[83] The outcome for US officials was disheartening: few of the 35,000 refugees from Eastern Europe in 1950–51 were considered of use to the Government. Spokesmen for the refugees said that they "came to West Germany anxious and eager to fight communism, but no program has been evolved to keep this fine spirit high".[84] Attempts by the Inter-agency Defector Committee to "stimulate" defections received a limited response, with statements over the Voice of America only encouraging about a dozen arrivals from the Soviet bloc. While the Mutual Security Act of 1951 had authorized up to $100 million for escapees "to form such persons into elements of the military forces supporting NATO or for other purposes", only 113 men had been enlisted in the US services by December 1951.[85]

The State Department liaison for covert operations summarized that the use of defectors was a "priority problem requiring a top-level governmental decision since no one agency is clearly tagged with responsibility".[86] The National Security Council finally responded in April 1951. To fulfill the objective of "placing the maximum strain on the Soviet structure of power through threatening the regime's control of its population", the NSC established "priority" categories of defectors: "(a) benefits to intelligence and related activities; (b) propaganda use and value; (c) denial of valuable personnel to Soviet and satellite regimes; (d) spread of increased disaffection and confusion within Soviet and satellite regimes; and (e) availability of personalities possessing background and knowledge, the acquisition of which would be in the national interest". To "encourage and induce the defection of the maximum possible number" of such people, the United States would make clear its policy to arrange asylum. For the first time, the Voice of America was authorized to use defectors on its broadcasts, primarily to encourage others to cross to the West.[87]

The PSB met the challenge with a two-phase plan. Phase A would "employ, resettle and care" for escapees from the Iron Curtain with more than $7 million of Government funds and private aid, notably $800,000 from the Ford Foundation. Training and education would be provided by the CIA-sponsored Free European University in Exile in Strasbourg, France. Phase B, code-named Engross, planned for the operational use of refugees "willing and capable of being responsive in some degree to the direction of agencies of the U.S. government", notably the Voice of America and the CIA. US officials would "encourage, assist, and guide the efforts of escapees . . . to increase popular dissidence behind the 'iron curtain', to expose Soviet tyranny, and to vitiate the effect of Communist propaganda throughout the world".[88] By the end of 1954, 14,354 refugees had been resettled and care had been provided for another 24,131. The program was also extended into China to ensure "leadership will be available in the event of a change in regime on the Chinese mainland". Refugee intellectuals were supported and re-employed in Hong Kong, with 200 specially trained to work in the the Nationalist Chinese Government; the ideas of the exiles were also "covertly utilized in Communist China to serve as a beacon of hope to the captive people".[89]

The military results of the defection program continued to be limited. By April 1953, only 360 escapees had joined the US Army, and Operation Crowbar for a highly visible Volunteer Freedom Corps of 50 divisions was repeatedly deferred throughout the 1950s for political and organizational reasons. Western European allies were especially wary of the units, fearing that they might resemble German "anti-Bolshevik" divisions of World War II.[90]

The payoff instead was psychological, with promotion of the image of a freedom-loving West welcoming those who fled from tyranny. The Voice of America and Radio Free Europe made good use of any defection stories. In September 1951, a Czech engineer took his train across the border into West Germany, where he and 30 passengers claimed asylum. The episode was inevitably set to the tune of *Casey Jones*. The popular bandleader Fred Waring performed the song on the Crusade for Freedom television spectacular (although it is not clear if the PSB was able to arrange for Ethel Merman to sing it), and the tune was included in the *Armed Forces Song Folio*. In August 1952 the *General Taylor* docked in New York with 44 escapees, including a family of five Czechs who had escaped in an amphibious jeep and a Czech student who had tunneled out of a prison camp and had been accepted by Yale Law School.[91]

In addition to the panel system, the PSB pursued its goal through its links with other groups in the Executive Branch. Through a regular liaison with the White House, the staff drafted or contributed to significant public statements,

such as Truman's 1952 State of the Union speech and the presidential statement rejecting clemency for the Rosenbergs, the couple convicted of passing
atomic secrets to the Soviets and executed in 1953.[92] It also converted Secretary of State Acheson's dedication of a library in Berlin into "a cultural polemic
in which the Secretary . . . would stress that the cultural heritage of 2,000 years
is the real monument of Western civilization, noting that in East Berlin the
Soviets are striving night and day to destroy any trace or vestige of the
free ideas which are contained in such books". The PSB helped develop the
propaganda campaign of the US delegation at the UN General Assembly,
arranging for "a series of five-minute punch speeches" on topics like "The
Communist Regime's Perversion of Marxism", and devised the psychological
exploitation of American nuclear programs, including the first tests of the
hydrogen bomb.[93]

The PSB was responsible for coordinating the overt work of the Voice of
America with the "light gray" output of Radio Free Europe.[94] The PSB's cooperation with Assistant Secretary of State Barrett and the Psychological Operations Coordinating Committee, established to oversee overt programs, was
close. Joint projects soon included propaganda to deal with "the excess of US
male [military] personnel with regard to the available Icelandic female population",[95] advice to the Far East Command on the Korean truce negotiations,
exposure of Soviet forced labor camps, and responses to Soviet "Hate America"
propaganda and charges of US bacteriological warfare in Korea. The PSB
developed an "international libel suit" against the report of the International
Scientific Commission alleging American use of bacteriological weapons in
Korea, while the State Department arranged for "indigenous discrediting of
certain scientists". Consideration was even "given to making narcotics charges
against Communist China".[96] Encouraged by the PSB, the POCC also strayed
into consideration of liberation, with Assistant Secretary of State Edward
Barrett considering "what 'gimmick' could be effective in allowing the population of the Soviet Union and satellite countries to express their dissatisfaction
with their present regimes but not to endanger their personal safety". Whether
his suggestion of jamming dial telephones was attempted is unknown, but
another proposal for photographs "to propagandize the existence of the Iron
Curtain [was] dropped since no good pictures [were] available".[97]

It was through covert operations, however, that the PSB came closest to
coordinating the offensive against Moscow. Barrett and Frank Wisner, the
head of the Office of Policy Coordination, set the precedent for cooperation
in mid-1950 by defining overt ("white") and covert ("black") activities.[98] NSC
10/5 consolidated the arrangement by adding two representatives from the
PSB to the Board of Consultants that oversaw covert plans. Liaison with the
CIA was initially hindered by the Agency's reluctance to release operational
details and by CIA Director Bedell Smith's belief that the PSB staff "should
be a small steering committee but instead had become a large papermill".[99]

However, as Bedell Smith gained confidence in the PSB as a coordinating body, Packet, the CIA's program "for a world-wide covert apparatus, including the establishment of facilities and the recruitment and training of personnel", was reviewed by the PSB to "(1) determine desirability and feasibility of covert programs and major projects, and (2) establish the scope, pace, and timing of covert operations". Bedell Smith further refined the procedure by ordering that every covert action be discussed by the CIA's Director of Plans with the Director of the PSB and his assistants.[100]

Within eighteen months of its creation, the PSB had developed a comprehensive psychological strategy to defeat the Soviet Union. The Budget of the Budget's annual audit concluded that "a healthy start [had] been made" with the "basic framework . . . proven sound" while Barrett, reviewing the Campaign of Truth, enthused, "The International Information and Education Exchange Program has been transformed into an alert, resourceful, and hard-hitting campaign to marshal the forces for freedom throughout the world and expose the treacheries and lies of international communism."[101]

A PSB report of October 1952 summarized the achievements. In Eastern Europe, information programs had "maintained hope of ultimate liberation among the peoples held captive by Soviet Communism". Psychological action in Western Europe had "contributed to an awareness of the communist danger in some countries, notably France and Sweden, to the development of pro-integration attitudes in West Germany, and to progress toward European functional and political unity". Although advances in Africa, Asia, and the Middle East had been limited, "there [had] been definite if modest progress, especially in building capabilities for future development". Methods ranged from the official, such as the Voice of America and embassy reading rooms, to the private, including Radio Free Europe and Government-subsidized publishers, to the unorthodox, notably broadcasting from ships, "three-dimensional moving pictures", and "the use of folk songs, folklore, folk tales, and itinerant story tellers".[102]

Yet both the PSB's pursuit of liberation and its search for a secure position in the Washington bureaucracy had an Achilles heel: the attitude of the State Department. The attempt of PSB Director Gordon Gray, supported by Assistant Secretary of State Barrett, to defuse the conflict by avoiding a precise definition of "psychological strategy" did not reduce the aversion of other officials, especially in the Policy Planning Staff, to the PSB as a coordinating body.[103] Indeed, State Department personnel were asserting that Gray really believed "the PSB should undertake the coordination of outstanding problems as soon as a staff is hired", telling the staff that "he [had] the highest authority for this method of procedure".[104] A PSB representative countered, "It was clear that the State members [of working groups] view the PSB as a separate and independent entity in the government rather than as an interdepartmental device which could be valuable to all agencies."[105]

By September 1951 panel work was already being disrupted by the "absence of any definition of what [the United States was] trying to come up with" because of "the only slightly disguised battle going on between certain elements of the PSB staff and the State Department".[106] The PSB was told by high-ranking State Department officials that its "real" purpose was evaluation or that its "function [was] primarily to monitor the Voice of America".[107] Charles Marshall of the Policy Planning Staff, after concluding, "The best conceivable thing to do about this Board would be to abolish it," gave the patronising summary that the State Department was "trying to throw a line to men who are in over their ears in getting their feet wet . . . [and] an organization which so far has demonstrated a potential only for causing a lot of irksome and profitless activity".[108]

The bureaucratic wrangle meant that, in the words of the CIA, "the U.S. has been unable to arrive at a definitive answer for the fundamental question of whether it is possible to live with the Kremlin or whether it must be destroyed".[109] Frank Wisner, now the CIA's Assistant Director of Plans, bluntly asked Tracy Barnes, seconded from the CIA to become the PSB's Deputy Director, "To what extent will the U.S. support counter-revolution in the slave states?"[110] as PSB staff evaluations complained:

> In Western Europe, we are not losing the Cold War, but we are not yet winning it. . . . At some strategically important points in Africa and Latin America, we are faced with the development of less imminent but potentially dangerous Communist satellites. . . . In certain areas of the Middle East and of South and Southeast Asia, we are in real and imminent danger of losing the Cold War.

American diplomacy, economic aid, and information programs like the Voice of America might achieve tactical successes but "they [did] not add up to an effective and successive global psychological strategy".[111]

PSB officials counter-attacked on a number of fronts. They contributed liberally, if "on background", to a six-part series by Anthony Leviero of the *New York Times* on "The War of Ideas". Leviero wrote that the PSB had "not been able to function too well" as a " 'part-time' group, forced to take a 'piecemeal approach' to the problems confronting it on a short-term, project-by-project basis".[112] Gordon Gray, leaving the PSB in early 1952 to return to the University of North Carolina, wrote a lengthy report to President Truman justifying the organization. He began with the ideological fervour that had led to the PSB's formation:

> We face today one of the great convulsions of history. The world in which we live is being changed by strong currents of thought and feeling – currents released by the American and French Revolutions in the 18th century, by the industrial revolution in the 19th, and by two destructive wars and the Russian Revolution in our own time. . . . Our role, as we have now expressed it in our national policies, is to

help lead the nations through this time of turmoil in such a way there will be an expansion – not a reduction – of the areas of freedom and knowledge.[113]

Gray was so intent on getting the upper hand over the State Department that he sought the publication of the report. The CIA, normally allied with the PSB, blocked this because of the sensitivity of the information; however, it did support a presidential statement to show "why we are in the cold war, the controlling principles and policies, the problems that are faced, the work so far accomplished, including the Board's part in that work, and the task ahead".[114] Even this was too much for the State Department, which delayed the statement until it was no longer timely.[115]

In the spring of 1952, PSB staff tried to grasp the nettle of a global offensive, proclaiming, "Perhaps more than anything else we need a way of verbalizing simply and strikingly the thought that the US is in fact leading a crusade for civilization against barbarism."[116] "PSB Planning Objectives" responded by trumpeting that the United States would use "basic moral and social forces such as religion, peace-aspiration, nationalism, internationalism, anti-colonialism, land hunger, racial tension, and the desire for social equality" to "UNDERMINE SOVIET POSITION IN EASTERN EUROPE", "MOBILIZE FREEDOM FORCES IN ASIA", and "DIVIDE THE DIVISIONISTS".[117] Barnes bluntly told the State Department "that the PSB had a role as wide as that of the National Security Council",[118] as the board's staff kept a wary eye on its adversary. It was even suspected that the appointment of Admiral Alan Kirk, a former ambassador to the Soviet Union, as PSB Director in the autumn of 1952 had "elements of a sell-out to the State Department".[119]

The PSB staff launched an all-out effort in May. George Morgan, the Assistant Director for Plans, wrote cogently, "Though it seems to be widely believed inside the Government as well as by the public that our policy is simply 'containment', it may be doubted whether it is or has been, except for public consumption." Barnes brought Packet, the CIA's program of covert operations, before the PSB Members – CIA Director Walter Bedell Smith, Undersecretary of State David Bruce, and Assistant Secretary of Defence William Foster – and asked:

1 Does U.S. policy . . . contemplate supplying overt physical support to revolutionary factions that might emerge in the wake of Stalin's death, if the situation offered a reasonable chance of changing a regime to suit U.S. interests without going to war?
2 Does U.S. policy . . . include or exclude efforts under any circumstances to overthrow or subvert the governments of the satellites of the USSR?

Barnes asked for confirmation of the principle "that OPC cannot create a useful apparatus unless it [is] authorized to develop an overall program in dollars and personnel, covering a period of, let us say, two or three years"?[120]

The PSB's Mallory Browne then produced an "Overall Strategic Concept for our Psychological Operations" which projected the achievement within five years of the goals of an "all-out psychological counter-offensive":

> Such an offensive concept of psycho-strategy requires less an official change of policy than a frank recognition of what is really implicit in our existing policy objectives, i.e.:
>
> (a) abandoning "containment" and openly espousing "liberation";
> (b) scrapping – not necessarily in public but in our strategic planning – the passive wishful thinking of "coexistence" and adopting a positive approach that acknowledges the vital necessity of overthrowing the Kremlin regime;
> (c) discarding our present strategy of fighting a defensive delaying action in the cold war while we prepare primarily to defend ourselves in a hot one, and substituting, therefore, a fully planned and phased global strategy of offensive underground fighting;
> (d) dropping the "Made in America" label on our aid programs and replacing it by a "Peace Partnership of Free Humanity" tag;
> (e) minimizing the government and official aspects of all our psychological operations, both inside and outside the Soviet orbit.

Browne acknowledged that uprisings within the next two to three years would be "fatally premature" but insisted that any delay beyond five years "would kill hope and leave no virile elements". He concluded with unshakable faith in the power of ideology:

> Humanity everywhere inherently treasures certain basic freedoms and rights, though these may differ in different parts of the world; . . . the free world – and ultimately the peoples not now free – will welcome American leadership, [if] we are genuine and humbly seek to help all humanity. . . .
>   This is the truly Christian approach and . . . , despite so many evidences to the contrary, it is essentially characteristic of the American people.[121]

Other PSB officials were more cautious, predicting 10 to 20 years for the campaign, and questioned Browne's call for an open espousal of "liberation", since the US public and foreign allies might not be supportive.[122] They also warned, "The possibility of provoking USSR military reaction must be carefully weighed before covert capabilities are fully exercised." For that reason, operations in Eastern Germany and Bulgaria should await "further development of Western military strength", and the liberation of Poland, Czechoslovakia, Rumania, Hungary, and the Soviet Union required "major development of Western military strength". Still, there was general agreement on renewed operations "to detach Albania from the Soviet bloc" and large-scale activity could be pursued in China, North Korea, and Viet Minh-held areas of Vietnam "without undue risk of general war".[123] Raymond Allen, who had succeeded Gordon Gray as Director, told the PSB members, "While conventional weapon strength had to be built, my impression was that our greatest potential strength and hope for victory lay in the direction of political warfare where 'containment plus' was a feasible doctrine."[124]

Inevitably, the biggest obstacle to the PSB's strategy was not Moscow but the State Department. Signs of forthcoming trouble came in late May when Paul Nitze and his Policy Planning Staff objected to the approval of Packet, the CIA's programme of covert action,[125] but the showdown came in July with the annual review of strategy in the NSC 68 series. The PSB sought the build-up of military strength to support liberation; as talks dragged on, its representative complained, "The country's most fundamental and decisive review of national strategy is for the most part merely a routine regurgitation of clichés currently prevalent in the middle levels of bureaucracy." He warned other members of the review panel, "Our capabilities behind the Iron Curtain had in the main been decreasing and . . . we had no clear way to increase them in sight." The CIA concurred that action had to be taken but the State Department's representative fell back on the long-term prospect. "If we made containment really work, the frustration of Soviet expansion would produce an internal cancerous condition which political warfare might exploit." The wooliness of this hope emerged in the caution of the State Department's Charles Bohlen, "It is out of the question to try to offer a blueprint: nobody can foresee how the struggle will end."[126]

While the PSB grappled with this opposition, other State Department officials ensured that the development of Browne's "Overall Strategic Concept" did not explicitly include liberation. Paul Nitze gloated that the "chief virtue" of the document was the admission that it could not propose a strategic concept because "(a) we do not have and cannot clearly foresee the time when we will have the capabilities and (b) because without adequate capabilities, the risks involved are clearly disproportionate to the probabilities of success".[127] By August, the CIA was confessing that, with the delays from the State Department's obstruction, Packet had lost a "good deal of its currency" and it was "doubtful that circumstances would permit the development in the immediate future of resources commensurate with the optimum program".[128]

The situation was further confused by the unraveling of covert operations in Eastern Europe and in China. For years, the OPC had tried to build resistance in Poland through Wolnosc i Niepodlenosc (WIN – Freedom and Independence). Leaders of the movement claimed that 100,000 people were available to support their core group of 500 men in the event of a fight with Government, but in December 1952 a Polish broadcast revealed the operation and indicated that the Soviet security services had run WIN to uncover and arrest potential Polish rebels. They gladly received, as a bonus, the gold provided by the OPC to finance WIN.[129] Air drops or sea landings of infiltrators into Albania repeatedly failed, ending in death or show trials. Some agents operated overland but failed to stimulate an internal resistance; however, the

Albanian secret police, who controlled the local "opposition" movement, led the Americans into further disastrous operations by broadcasting the "success" of the agents back to the US base in Greece.[130]

Reverses were also experienced in the Baltic States, where the Soviets had suppressed the partisan resistance by the time large-scale US support arrived, and in the Ukraine, where 16 agents were lost in five missions in a year.[131] Frank Lindsay, who had developed the émigré program since 1948, wrote a pessimistic report for the CIA suggesting that US support of the resistance network should be terminated. Had it not been for Allen Dulles, Lindsay's report might have been accepted; Dulles, destined to become Director of Central Intelligence in the Eisenhower Administration, bluntly responded, "Frank, you can't say that."[132] Despite the lack of success, incursions into Albania, the Baltics, and the Ukraine would continue into 1953.[133]

Failure abroad was compounded by the demands of the émigré groups. A comprehensive survey stressed the "lack of effective coordination" with "instances . . . in which different information agencies of the American Government have extended support to the same foreign group". One desperate Russian émigré group, the Central Union of Post-war Émigrés, blew up its headquarters and blamed the KGB in an attempt to obtain more funding.[134] Returns were low. A charitable interpretation was that of the CIA's Thomas Braden: "[It] got to be just horrendous. They were eating up everybody's time. . . . The intelligence they were giving us was nothing but gossip. . . . They came up with these theses and bored Allen [Dulles] for two hours with them." A harsher observation would be that the inflated speculations of imminent revolution fueled the CIA's support of the disastrous failures in Eastern Europe.[135]

An assessment of CIA activity persisted with the assertion, "U.S. capabilities for future covert operations [in Eastern Europe] have increased, particularly in Poland and East Germany. . . . CIA now possesses capabilities for influencing large segments of labor, youth, refugees, persecutees, women, religious groups, and political parties." The problem was that "the power and influence of the Kremlin within the USSR [had] not been affected by U.S. covert activities, and short-term possibilities in this direction [were] so slight as to be insignificant".[136] Given this, the CIA's intelligence analysts continued to lack the confidence of their counterparts in covert operations. "The liberation of the Russian people [was] not considered to be a feasible undertaking for the next several years. . . . The chances of effecting the [detachment] of the satellites [was] regarded as more feasible, but barring developments not presently foreseen . . . [was] not considered a likely near-term possibility."[137]

The pattern was the same in Asia. CIA-backed forces of General Li Mi again invaded China from Burma in 1952, penetrating 60 miles into Yunnan Province, but, as in the previous year, there was no peasant rising and the offensive was vanquished. Li Mi gave up the quest, preferring to run opium from his Burmese fiefdom. Further embarrassment followed with the parachuting of agents, trained at a $28 million CIA complex on the island of Saipan, into Manchuria. Two operatives, John Downey and Richard Fecteau, were captured when flying into China to retrieve agents in November 1952. Less publicized but more striking was the abysmal record of the Chinese agents: of 212 infiltrated into the mainland between 1951 and 1953, 101 were killed and 111 were captured. The CIA's stock of $152 million of foreign weapons for the insurgency lay idle.[138]

US officials also had to contend with the disquiet of allies. British unease culminated in a clash between Truman's advisors and Prime Minister Winston Churchill in January 1952. Aboard the presidential yacht *Williamsburg*, Churchill insisted that, with the Stalinist system dependent on fear of the West, a harsh Anglo-American policy would only help Moscow. The American delegation, who had already leaked to the press that they could not accept the British position since it indicated acceptance of an "amoral" regime, dismissed the argument, but Foreign Minister Anthony Eden reiterated the British warning against liberation.[139]

Despite these setbacks, PSB officials were still hopeful that the review of global strategy at the end of 1952, labeled NSC 135, would go "back essentially to the portion of NSC 20/4 [of 1948] which lays down policy regarding reduction and retraction of Soviet power and influence".[140] The PSB's general plan to exploit Moscow's vulnerabilities was completed in November with three "broad fields of activities", including "weakening of Kremlin control over the Soviet-controlled bloc, and increasingly occupying the Kremlin with problems within this area". Among six missions for the CIA were the detachment of Albania from the Soviet bloc, "breeding suspicion and dissension within the Communist system", and economic sabotage "with particular emphasis on Czechoslovakia".[141]

The PSB's hopes were stymied, however, as the Truman Administration continued to fudge the issue in the face of the Policy Planning Staff's opinion, "We do not feel confident that we have sufficient strength to make the risks of [liberation] acceptably low". The outcome of the review aspired to "the exploitation of rifts between the USSR and other communist states and between the satellite regimes and the peoples they are oppressing"; however, the NSC agreed "there should be no further increase at present in the allocation of resources" to operations against the Soviet bloc. The policy concluded with language proposed by the State Department's Paul Nitze:

> Where operations can be conducted on terms which may result in a relative decrease in Soviet power without involving unacceptable risks, the US should pursue and, as practicable, intensify positive political, economic, propaganda, and paramilitary operations against the Soviet orbit, particularly those operations designed to weaken Kremlin control over the satellites and the military potential of the Soviet system. However, we should not overestimate the effectiveness of the activities we can

pursue within the Soviet orbit, and should proceed with a careful weighing of the risks against the possible gains in pressing upon what the Kremlin probably regards as its vital interests.[142]

The State Department was now so hesitant that even the idea of having President-elect Dwight Eisenhower make a Christmas gift of "one million copies of the Scriptures" to the Soviets was set aside.[143] PSB officials concluded with regret, "We are unable at present to propose a strategic concept which outlines a program designed to bring about a final solution of the cold war because: (a) we do not have and cannot clearly foresee the time when we will have the capabilities, and (b) because without adequate capabilities the risks involved are clearly disproportionate to the probabilities of success".[144] CIA representatives agreed, regretting that its operational program, Packet, had lost a "good deal of its currency", as it was "doubtful that circumstance will permit the development in the immediate future of resources commensurate with the optimum program".[145]

With no firm decision forthcoming, the campaign for liberation proceeded on an *ad hoc* basis through the State–private network. In contrast to its "dull" and "patronizing" broadcasts to Western Europe, Voice of America propaganda to the Soviet bloc was "hard-hitting" and "dynamic", as it "adopted a number of the distinctive techniques developed by Radio Free Europe".[146] The National Committee for a Free Europe, with CIA support, proceeded on the criteria of "1. Adequate Funds. 2. No Holds Barred. 3. No Questions Asked".[147] Radio Free Europe's mandate was clear:

1 Keeping alive the hope of liberation in the satellite states and telling the various peoples that they are not forgotten by the free world;
2 Stimulating and increasing the difficulties of the satellite regimes in their efforts to achieve full control of production and economic integration with the USSR;
3 Creating doubts and fears among the quislings of the satellites by character assassination and talking of ultimate retribution, and at the same time drawing a distinction between Communist puppets and those who follow the party line in order to survive. [*Following passage deleted.*][148]

An outside report on RFE by assessors from General Motors concluded, "Support of this organization is one of the very best investments American business and American citizens can make in their effort to win the cold war."[149] PSB officials recognized, "RFE specializes in a number of hard-hitting programs addressed particularly to those Czechs and Hungarians who for one reason or another are discontented with the existing regimes, and who are or could become a nuclei of resistance groups."[150] The programs featured, according to *Life* magazine, "skits and prizes of nylon stockings, tobacco, and other items hard to get in the communist countries".[151]

The most significant operation had been aimed at Czechoslovakia. In April 1951 a high-powered transmitter was open at Holzkirchen, West Germany, for Czech and Slovak broadcasts. General Lucius Clay, the chairman of the Crusade for Freedom, trumpeted:

> Native Czechs and Slovaks – exiles and recent escapees from behind the Iron Curtain – will write the programs and tell the truths of the free world. . . . They will expose Communist quislings behind the Iron Curtain, undermine the authority of Moscow's puppet government and, insofar as is possible, help the prisoner peoples prepare for their day of liberation.[152]

The broadcasts were complement by balloon drops of thousands of leaflets and fake currency to destabilize the Czech economy and undermine its regime. Clay's successor, Harold Stassen, joined journalist Drew Pearson and NCFE officials in a ceremony in Bavaria to release the first 2,000 balloons carrying the leaflet. "A new wind is blowing. New hope is stirring. Friends of freedom in other lands have found a new way to reach you. . . . Tyranny cannot control your winds, cannot enslave your hearts. Freedom will rise again."[153] RFE followed with 20 hours of broadcasts each day on five different transmitters.[154]

Inevitably the program ran afoul of the State Department's caution. Requests for further balloon operations were blocked by the department's liaison officers with the NCFE. By spring 1952, NCFE President C. D. Jackson was complaining to an emergency meeting:

> Despite all the flowery directives, all RFE-NCFE really was told was "do *something*". Not only did we do something, we were on the way to IT. Went further, faster, than anyone dreamt possible.
>
> Problem: How do we preserve the dynamic of this thing without having to pull in our horns?
>
> There is no present answer to this because of the absolute paucity of policy in Washington. Complete vacuum. There is essentially nothing on
>
> WHAT DO WE WANT?
>
> WHERE ARE WE GOING?
>
> WHAT IS OUR PLAN?[155]

Frustrated, the activists set their sights on working with the next Administration. An editorial in the London *Economist*, entitled "Containment Plus" and published in late April, bore the imprint of their complaints:

> The discreet silence of Western diplomacy about its hopes and purposes in Eastern Europe becomes more and more conspicuous. . . .
>
> From the viewpoint of the Kremlin this silence of embarrassment must look like the silence of conspiracy. From London and Paris, from the land and sea stations of the Voice of America, from Radio Free Europe in Munich, and from such guerrilla bases as Madrid and Belgium and so-called "black" stations, there comes hour after hour a stream of criticism and exhortation directed at the Soviet Union and

its satellites. The effort is comparable only to that of the Cominform itself. To Moscow monitoring services, and to the Russians who read analyses of Western output, it must all look systematic and sinister. To experienced Communists, who themselves plan ahead and think in terms of political warfare, it must seem incredible that all this activity is not harnessed to a plan for war and civil war among the western marshes of the Soviet Union. To encourage resistance by words and to have no intention of supporting it later by arms does not, the Russians would argue, make sense.[156]

Jackson, who had been Dwight Eisenhower's propaganda specialist in World War II, claimed that Washington's hesitancy would "horrify Ike. It is contrary to his whole philosophy and method of operation. He is going to turn to somebody and say 'Get something on this'."[157] What was required was a brainstorming session to set the agenda for psychological warfare. So in May 1952, an extraordinary gathering of 28 Government officials and "private" crusaders convened for two days in Princeton, New Jersey. Allen Dulles represented the CIA, Charles Bohlen the State Department, and George Morgan the PSB. Jackson was joined by Walt Rostow and Lloyd Berkner of MIT's Project Troy, Joseph Grew and Adolf Berle of NCFE, Radio Free Europe's top personnel, and Alan Valentine, the head of the Committee for Free Asia.

The "private" practitioners opened the meeting with a litany of opportunities squandered by the Government, Jackson again venting his bitterness about the failure to follow up NCFE's sabotage of the Czech economy. He claimed that only five hours of "infrequent radio messages" on a currency devaluation had started a nationwide panic and concluded angrily:

> We created one or more salients into the hearts and minds of our friends behind the Iron Curtain; into the fears and mistrust of Communist officials behind the Curtain; and possibly created a frown on Uncle Joe's brow.
>
> Well, when these salients had been created, and we looked around for who was to close up, on the flanks. . . . There was no one there, and the reason was not because the country is not brave, or because people didn't want to be there, but because no one had thought that these salients could be created as deep and as fast.[158]

Jackson's view was echoed by most of the "private" conferees. They again noted the recent editorial in the *Economist*, which pointed to the contradiction within US policy: "What is dangerous is that an unofficial and covert policy of 'actively supporting passive resistance' should run parallel with an official policy of doing next to nothing about Eastern Europe."[159] MIT's Lloyd Berkner asserted, "We simply cannot build a defensive situation and wait for a *status quo*. Time can now play against us." Adolf Berle spoke for RFE: "Something must happen – either we tell [the émigrés] to go home, or start composing music, or drop out of the picture, or we suggest a goal for the US or the West."

Government officials remained silent on the point, however, and the meeting soon bogged down over the issue of concrete measures, specifically whether a presidential statement on Eastern Europe should encourage uprisings. Jackson was one of the few who was undeterred by the possibility of a Soviet military reaction, arguing that an aggressive move towards liberation was necessary to prevent World War III:

> Had it been possible for George Gallup or Elmo Roper to get into these countries and ask the question, "What do you believe is the only way in which your country can be liberated?", the answer in 99.9 percent of the cases would have been "By war between the US and Russia".
>
> When you have that as national psychosis, you have got to have more than pap to hand these people in order to enlist them in any plan that we may devise.

Allen Dulles blustered:

> I don't worry so much about the effect of a statement. I am not sure that one of the things that we have lacked in these countries is maybe a martyr or two to inspire these people. . . . After all we have had over 100,000 casualties in Korea, but there are more than 80 million in Eastern Europe, and if we have been willing to accept those casualties, I wouldn't worry if there were a few casualties or a few martyrs behind the Iron Curtain without desiring to stir up a situation of revolt.

However, when Berkner asked, "Are we prepared, officially and generally, to encourage the Czechoslovaks [into an uprising]?" the Government's covert operators beat a retreat. Allen Dulles explained, "We should clearly state that peaceful means are envisaged. Negatively the idea is that we are going to war to liberate those countries." Robert Joyce, the State Department liaison for covert operations, bluntly added, "We are not going to send a panzer division into Hungary to save [a] lady. . . . There is no courage, no blueprint, no timetable because we don't believe you can have one at this time."

The "private" group counter-attacked with a call to ideological arms. Frank Altschul, NCFE's head of broadcasting, contended, "I don't think the crisis has been sufficiently dramatized. I don't think [the American people] realize that the civilization of which they are a part is in jeopardy, and against that the question of whether their living standards are maintained at the present level for a few years is literally a matter of relative unimportance." Jackson added, "What we are appealing for is an intangible," while MIT's Walt Rostow warned, "On the other side of the Iron Curtain, if you fail to make this statement, you must know that every day that goes by the vacuum is being filled" by the Soviet Union.

The arguments were in vain. The "private" campaign could have only a limited effect without presidential endorsement, and the State Department was not going to acquiesce in a hard-hitting statement by Truman. Charles Bohlen insisted, "Anything which can be done [for political warfare] is being tried," and then offered a number of objections to any new initiative, notably the

worries of Western European allies over a liberation policy, before concluding, "I am not saying [the statement] is impossible, but it is not quite as easy
as it sounds." Jackson snapped in frustration, "I think that the NCFE, the
Committee for Free Asia, [the PSB], and the VoA [Voice of America] should
go out of business because what we are doing is handling it like something
you pick up at [the toy store] F. A. O. Schwarz. We are neither conveying
America, nor freedom for the future, and all we will eventually succeed in
doing is get some damn good guys killed." Bohlen merely repeated Jackson's
final words for effect while sustaining the line of caution: "The present end
result of the operations of VoA and RFE would be to get people killed."[160]

After another frustrating day of discussions, the compromise statement
approved by the conference was so watered down that it was more cautious
than Truman's recent speeches, such as the assertion to the American Action
Committee against Mass Deportations in Rumania: "[Rumania is] going to
survive as free country. You are going to get our wholehearted cooperation in
trying to survive. And if I can continue our program which I have inaugurated, you are going to be a free country again, before you pass on to the next
world."[161]

The Cold Warriors reluctantly recognized that their *ad hoc* activity was no
substitute for a coherent policy directed from the highest levels. When
John Foster Dulles, the future Secretary of State in the Eisenhower Administration, criticized "containment" in a lengthy article in *Life* magazine in
May 1952, Gordon Gray congratulated him: "I argued very strongly during
the period that I served as Director of the PSB that containment was not
enough. However, I am not sure that I succeeded in convincing anyone but
myself and my associates in the staff of the Board."[162] C. D. Jackson fretted
angrily:

> The Potomac residents are in such a tailspin, what with one thing and another, that
> I don't think anybody will ever get around to doing anything between now and
> January. Meanwhile, Uncle Joe and his Kremlin Kronies seem to have the field to
> themselves except for the relatively few sensitive characters like Irving Brown [the
> American Federation of Labor's representative in Europe and an important conduit
> of CIA funds].[163]

Notes

1 Draft Senior NSC Staff Report NSC 114 and Annex 5, 27 July 1951, US DDRS, 1980
   284B–285A
2 Elsey to Truman, 26 October 1950, HST, Elsey Papers, Box 65, Foreign Relations – Voice
   of America; Draft Senior NSC Staff Report NSC 114 and Annex 5, 27 July 1951, US DDRS,
   1980 284B–285A
3 Berkner to Acheson, 27 December 1950, USNA, Department of State, Records Relating to
   Project Troy, Box 1

4 The chief documents concerned were NSC 59/1 and NSC 74. See the summary in Lay memorandum, 10 July 1950, US DDRS, 1977 305A

5 Micocci to Kohler, 9 November 1951, USNA, Department of State, Central Decimal File, Box 2243, 511.00/11-951

6 Report of Project Troy, 4 February 1951, USNA, Department of State, Records Relating to Project Troy, Box 1

7 POCC internal newsletter, January 1952, USNA, HST, Department of State, Records Relating to International Information Activities, Box 17, Miscellaneous; POCC internal newsletter, December 1951, USNA, HST, Department of State, Records Relating to International Information Activities, Box 18, Reports: Planning for a Psychological Offensive against the USSR

8 Air Force memorandum, "Cost of Psychological Warfare," 24 March 1951, USNA, HST, Department of State, Records Relating to International Information Activities, Box 17, Miscellaneous

9 Connors/Young/Bohnnker to Consultants, 13 October 1951, USNA, HST, Department of State, Records Relating to International Information Activities, Box 15, National Psychological Strategy Board

10 See Ernest May and Richard Neustadt, *Thinking in Time: The Uses of History for Decisionmakers* (New York, 1986), 34–48

11 Directive for Occupation of North Korea, 28 October 1950, *Minutes*, Reel 2

12 Barrett to Webb and subsequent note, 5 December 1950, FRUS, 1950, I, 423–5

13 Evan Thomas, *The Very Best Men: Four who Dared in the Early Years of the* CIA (New York, 1995), 64

14 Annex to OCB Special Study, "Review of US Policies on Exploitation of Soviet Vulnerabilities," 8 June 1954, USNA, Department of State, Lot 62 D 430, Records Relating to State Department Participation in the OCB and the NSC, 1947–1963, Box 31, Soviet Vulnerability

15 Bedell Smith memorandum, 20 February 1951, US DDRS, 1991 1919; Barnes briefing to PSB, 7 May 1952, US DDRS, 1991 2310

16 Shulman to Acheson, 15 May 1951, USNA, Department of State, Lot 64 D 563, Records of the Policy Planning Staff, 1947–1953, Subject Files, Box 11A, Political and Psychological Warfare 1951–1953

17 See Webb to Director of the Bureau of the Budget, 12 March 1951, USNA, Department of State, Lot 52 D 483, Records Relating to Project Troy

18 Lilly memorandum, "Development of American Psychological Operations, 1945–1951," US DDRS 1991 2302; Truman directive, 4 April 1951, US DDRS, 1991 2244

19 Gray briefing, 26 November 1951, US DDRS, 1991 540; PSB staff meeting, 5 May 1952, HST, Staff Memoranda and Office Files, PSB Files, Box 27, 337 Staff Meetings

20 Humelsine to Webb, 8 March 1949, USNA, Department of State, Lot 66 D 148, Records Relating to State Department Participation in the NSC 1947–1963, Box 124, CIA and Dulles Reports

21 White to Truman, 19 July 1951, HST, Gray Papers, Box 1, PSB File 1290-D, Miscellaneous

22 Murrow to Barrett, 11 July 1951, Department of State, Edward Barrett Files, Box 2. Gray's first full-time deputy was Robert Cutler, a Boston financier who would later be National Security Advisor under President Eisenhower. After a few months, Cutler was succeeded by Tracy Barnes, who had been seconded from the Office of Policy Coordination. Other OPC personnel were reassigned to the PSB to ensure tight control of covert operations. (Davis memorandum, 24 October 1951, HST, Staff Memoranda and Office Files, PSB Files, Box 31, 381 List of Planning Projects Authorized by the Board)

23 Truman to Gray, 31 May 1951, HST, Gray Papers, Box 1, PSB File 1290-D

24 Quoted in Assistant Director for Intelligence Coordination to Departments, 1 June 1951, US DDRS, 1991 1809

25 CIA to PSB Staff, 23 July 1951, US DDRS, 1991 3536
26 Philbin to PSB Staff, 26 July 1951, US DDRS, 1991 2252
27 PSB paper, 31 July 1951, US DDRS, 1991 1679
28 Marshall to Nitze, 29 July 1951, USNA, Department of State, Policy Planning Staff, Subject Files, Box 11A, Political and Psychological Warfare 1951–1953
29 Gordon Gray oral history, HST, Oral History Collection
30 Truman Papers, Staff Memoranda and Office Files, PSB Files, Box 25, PSB Staff Coordination and Liaison with the White House, Barrett to Webb, 13 August 1951; Gray to PSB Staff, 13 August 1951, US DDRS, 1991 1681; Gray briefing, 26 November 1951, US DDRS, 1991 540
31 Cutler to Gray, 23 September 1951, US DDRS, 1991 1117
32 Cutler address to American National Security Committee, 12 October 1951, HST, Gray Papers, Box 3, President Truman, PSB 1951
33 Quoted in Korns to Cutler, 30 October 1951, US DDRS, 1988 3536
34 NSC 114/2, 17 October 1951, *Minutes*, Reel 2
35 Progress report on NSC 58/2, 22 May 1951, US DDRS, 1988 1661
36 NSC 114/2, 17 October 1951, *Minutes*, Reel 2; Progress report on NSC 58/2, 22 May 1951, US DDRS, 1988 1661
37 NSC 118/2, 19 December 1951, *Minutes*, Reel 2
38 Ninety-first NSC meeting, 16 May 1951, *Minutes*, 2nd Supplement, Reel 1
39 NSC 48/5, 17 May 1951, *Documents*, Reel 2
40 Current Policies of the Government of the USA Relating to the National Security, Volume I, Part III, Far East–Communist China, 1 November 1952, US DDRS, 1989 991
41 NIE-33, 7 November 1951, US DDRS, 1986 1813
42 Progress report on NSC 58/2, 22 May 1951, US DDRS, 1988 1661
43 Progress report on NSC 58/2, 22 May 1951, US DDRS, 1988 1661
44 Ninetieth NSC meeting, 3 May 1951, US DDRS, 1994 401
45 "Objectives," undated, US DDRS, 1988 1241; Gleason memorandum, 27 June 1951, US DDRS, 1990 1430; PSB D-31, "A Strategic Concept for a National Psychological Program," 26 November 1952, USNA, Department of State, Lot 62 D 333, PSB Working File, 1951–1953, Box 5, PSB D-31
46 McFarlane to Scowcroft, 29 March 1975, US DDRS, 1993 2923
47 Carroll to Gray, 12 September 1951, US DDRS, 1991 1683; Carroll memorandum, undated, US DDRS, 1991 3539; Carroll to Gray, 20 September 1951, US DDRS, 1991 1039
48 Kennedy to Gray, 5 November 1951, US DDRS, 1991 3539
49 Putnam memorandum, 1 November 1951, US DDRS, 1991 3539
50 Planning Framework, 13 November 1951, HST, Staff Memoranda and Office Files, PSB Files, Box 23, 334 Director's Group
51 See HST, Staff Memoranda and Office Files, PSB Files, Box 34, 387.4 Korea, File 1
52 POCC newsletter, November 1951, USNA, Department of State, Records Relating to International Information Activities, Box 23; Browne to Sherman, 1 May 1952, HST, Staff Memoranda and Office Files, PSB Files, Box 34, 387.4 Korea, File 2
53 State Department Infoguide Bulletin 92, 17 September 1952, USNA, Department of State, Central Decimal File, Box 2245, 511.00/9-1752
54 POC agenda A-10, 2 July 1951, USNA, Department of State, Records Relating to International Information Activities, Box 23; MacDonald to Browne, 14 May 1952, HST, Staff Memoranda and Office Files, PSB Files, Box 32, 383.6 Report on Situation with Respect to Repatriation of PoWs
55 Cutler memorandum, 27 September 1951, HST, Staff Memoranda and Office Files, PSB Files, Box 24, 334 National Security Council; Phillips to Under-secretary of State, 2 April 1953, USNA, Department of State, PSB Working File 1951–1953, Box 1, PSB D-10

56 Acheson to Marshall, 27 August 1951, USNA, Department of State, PSB Working File 1951–1953, Box 1, PSB D-6
57 Norberg memorandum, 28 January 1952, US DDRS, 1990 600
58 PSB memoranda in HST, Staff Memoranda and Office Files, PSB Files, Box 25, 334 PSB Staff Coordination and Liaison with the White House; Davis memorandum, 20 May 1952, HST, Staff Memoranda and Office Files, PSB Files, Box 32, 383.6 Report on Situation with Respect to Repatriation of POWs; Taylor to Allen, 24 January 1952, HST, Staff Memoranda and Office Files, PSB Files, Box 34, 387.4 Korea
59 Barrett–Wisner meeting, 16 January 1952, HST, Staff Memoranda and Office Files, PSB Files, Box 32, 383.6 Report on Situation with Respect to Repatriation of PoWs
60 "Basic Factors in Korean Situation," undated, US DDRS, 1989 782
61 Craig memorandum, 12 May 1953, US DDRS, 1988 2337
62 USITO 21, 15 August 1953, FRUS, 1952–1954, II, 1735–6
63 Bonbright to Matthews, 7 July 1951, HST, Staff Memoranda and Office Files, PSB Files, Box 11, 091.4 Europe #1
64 NSC 67/1, 20 April 1950, Minutes, Reel 2
65 Bonbright to Matthews, 7 July 1951, HST, Staff Memoranda and Office Files, PSB Files, Box 11, 091.4 Europe #1
66 "French and Italian Elections," 6 July 1951, US DDRS, 1988 3302
67 "Reduction of Communist Strength and Influence in France," 22 October 1951, US DDRS, 1991 1584; Cox to Sherman, 30 June 1952, US DDRS, 1991 3401; Irwin Wall, The United States and the Making of Postwar France, 1945–1954 (Cambridge, UK, 1991), 108–9 and 213–15. See also USNA, Department of State, Lot 62 D 333, PSB Working File, 1951–1953, Box 2, PSB D-14
68 Psychological Operations Plan for the Reduction of Communist Power in France, 31 January 1952, US DDRS, 1989 3524; Norberg memorandum, undated [September 1952], HST, Staff Memoranda and Office Files, PSB Files, Box 11, 091.4 Europe #2
69 See the plan of action in US DDRS, 1997 2557
70 Cloven/Demagnetize Coordinating Committee meeting, 19 March 1952, and subsequent minutes, US DDRS, 1991 3398; Briefing Papers for De Gasperi Talks, "Common Action against Communism," 18 September 1951, US DDRS, 1992 1958; Briefing Papers for De Gasperi Talks, "Psychological Action to Counter Totalitarian Propaganda," 20 September 1951, US DDRS, 1992 1966; "PSB Planning Activities," 2 July 1952, US DDRS, 1992 2287; "Plan 'B' Action Checklist (for Italy)," 22 October 1951, US DDRS, 1991 1617
71 Acheson–De Gasperi meeting, 1 October 1951, USNA, Department of State, Policy Planning Staff, Country and Area Files, Box 18; Cloven/Demagnetize Coordinating Committee meeting, 19 March 1952, and subsequent minutes, US DDRS, 1991 3398; Kirk to Acheson, 27 October 1952, HST, Staff Memoranda and Office Files, PSB Files, Box 22, 319.1 Report by PSB on the Status of the Psychological Program; "Guidelines of U.S. Policy toward Italy," 1 July 1961, US DDRS, 1991 3190; "Italy: Department of State Guidelines for Policy and Operations," January 1962, US DDRS, 1992 1393
72 William Colby, Honourable Men: My Life in the CIA (London, 1978), 108–40; "Guidelines of U.S. Policy toward Italy," 1 July 1961, US DDRS, 1991 3190; "Italy: Department of State Guidelines for Policy and Operations," January 1962, US DDRS, 1992 1393
73 PSB D-27, "Psychological Strategy Program for Japan," 30 January 1953, USNA, Department of State, Lot 62 D 333, PSB Working File, 1951–1953, Box 4, PSB D-27
74 Trisko to PSB Panel F, 24 April 1952, US DDRS, 1992 1316; Norberg to Johnson, 11 September 1952, US DDRS, 1991 1132; PSB D-22, 6 February 1953, US DDRS, 1992 2911
75 Mann to Murphy, 11 December 1952, US DDRS, 1977 336B
76 Gray to Dulles, 18 October 1951, HST, Staff Memoranda and Office Files, PSB Files, Box 1, 000.8 Report of Mr De Chant's Second Michigan Study

77 "Project for the NPSB," undated, USNA, Department of State, Lot 62 D 333, PSB Working
   File, 1951–1953, Box 4, PSB D-26
78 PSB D-21, 9 September 1951, USNA, Department of State, Lot 62 D 333, PSB Working File,
   1951–1953, Box 3, PSB D-21, Germany
79 HST, Staff Memoranda and Office Files, PSB Files, Box 6, 091 Germany, Records of Working
   Group Meetings, 23 January–8 July 1952; Kirk to Smith, 27 October 1952, HST, Staff
   Memoranda and Office Files, PSB Files, Box 22, 319.1 Report by PSB on Status of the Psychological Program; Taylor to Allen, 11 September 1952, HST, Staff Memoranda and Office
   Files, PSB Files, Box 33, Report on Escapee Program
80 PSB D-21, 9 September 1952, USNA, Department of State, Lot 62 D 333, PSB Working File,
   1951–1953, Box 3, PSB D-21, Germany; PSB Staff Meeting, 18 April 1952, US DDRS, 1990
   557; Kirk to Smith, 27 October 1952, HST, Staff Memoranda and Office Files, PSB Files,
   Box 22; Taylor memorandum, 11 July 1952, US DDRS, 1991 598; Barnes memorandum, 5
   June 1952, US DDRS, 1992 1793
81 See USNA, Department of State, Lot 62 D 333, PSB Working File, 1951–1953, Box 6, PSB
   D-43; PSB D-39, 4 June 1955, USNA, Department of State, Lot 62 D 430, Records Relating to State Department Participation in the OCB and the NSC, 1947–1963, Box 13, Dis-
   position of PSB Papers
82 Souers memorandum, 21 April 1948, US DDRS, 1991 1532; UM D-61A, 9 December 1949,
   USNA, Department of State, General Records of the Office of the Executive Secretariats,
   Position Papers and Reports for the Undersecretary's Meetings, 1949–1952, Box 2
83 See Kennan to Webb, 30 March 1950, USNA, Department of State, Lot 64 D 563, Records
   of the Policy Planning Staff, 1947–1953, Box 11A, Political and Psychological Warfare
   1947–1950
84 Coverdale to Gray, 20 November 1951, HST, Staff Memoranda and Office Files, PSB Files,
   Box 32, 383 Psychological Aspects of Phase A Defection Program; Associated Press, "Legion
   of ex-Czechs Urged to Fight Reds," 1 November 1952, HST, Staff Memoranda and Office
   Files, PSB Files, Box 33
85 Godel to Cutler, 19 December 1951, US DDRS, 1991 1578; "Psychological Operations Plan
   for Soviet Orbit Escapees," 20 December 1951, US DDRS, 1991 1139
86 MacKnight to Frank, 20 September 1950, USNA, Department of State, MacKnight Files,
   Box 9, General
87 NSC 86/1, 18 April 1951, Minutes, Reel 2
88 Godel to Cutler, 19 December 1951, US DDRS, 1991 1578; "Psychological Operations Plan
   for Soviet Orbit Escapees," 20 December 1951, US DDRS, 1991 1139; Truman Papers, Staff
   Memoranda and Office Files, PSB Files, Box 33, 383.7 Report on Escapee Program, Bruce
   to PSB Staff, 7 August 1952, and Cox to Sherman, 5 September 1952; USNA, Department
   of State, Lot 62 D 333, PSB Working File, 1951–1953, Box 2, PSB D-18; "A National Psychological Program with Respect to Escapees from the Soviet Orbit: Phase B," 15 January
   1953, US DDRS, 1997 2954
89 Bruce to PSB Staff, 7 August 1952, US DDRS, 1991 1721; Devine to Godel, 23 November
   1951, US DDRS, 1992 822; Phase B meeting, 14 March 1952, US DDRS, 1991 2379; Taylor
   memorandum, March 1952, US DDRS, 1991 3547; "10/5 Planning Problem," undated, and
   subsequent memoranda, US DDRS, 1992 1132–4; Kirk to Smith, 27 October 1952, US
   DDRS, 1991 3556; Allen memorandum, 31 July 1952, US DDRS, 1992 1546; FOA report,
   23 December 1953, US DDRS, 1993 2951
90 Operation Crowbar is outlined in Department of Defense report, 18 November 1951, US
   DDRS, 1990 3088. The formation of paramilitary units probably occurred, but evaluation
   of their effectiveness is hindered by the continued classification of Government documents
91 Blackstock memorandum, 18 September 1951, HST, Staff Memoranda and Office Files, PSB
   Files, Box 5, 091 Czechoslovakia; Kolarek to Devine, 18 January 1952, HST, Staff Memo-

randa and Office Files, PSB Files, Box 32, Psychological Aspects of Phase A Defection Program. The aftermath of the Czech train incident was not publicized, however. Most of the defectors were settled in Canada, but both the engineer and the despatcher of the train wrote to Government officials, "After all that glory [of touring the United States], there came the sobering up. We are working at the Lionel firm, and all those promises made by Mr Johnson in Germany turn out to be hollow words. . . . The thing that irks is that everyone around us is trying to make money on us to this day, and we feel we can trust no one"

92 Sherman to Gray, 24 August 1951, HST, Staff Memoranda and Office Files, PSB Files, Box 25, 334 PSB Staff Coordination and Liaison with the White House; Draft presidential statement, 30 December 1952, HST, Staff Memoranda and Office Files, PSB Files, Box 32, 383.4 Rosenberg Cases

93 Norberg to Gray, 16 October 1951, US DDRS, 1991 3542; Gleason to Truman, 24 October 1952, US DDRS, 1978 251A

94 Sherman to Taylor and Browne, 4 March 1952, US DDRS, 1991 1666

95 Norberg to Wilber, 22 January 1952, US DDRS, 1991 2304

96 Norberg to Sherman, 10 October 1952, US DDRS, 1991 397; Morgan to PSB members, 15 July 1952, US DDRS, 1991 1559; Norberg memorandum, 30 September 1952, US DDRS, 1991 1626; Browne to Allen, 5 August 1952, US DDRS, 1991 1716

97 Hargus to Fritchey, 4 March 1952, and subsequent memoranda, US DDRS, 1991 1559; Sargeant Papers, Box 2, Psychological Operations Coordinating Committee, POC D-50/1, 2 January 1953; Lay memorandum, 20 February 1953, US DDRS, 1978 388B. For records of POCC meetings, see Norberg memoranda, December 1951–September 1952, US DDRS, 1991 3546, and Norberg memorandum, 15 July 1952, US DDRS, 1991 1625. The Barrett suggestion is in Norberg's record of the meeting of 19 December 1951

98 Barrett memorandum, 1 August 1950, USNA, Department of State, Lot 53 D 47, Records Relating to International Information Activities, Box 13, Intelligence. In the "light gray" area, where operations were not acknowledged by the Government but where they might affect State Department acitivities, no project would be undertaken without the clearance of Barrett or his liaison with OPC

99 *The Director of Central Intelligence Historical Series: General Walter Bedell Smith,* Volume IV, 1 December 1971, US DDRS, 1991 63

100 Memorandum for Deputy Director (Plans), 13 October 1952, US DDRS, 1992 543

101 Bureau of the Budget report, 21 April 1952, HST, Staff Memoranda and Office Files, PSB Files, Box 25, 334 PSB Staff Coordination and Liaison with the White House, File 3; Barrett memorandum, 18 January 1952, HST, Sargeant Papers, Box 2, Correspondence, Assistant Secretary of State for Public Affairs, 1952

102 Kirk to Smith, 27 October 1952, HST, Staff Memoranda and Office Files, PSB Files, Box 22; National Security Council progress report, 31 December 1952, US DDRS, 1992 368; Status Report on the National Psychological Effort, 1 August 1952, US DDRS, 1992 1715

103 Barrett to Webb, 13 August 1951, HST, Staff Memoranda and Office Files, PSB Files, Box 25, 334 PSB Staff Coordination and Liaison with the White House

104 Barnes to Webb, 10 August 1951, USNA, Department of State, PSB Working File, Box 1, PSB D-1

105 Irwin to Norberg and Hirsch, 7 May 1952, HST, Staff Memoranda and Office Files, PSB Files, Box 23, 334 LENAP

106 Schaetzel to Phillips, 11 September 1951, HST, Staff Memoranda and Office Files, Box 1, 040 State Department

107 Morgan memorandum, 1 May 1952, HST, Staff Memoranda and Office Files, PSB Files, Box 24, 334 Panel I (Southeast Asia); Putnam to Johnson, 1 May 1952, HST, Staff Memoranda and Office Files, PSB Files, Box 3, 040 State Department

108 Marshall to Nitze, 19 November 1952, USNA, Department of State, Lot 64 D 563, Records

of the Policy Planning Staff, 1947–1953, Subject Files, Political and Psychological Warfare 1951–1953

109 Draft Staff Study, "Preliminary Estimate of the Effectiveness of US Psychological Strategy," 5 May 1952, US DDRS, 1991 546

110 Wisner to Barnes, 28 March 1952, US DDRS, 1991 2008

111 Browne to Allen, 7 May 1952, US DDRS, 1991 1697. See also the report of the US Advisory Commission on Information for 1952 in HST, Hulten Papers, Box 13

112 *New York Times*, 15 December 1951

113 Gray report to Truman, 22 February 1952, HST, Staff Memoranda and Office Files, PSB Files, Box 25, 334 PSB Staff Coordination and Liaison with the White House

114 Wisner to PSB, 6 March 1952, USNA, Department of State, PPS Records, Subject Files, Political and Psychological Warfare 1951–1953

115 Nitze to Sargeant, 14 March 1952, and Bruce to Smith, 21 May 1952, USNA, Department of State, Lot 64 D 563, Records of the Policy Planning Staff, 1947–1953, Subject Files, Political and Psychological Warfare 1951–1953; Marshall to Matthews, 18 March 1952, USNA, Department of State, PPS Records, Chronological File, Chronological January–December 1952

116 Taylor to Barnes, 7 February 1952, HST, Staff Memoranda and Office Files, PSB Files, Box 31, 381 List of Planning Projects Authorized by the Board

117 "PSB Planning Objectives," 7 April 1952, US DDRS, 1993 1149

118 Marshall to Nitze, 3 April 1952, USNA, Department of State, Lot 64 D 563, Records of the Policy Planning Staff, 1947–1953, Subject Files, Political and Psychological Warfare 1951–1953

119 Barnes to Gray, 12 May 1952, HST, Gray Papers, Box 1

120 Morgan to Allen, 10 April 1952, US DDRS, 1991 1693; Barnes briefing to PSB Members, 8 May 1952, US DDRS, 1991 2310

121 PSB staff study, "Overall Strategic Concept for our Psychological Operations," 7 May 1952, HST, Staff Memoranda and Office Files, PSB Files, Box 15, 091.412 The Field and Role of Psychological Strategy in Cold War Planning

122 Korns to Sherman, 14 May 1952, and Cox to Sherman, 16 May 1952, HST, Staff Memoranda and Office Files, PSB Files, Box 15, 091.412 The Field and Role of Psychological Strategy in Cold War Planning

123 Draft memorandum, "Phasing of Covert Operations Designed to Reduce and Retract Soviet Influence and Power," undated, US DDRS, 1991 1772; Sherman to Taylor, 23 June 1952, HST, Staff Memoranda and Office Files, PSB Files, Box 1, 000.1 Rand Corporation study

124 PSB meeting, 21 August 1952, HST, Staff Memoranda and Office Files, PSB Files, Box 28, 337 PSB Luncheon Meetings

125 Barnes to PSB, 29 May 1952, US DDRS, 1991 2314

126 Morgan memoranda, 8–10 July 1952, HST, Staff Memoranda and Office Files, PSB Files, Box 24, 334 NSC

127 Nitze to Bruce, 26 August 1952, USNA, Department of State, Lot 64 D 563, Records of the Policy Planning Staff, 1947–1953, Chronological File, Chronological January–December 1952

128 CIA representative to Barnes, 18 August 1952, US DDRS, 1991 2321

129 John Ranelagh, *The Agency: The Rise and Decline of the CIA* (New York, 1987), 227–8

130 John Prados, *Presidents' Secret Wars: CIA and Pentagon Covert Operations from World War II to Iranscam* (New York, 1986), 50–1; Thomas Rees, "Blunder and Betrayal in the Balkans," *Guardian Weekend* (London), 10 October 1998

131 Prados, *Presidents' Secret Wars*, 43 and 58

132 Thomas, *The Very Best Men*, 73

133 Prados, *Presidents' Secret Wars*, 59

134 Report of the President's Committee on International Information Activities, 30 June 1953, US DDRS, 1997 2351; Thomas, *The Very Best Men*, 36. See also the litany of complaints by a CIA liaison – ACLPR "is an almost complete failure", "too much paid to the wrong people", "it has been run by incompetents or people with their own axe to grind" – and the comment of another observer that it was "clear that the [Russian nationalist movement] NTS was getting substantial funds from sources other than the Committee [ACLPR], on the basis of which it is almost arrogant in its independence". (W. G. J. to Blum, undated, US DDRS, 1991 752, and Scott to Smith, 20 September 1952, 1991 1130)

135 Thomas Braden oral history, 5 May 1982, Hoover Institution, Sig Mickelson Collection, Audiotape 11

136 PSB-30, "Summary of a Report from the Central Intelligence Agency," 1 August 1952, PSB D-30, "Status Report on National Psychological Effort and First Progress Report," Annex D, 1 August 1952, USNA, Department of State, Lot 62 D 333, PSB Working File, 1951–1953, Box 4, PSB D-30

137 Outline of Means Papers, 15 May 1952, HST, Staff Memoranda and Office Files, PSB Files, Box 13, 091.411 Agenda for PSB Meetings

138 Ralph McGehee, *Deadly Deceits: My Twenty-five Years in the CIA* (New York, 1983), 26; David Wise and Thomas B. Ross, *The Invisible Government* (New York, 1964), 112–15; William Corson, *The Armies of Ignorance: The Rise of the American Intelligence Empire* (New York, 1977), 320–3; Thomas, *The Very Best Men*, 52–3

139 John Young, "Britain and Liberation," paper to University of Birmingham Modern History Seminar, 7 May 1997

140 Browne memorandum, 18 December 1952, HST, Staff Memoranda and Office Files, PSB Files, Box 22, 319.1 Report by PSB on Status of the Psychological Program

141 PSB D-31, "A Strategic Concerpt for a National Psychological Program," 26 November 1952, USNA, Department of State, Lot 62 D 333, PSB Working File, 1951–1953, Box 5, PSB D-31

142 FRUS 1952–1954, II, 67 and 229; Lay memorandum, 19 January 1953, US DDRS, 1977 44B; NSC Report on Status of U.S. Programs for National Security, 1 December 1952, US DDRS, 1992 368; Lay memorandum, 15 August 1952, *Documents*

143 Darlington to Kirk, 28 October 1952, and subsequent memoranda, HST, Staff Memoranda and Office Files, PSB Files, Box 1, 000.3 Russia for Ideological Warfare

144 "Review of US Policies on Exploitation of Soviet Vulnerabilities," 8 June 1954, USNA, Department of State, Lot 62 D 430, Records Relating to State Department Participation in the OCB and the NSC, 1947–1963, Box 31, Soviet Vulnerability

145 CIA representative to Barnes, 18 August 1952, US DDRS, 1991 2321

146 Morgan to Craig, 8 September 1952, US DDRS, 1991 1193; Sherman to Taylor and Browne, 4 March 1952, US DDRS, 1991 1666

147 Jackson to Biddle, 17 March 1952, DDE, Jackson Papers, Box 28, Anthony J. Biddle

148 Sherman to Taylor and Browne, 4 March 1952, US DDRS, 1991 1666

149 General Motors Research Staff, "Report on Radio Free Europe," 15 December 1952, DDE, Jackson Papers, Box 45, Free Europe Committee

150 Browne to Allen, 12 February 1952, US DDRS, 1988 2918

151 Cited in Walter Hixson, *Parting the Curtain: Propaganda, Culture, and the Cold War, 1945–1961* (New York, 1997), 62

152 Crusade for Freedom, 29 April 1951, FDR, Eleanor Roosevelt Papers, Correspondence 1945–1952, Box 3275, Crusade for Freedom

153 Hixson, *Parting the Curtain*, 65. Between 1951 and 1956, Czech authorities claimed that 79 political murders were carried out by enemies of the state. Thirty-five of those assassinations occurred in 1952. (Vojtech Mastny, *The Cold War and Soviet Insecurity: The Stalin Years* (New York, 1996), 118)

154 "The Crisis in Czechoslovakia," undated, DDE, Jackson Papers, Box 65, Operation Marshmallow
155 Altschul–Jackson–Washburn meeting, 28 April 1952, DDE, Jackson Papers, Box 69, 1952 Princeton Meeting, 10–11 May 1952
156 *The Economist*, "Containment Plus," 26 April 1952
157 Altschul–Jackson–Washburn meeting, 28 April 1952, DDE, Jackson Papers, Box 69, 1952 Princeton Meeting, 10–11 May 1952
158 The account in the following paragraphs is based upon Record of Princeton Meetings, 10–11 May 1952, US DDRS, 1988 1164
159 *The Economist*, "Containment Plus," 26 April 1952
160 Record of Princeton Meetings, 10–11 May 1952, US DDRS, 1988 1164
161 Allen to PSB, 9 June 1952, USNA, Department of State, Lot 62 D 333, PSB Working File, 1951–1953, Box 4, PSB D-26
162 Gray to Dulles, 16 June 1952, HST, Gray Papers, Box 1
163 Jackson to Brown, 22 April 1952, DDE, Jackson Papers, Box 31, Irving Brown

10

A crusade of indecision

In January 1953, President Dwight D. Eisenhower was inaugurated on a keynote message of "MORALITY, FAITH, and PEACE". In his inaugural address, he set out his conception of the American ideology: "We are called, as a people, to give testimony, in the sight of the world, to our faith that the future shall be free. . . . It is our faith in the deathless dignity of man, governed by eternal moral and natural laws."[1]

Eisenhower's commitment to that ideology was far different, at least in public, from that of his predecessor. He had come to office on a Republican platform which condemned "the negative, futile, and immoral policy of 'containment'" and promised, "The policies we espouse will revive the contagious, liberating influences which are inherent in freedom. They will inevitably set up strains and stresses within the captive world which will make the rulers impotent to continue in their monstrous ways and mark the beginning of their end."[2] The candidate had, in John Foster Dulles, a Secretary of State famed for his almost Messianic conviction that the United States must triumph over the evils of Soviet Communism. The attitude was not just a public posture: Eisenhower's press secretary, James Hagerty, labeled Foster Dulles a Roundhead who "had not only a conviction and belief, but . . . a spiritual belief and a spiritual conviction that drove him as well".[3] Another official caustically noted that Foster Dulles "seemed to feel that he had a 'pipeline on high'".[4]

As early as February 1949, Eisenhower, then *de facto* Chairman of the Joint Chiefs of Staff, had urged the National Security Council to expand the use of psychological warfare. He served on the Board of the National Committee for Free Europe and was closely connected with the Crusade for Freedom. It was his presidential campaign, however, that brought liberation to the fore. In the same week that "private" activists were convening in Princeton, New Jersey, to overcome Government hesitation and renew efforts at liberation, Foster Dulles was publishing the manifesto "A Policy of Boldness" in *Life* magazine. The article is now famous for its introduction of the doctrine of "massive retaliation"; overlooked and, arguably, more significant was Dulles's call for a "political offense". Although he specifically ruled out US military intervention or "a series of bloody uprisings" within the Soviet bloc, he insisted, "We can be confident that within two, five or 10 years substantial parts of the present captive world can peacefully regain national independence." The present Government had been delinquent in supporting this movement, Dulles insisted; he recommended task forces to aid escapees and defectors, coordination of official services like the Voice of America, and support of other efforts like Radio Free Europe.

Were the Princeton conference and Dulles's article, ostensibly prepared for his meeting with Eisenhower in Paris in early May, two halves of an offensive by "private" operators and some Government officials, directed at the next Administration rather than the present one? Dulles's allusion to "some highly competent work . . . being done at one place or another to promote Liberation" and his call for a strong presidential statement establishing peaceful liberation as a US goal certainly parallel the Princeton proceedings. While there is no firm evidence that he met with any of the Princeton conferees to discuss "A Policy of Boldness", the presence of Allen Dulles at Princeton is intriguing. So is the fact that Emmet Hughes, a close colleague of C. D. Jackson at Time-Life, helped draft Foster Dulles's article.[5]

Abbott Washburn, who joined Eisenhower's campaign staff shortly after the Princeton conference, communicated the details to the candidate. He made clear that he and C. D. Jackson had organized the conference "with the agreement of General [Lucius] Clay" – Washburn had worked with Clay at the Crusade for Freedom, and the General just happened to be one of the leaders of the Eisenhower for President movement. Washburn conveniently omitted any reference to compromise with the State Department lobby and emphasized a hard-line consensus "that the policy of mere 'containment' or holding of the line against further Soviet expansion has outlived its usefulness and should be replaced with a more dynamic and positive policy of ultimate liberation of the enslaved nations, in line with our fundamental American concept of man's God-given right to individual freedom".[6]

Washburn prompted Eisenhower to use the Princeton material in speeches "to show that the new Republican Administration's foreign policy will reveal a new, dynamic quality that will wrest the offensive away from Moscow in the cold war".[7] In late August 1952 the candidate declared to the American Legion convention, "The American conscience can never know peace until these peoples [of the Soviet bloc] are restored again to being masters of their own fate. . . . We must tell the Kremlin that never shall we desist in our aid to every man and woman of those shackled lands who seeks refuge with us, any man who keeps burning among his own people the flame of freedom or who is dedicated to the liberation of his fellows."[8]

Eisenhower deliberately omitted the word "peaceful" from his speech. Dulles was more careful, after a long conference with the candidate, to clarify "violent" and "non-violent" paths to liberation, specifying an internal revolution rather than US military action, but his call was no less strident: "What we should do is try to split the satellite states away from the control of a few men in Moscow. The only way to stop a head-on collision with the Soviet Union is to break it up from within." This would be done through passive resistance, slowdowns, and non-cooperation, stirred up by "the Voice of America and other agencies" and supplied via air drops from groups like the National Committee for Free Europe.[9]

These statements raised concern in some quarters. The *Washington Post*, for example, fretted, "The sad truth is that there is no quick and easy way of liberating the captives in eastern Europe. . . . It is nothing but a salve for the American conscience for campaign speakers to talk of 'liberation' as if a few propaganda blasts or manifestoes could accomplish it."[10] Even Radio Free Europe moved to dampen speculation which could lead to premature revolt: "We of RFE . . . cannot comment upon these statements with unqualified optimism, for to do so would be to deceive our listeners by inspiring in them exaggerated hope of Western intervention . . . Not one word in these statements can be used to encourage militant anti-communists to go over from passive to active resistance in the expectation that such resistance will be supported by Western elements."[11]

Eisenhower later claimed that he heeded such words and instructed Foster Dulles to emphasize "all peaceful means" to liberation.[12] Speaking to the Council on Foreign Relations in October, the future Secretary of State explained, "[Liberation would] activate the strains and stresses within the Communist empire so as to disintegrate it. . . . Activation does not mean armed revolt. The people have no arms and violent revolt would be futile; indeed it would be worse than futile, it would precipitate massacre."[13] Yet Eisenhower, without explaining how liberation could occur without confrontation, continued to pledge the achievement of universal freedom. In another campaign speech, he insisted, "These lands [in Eastern Europe] cannot be written off as irrevocably lost. The free world cannot permit their burial to the accompaniment of either Leninist requiems or fatalists' casual post-mortems. To do this would not merely seal Soviet domination in Europe; it would signify the free world's abdication of its own conscience."[14]

Eisenhower linked his invocation of "freedom" to a unified psychological strategy for total victory. He wrote in his diary, "We are proud of our guarantees of freedom in thought and speech and worship. Of such value are all these things to us that, unconsciously, we are guilty of one of the greatest errors that ignorance can make – we assume that our standard of values is shared by all other humans in the world."[15] This concept of the "peaceful means" to liberation was further developed in a letter to Foster Dulles: "Psychological warfare can be anything from the singing of a beautiful hymn to the most extraordinary kind of physical sabotage."[16] For this, he told audiences, "Every department and every agency of government that can make a useful contri-

bution [would] bring its full strength to bear under a co-ordinated program."
He concluded, just before the election, to a large crowd in the Cow Palace in
San Francisco:

> Our aim in the "cold war" is not conquering of territory or subjugation by force.
> Our aim is more subtle, more pervasive, more complete. We are trying to get the
> world, by peaceful means, to believe the truth. . . .
>   The means we shall employ to spread this truth are often called "psychological".
> Don't be afraid of that term just because it's a five-dollar, five-syllable word.
> "Psychological warfare" is the struggle for the minds and wills of men.[17]

The new President's dedication to a renewed offensive within the Soviet bloc
was reinforced by a budget of $100 million for CIA operations in Eastern
Europe and by his choice of advisors. Significantly, he created the post of
Special Assistant for psychological operations and appointed C. D. Jackson,
Eisenhower's chief psychological warfare officer in World War II. Jackson had
pressed in 1947 for the General to become President, asking Time-Life publisher Henry Luce to support the effort.[18] He was a zealot for those causes
in which he believed, taking up liberation as President of the National Committee for Free Europe from 1950 before joining Eisenhower's campaign team
two years later. He was a staunch advocate of free enterprise everywhere –
even the British Welfare State was an evil "socialist revolution . . . debasing
the middle class to proletarian status".[19]

Jackson was, to put it mildly, a flamboyant presence in the White House,
an extrovert who "loved grand intrigue, . . . absolutely fascinated with being
there at that great center of power in the world".[20] Jackson's deputy, Abbott
Washburn, profiled his boss: "Enormous persuasiveness in his own right,
tremendous effect on others who came in contact with him. A lot of drama,
a lot of flair, great user of words."[21] Howland Sargeant, Assistant Secretary of
State for Public Affairs and later head of Radio Liberty, asserted, "[C.D.] was
a Renaissance man. He should have lived in the time of Elizabeth."[22]

Jackson was also renowned for a modern passion for fast cars and motor
bikes. On one occasion, he announced to his staff, "Yeah, I'm off," on a
mission to Western Europe. Thirty-six hours later, he sent the cable, "Slight
motorcycle accident at Shannon Airport, left leg in cast up to hip. Don't worry,
I'm going to make it to Rome."[23] Writing to Jackson about economic matters,
Joseph Dodge, the Director of the Bureau of the Budget, added, "I sincerely
hope you and your MG have not got into any serious trouble." Jackson replied
that the MG was "still going strong" but he was thinking of trading it for a
Corvette.[24]

Jackson's creative approach to all aspects of psychological strategy was
epitomized by his handling of the death sentences of the convicted spies Ethel
and Julius Rosenberg. By January 1953 the two had almost exhausted their
avenues of appeal, and their execution was imminent. The case was causing

serious problems for the United States with Western Europeans, many of whom believed that the Rosenbergs were innocent or that they should be granted clemency. The CIA was so concerned that it despatched 18 pages of specially prepared material to its station chiefs to counter "pro-Rosenberg propaganda".[25]

As soon as the Eisenhower Administration took office, Jackson wrestled with the problem. His original idea, passed to Attorney General Herbert Brownell, was "one more try to crack at least one of the Rosenbergs, now that we have the added psychological leverage of Soviet anti-semitism". A Jewish psychiatrist such as Karl Binger should "insinuate himself into their confidence during the next 30 days, and if they did show signs of coming along, a stay of execution for another 30 or 60 days could be arranged while the work progressed". Jackson assured Brownell, "I am sure you understand that my interest is not in saving the Rosenbergs. They deserve to fry a hundred times for what they have done to this country, but if they can be cracked, what they can tell us may save the lives of hundreds of thousands of Americans later."[26] Director of Central Intelligence Allen Dulles spelled out the benefits of the initiative:

> [The Rosenbergs'] recantation would entail backfiring of this entire Soviet propaganda effort. It would be virutally impossible for world communism to ignore or successfully discredit the Rosenbergs. The couple is ideally situated to serve as leading instruments of a psychological warfare campaign designed to split world communism on the Jewish issue, to create disaffected groups with the membership of the Parties, to utilize these groups for further infiltration and for intelligence work.[27]

Jackson was persisting with his scheme in late May, three weeks before the execution, urging Brownell "to play a war of nerves with the Rosenbergs". Brownell replied, "The matron had managed to ingratiate herself and . . . they had hopes in that direction."[28] Days later, Eisenhower authorized Jackson to explore with Brownell and FBI Director J. Edgar Hoover the possibility of commuting Ethel Rosenberg's sentence.[29]

For better or worse, Jackson's creativity was fueled by self-belief and vanity. On one occasion, the Director of Central Intelligence, Walter Bedell Smith, praised Jackson "as the most successful psychological warrior he had ever known". As Jackson preened, Bedell Smith explained that his estimate was based on a leaflet drop on Polish and Russian "slave labor" camps in Germany in World War II. The leaflet containers failed to open; however, they struck a barge, sinking it and blocking the Rhine.[30]

Jackson perceived his immediate mission to be the establishment of an integrated system for his operations. Ignoring the existence of the PSB, he argued that the State Department, CIA, and military services were "highly competitive, in fact to the point of sabotage . . . because the Government of the US has neither policy nor plan for conducting the cold war".[31] His "Great Opportunity" came when the review of the Government's structure for psychological operations, urged by the 1952 Princeton meeting, was authorized by Eisenhower immediately after his election. Chaired by William Jackson, another veteran of World War II psychological warfare and a former Deputy Director of Central Intelligence, the committee was to conduct "a *real* survey of what is being done now in political warfare and information by this country, in Government, in private organizations, and in para-Government or para-private organizations".[32]

C. D. Jackson was further encouraged when some of the NSC's initial decisions under Eisenhower pointed to the implementation of an offensive. On 11 February, the council reviewed the use of radio for psychological operations, a matter so sensitive that the Record of Action is still classified by the US government.[33] Over the next two weeks, the NSC discussed the formation of the Volunteer Freedom Corps, made up of 250,000 refugees from Eastern Europe, with the proposal that "ultimately they . . . be trained and armed to replace US forces in Korea".[34] Eisenhower commented favourably not only about the "good fighting material at a much cheaper rate" but also of the potential to "create anxiety and unrest in the USSR".[35] The programme to stimulate the defection of "key individuals" from the Soviet bloc was also reviewed and expanded.[36]

Draft policy on Communist China was just as explicit. The United States would seek "the reorientation or replacement of the Peiping regime" through "political, military, and economic pressures . . . influencing the leaders and people in China to oppose the Peiping regime". Operations would "foster and support anti-Communist Chinese elements both outside and within China, with a view to developing and expanding resistance in China to the Peiping regime's control".[37] Some officials in the International Information Administration were even prepared to jettison the State Department's caution, arguing, "We should aim at a greater concert of effort at ideas which may be expected to promote disunity and eventual political disintegration behind the Iron Curtain, especially in the satellite countries."[38]

Yet the Eisenhower Administration, for all its bluster about "freedom", would not commit itself to an all-out campaign. Its first general statement of global policy, NSC 141, restated the objective of "exploitation of rifts" in the Soviet bloc but did not answer the question posed by the National Security Advisor, Robert Cutler, "Should the U.S. really go in to match the Soviets in undercover activities?"[39] Papers prepared for the Jackson Committee highlighted division between agencies. Representatives of the Departments of State and Defense simply noted that the present policy did not encourage rebellion while the CIA's submission complained, "Our present Cold War techniques directed toward limitation or reduction in Soviet power within the Bloc are not adequate to produce the desired results."[40]

The conflict between rhetoric and practice was highlighted in the controversy over the Yalta agreements of 1945. In his State of the Union address, Eisenhower won Republican applause with the commitment to "an appropriate resolution making clear that this government recognizes no kind of commitment contained in secret understandings of the past with foreign governments which permit this kind of enslavement".[41] Foster Dulles effused to Congressional leaders, "The resolution would help allay the fears of some enslaved peoples that the US is abandoning them to their fate; instead, this might cause a 'little indigestion' behind the Iron Curtain."[42]

The initiative backfired when the State Department intervened to warn that US repudiation would allow the Soviets to do the same, jeopardising the Western position in Italy, Germany, and Austria. Caught between Republican pressure and diplomatic risks, the Administration offered the woolly compromise which "did not involve any repudiation of actual agreements, but merely involved rejection of perverted interpretations of these agreements which had led to the subjection of free peoples".[43]

The Yalta question was superseded by an even more definitive setback for the Administration. Ironically, it emerged from the perfect opportunity to promote discord within the Soviet bloc. On 4 March, Joseph Stalin, the greatest menace to the Free World, suffered a fatal stroke, leaving a vacuum in Moscow's structure of power.

Although Stalin's demise was sudden, the Psychological Strategy Board had drawn up Operation Cancellation for such a situation; the plans were approved by the PSB's members in October 1952.[44] Besides calling for further information and analysis of the Soviet leadership, Cancellation sought study and implementation of "ways of enhancing top-level conflicts in a useful manner before Stalin's passing" combined with "exploitation of salient vulnerabilities in the Soviet or Orbit control apparatus".[45] There was even the possibility of accelerating Cancellation through the assassination of Stalin, allegedly through a special CIA unit led by Colonel Boris T. Pash. In August 1952, amidst rumors that the Soviet leader would propose a four-power summit in Paris, proposals for the "liquidation" of Stalin were sent to Frank Wisner and Allen Dulles before Walter Bedell Smith, then Director of Central Intelligence, finally rejected the plan.[46]

C. D. Jackson's immediate reaction to Stalin's stroke noted the planning for "everything possible to overload the enemy at the precise moment when he is least capable of bearing even his normal load. . . . It is not inconceivable that out of such a program might come further opportunities which, skillfully exploited, might advance the real disintegration of the Soviet empire." Jackson added the suggestion that the Government "activate immediately the long-deferred and several-times-cancelled plan for an Albanian *coup d'état*".[47] Within hours, an informal meeting of the PSB's members approved a working party to implement the plan.[48]

The problem was that the State Department had already undermined Cancellation. The PSB had clearly called for an "agreed Government position ... for stand-by instruction" to the media,[49] but the department hesitated at the PSB's enumeration of the possibilities: "(1) To create frictions within this structure before Stalin has passed from power; (2) To manipulate frictions which may develop after his passing from power; (3) To manipulate frictions which might develop should one of Stalin's apparent heirs disappear while Stalin is still in power." The department claimed ingenuously "that insufficient hard intelligence exists at present to proceed on any of these lines without further study"; the reality was that its officials had vetoed the initial proposal of the PSB working group for a well defined offensive.[50] Thus, Eisenhower supposedly lamented to his Cabinet, "Ever since 1946, I know that all the so-called experts have been yapping about what would happen when Stalin dies and what we, as a nation, should do about it. Well, he's dead. And you can turn the files of our government inside out – in vain – looking for any plans laid. We have no plan."[51]

When the time came for a decision, the National Security Council could not agree on an aggressive strategy. The President argued that "the moment was propitious for introducing the right word directly into the Soviet Union", with Jackson bolstering him:

> This was the first really big propaganda opportunity offered to our side for a long time. It enabled us to stress our devotion to peace, and it would enable us to counteract with real forcefulness the "hate America" campaign in the Soviet orbit and to calm anxieties elsewhere in the world by reassuring peoples everywhere of America's devotion to peace.

It was Foster Dulles, the great liberator of the 1952 campaign, who balked. He considered the draft of Eisenhower's statement counterproductive, since "it would be interpreted as an appeal to the Soviet people to rise up against their rulers in a period of mourning, at a time when they were bound to regard Stalin more reverentially than ordinarily".[52] Only the appointment of another working party offered slim hope for the activists.

Eisenhower's first actions on 5 March, as Stalin lay dying, were limited to a prayer asking God to bring "peace and comradeship" and a muddled, meaningless statement at a press conference: "So it comes down to it that it is a part, again, of this whole world effort that we are making, and which is going to be successful only as all America – indeed, all the free world – keeps its heart right into the job."[53] In Berlin, two frustrated CIA officers distributed some leaflets and sang, to an old Tsarist army melody: "It happened in Berlin/A great event, oh friends/We presented leaflets/On the day of Stalin's death."[54]

Still, Jackson persisted. Assisted by Walt Rostow, he called for an all-out offensive with "no mere pious platitudes but a real bite". A task force would explore the "twilight area where overt military and diplomatic action is inseparable from psychological warfare". Meanwhile, a four-power meeting of Foreign Ministers would "overload" the Soviets through US proposals on Korea, Europe, and Latin America, a message from Eisenhower to the Soviet people would exploit the "great emotional shock" of Stalin's death as a "unique Soviet vulnerability".[55] Jackson and Rostow pressed the NSC's working party to recommend measures to show strength such as "apparent acceleration of our military buildup" with fleet visits and aerial demonstrations, development of Volunteer Freedom Corps among Chinese and North Korean prisoners of war and Eastern European refugees, and overt preparations for an offensive in Korea. There was even a proposal for a meeting between the Director of Central Intelligence, the Under-secretary of State, and Lavrenti Beria, the head of the KGB, to discuss "the safe conduct and orderly passage of those who wish to leave the Soviet Union to come out into the Western world". The working group argued that "Beria's leaving the center of power, and even the consideration of it, would increase uneasiness and suspicion, and at the same time the humanitarian interest in refugees, with its special appeal to many groups in the free nations, [would be] apparent".[56]

Jackson and Rostow also had some support within the NSC, notably from the Director of the Mutual Security Administration, Harold Stassen, who lobbied for guidelines "to foster any and all divisive forces within the top hierarchy of the Kremlin".[57] All the time, however, State Department officials were reminding their superiors, "A direct frontal assault on the Soviet structure or leadership would only have the effect of consolidating their position."[58] The department's immediate guidance established:

> In regard to [the] Soviet popular masses, our actions must not appear [to] offend their sensibilities or exceed [the] bounds [of] good taste, thereby confirming Soviet propaganda image of Americans as crude barbarians and tending [to] unite popular opposition to US. Specifically we must take into account [the] fact that for generations Stalin has been [the] only leader people have known; he has been carefully sheltered from popular resentment against bureaucratic, doctrinal regime; moreover, he has been systematically built up as symbol of [the] power and prestige acquired by [the] Soviet state in war and peace.[59]

The bureaucratic conflict, which had precluded any immediate US response, now produced days of wrangling, culminating in a series of meetings in the White House. The first skirmish pitted Jackson against Charles Bohlen and Paul Nitze. Jackson insisted upon a four-power conference, but the State Department was locked into inactivity. Bohlen, contending that the "immediate present is probably not the time of maximum opportunity. . . . Stress and dissension will take time, some weeks or months, to manifest themselves," insisted that Eisenhower make no proposal before Britain and France were consulted.[60] Bedell Smith, the former Director of Central Intelligence who had become Under-secretary of State, loyal to his department rather than the CIA's penchant for covert operations, drove home the point in correspondence with the PSB: "Aggressive heightening of cold war pressures . . . [would] probably tend to assist the new regime to consolidate its position." He opposed any presidential speech, since "the initial shock of Stalin's death has produced for the time being unity and coherence in the regime".[61]

Jackson took the case to the top by writing Foster Dulles, who had been at his vacation retreat on Duck Island on the New York–Canada border while the bureaucratic battle was raging. He gave detailed responses to the State Department's objections and reiterated, "Stalin's death provides us with the first real, normal opportunity to assume a position of initiative toward (a) Russia, (b) the satellites, (c) Western Europe, (d) Asia, (e) our own people." Jackson then concluded, perhaps with a lack of tact, "One important by-product of this central decision would be a reinvigorated Department of State whose personnel would be able to participate actively in a crusade of the highest magnitude, and thereby emerge from the national doghouse in which they unfortunately find themselves today."[62]

The climactic meeting came in the NSC on 11 March. Eisenhower was still indecisive, his opening statement a strange homily that "Russia would have sought more peaceful and normal relations with the rest of the world" if Stalin had been in control of the Politburo. Jackson stepped in to introduce his plan, which he argued was based on policy dating from NSC 20/4 in 1948. He called on Eisenhower to make his speech, including the call for a conference of Foreign Ministers, within the next week. Insisting "this was the greatest opportunity presented to the US in many years to seize the initiative", he added, "From the moment of delivery of that speech, all the arms of the US Government, all the Embassies and missions abroad, all the other facets of American power and influence were to be linked close together in the pursuit of the objective [of upsetting the Soviet bloc]. The follow-up would have to be swift, sure, and coordinated."

Foster Dulles initially encouraged this strategy, asserting, "What we must do was to play up this nationalism and discontent for all it was worth, to seize every opportunity by this device to break down the monolithic Soviet control over the Satellite states," but then, with consummate irony, the former trumpeter of liberation abandoned any support for action:

> It seemed especially doubtful . . . as to whether this was the appropriate moment to carry the offensive direct to the Soviet Union. The Soviets were now involved in a family funeral and it might be best to wait until the corpse was buried, and the mourners gone off to their homes to read the will, before we begin our campaign to create discord in the family. If we moved precipitately, we might very well enhance Soviet family loyalty and disrupt the free world's.

Jackson's proposal of a conference of Foreign Ministers might have "quite disastrous effects", as Western Europe "would believe [US] leadership erratic,

venturesome, and arbitrary". Any speech by Eisenhower "should substitute
... a call for the end of hostilities in Asia generally, and in Korea and
Indochina specifically, under appropriate safeguards".

The President now re-entered the discussion. In a maneuver which
would often occur in NSC meetings, he avoided the crux of the dispute and
embarked on a tangent. A speech, instead of appealing on a specific issue
like Korea, should "concentrate on our determination to raise the general
standard of living throughout the world. We do need something dramatic to
rally the peoples of the world around some idea, some hope, of a better
future."

Whatever the merits, both as propaganda and as policy, of Eisenhower's
"focus ... on the common man's yearning for food, shelter, and a decent standard of living", its immediate effect was to suspend the strategy of liberation.
The appeal to economic prosperity could only be a long-term aspiration rather
than a psychological call to arms. The President had shelved Jackson's plans;
in passing, he mentioned that he shared Foster Dulles's "anxiety" about the
conference of Foreign Ministers.[63]

To the amazement of those who had been denied an offensive, Foster Dulles
continued to promote in public the general concept of upsetting the Soviet
bloc. He spoke to a special meeting of civilian consultants about

ending the peril of the Soviet Union. . . . This could be done by inducing dintegra-
tion of Soviet power. This power is already overextended and represents tyrannical
rule over unwilling peoples. If we keep our pressures on, psychological and other-
wise, we may either force a collapse of the Kremlin regime or else transform the
Soviet orbit from a union of satellites dedicated to aggression into a coalition of
defense only.[64]

In contrast, C. D. Jackson concluded with dismay, "If we do not take the initiative and capitalize on the dismay, confusion, fear, and selfish hopes brought
about by this opportunity, we will be giving the enemy the time to pull himself
together, get his wind back, and present us with a new monolithic structure
which we will spend years attempting to analyze."[65] Jackson tried to keep
American options open through meetings with Eastern European emigres such
as Stanislaw Mikolajczyk, a leader of the Polish Government in exile during
World War II.[66]

The Administration's hesitancy was fully exposed on 15 March when the
Soviet leadership seized the initiative. The new Prime Minister, Georgi
Malenkov, called for a new era in US–Soviet relations and "resolution through
peaceful means" of outstanding problems with all States. Moscow dwelt upon
the necessity of a truce in the Koren War while internal measures included
an amnesty for convicts and withdrawal of the "Doctors' Plot" allegations
made by Stalin in 1952.[67] Rostow captured the frustration of the activists:
"Malenkov's speech and our dallying makes me mad. We never should have

been in the position of replying; and we'll have to meet the bugger anywhere. We must learn to move fast and like grown-ups, God damn it."[68]

According to speech writer Emmet Hughes, Eisenhower now tried to regain the initiative with a plea for peace. He allegedly waxed lyrical:

Here is what I would like to say.

The jet plane that roars over your head costs three-quarters of a million dollars. That is more money than a man earning ten thousand dollars every year is going to make in his lifetime. What world can afford this sort of thing for long? . . .

Now there could be another road before us – the road of disarmament. What does this mean? It means for everybody in the world: bread, butter, clothes, homes, hospitals, schools – all the good and necessary things for decent living.

So let *this* be the choice we offer. If we take this second road, all of us can produce more of these good things for life – and we, the United States, will help them still more. How do we go about it? Let us talk straight: *no* double talk, *no* sophisticated political formulas, *no* slick propaganda devices.[69]

Hughes's account of a President dramatically altering the debate is not borne out by documents, nor is it clear that Eisenhower's thoughts were really upon peace rather than propaganda. What did emerge, after more than five weeks of wrangling, was not Jackson and Rostow's crusade for freedom but the State Department's strategy of a subtle challenge emphasizing the positive effects of reduced military expenditure.[70] The approach was unveiled as "A Chance for Peace" in an address by Eisenhower to the American Society of Newspaper Editors on 16 April. He offered an accommodation with the Soviets, provided Moscow helped end the Korean War, signed a peace treaty for Austria, accepted a "free and united Germany", allowed free elections in Eastern Europe, and made other concessions.[71]

The address, supplemented by a speech by Foster Dulles to the same group, was never a serious effort at negotiation; no one in the Administration expected the Soviets to accept the US conditions. Despite the State Department's disclaimer that it was "not a psychological warfare maneuver",[72] it was a concerted effort to win over world opinion. The speech was distributed worldwide not only by the Voice of America but also through "unofficial" channels like Radio Free Europe, Radio Free Asia, and the International Confederation of Free Trade Unions.[73] A British Broadcasting Corporation programme reached 20 million people.[74]

Although Eisenhower's delivery of the speech was hindered as he suffered stomach cramps, initial reactions were positive. The *New York Post* called the address "America's voice at its best" while the *New York Times* saw it as "magnificent and deeply moving".[75] The State Department effused that the talk had elicited "more public interest and excited more favorable comment throughout the word than any official statement of high policy" since the Marshall Plan, and Jackson acknowledged, "We had most certainly seized the initiative and the President had secured better results than had been anticipated."[76] The impact soon wore off, however, as the Soviets continued to promote "peace" without taking the steps demanded by the US. The speech was also overtaken by Winston Churchill's sudden and dramatic call on 11 May for an immediate summit of the British, Soviet, and US leaders.

Far from being the catalyst for US victory, the episode only highlighted weaknesses in US policy-making, with Jackson and the State Department established as adversaries. In the aftermath of the "Chance for Peace", the department portrayed, through friendly journalists, "the enthusiasm of the amateurs pitted against the experience and caution of the professionals".[77] US News and World Reports added, "The President's underlying intention [is] to apply an unrelenting pressure that will drive the Russians onto the defensive – for the first time since the cold war started – and keep them there. . . . The President is meanwhile warning quietly warning his aides against attempting any fancy maneuvers designed simply to show up the Soviets for propaganda reasons. Such high jinks, conceivably, might defer a cold-war solution."[78]

Eisenhower, rather than providing leadership, had allowed Foster Dulles to make the key decisions by default; his fetish for a dramatic speech proved no substitute for a coherent strategy. Amidst the squabbling, the CIA, led by Allen Dulles, the brother of the Secretary of State, was unwilling or unable to press for liberation. Instead, Radio Free Europe filled the vacuum:

> We should say to our listeners that this is the time for them to demand the punishment of those who oppress them in the village, the factory, the mine, the kolkhoz. They should demand purification of the regime from top to bottom, expose petty thieves, foremen or managers who molest girl workers, bosses who live in luxury, civil servants who are arrogant and ill-mannered, lick-spittle favorites in universities and youth organizations, [and] manifestly ignorant professors.[79]

Most importantly, the Washington bureaucracy had sabotaged the coordination of the Cold War offensive through the Psychological Strategy Board. The State Department had always resented what it perceived as an intruder into its domain, and Jackson, rather than challenging an established agency, turned to the PSB as a scapegoat. Complaining about the "gaps in organizations and coordination", Jackson claimed that "the PSB paper [on Cancellation], which should have been a key document . . . , is worthless", never admitting that it was the State Department's foot-dragging, rather than the PSB's ineptitude, that had limited the plans.[80]

For example, the working party led by PSB officials had persisted with planning for the exploitation of Stalin's death. Their blueprint "to foster any and all divisive forces within the top hierarchy of the Kremlin", finally approved on 23 April, confronted Communist leaders "with difficult major choices in a way which does not encourage them to close ranks, but which tends to isolate them and divide their counsels, while uniting humanity, especially the free world, with us".[81] Specific operations, however, were limited because of the

State Department's hesitancy. The CIA's intelligence assessment was perceptive about the nature of the PSB's work: "[This] merely claimed to be an interim strategic concept. It did not purport to offer the final solution of the Cold War and thus left the vacuum which resulted from the lack of a strategic plan against which the efforts of all instruments of US national policy could be harnessed."[82]

Jackson summarized his own difficulties in a long and vehement letter to Eisenhower in early April:

> If you were to ask me how I would evaluate in one word these first six weeks, that would have to be "failure". . . . I was unable to persuade you or the Secretary of State, plus quite a few lesser characters, that it was essential to move immediately on the single most important event since V-J Day – the death of Stalin. The result has been that, for a month, we have given a virtual monopoly to the Soviets over the minds of people all over the world – and in that month, they have moved with vigor and disarming plausibility.

Most telling was Jackson's recitation of the bureaucratic obstacles he faced, an assessment which revealed that he was beset with the same problems that had affected the PSB:

> So long as [Jackson] sticks to the script of a radio program, or the contents of a booklet, or advising a Cabinet Officer on how a situation should be handled, he is safe. But, as soon as he gets into the real guts of his job, which is well over and beyond radio and booklets and off-the-cuff advice, he is in trouble, because he is actually moving into areas where a Secretary of State, a Secretary of Defense, a Director of the CIA, a Director of the MSA [Mutual Security Administration] could quite truthfully and with complete administrative logic, say, "Hey, who's running this department?"[83]

What Jackson would not admit, either from loyalty or from misguided adulation of Eisenhower, was that the problem was exacerbated by the president's lack of leadership. Jackson praised, "You felt that psychological warfare had to be an integral and coordinated part of the foreign diplomatic and military policy of the United States; and you selected a man to bring about that integration and coordination."[84] Yet, in the end, it was Eisenhower's failure to take charge that had hindered action. Years later, Jackson would reach the conclusion, "[The President is] not a national or a political leader. . . . While he can become momentarily fascinated by individual pieces of the international jigsaw puzzle, he does not seem to be able to see what the picture would look like when all the pieces were put together."[85]

This change of heart would come far too late for the PSB. Its fate was sealed by the coincidence that, as the State Department and Jackson squabbled, the special committee reviewing psychological strategy, the Jackson Committee, was issuing its report. Logically the committee should have focused upon the conflict between the principle of liberation and the State Department's caution.

Indeed, its final report recognized, "While the Psychological Strategy Board has concentrated heavily on planning, it has possessed neither sufficient power to exercise effective coordination nor the techniques adequate to produce meaningful evaluations. Even the planning function has been carried on in the midst of ambiguity and serious interdepartmental controversy." A central organization was required "to pull these things together . . . so a symphonic theme can be played which will be heard and enjoyed by the people of the world and our people".[86]

The obvious solution was to challenge the State Department and build upon the PSB's coordinating function, but, like C. D. Jackson, the Jackson Committee preferred to shoot at an easy target. It set up the pretext, based on the testimony of the State Department's Charles Bohlen, that the board was "founded on the misconception that psychological strategy exists apart from offical policies and actions" to recommend its abolition. The PSB had never made such a claim – indeed, its entire *raison d'être* was to integrate the policies of different departments into a comprehensive strategy – but the State Department was glad to back the Jackson Committee, and Eisenhower merely rubber-stamped the recommendations.[87] By May, more than a month before the Committee officially reported, press reports summarized the prevailing sentiment, "True psychological warfare, properly defined, is so bound up with the conduct and demeanor of the whole American Government, that you cannot establish a separate department of psychological warriors."[88]

The PSB was replaced by the Operations Coordinating Board (OCB), an interdepartmental body mandated to implement the guidelines of the National Security Council. The new arrangement had some organizational advantages: sheltered by the NSC from the departmental obstructions that had undermined the PSB, the OCB was effective in developing regional and country programs and was also authorized to review certain covert projects. Robert Tufts, who first proposed the OCB to the Jackson Committee, explained, "The jurisdiction of the Operations Board would be as wide as that of the National Security Council. All actions in the cold war have an impact on the wills and attitudes of other governments and peoples. . . . This fact would be recognized without falling into the mistake of attempting to single out some indefinable elements which are peculiarly psychological."[89]

The fundamental issue was still avoided, however. Was the United States committed to an all-out global offensive against Soviet Communism? The PSB's chief specialist on psychological and ideological warfare, Edward Lilly, wrote to C. D. Jackson:

> Our present national policy of reducing the power and influence of USSR is as dynamic as yeastless dough. Reduce Soviet power to what size and for what? Is there any certainty that communist power will stay reduced? Or do we just let the next generation worry about that? We pass to our children the problem we did not have the guts to solve.[90]

In contrast, Bohlen poured cold water on any expansion of operations, since "the expectations had been greater than the facts would justify". He asked, "Is it wise to nail to our masthead the objective of liberation?"[91] The Jackson Committee did not resolve the dispute, and a policy document of June 1953 persisted with the vague injunction that the United States, "without taking undue risks, [should] place the maximum strain on Soviet–satellite relations and try to weaken Soviet control over the satellite countries".[92]

Intriguingly, Foster Dulles was on the verge of abandoning his State Department staff and returning to liberation. He gave Eisenhower and other officials a picture of doom in the battle for mankind: "The existing threat posed by the Soviets to the Western world is the most terrible and fundamental in the latter's 1,000 years of domination. This threat differs in quality from the threat of a Napoleon or Hitler. It is like the invasion by Islam in the 10th century. Now the clear issue is: can Western civilization survive?" In sharp contrast to his reaction to Stalin's death, he claimed, "The present course we are following is a fatal one for us and the free world. It is just defensive."

Foster Dulles now pondered how to "turn the Soviet bloc into a loose alliance without capacities, far different from Stalin's monolith", asking, "Where can we have a success?" within Moscow's sphere of influence. He offered as possibilities the liberation of Korea "if the armistice [broke] down", of Hainan with Chinese Nationalist troops "and U.S. naval and air power", and of Albania. Foster Dulles even raised the question of freeing Hungary, Bulgaria, and Czechoslovakia. Although "to do any one of these might take two years to accomplish", this was "all the more reason to begin at once".[93]

To establish its long-term strategy, the Administration embarked upon Operation Solarium, in which three teams of State Department personnel, military leaders, and selected academics were given different mandates and commanded to produce overall strategies and programmes. Team A, chaired by George Kennan, accepted that the United States "must try to weaken Soviet power and bring about its withdrawal within traditional boundaries . . . [but] rather than pressing for the destruction of the Soviet state, [the United States] should wait for an evolution in Soviet life and patterns of behavior". This evolution would be encouraged by exploiting the "vulnerabilities of the Soviet Bloc . . . by various covert and overt means", but the emphasis would be on persuading "the Soviet leaders that it is not too late to turn back from their present course."[94] Team B agreed but added that the United States should accelerate the evolution "with the warning of general war", including nuclear attacks, "as the primary sanction against further Soviet bloc aggression". General war would be prompted by "any advance of Soviet bloc military forces beyond [their] present borders".[95]

In contrast, Team C insisted, "The US cannot continue to live with the Soviet threat. So long as the Soviet Union exists, it will not fall apart, it must and can be shaken apart." Criticizing existing policy, Team C insisted that the

United States must confront the "lack of a national strategy to end the Cold War by winning it". Within five years, the United States would secure the unification of Germany and Korea, an Austria free from Soviet troops, and a Nationalist stronghold on the mainland of China. By 1965, an "all-out offensive" to bring Soviet satellites into "the family of Free Nations" would be completed. After that would come "the elimination of the Communist conspiracy" and "the overthrow of the Communist regime in China".[96]

Solarium dissolved into disagreement. Meeting the teams, Eisenhower offered no lead but meandered along a tangent: "The only thing worse than losing a global war was winning it. . . . There would be no individual freedom after the next global war." He worried about the paradox that, the more aggressive the strategy to advance freedom, "the more you lose the individual liberty which you are trying to save and become a garrison state". This did nothing to resolve the conflict between the teams, especially Team A and Team C, who were locked "in strong disagreement . . . differing on the intentions and objectives of the Russians". Told that six weeks of discussions had not reconciled the differences, Eisenhower "seemed very put out" but left it to the NSC staff "to work out" a plan and present it to the National Security Council on 30 July.[97]

On the surface, the NSC's discussion turned against Task Force C, with Allen Dulles presenting the CIA's assessment that, while the Soviets might "lack vitality over the long run", their collapse might "not show up critically for 10 or 15 years yet". However, the NSC not only maintained the option of individual operations to weaken the Soviet bloc but encouraged such initiatives. Allen Dulles had already called for a renewed US effort to destabilize the Guatemalan Government; now he and Foster Dulles proposed that the United States should coordinate its planning to overthrow the Albanian regime, with an interdepartmental task force being established "under one competent individual". Eisenhower asked for careful consideration of the plans "because of the question of who gets it and who gets hurt".

The NSC did not endorse any proposals but directed its Planning Board, working with the three teams, to draft a new basic national security policy and recommend any immediate measures, "including proposed specific actions with respect to particular Communist-controlled nations". Foster Dulles reinforced this case-by-case approach to liberation by explaining, "A start could be made on a more positive policy in Albania without the risk of war. Such was not the case in Hainan [an island off the coast of Communist China], which could be taken only by overt military action."[98]

Eisenhower revisionists, committed to the portrayal of a strong President, have portrayed Solarium as a supreme example of the President's leadership. Yet, apart from a burst of rhetoric at the end of the NSC meeting, it is difficult to see what Eisenhower resolved. C. D. Jackson was "disturbed at President's closing remarks which, although flattering to participants, virtually threw cold water on all action",[99] yet it was the Dulles brothers, not the President, who grappled with the issue of how far the United States should go in its confrontation with Moscow. More importantly, Eisenhower's failure to get a clear NSC directive on liberation allowed the general struggle between Jackson's activism and the State Department's caution to continue.

The effect of this indecision was exacerbated because, as Solarium was being discussed, the Administration was presented with a second opportunity to exploit instability within the Soviet sphere. On 17 June 1953, after spontaneous strikes led by construction workers, 5,000 demonstrators gathered in the streets of East Berlin. Ostensibly they were protesting at the economic policy of the East German government, in particular a 10 percent increase in work norms issued in late May, but the rally soon became a general challenge to the regime. When a Cabinet Minister addressed the marchers, he was pushed aside by a worker who roared, "What you have declared here is of no interest to us. We want to be free. Our demonstration is not against norms. . . . This is a people's revolt."

Up to 30,000 people gathered the next day on the Potsdamer Platz in the centre of East Berlin, overturning police shelters, tearing up Communist banners and posters, and taking down the Soviet flag from atop the Brandenburg Gate. The Peoples' Police opened fire to no effect; the crowds grew – estimates ranged from 50,000 to several hundred thousand – chanting, "Ivan go home". An official in the Soviet embassy later claimed that he was on the phone with East German leader Walter Ulbricht as "drunks" smashed windows outside the offices of the ruling Socialist Unity Party when "Ulbricht put down the phone and said, 'It's all over.' He said it in a way which translates roughly in Russian, 'It's the end.'" The Soviet official thought this peculiar, since it would take only "five minutes to sort [the demonstrators] out". Within hours, the Soviets had moved three armored divisions into East Berlin to quell the marchers.[100]

US psychological warfare played its part in the demonstrations. A week earlier, special guidance on an attempt by the East German government to ease opposition to the increased work norms through conciliatory economic and social policies commented:

> [The East German people] have successfully resisted Moscow's . . . puppets and have won immense concessions. . . . This should give new heart to East European farmers, workers, priests, and youth. They should continue their passive resistance to the further Sovietization of their country. A rollback of the Soviet power may have begun.[101]

Discontent was encouraged by Radio in the American Sector (RIAS), which had had five daily broadcasts and "special labor programs . . . working up a mood of rebellion in East German factories since 1950".[102] When the uprisings began, the station emphasized, "free world solidarity with oppressed peoples of Communist-controlled East Germany, . . . endorsing the substance of the demands made by the workers and population of East Germany for a general improvement of the harsh and unsatisfactory conditions".[103] To ensure its message was not jammed by the Soviets, RIAS doubled its programming, taking over three medium-wave frequencies.[104] The German Trade Union Federation in West Berlin used the station to support the marchers and their demands for tolerable work norms, prompt payment of wages, and a decreased cost of living.[105] Support for RIAS was lent by the US Armed Forces Network, which broadcast to American troops but also had an estimated "eavesdropper" audience of up to 60 million.[106]

Allen Dulles tried to distance RIAS from events, telling the National Security Council, "The US had nothing whatsoever to do with inciting these riots. . . . Our reaction thus far had been to confine ourselves, in broadcasts which were not attributable, to expressions of sympathy and admiration with an admixture of references to the great traditions of 1848."[107] The denial was disingenuous. US-sponsored broadcasts may not have instructed the demonstrators to take to the streets, but their references to freedom, economic rights, and "the great traditions of 1848" helped fuel the protests. In January, RIAS had declared its objective of "constructive subversion" by "maintain[ing] contact with the people of the Soviet Zone and East Berlin in order to strengthen their belief in democratic principles, maintain their hope for freedom, stiffen their spirit of resistance to Soviet Communist rule, and maintain their confidence in the policies of the Western powers".[108] The Jackson Committee reported:

> RIAS has made an important contribution in impressing on the population of eastern Germany the determination of the West and in sustaining their hopes for eventual liberation from the Soviet Union. . . . It has built up a large and devoted following among the German population in the Soviet Zone and is generally believed to be accepted by many of its German listeners as a *bona fide* German station.[109]

In late May, the PSB had expressed its "special interest in RIAS in view of its great importance for psychological operations. . . . Effective operation of RIAS should be insured by stepping up its facilities as necessary and feasible."[110]

Testimonials to the role in the uprising of RIAS, described by the US High Commissioner in Germany, John McCloy, as "the spiritual and psychological center of resistance in a blacked out area of Communist domination"[111] were numerous. C. D. Jackson confirmed to Representative John Taber, the Chairman of the House Appropriations Committee, that RIAS's output was "detailed, factual and timely. . . . The broadcasts were commenced aggressively on 16 June and have continued up to . . . 17 July along lines calculated to exploit popular unrest."[112] Taber, normally a savage critic of Administration expenditure, needed no convincing – he had surprised witnesses in the spring by remarking, "We don't need to spend much time on RIAS; we all know what a wonderful job it's doing."[113] The CIA's director of covert operations, Frank Wisner, later noted, "RIAS [was] an extremely valuable psychological warfare asset [with] a demonstrable and substantial impact within the Soviet Zone" and an "especially creditable" performance during the East German uprising.[114] As Edmond Taylor, a former PSB employee, summarized, "No 'psychological warriors' in history have ever furnished a more dramatic illustration of their art."[115]

RIAS's role was accentuated by the decision of its director, Gordon Ewing, to encourage the spread of the revolt. Ewing recognized "that he would be pouring gasoline on the flames" but believed that, despite the inevitable crushing of the demonstrations, "the spirit of resistance . . . would be immeasurably strengthened by even a temporary victory over the Communist regime".[116] On the evening of 16 June, Ewing authorized a commentary that emphasized the success of the demonstrations and called for more action. If protesters tolerated a resumption of the Government's policies, East Germany would be "so valuable for the Soviets that [it] . . . would become too important to be a bargaining object in the diplomatic market, too good to be given up". The commentary concluded, "Dear listeners, we would be delighted to inform you of more victories in days to come."[117] RIAS was supported by Radio Liberation, which targeted Soviet troops stationed in Berlin. A typical broadcast made the appeal, "Soldiers and officers of the Soviet Army, the German workers' struggle against Kremlin oppression is unfolding before your eyes. . . . [On an] order to fire on the demonstrators remember they are not enemies of our country but are defenders of freedom. . . . The workers of East Berlin are fighting for the cause of all mankind and for the delivery of the whole world, including our motherland, from communism. Help them!"[118]

The State Department, while noting "it is now pretty clear that [RIAS] played a major role in spreading demonstrations from East Berlin to the Zone",[119] played a double game. It used the protests – "factually and as fully as possible", of course – to "demonstrate the true relationship between Soviet Communists and the workers and population of East Germany". It was not so confident, however, that it would nail US colours to the mast. It would not disseminate a high-level statement "because we do not wish to run the risk of identifying ourselves with the demonstrations".[120] Washington journalists used leaks to report, "State Department officials . . . apparently feel that Mr. Ewing ran grave risks in the lengths to which he went in helping stir up and urge on the anti-Communist riots."[121]

Caught by surprise by the intensity of the riots, the NSC was again paralysed. C. D. Jackson urged support for the demonstrators, who had shown "for the first time since their enslavement that the slaves of the Soviet Union felt that they could do something. . . . The $64 question was how far that US was prepared to go if this gets really cracking." Initially Eisenhower was receptive to aggressive action. Assured by Jackson that the United States could not only prevent a Soviet "slaughter of the population" but could assist the "beginning of the disintegration of the Soviet Empire", the President agreed that the United States should consider arming the population, although the "revolution would have to be more widespread before the US could consider intervening". Foster Dulles was noncommittal, however, so Eisenhower would do no more than ask for a report on action over the next 60 days.[122]

So when Soviet forces quelled the protests the Administration did not intervene, apart from an increase in aid to West Berlin and a letter from Eisenhower to West German leader Konrad Adenauer. A proposal from the CIA base chief in Berlin to hand out pistols, rifles, and Sten guns to the protesters was rejected by Wisner and John Bross, responsible for Eastern European operations. The rioters could be given asylum and sympathy but nothing more. When Allen Dulles returned to duty the next morning, the Soviets had already moved in an armored division. The opportunity had been lost. As Bross recalled, "It was the one time that I saw Allen angry and disappointed in me."[123]

Still, the doomed PSB clung to the possibility of action. Acting quickly on Eisenhower's request, they produced a battle plan within a week for the National Security Council. The US Government should "nourish resistance to Communist oppression through satellite Europe, short of mass rebellion" and "exploit satellite unrest as demonstrable proof that the Soviet Empire is beginning to crumble". Within 60 days, the United States would "covertly stimulate acts and attitudes short of mass rebellion", "establish, where feasible, secure resistance nuclei capable of further large-scale expansion", "intensify defection programs", "stimulate free world governmental, religious, and trade union activities capable of psychological effect behind the Iron Curtain", and "encourage elimination of key puppet officials". The United States would then "organize, train and equip underground organizations capable of launching large-scale raids or sustained guerrilla warfare" and press for elections in Eastern Europe, inclusion of Soviet nationals in the Volunteer Freedom Corps, and renewal of balloon operations to drop leaflets behind the Iron Curtain.[124] Far from blocking any steps which could lead to a repetition of the uprising, the NSC expressed "considerable enthusiasm" for the proposals.[125]

The Eisenhower Administration had twice declined to press US intervention in Eastern Europe, yet the President lacked the will to rule out liberation. This self-imposed ambiguity continued in the aftermath of Solarium. The Planning Board's review of global strategy, commissioned by the NSC in July, finally rejected Team C's program for the "conquering" of the Soviet Union and concluded, "Short of general war, acceptable negotiated settlements with the USSR are the only means of substantially reducing the Soviet threat." Division continued, however, over an offensive within the Soviet bloc to force diplomatic concessions. One side within the Planning Board was ready "to forego pressures at least against the USSR itself [and] to attempt to reduce tensions on secondary issues", but Side B sought "to maintain pressures against the USSR which do not involve grave risk of general war".[126]

The National Security Council met three times in October to resolve the debate, but if its "New Look" global strategy, NSC 162/2, emphasized the build-up of nuclear forces to deter the Soviets, it was far less clear on non-military plans. At a session on 7 October, Eisenhower said simply that he preferred Side B's recommendation for the maintenance of pressure against the Soviet bloc. So debate over the policy was deadlocked, with the State Department, supported by the CIA's Deputy Director of Intelligence, Robert Amory, linking covert action to "conditions which will induce the Soviet leadership to be more receptive to acceptable to negotiated settlements" and the Department of Defense preferring the break-up of the Soviet bloc without recourse to negotiation.[127]

The NSC made no final decision until meetings on 22 and 29 October, and it was Foster Dulles, not the President, who made the key contribution. Having flirted with a more aggressive stance in the spring, he once more chose caution, warning against "providing a blank check for US support of all the aspirations of all peoples everywhere for freedom and independence". The United States should merely issue its "endorsement of the legitimate aspirations of these peoples". The Secretary of State now questioned the "detachment of Albania from the Soviet bloc as well as an assault on Hainan Island".[128] The NSC agreed that "the detachment of any major European satellite from the Soviet bloc does not now appear feasible except by Soviet acquiescence or by war".[129]

A similar process occurred with policy towards Communist China, adopted by the NSC on 5 November. Again Eisenhower was peripheral in the discussion. The Joint Chiefs of Staff had proposed as an "ultimate, though not an immediate, objective the removal of the present Chinese Communist regime and its replacement by a regime not hostile to the US". Under-secretary of State Bedell Smith accepted the long-range objective but noted crisply that the NSC was considering a situation in which there was "very little prospect of upsetting the present regime". Thus the council retreated from any offensive "in the absence of further Chinese Communist aggression or a basic change in the situation," although it maintained the objective of building up Chinese Nationalist forces "for raids against the Communist mainland and seaborne commerce with Communist China and for such offensive operations as may be in the US interest".[130]

Yet the language of the NSC's decisions, as usual, was not definitive. In NSC 162, liberation might not have been identified as an objective of measures to push Moscow into negotiations. However, the injunction "to create and exploit troublesome problems for the USSR, impair Soviet relations with Communist China, complicate control in the satellites, and retard the growth of the military and economic potential of the Soviet bloc"[131] allowed activists to persist with plans with no thought of a peaceful settlement with the Soviets.

The confusion culminated in the National Security Council's revision of policy on Eastern Europe in December 1953. NSC 174 insisted, "Full advantage should be taken of the means of diplomacy, propaganda, economic policy, and covert operations to maintain the morale of anti-Soviet elements, to sow confusion and discredit the authority of the regimes, to disrupt Soviet–satellite relationships, and generally to maximize Soviet difficulties," but then added the caveat, "The US should not encourage premature action on [the] part [of peoples in the Soviet bloc] which will bring upon them reprisals involving further terror and repression."

The NSC agreed that it would encourage passive resistance, "foster satellite nationalism", and "cooperate with ... forces such as religious, cultural, and social which are natural allies in the struggle against Soviet imperialism"; however, it balked at the uprisings that were a logical outcome of those measures: "Continuous and careful attention must be given to the fine line, which is not stationary, between exhortations to keep up morale and to maintain passive resistance, and invitations to suicide." So the United States would "encourage defection of key satellite personnel ... but not mass defection" and "support or make use of refugees ... [who] can contribute to the attainment of US objectives, but do not recognize governments in exile". The special case of Albania would "be kept under continuous review".[132] The National Security Advisor, Robert Cutler, was honest enough to note the inadequacy of the NSC's resolutions. He called for a "more comprehensive policy formulation concerning the exploitation of Soviet vulnerabilities", noting for example that there were "no adequate guidelines ... [on] whether the US should pursue a policy ... to support in some form the independence of the nationalities of the Soviet Union".[133]

The NSC may not have endorsed the aggressiveness of C. D. Jackson and his supporters within the CIA; however, by failing to draw a firm line, Eisenhower and his advisors gave the activists the space to pursue their operations. A week before the East German uprising, the President told the National Young Republican Organization of his efforts "to encourage strains and stresses within the ranks of the 800 millions in the Soviet world now deprived the hopes and the rewards of a free life".[134] The following month, he told Britain's Acting Foreign Secretary, Lord Salisbury, and the French Foreign Minister, Georges Bidault, that "he wanted to harry the Communists by every means" and pressed the idea of a "Free Corps" of East European refugees. Photographers were quickly herded into the room before Salisbury or Bidault could respond.[135]

Jackson exploited the possibilities in East Germany. He eschewed overt stimulation of uprisings, writing a journalist who had suggested US intervention, "It would be immoral and inefficient to provoke massacres, which would not only kill off the best men but also destroy our position in the minds of the people behind the Iron Curtain."[136] At the same time, he was eager for a high-profile symbol of US support for "freedom", for example, through the provision of free food to the East German population. Shipments to Eastern Europe had been considered months before the June demonstrations, with advocates like the US Minister to Hungary writing eloquently, "The force to lick hate is love. Giving food to the needy is good neighborliness, the basic concept of Western civilization."[137] The idea was set aside because the deliveries required the consent of local governments,[138] but this was not the case in Berlin, where East Berliners could collect food from Western zones.

Jackson, using a report by a working group chaired by Foster and Allen Dulles's sister Eleanor,[139] quickly obtained Eisenhower's support for the program. The President was "most anxious that this be done immediately while matters are still hot", adding the embellishment that Danish cheese should be bought with $1 million from the CIA. He was also ready to extend the food distribution to Czechoslovakia, Hungary, and Poland.[140] The President's approval was reinforced by the illusion of more cautious officials that the initiative could be distinguished from US psychological strategy. As the US embassy in Bonn labelled the situation, "Food, yes. Propaganda, no."[141]

On 17 July, as 4,500 tons of food were sent by ship to Western Germany, an estimated 8,000 to 15,000 people queued 10 to 12 abreast for the deliveries, some people standing for up to 14 hours. The first phase of the program lasted a month, and the second set of deliveries began at the end of August. Significantly, approximately two-thirds of the food was handed out to people who lived outside East Berlin, many of them residing deep within the Communist zone.[142] The US embassy enthused that the West was "once more a real, vital force in their lives".[143] As usual, C. D. Jackson saw a beachhead for further action: "[This was the] fastest and smoothest joint operation that I have seen since I have been down here. We are prepared to swing into action for Hungary whenever you blow the whistle."[144]

Amidst the warning of embassy staff in Germany against "a blatant propaganda campaign to ram home the American role",[145] reduced distribution because of harsher East German restrictions on travel, and the worries of European allies, the food programme was ended in early October but not before West Berlin mayor Ernest Reuter called it "no less than a continuation of the events of 17 June by other means".[146] Jackson finally had his aggressive campaign, notably through the renewed use of balloons to drop leaflets and "freedom" currency into Eastern Europe. Only weeks before the East German uprising, there had been riots in factories and cities throughout Czechoslovakia over economic restrictions, and the National Committee for Free Europe had tried to seize the advantage with another propaganda offensive. Radio Free Europe targeted the police and the army, asking whether they would fire upon their countrymen. Officials were encouraged to sabotage bureaucratic processes and students were told to prepare for the day of freedom. While they should "be suspicious . . . [about] strangers who talk about resistance?" They should also

> think about what you can do, what part will be yours when the time comes. And when you think, remember how great will be the reward – to be a free man rebuilding a free country in a free, fraternal United Europe; to have *Koruno* that will actually buy something – an English motor-bike, a French literary review, a novel by Hemingway, a honeymoon on the Italian lakes, all in a world without police.[147]

Two days after the East German demonstrations, Jackson was demanding that Radio Free Europe call Czechs on to the streets. He provoked an argument with Robert Lang, the Director of RFE, who protested, "You've got the wrong idea what propaganda can do. Are there American troops going to the border?" When Lang continued, "If you want somebody to do this, you're going to have to send somebody else," he was instructed by his superiors, "It isn't yours. It belongs to us and you will do what you're told." Lang recalled, "I said I won't do it and then I went in the bathroom and had a good cry."[148]

After a meeting with Foster and Allen Dulles, Lang won a postponement of the initial plan, but Jackson persisted with the offensive through the stockpiling of 100,000 balloons and the use of US military aircraft. He promoted the idea, passed to him from a private contact, of a "Gifts from Heaven" initiative to carry "vitamins, razor blades, seeds, knitting wool, etc." into the Soviet bloc.[149] Initially held up by the fear that the Soviets would charge the United States with using the balloons for biological warfare, the plan was adopted in the wake of the East German uprising and RFE's success in Czechoslovakia.[150]

In homage to Shakespeare, the new operations were codenamed Caliban and Prospero with a "strange mixture of frenzy, humor, and goodwill (to say nothing of good luck), which combined to make Prospero's magic potent".[151] In five days, 12 million leaflets, pictures of the East German demonstrations, and replicas of coins were scattered across Czechoslovakia, supported by Radio Free Europe's Voice of Free Czechoslovakia.[152] RFE analysts gave a glowing report of success: "All last week people were jumping like frogs to catch the leaflets as they came down. Many people wore the coins around their necks." Soldiers, police, and even schoolchildren were despatched to collect the leaflets, MiGs were scrambled to try to shoot down the balloons, and postmen had orders to ask customers if they had any of the dropped materials.[153] There was even a prohibition on swimming in certain rivers to prevent the collection of leaflets.[154]

Support from "private" US organisations for their Eastern European counterparts was a key element of Jackson's strategy. After an appeal by Eisenhower, religious organisations worked with CARE and the American Red

Cross to orchestrate a clothing drive for East Germany.[155] Jackson ensured that East Germans learned of the declaration of the International Confederation of Free Trade Unions, "We call upon the Government of the US immediately to take the initiative in aiding the workers of Soviet-occupied Germany in their struggle against Soviet totalitarianism." The message was supplemented with the warm wishes of George Meany of the American Federation of Labor and Walter Reuther of the United Auto Workers for their struggling compatriots behind the Iron Curtain.[156] Public commemorations of "freedom" were emphasized, for example, through a Memorial to Martyrs of Freedom or "Hall of Heroes" to be located in West Berlin.[157] Jackson, spurred by a "very excited" Henry Luce, latched on to the symbol of Willi Goettling, an East German worker shot without trial during the uprising.[158]

There were also unorthodox symbols of Western superiority, notably the offer of $100,000 to the first pilot to defect with a Soviet-made MiG fighter. The plan dated from the early days of the OPC when Frank Wisner authorized $400,000 for a former officer of the Polish Air Force who insisted he could buy a MiG on the black market. The pilot spent the money in an expensive hotel on as many women and as much champagne as possible; no MiG materialized. The challenge was renewed in 1952 by General Mark Clark in Korea but it was spurred by the defection in March 1953 of a Polish airman to a Danish island, an event exploited by British propaganda.[159] In September 1953 the US reward was finally taken up by a pilot in Korea; however, the *coup* backfired when Eisenhower worried that it would appear as a US provocation violating the Korean armistice. After much deliberation, the $100,000 was finally paid, along with the CIA's provision of a free education through a US university or the Committee for Free Asia, but the defection was not publicized.[160]

Most significantly, there were the radio operations. Radio in the American Sector did not shut down after the failure of the East Berlin demonstrations. On the contrary, it encouraged the defection of members of the East German security police. The text of liberation was clear:

> Fellow Germans, Germany is certain again to be united and free. We know that with God's help that day is coming. How can you risk shooting and maltreating other Germans whose other crime is that they are hungry? They will not forget. Come over to the side of freedom. You are welcome here.[161]

If the State Department ensured that RIAS removed references to "imminent" freedom, Radio Free Europe escaped restriction. Broadcasts to Czechoslovakia were explicit about the US objective: "We say to you . . . that in this new situation it is possible not only to hope for liberation but to work for it effectively." Commentaries encouraged economic warfare – "Here the people either work or they sabotage, which is the only true voting in a dictatorship. . . . So far no satellite government nor even the Russians themselves have invented an expedient by which to counter this popular plebiscite" – and hinted at even more forceful action: "Higher wages – lower prices: only the fall of the government can solve this problem. . . . These governments are but shadows, like those cast by Russian soldiers on to the walls in the satellite countries."

RFE might have warned that the revolution might not occur immediately, but this was not an acceptance of the State Department's line against "inciting" an uprising; rather, it was case of waiting for the right moment. "It would be a revolutionary error and no revolutionary asset were valuable cadres of determined and experienced men sacrificed prematurely. The classical revolutionary situation sets in when the internal and external opportunities blend, when on both sides of the Iron Curtain the word will be spoken: NOW." Most importantly, RFE was assuring US support for direct action: "You were the first to furnish all necessary arguments for the liberation policy. You have brought about the decision that the liberation policy shall not be forgotten."[162]

The passage of the "New Look" had done nothing to alter the division between caution at certain levels and activism in others. If the National Security Council was keeping liberation at arm's length, its passionate words about eventual triumph allowed the network of psychological warriors to persist. C. D. Jackson wrote Eisenhower, "The internal stresses among the satellites and within Russia itself are working for us, and will continue to work for us so long as we move forward."[163] The President was happy to approve Jackson's statement, made to a group commemorating the thirty-fifth anniversary of the Czech Republic, that he "would never forget that between free West and the Soviet Union lie countries whose present condition of enforced servitude must never be acceptable".[164]

So the programme of food distribution proliferated, including special plans for Christmas parcels into both Eastern and Western Europe. By February 1954 the distribution involved six different groups, including the Operations Coordinating Board, the Voice of America, the relief agency CARE, and the Freedom Foundation. So many people were now involved that Jackson had to appeal to the National Security Council to take charge of the sprawl of organisations.[165] A new balloon initiative was agreed between Jackson's staff and the National Committee for Free Europe, with the CIA overseeing the implementation,[166] and wide-ranging measures for the stimulation of defections were implemented.[167]

There were even more dramatic plans in store. With Leo Cherne, the head of the International Rescue Committee, and other "private" leaders, Jackson considered "possible support and use of June 17 rioters still in West Berlin" (the CIA was eventually authorized "to exploit any future disturbances" without reference to the NSC), and he agitated for manipulation of future riots in East Germany, though adding hastily that he was "not suggesting an airlift of 75-millimeter recoilless rifles".[168] An appeal for US recognition of the Ukraine was scotched by Bedell Smith,[169] but Jackson did work with the CIA's

Director of Plans, Frank Wisner, for "Radio Free Europe [to] pick up Baltic broadcasts".[170] Allen Dulles supported Jackson's call to review policy on Soviet "nationalities" since existing plans "may not have given the most appropriate emphasis to the exploitation" of nationalism to cause discord within the Soviet Union.[171] Moreover, despite Foster Dulles's injunction against the operation, Jackson and the CIA persisted with the forlorn hope of liberating Albania. Jackson continued to meet with British intelligence officers, Adam Watson, the British liaison for psychological warfare, and Julian Amery, a Member of Parliament involved with covert action in Albania since World War II, who were "enthusiastic" about proceeding with the plans for "Country A".[172]

For China, Jackson developed a "winter of discontent". The origin of the proposal lay in news reports of June 1953 of a Chinese famine affecting 10 million people, characterized indelicately by US officials as a "rather fertile field" for US propaganda to discredit Mao Tse-tung and highlight the possibility of American food relief. By November, a comprehensive "high-priority" programme to exploit agricultural and economic conditions was in progress.[173] Once again, Jackson was supported by Walt Rostow, who carried out a comprehensive study on the use of propaganda within China.[174] The typical line was "If Soviet agriculture is so advanced, why is it necessary for backward China to send the USSR rice and other foodstuffs from its slim surplus?"[175]

Rostow also contributed to the most intriguing and most provocative US project. In late 1953, he offered suggestions for "Project Control", a plan for the "political use of air power" by the US Air Force. The study was for a "persuasive reconnaissance offensive" which could lead to the use of "American atomic delivery capability to produce a partial or total resolution of certain key problems between the USSR and the US". In simpler terms, the Air Force would send planes over Soviet territory not only to undertake photographic reconnaissance, not only to demonstrate and publicize US superiority in the air, but to press political demands upon the Soviets such as withdrawal from Eastern Europe, dissolution of the Cominform, and release of political and military prisoners. If Moscow caved in, the United States would win an important psychological and political battle; if the Soviets tried to stop the aircraft, the United States would respond with a nuclear strike.

Was the United States, in the name of "psychological warfare", close to the use of atomic bombs? White House staff insisted "that [Eisenhower] would not have members of the armed forces flying over the USSR. That amounted to an act of war"; however, the head of the Strategic Air Command, General Curtis LeMay, may have acted without presidential authority.[176] Aircraft did fly over the Soviet Union; on at least one occasion Soviet MiGs fired at a US plane. LeMay congratulated the returning crew on "a mission well done" and then commented, "Maybe if we do this overflight right, we can get World War Three started."[177]

To call global policy muddled at the end of Eisenhower's first year would be an understatement. The Administration, while persisting with public rhetoric which verged on the irresponsible, continued to hedge its bets on Eastern Europe. Its policy in NSC 174, "U.S. Policy toward the Soviet Satellites", warned:

> In its efforts to encourage anti-Soviet elements in the satellites and keep up their hopes, the United States should not encourage premature action on their part which will bring upon them reprisals involving further terror and suppression. Continuing and careful attention must be given to the fine line, which is not stationary, between exhortations to keep up morale and to maintain passive resistance, and invitations to suicide.[178]

Yet the document maintained that the United States would "foster satellite nationalism as a force against Soviet imperialism", "stimulate and exploit conflicts within the communist ruling groups in each satellite", and "encourage democratic, anti-communist elements in the satellites".[179] A progress report on NSC 174 summarized the fundamental problem:

> Effective implementation . . . is inhibited by the cautions and limitations written into [this] document, by the practical difficulties of operating effectively on any scale in or into the denied area and by the fact that the results of aggressive action to carry them out would seriously risk producing results in conflict with other U.S. policy objectives. . . .
> Action and planning must be largely confined to overt diplomatic action, encouraging passive resistance, trying to keep alive the hopes of the satellites' peoples, and propaganda sent into the area by radio, balloon, rocket, or infiltrated.[180]

A CIA assessment was even more to the point: "Results produced thus far do not meet operational requirements."[181]

Notes

1 State Department Circular 779, 19 January 1953, FRUS, 1952–1954, II, 1652–3
2 Quoted in Department of State Special Report on American Opinion, "Public Attitudes toward a US Policy of 'Liberation'," USNA, Department of State, PSB Working File, Box 4, PSB D-26
3 James Hagerty oral history, 2 March 1967, DDE, Oral History Collection
4 George V. Allen oral history, 7 March 1967, DDE, Oral History Collection
5 "A Policy of Boldness," Life, May 1952; Emma Lambert, "Cultural Cold Warriors? Time Inc. and the Eisenhower Administration," University of Birmingham research seminar, 18 November 1998; Townsend Hoopes, The Devil and John Foster Dulles (Boston, MA, 1973), 125–8
6 Washburn to Eisenhower, undated [1952], DDE, Jackson Papers, Box 69, Princeton Meeting, 10–11 May 1952
7 Washburn to Eisenhower, undated [1952], DDE, Jackson Papers, Box 69, Princeton Meeting, 10–11 May 1952

8 Cited in *Bulletin of American Friends of Russian Freedom*, November 1952, DDE, Jackson Papers, Box 24, America Miscellaneous
9 See *Washington Evening Star*, "Mr. Dulles on 'Containment'," 28 August 1952, and Vojtech Mastny, *The Cold War and Soviet Insecurity: The Stalin Years* (New York, 1996), 146. Robert Bowie, head of the State Department's Policy Planning Staff during the Eisenhower Administration and later the author of books on the Adminstration, has repeatedly claimed that Eisenhower held back an aggressive Foster Dulles. In *The Cold War* documentary series, Bowie repeated, "Dulles had talked about liberation but Eisenhower insisted that . . . he couple it with 'peaceful means'." (BBC Television, *The Cold War*, Part 7, 7 November 1998.) Bowie is a spirited defender of Eisenhower but the historical record fails to sustain his assertion
10 *Washington Post*, "Freeing the Satellites," 28 August 1952
11 Quoted in Robert Holt, *Radio Free Europe* (Minneapolis, MN, 1958), 24
12 Stephen Ambrose, *Eisenhower the President* (London, 1982), 276
13 J. R. Beal, *John Foster Dulles* (New York, 1959), 312
14 Cited in *Bulletin of American Friends of Russian Freedom*, November 1952, DDE, Jackson Papers, Box 24, America Miscellaneous
15 Eisenhower handwritten notes, 7 February 1954, *Diaries*, Reel 1
16 Eisenhower to Foster Dulles, 24 October 1953, US DDRS, Retrospective 897A
17 Eisenhower address, 8 October 1952, DDE, Jackson Records, Box 2, Robert Cutler
18 Jackson to Luce, 19 November 1947, DDE, Jackson Papers, Box 57, Henry R. Luce, 1943–1948
19 Jackson to Luce, 9 October 1947, DDE, Jackson Papers, Box 57, Henry R. Luce, 1943–1948; Evan Thomas, *The Very Best Men: Four who Dared in the Early Years of the CIA* (New York, 1995), 37–8
20 James Shepley oral history, 23 August 1967, DDE, Oral History Collection
21 Abbott Washburn oral history, 20 April 1967, DDE, Oral History Collection
22 Howland Sargeant oral history, 15 December 1970, HST, Sargeant Papers, Box 3
23 Howland Sargeant oral history, 15 December 1970, HST, Sargeant Papers, Box 3
24 Dodge to Jackson, 17 August 1954, and Jackson to Dodge, 15 October 1954, DDE, Jackson Papers, Box 38, Joseph Dodge
25 CIA memorandum, 30 January 1953, US DDRS, 1988 2006
26 Jackson to Brownell, 23 February 1953, DDE, Jackson Records, Box 2, Herbert Brownell
27 Cited in Peter Grose, *Gentleman Spy: The Life of Allen Dulles* (Boston, MA, 1994), 341–2
28 Jackson memorandum, 27 May 1953, DDE, Jackson Records, Box 5, R
29 Jackson daily log, 4 June 1953, DDE, Jackson Records, Box 56, Log 1953 (1)
30 *The Director of Central Intelligence Historical Series: General Walter Bedell Smith*, Volume IV, US DDRS, 1991 63
31 Jackson to Eisenhower, 17 November 1952, US DDRS, 1986 3555
32 Jackson to Rostow, 31 December 1952, DDE, Jackson Papers, Box 75, Walt W. Rostow to 1956
33 131st NSC meeting, 11 February 1953, *Minutes*, 1st Supplement, Reel 1
34 134th NSC meeting, 25 February 1953, US DDRS, 1987 2918; Eisenhower to Lay, 1 February 1953, US DDRS, 1986 3591
35 132nd NSC meeting, 18 February 1953, *Minutes*, 1st Supplement, Reel 1
36 Comstock briefing, 26 March 1953, DDE, Jackson Papers, Box 1, OCB, Miscellaneous Memoranda
37 NSC 148, "US Policies in the Far East," 6 April 1953, *Documents*, Reel 3
38 Compton report, 31 December 1952, FRUS, 1952–1954, II, 1644
39 Notes for Briefing of NSC Consultants, 11 March 1953, US DDRS, 1991 975
40 Cited in Hoopes memorandum, 6 February 1953, US DDRS, 1988 565

41 Cited in Robert Donovan, *Eisenhower: The Inside Story* (New York, 1956), 47
42 Legislative Leadership Meeting, 26 February 1953, *Diaries*, Reel 2
43 Foster Dulles to Eisenhower, 13 February 1953, US National Archives, Department of State, Central Decimal File, 760.00/2-1353; Legislative Leadership Meeting, 2 March 1953, *Diaries*, Reel 2
44 PSB Office of Plans and Policy Status Report 24 February–7 March 1952, undated, US DDRS, 1992 2296; sixteenth PSB meeting, 30 October 1992, US DDRS, 1993 1775
45 PSB-24, "Program of Psychological Preparation for Stalin's Passing from Power," 1 November 1952, USNA, Department of State, Lot 62 D 333, PSB Working File, 1951–1953, Box 4, PSB D-24
46 Grose, *Gentleman* Spy, 328–9; William Corson, *The Armies of Ignorance: The Rise of the American Intelligence Empire* (New York, 1977), 360–6
47 Jackson to Cutler, 4 March 1953, US DDRS, 1997 0945
48 Informal PSB meeting, 5 March 1953, USNA, Department of State, Lot 62 D 333, PSB Working File, 1951–1953, Box 1, PSB D-10
49 USNA, Department of State, Lot 62 D 333, PSB Working File, 1951–1953, Box 4, PSB D-24
50 Phillips to Bruce, 29 October 1952, USNA, Department of State, Lot 62 D 333, PSB Working File, 1951–1953, Box 4, PSB D-24
51 Quoted in Emmet Hughes, *The Ordeal of Power: A Political Memoir of the Eisenhower Years* (New York, 1963), 101
52 135th NSC meeting, 4 March 1953, US DDRS, US 1990 914
53 *Public Papers of the President: Dwight David Eisenhower*, 1953, 76
54 Thomas, *The Very Best Men*, 356
55 Jackson to Cutler, 4 March 1953, US DDRS, 1980 115D; Eisenhower draft message to Soviet Union, undated, US DDRS, 1992 322; W. W. Rostow, *Europe after Stalin: Eisenhower's Three Decisions of March 11, 1953* (Austin, TX, 1982), 3–4
56 Draft plan of action in Morgan to PSB, 13 March 1953, USNA, Department of State, Lot 62 D 333, PSB Working File, 1951–1953, Box 4, PSB D-30
57 Stassen to Smith, 10 March 1953, DDE, Jackson Records, Box 1, PSB Plans for Psychological Exploitation of Stalin's Death
58 Bohlen memorandum, 7 March 1953, USNA, Department of State, Lot 64 D 563, Records of the Policy Planning Staff, 1947–1953, Subject Files, Box 23, Soviet Union
59 State Department Circular 925, 5 March 1953, FRUS, 1952–1954, II, 1681–2
60 Hughes to Eisenhower, 10 March 1953, *Diaries*, Reel 15
61 Smith to Morgan, 10 March 1953, DDE, Jackson Records, Box 1, PSB Plans for Psychological Exploitation of Stalin's Death
62 Jackson to Dulles, 10 March 1953, DDE, Box 85, Stalin's Death
63 136th NSC meeting, 11 March 1953, *Minutes*, 1st Supplement, Reel 2
64 Special meeting with civilian consultants, 31 March 1953, *Minutes*, 1st Supplement, Reel 2
65 Jackson to Cutler, 4 March 1953, US DDRS, 1980 115D
66 Jackson daily log, 30 March 1953, DDE, Jackson Papers, Box 56, Log 1953 (1)
67 State Department Circular Telegram 958, 16 March 1953, USNA, Department of State, Central Decimal File, 511.00/3-1653, Box 2247; State Department Circular Telegram 974, 24 March 1953, USNA, Department of State, Central Decimal File, 511.00/3-2453, Box 2247; "Soviet Lures and Pressures," 26 March and 15 April 1953, US DDRS, 1986 3571; 139th NSC meeting, 8 April 1953, US DDRS, 1987 2885
68 Rostow to Jackson, 13 March 1953, DDE, Jackson Papers, Box 6, Walt Rostow (1)
69 Hughes, *The Ordeal of Power*, 103–4
70 See the drafts in US DDRS, 1991 576, 1991 582 and 1991 584
71 *Public Papers of the President*, 1953, 179–86

72 State Department Circular Telegram 1036, 16 April 1953, USNA, Department of State, Central Decimal File, 511.00/4–1653, Box 2247

73 Jackson to Morgan, 11 April 1953, DDE, Jackson Papers, Box 4, George Morgan

74 Status of the Psychological Program, 30 July 1953, US DDRS, 1986 2979

75 Cited in Grose, *Gentleman Spy*, 352–3

76 141st NSC meeting, 28 April 1953, US DDRS, 1987 2906

77 Joseph Harsch, "The Affairs of Nations: The Battle for a Career Foreign Service," undated, DDE, Jackson Papers, Box 2, C

78 "Washington Trends," *US News and World Reports*, 27 April 1953

79 Special Guidance to Radio Free Europe #7, 10 April 1953, US DDRS, 1997 2630

80 Jackson to Cutler, 4 March 1953, US DDRS, 1980 115D. Jackson's deputy, Abbott Washburn, shared his superior's opinion, commenting that the death of Stalin "offered a Lot of opportunities that we really didn't take advantage of, because not enough preliminary planning had been done. . . . Jackson and I were amazed that there wasn't Plan A, Plan B, Plan C." (Abbott Washburn oral history, 20 April 1967, DDE, Oral History Collection)

81 PSB D-40, "Plan for Psychological Exploitation of Stalin's Death," 23 April 1953, USNA, Department of State, Lot 62 D 333, PSB Working File, 1951–1953, Box 6, PSB D-40

82 CIA Memorandum, "Objectives," undated, US DDRS, 1992 2413

83 Jackson to Eisenhower, 2 April 1953, DDE, Jackson Papers, Box 41, Eisenhower – Correspondence through 1956 (1)

84 Jackson to Eisenhower, 2 April 1953, DDE, Jackson Papers, Box 41, Eisenhower – Correspondence through 1956 (1)

85 Jackson log, 24 July–13 August 1958, DDE, Jackson Papers, Box 57, Log 1958

86 Final report of the Jackson Committee, 30 June 1953, US DDRS, 1987 1120

87 Final report of the Jackson Committee, 30 June 1953, US DDRS, 1987 1120; Lay memorandum, 23 July 1954, US DDRS, 1977 305B

88 "No Mirrors Found for Cold War," *Washington Post*, 24 May 1953

89 Tufts to Jackson Committee, 28 March 1953, US DDRS, 1990 405

90 Lilly to Jackson, 3 June 1953, US DDRS, 1997 0072

91 Bohlen to Jackson Committee, 24 February 1953, US DDRS, 1988 547

92 NSC 153, "Restatement of Basic National Security Policy," 1 June 1953, *Documents*, Reel 3

93 "Solarium Project: Principal Points Made by J.F.D.," 8 May 1953, USNA, Department of State, Lot 64 D 563, Records of the Policy Planning Staff, 1947–1953, Box 64, NSC 131/141/153

94 Task Force A report, undated, USNA, Department of State, Lot 66 D 148, Records Relating to State Department Participation in the OCB and the NSC, 1947–1963, Box 129

95 Task Force B report, undated, US DDRS, 1992 851

96 Task Force C report, 16 July 1953, USNA, Department of State, Lot 66 D 148, Records Relating to State Department Participation in the OCB and the NSC, 1947–1963, Box 129

97 "Project Solarium," 16 July 1953, *Minutes*, 1st Supplement, Reel 2

98 157th NSC meeting, 30 July 1953, *Minutes*, 1st Supplement, Reel 2

99 Jackson daily log, 16 July 1953, DDE, Jackson Papers, Box 56, Log 1953 (2). A 1984 newspaper account claimed that Eisenhower stood up and summarized that rollback would strain American alliances and represented "a departure from our traditional concepts of war and peace". There is no indication of the remarks in the official record, however. (*Washington Post*, 7 December 1984)

100 CIA Office of Current Intelligence, "Comment on East Berlin Uprising," 17 June 1953, DDE, Jackson Records, Box 3, Germany; Alexander Bogomolov interview in BBC Television, *The Cold War*, Part 7, 7 November 1998

101 Special Guidance to Radio Free Europe #12, 11 June 1953, US DDRS, 1997 3400

102 Edmond Taylor, "RIAS: The Story of an American Psywar Outpost," in William Daugherty and Morris Janowitz (eds.), *A Psychological Warfare Casebook* (Baltimore, MD, 1958), 146. RIAS officials estimated that 50–70 percent of the 18 million population in the Soviet Zone of East Germany listened to broadcasts. (Walter Hixson, *Parting the Curtain: Propaganda, Culture, and the Cold War* (New York, 1997), 74)

103 Information Policy #380, Circular 1214, 17 June 1953, US National Archives, Department of State, Central Decimal File, 511.00/6-1753

104 Status of the USIA Program, 1 March 1954, US DDRS, 1993 488

105 CIA Office of Current Intelligence, "Comment on East Berlin Uprising," 17 June 1953, DDE, Jackson Records, Box 3, Germany

106 Kyes to OCB, 12 January 1954, US DDRS, 1987 674

107 150th NSC meeting, 18 June 1953, US DDRS, 1986 2118

108 Taylor, "RIAS," in Daugherty and Janowitz, (eds), *A Psychological Warfare Casebook*, 149; Memorandum on RIAS, undated, US DDRS, 1987 166

109 Final report of the Jackson Committee, 30 June 1953, US DDRS, 1987 1120

110 Morgan memorandum, 28 May 1953, USNA, Department of State, PSB Working File, Box 4, PSB D-23, Thailand

111 Christian Ostermann, "The Eisenhower Administration: Psychological Warfare and the East German Uprising of 1953," paper at Annual Conference of Society for Historians of American Foreign Relations, 22 June 1997

112 Jackson to Taber, 22 July 1953, DDE, Jackson Records, Box 5, Radio Free Europe

113 Taylor, "RIAS," in Daugherty and Janowitz (eds), *A Psychological Warfare Casebook*, 145

114 Wisner to Jackson, 20 July 1953, DDE, Jackson Records, Box 5, Radio Free Europe. A report from the US Information Agency acknowledged that RIAS had a "major role in the exploitation of the June 17 uprisings" as well as pointing to USIA efforts "encouraging the view that Soviet power in the satellite world was not impregnable, that resistance manifested by the East Germans had achieved concrete successes, and that the potentials of popular resistance were greater than many had dared imagine". (Status of the USIA Program, 1 March 1954, US DDRS, 1993 488)

115 Taylor, "RIAS," in Daugherty and Janowitz (eds), *A Psychological Warfare Casebook*, 146

116 Taylor, "RIAS," in Daugherty and Janowitz (eds), *A Psychological Warfare Casebook*, 147–8

117 Quoted in Joseph Harsch, "RIAS Deputy Chief Shows Value and Risk of West Berlin Radio," *Christian Science Monitor*, 8 July 1953

118 Quoted in Sig Mickelson, *America's Other Voices: Radio Free Europe and Radio Liberty* (New York, 1983), 69

119 Hixson, *Parting the Curtain*, 75

120 Straus to Phillips, 17 June 1953, DDE, Jackson Records, Box 3, Germany

121 Quoted in Harsch, "RIAS Deputy Chief"

122 Ostermann, "The Eisenhower Administration"

123 Burton Hersh, *The Old Boys: The American Elite and the Origins of the CIA* (New York, 1992), 377; Thomas Powers, *The Man who Kept the Secrets: Richard Helms and the CIA* (New York, 1979), 56; Gross, *Gentleman Spy*, 356–7

124 Morgan to PSB, 29 June 1953, USNA, Department of State, Lot 63 D 351, Records Relating to State Department Participation in the OCB and the NSC, 1947–1963, Box 73, NSC 158

125 Jackson daily log, 25 June 1953, DDE, Jackson Papers, Box 56, Log-1953 (1)

126 165th NSC meeting, 7 October 1953, *Meetings*, 1st Supplement, Reel 2. Another study on rollback was carried out for the CIA by the Ford Foundation's Richard Bissell. Within a year, Bissell would join the Agency, supervising the creation of the U-2 spy plane. (Thomas, *The Very Best Men*, 87)

127 Amory memorandum, October 1953, USNA, Department of State, Lot 62 D 333, PSB
     Working File, 1951–1953, Box 65, NSC 135/141/153
128 167th NSC meeting, 22 October 1953, US DDRS, 1991 2021; 168th NSC meeting, 29
     October 1953, US DDRS, 1991 1988
129 See USNA, Department of State, Lot 62 D 333, PSB Working File, 1951–1953, Box 65, NSC
     135/141/153
130 169th NSC meeting, 5 November 1953, US DDRS, 1992 2680; NSC 146/2, 6 November
     1953, US DDRS, 1989 3570
131 NSC 162/2, 30 October 1953, *Documents*, Reel 3
132 NSC Planning Board report on NSC 174, 11 December 1953, US DDRS, 1987 2873
133 Cutler to Smith, 24 November 1953, US DDRS, 1992 1714
134 *Public Papers of the President*, 1953, 401
135 John Young, *Winston Churchill's Last Campaign: Britain and the Cold War, 1951–1955*
     (Oxford, 1996), 188
136 Jackson to Speer, 4 August 1953, DDE, Jackson Papers, Box 1, OCB, Miscellaneous
     Memoranda (2)
137 Ravndal to Jackson, 14 April 1953, USNA, Department of State, Lot 62 D 333, PSB Working
     File, 1951–1953, Box 8, Informal PSB Meetings
138 Jackson to Ravndal, 22 May 1953, and Morgan to Jackson, 8 June 1953, DDE, Jackson
     Papers, Box 1, OCB, Miscellaneous Memoranda (2)
139 Morgan memorandum, 8 July 1953, USNA, Department of State, Lot 62 D 333, PSB
     Working File, 1951–1953, Box 8, Informal PSB Meetings
140 Jackson to PSB Board Members, 11 July 1953, DDE, Jackson Papers, Box 1, OCB, Miscel-
     laneous Memoranda (2)
141 Bonn to State Department, Cable 290, 18 July 1953, DDE, Jackson Records, Box 3, Germany
142 Bonn to State Department, Cable 280, 18 July 1953, DDE, Jackson Records, Box 3,
     Germany; O'Connor to Jackson, 31 August 1953, DDE, Jackson Records, Box 1, OCB,
     Miscellaneous Memoranda
143 Bonn to Mutual Security Administration, Cable TOMUS 81, 2 August 1953, DDE, Jackson
     Records, Box 3, Germany
144 Jackson to Ravndal, 7 August 1953, DDE, Jackson Records, Box 5, R
145 Bonn to Mutual Security Administration, Cable TOMUS 81, 2 August 1953, DDE, Jackson
     Records, Box 3, Germany
146 Ostermann, "The Eisenhower Administration"
147 Quoted in Holt, *Radio Free Europe*, 149; "Analysis of Soviet Policy and Current Develop-
     ments in East Germany and Czechoslovakia," 12 June 1953, US DDRS, 1997 2631
148 Robert Lang oral history, Hoover Institution, Sig Mickelson Collection, Audiotape 29
149 Tigrid to Jackson, 18 March 1953, and Jackson to Tigrid, 31 March 1953, DDE, Jackson
     Records, Box 6, T
150 Jackson daily log, 6 April 1953, DDE, Jackson Papers, Box 56, Log 1953 (1); Jackson to
     Ayer, 3 August 1953, DDE, Jackson Records, Box 2, Balloons
151 Walker to Jackson, 22 July 1953, DDE, Jackson Records, Box 2, Balloons
152 Jackson to OCB, 22 September 1953, USNA, Department of State, Lot 62 D 333, PSB
     Working Files, 1951–1953, Box 6, PSB D-38. See also Griffith to Lang, 7 August 1953,
     Project Vista Collection, National Security Archive, George Washington University,
     Washington, DC
153 Michie to Walker, 24 July 1953, DDE, Jackson Records, Box 2, Balloons Memorandum on
     Free Europe Press operations, 8 February 1956, USNA, Department of State, Lot 59 D 233,
     Miscellaneous Office Files of the Assistant Secretary of State for European Affairs,
     1943–1957, Box 28, Balloons

154 Jackson to OCB, 22 September 1953, Department of State, Lot 62 D 333, PSB Working Files, 1951–1953, Box 6, PSB D-38
155 Dulles to Eisenhower, undated, US DDRS, 1986 2664
156 Carroll to Dulles, 8 July 1953, DDE, Jackson Records, Box 3, Germany
157 Jackson to Washburn, 18 August 1953, DDE, Jackson Records, Box 1, OCB, Miscellaneous Memoranda; O'Connor to Washburn, 18 August 1953, DDE, Jackson Records, Box 1, PSB, Exploitation of Unrest in Satellite Europe
158 Jackson to Braden, 28 July 1953, DDE, Jackson Records, Box 2, B
159 Thomas, *The Very Best Men*, 65; Daugherty and Janowitz (eds), *A Psychological Warfare Casebook*, 156; BBC Central European Service (Polish) broadcast, 30 March 1953, DDE, Jackson Records, Box 5, P
160 Eisenhower to Smith, 21 September 1953, *Diaries*, Reel 1; Jackson daily log, 23 September 1953, DDE, Jackson Papers, Box 56, Log 1953 (1); Jackson to Smith, 5 November 1953, DDE, Jackson Records, Box 6, Walter Bedell Smith
161 Bonn to US Information Agency, Cable TOUSI 12, 13 August 1953, DDE, Jackson Records, Box 3, Germany
162 "Ferdinand Peroutka's Sunday Talk," 28 June and 5 July 1953, and "Peroutka's Special Commentary," DDE, Jackson Records, Box 5, Radio Free Europe
163 Jackson to Eisenhower, 21 September 1953, DDE, Jackson Papers, Box 41, Eisenhower, Correspondence through 1956 (1)
164 Eisenhower appointments diary, 27 October 1953, *Diaries*, Reel 1
165 Jackson to Cutler, 26 February 1954, DDE, Jackson Records, Box 2, Robert Cutler
166 Jackson daily log, 16 and 17 October 1953, DDE, Jackson Papers, Box 56, Log 1953 (2)
167 Foreign Operations Administration, "A Report for OCB Examination on Effectiveness of the Escapee Program," 23 December 1953, US DDRS, 1993 2951
168 Jackson daily log, 6 November 1953, DDE, Jackson Papers, Box 56, Log 1953 (2); Staats memorandum, 8 January 1954, USNA, Department of State, Lot 62 D 430, Records Relating to State Department Participation in the OCB and the OCB and the NSC, 1947–1963, Box 1, OCB Minutes; Jackson to Smith, 16 November 1953, DDE, Jackson Records, Box 1, OCB Miscellaneous Memoranda (2)
169 Smith to Jackson, 24 December 1953, US DDRS, 1979 85C
170 Jackson daily log, 15 July 1953, DDE, Jackson Papers, Box 56, Log 1953 (2)
171 Allen Dulles to Jackson, 25 September 1953, DDE, Jackson Records, Box 1, OCB, Miscellaneous Memoranda (2)
172 Jackson daily log, 15 October 1953 and 11 November 1953, DDE, Jackson Papers, Box 56, Log 1953 (2)
173 McNair to Morgan, 12 June 1953, DDE, Jackson Records, Box 2, C; Staats to OCB, 3 December 1953, DDE, Jackson Records, Box 1, OCB, Miscellaneous Memoranda (3); Staats to Jackson, 14 January 1954, DDE, Jackson Records, Box 1, OCB, Miscellaneous Memoranda (2)
174 Rostow to Lindsay, 8 January 1954, US DDRS, 1979 99A
175 Hong Kong to State Department, Cable 2287, 8 May 1954, USNA, Department of State, Central Decimal File, 511.00/5-854
176 Told by an advisor on another occasion that pre-emptive bombing "wasn't national policy", LeMay responded, "I don't care. It's my policy. That's what I am going to do." (Paul Lashmar, "Killer on the Edge," *New Statesman and Society*, 15 September 1995)
177 Rostow to Jackson, 18 November 1953, US DDRS, 1987 2379; Lashmar, "Killer on the Edge"; Tami Davis Biddle, "Handling the Soviet Threat: 'Project Control' and the Debate on American Strategy in the Early Cold War Years," *Journal of Strategic Studies*, September 1989, 273–302

178 Quoted in Murphy to Dulles, 11 July 1956, USNA, Department of State, Lot 63 D 351, Records Relating to State Department Participation in the OCB and the NSC, 1947–1963, Box 88, NSC 5608

179 Draft NSC 174, 11 December 1956, , USNA, Department of State, Lot 63 D 351, Records Relating to State Department Participation in the OCB and the NSC, 1947–1963, Box 76, NSC 174

180 167th NSC Meeting, 22 October 1953, US DDRS, 1991 2021; 168th NSC meeting, 29 October 1953, US DDRS, 1991 1988; OCB List of Actions, 20 August 1954, US DDRS, 1990 2383; Progress Report on NSC 174, 16 July 1954, US DDRS, 1987 2874

181 CIA memorandum, "The Foreign Intelligence Program," 4 August 1953, US DDRS, 1993 2416

11

A policy of candor

The debate over liberation was one preoccupation of the Eisenhower Administration in 1953, but it was far from the only concern over the use of "psychological strategy". While Government officials and their private contacts argued over covert action behind enemy lines, there was also a comprehensive review of overt propaganda. In particular, Eisenhower and his advisors would confront the challenge of the atom, trying to convince audiences at home and abroad that the Government was a trustworthy guardian seeking progress rather than destruction.

At first glance, the hearings of the Jackson Committee on psychological strategy had produced a valuable reorganization of Government services. The Psychological Strategy Board had been replaced by the Operations Coordinating Board while the dissemination of propaganda abroad took on a higher profile with the conversion of the State Department's International Information Administration into the autonomous US Information Agency. Despite the chaotic reaction to Stalin's death, Eisenhower's 16 April "Chance for Peace" speech, with its call to convert military expenditure into spending on hospitals, schools, and other services, could be upheld as a "softly, softly" alternative to strident anti-Commmunism.

A number of pressing problems remained for the Administration, however. Some were due to personalities, for example, Press Secretary Carl McCardle. A Philadelphia newspaperman, McCardle was known more for his drinking than for his journalism. Theodore Streibert, the head of the US Information Agency, understated the case by labelling McCardle "inept" and "not cooperative".[1] Jackson more colorfully called him a "horse's ass . . . [a] triple menace, guaranteed either not to understand the question, or give the wrong answer, or be drunk at 10 AM".[2] The defense establishment also lacked a subtle appreciation of propaganda. For example, a General McNarney had to be told that the use of atomic-bomb pictures from Hiroshima was not quite appropriate to celebrate the fiftieth anniversary of flight.[3] Secretary of Defence Charles Wilson couldn't "get the role of [the] press through his head", repeatedly making unauthorized statements about the wonders of new US weapons.[4]

There were also difficulties associated with US allies. The Volunteer Freedom Corps, the once exciting initiative for elite military units of émigrés, finally collapsed amidst worries of the effect upon nervous Western European Governments.[5] Even more significant for the projection of "free" East Europeans were the recurrent difficulties in sustaining united National Committees in Exile. George Kennan advised Jackson to use the "greatest caution" with the committee and offered a "special word of warning" on the Ukrainians, who were "probably selling the US Government a dangerous bill of goods". He concluded, "I am extremely skeptical about the wisdom of getting ourselves hooked to the ambitions of noisy, immature, and extremist exile figures who announce themselves as the 'national' leaders of various linguistic groups in Eastern Europe."[6]

Even Jackson's enthusiasm was tempered by the exasperation of mediating rivalries or dealing with leaders who did not necessarily fulfill the "democratic" model. For example, he described the League of Free Romanians as "nice, honest, but slightly gaga old Generals like Radescu or conniving . . . characters like most of the rest of them".[7] By November 1953, he was so frustrated that he wrote, "Am personally convinced by now we must not go in for predetermination of minorities anywhere."[8] His spirits were not helped by informants giving graphic descriptions of the American Committee for the Liberation of the Peoples of Russia:

> Chief problems being Nicolaevsky's Marxism, Kerensky's political impotence, Otis Swift's screwballishness, Marxist allegations against Kuniholm, State Department Character assigned to Admiral Stevens [the head of ACLPR], and ridiculous situation of exile politicoes in same town with radio people. This is about my sixth attempt on this one. Hope it is successful this time.[9]

"Right-wing" Russians told Jackson that any constituency to the right of socialism was "completely ignored by the previous Administration" and claimed Marxist influence in the ACLPR.[10] One of the most powerful émigré groups, the Ukrainian movement NTS, refused to cooperate with other elements, a position worsened because "NTS [was] getting substantial funds from sources other than the [ACLPR], on the basis of which it [was] almost arrogant in its independence".[11] Arguments among Czechoslovak émigrés were so intense that the "Slovak Liberation Committee" accused leading Czech commentators for Radio Free Europe of Communist sympathies.[12] Conversely, Stanislaw Mikolajczyk, the prominent Polish leader, protested about the "growing tendency in the United States to accept at face value certain accusations against democratic émigrés made by extreme rightists".[13]

The greatest threat to the psychological program remained the US Congress. Traditional antipathy on Capitol Hill to propaganda was reinforced by the growling presence of Joe McCarthy. The Senator from Wisconsin may have been a fervent anti-Communist, but the combination of his political ambition and his paranoia meant that he treated the Eisenhower Administration as an adversary rather than an ally in the fight against the Soviets.

McCarthy targeted the information services as a sanctuary for left-wingers. The charge had long circulated among Republican Congressmen and was used as a powerful argument to restrict the funding of the Voice of America, but McCarthy brought it wider publicity in 1953. Within weeks of the inauguration, he was cultivating sources who insisted "people working for RFE ... were either ex-Communists or ex-Socialists who were utterly discredited in their own country and who were doing us more harm than good".[14] Radio in the American Sector was also alleged to have current Communists on its payroll; more importantly for right-wing Republicans, its head, Gordon Ewing, was a member of the Democrat-dominated Americans for Democratic Action.[15] The charges resonated in editorials like that of the *New York Daily Mirror*: "The wartime OWI [Office of War Information] and its peacetime progeny, the Voice of America, were remarkable failures. The former got clabbered up with people like Owen Lattimore [the expert on Asia attacked in the 1950s for being soft on Communist China]. The 'Voice' has never been the voice of America, but has spoken to Europe in the accents of Socialism."[16]

The Senator's fiercest and most damaging assault was upon the US Information Agency's predecessor, the International Information Administration. Congress once again, was savaging the budget. The House of Representatives slashed the requested $123 million by more than 50 percent and the Senate restored only a small portion of the cut; as a result, the number of personnel collapsed from 13,500 to 9,281. McCarthy went even further with hearings in February 1953 vilifying IIA Deputy Administrator Reed Harris as his assistants, Roy Cohn and David Schine, toured Western Europe to identify "Communist" authors on the bookshelves of libraries in US embassies.

The book hunt was a red herring. Only eight Communist authors had books in embassy libraries, and none of those had been purchased since 1946. The real objective was publicity for McCarthy and a purging of "fifth columnists", i.e. left-wing critics of US policy such as the novelists Dashiel Hammett and Howard Fast, Paul Robeson's wife Eslanda and his biographer Shirley Graham, the historian Herbert Aptheker, and the African-American activist W. E. B. DuBois. Their works were withdrawn in April; Jean-Paul Sartre was also blacklisted because of his participation in the Vienna Peace Congress. Even the 1946 *Annals of the American Academy of Political and Social Science* were destroyed because they advocated "one world government or one world citizenship".[17]

The damage was exacerbated by Foster Dulles's craven response to the investigation. Instead of defending the book policy, the Secretary of State commanded his department and embassies not to use "Communist" books, to withdraw any magazines with "material detrimental to US objectives" and "not to identify by name any living international communist unless absolutely necessary".[18] The Director of the International Information Administration, Robert Johnson, tried to defend the practice of stocking books by Communist authors that "advanced American uses", but McCarthy turned the tables by declaring, "I cannot conceive of anyone in charge of the information program actually believing that an individual under Communist discipline is attempting to 'serve the ends of democracy'," ordering Johnson to testify before his subcommittee and demanding the names of those responsible for purchasing books.[19]

Panicked, the Administration told Congressmen that Johnson would be replaced and desperately searched for a successor. After one prospect, Philip Reed of General Electric, replied that he was "not too enthusiastic" and turned down a direct appeal from Eisenhower, Jackson lamented, "No one in his right mind would take the job."[20] It was an ironic echo of Johnson's own claim, "I did not want the job any more than a dog wants fleas."[21]

The President raged that returning tourists reported "the name of McCarthy was on everyone's lips and he was constantly compared to Adolf Hitler". He asked "whether any use could be made of the covert radio to attack and ridicule McCarthy".[22] However, Eisenhower was so jittery that, rather than condemning the Senator, he asked for further investigations of his own personnel. He told the National Security Council, "It might be possible in some fashion to send to these various foreign countries observers who were really loyal to the new Administration to find out what is going on overseas. It would be very helpful to find out who are the traitors in these various missions."[23]

The situation eased somewhat when Theodore Streibert, the co-founder of the Mutual Broadcasting System, agreed to take charge when the International Information Administration officially became the US Information Agency on 31 July. Streibert could be a terrifying leader, "humiliating his executives in public", but he was respected by his staff and "also persuaded with great charm".[24] C. D. Jackson anointed him "a real find" after the new Director, within two weeks of assuming his post, persuaded key Congressmen to restore $20 million to the budget and to remove restrictions on the hiring of personnel.[25] Streibert not only assuaged critics but also positioned his agency within the Administration's "psychological strategy" through a clear statement of "USIA Strategic Principles":

> Although our public assigned mission does not explicitly point to our role as a weapon of political warfare, the current conflict of interests between the US and the Soviet Union, in which each seeks its aims by methods other than the use of armed force, constitutes political warfare.
>
> Appropriate subjects of information programs are those aspects of the US which show its people sharing fundamental beliefs and basic values with the millions of men and women the US is attempting to win to its side. Examples include belief in a deity, in individual and national freedom, in ownership of property and in human rights, in a peaceful world and the common humanity of men and nations com-

promising their differences and cooperation in the United Nations. The military strength of the US, its economic system, its standard of living, its technical development and productive capacity make fruitful and effective subjects of propaganda if presented without self-praise in ways which show US capacity to resist aggression and to give powerful assistance in the creation of a peaceful world order.[26]

McCarthy was finally curbed after he sought a public purge of "left-wingers" in the CIA. Even then, his pressure led to the dismissal of key operatives such as Carmel Offie, who had been instrumental in the CIA's developing use of refugees and then became a case officer for the Agency's covert cultural efforts in Europe, and harassment of others.[27] More subtly, McCarthy's witch hunt had a lasting effect in turning the attention of the President and the National Security Council from liberation abroad to public opinion at home. The concern was not a new one, of course: NSC 68 had stressed the need to ensure that the population would make the necessary sacrfices, such as the payment of higher taxes, in the contest with the Soviet Union. Eisenhower was particularly concerned with the public's response to a "national security state", insisting, "Since the Soviets are totalitarians, they could assign whatever proportion of national income they desire to warlike purposes. We, who are dedicated to raising the standards of living for all peoples, are inhibited from such methods."[28]

The central issue was disarmament. In late 1951, the Truman Administration had pursued a major initiative, culminating in a presidential speech at the United Nations, but there was little substance to the campaign and it faded into fruitless talks between the nuclear powers.[29] Several months later, a consultant to the PSB, Dr Stefan Possony, gave the issue a different slant, "It must ... be realized that the atom as a peace and prosperity maker will be more acceptable to the world than the atom as a war maker or even as a military victor, and that even the destructiveness of the bomb will be accepted far more readily if at the same time atomic energy is being used for productive ends."[30]

The Eisenhower Administration took up the theme as soon as it assumed office. A report by a panel of consultants chaired by Robert Oppenheimer and including Vannevar Bush, head of the US science program in World War II, and Allen Dulles was submitted to the State Department days before Eisenhower's inauguration. It recommended "Candor to the American Government and People". The consultants foresaw that "the Soviet Union may [sson] have many hundred atomic bombs; within 10 or 15 years she could have several thousand". It was "a matter of urgency that ... awareness [of this] should become much more widespread", since "no matter how many bombs we may be making, the Soviet Union may fairly soon have enough to threaten the destruction of our whole society".[31]

The panel's call for a public alert was reinforced by its conclusion that discussions with the Soviets on atomic weapons were useless. This was endorsed by Eisenhower's National Security Council in the following weeks: "The Soviet

conception of negotiating in good faith . . . is a coldly calculated product of a
system of power and behavior which is deeply hostile to the whole concept of
human liberty in general and the United States Government in particular. . . .
It is obvious that continued disarmament discussions in the United Nations
will be unproductive and disadvantageous to the United States, in view of their
misleading effect on public opinion and the opportunity they afford for Soviet
propaganda."[32]

In essence, the Administration was campaigning for "psychological rearmament" so the citizenry would accept a war economy in peacetime and the
use of atomic bombs. The Jackson Committe on US information services concluded, "[The American people] do not yet grasp the import of the President's
recent words that we live in an age, not an instant, of peril. They do not fully
understand the dangers that confront them, the power of the enemy, the
difficulty of reducing that power, and the probable duration of the conflict."[33]
With Foster Dulles urging no relaxation of pressure on the Soviet bloc, even
after Stalin's death, another panel of civilian consultants reiterated the need
for "much greater candor by the Administration in setting forth to the American people the nature of the Soviet threat, the grave fiscal situation, and the
resulting dilemma".[34] C. D. Jackson asked Gordon Dean, the chairman of the
Atomic Energy Commission, to write an article when he left the commission,
since Jackson did "not think there is too much time before us on this business
of changing the attitude of people in this country toward this activity". He
chided Dean, "The scientists themselves could be of great help in this work.
After all it was their original breast-beating in the fall of 1945 which started
the nation on its 'sin' complex, and I feel that they have a grave responsibility toward the American people in helping to get rid of that complex."[35]
Jackson's pressure was somewhat unnecessary, since Dean had publicly stated
two years earlier, "Our fundamental concepts of what atomic warfare is and
what it might mean to us must undergo a revolutionary change for an era
when we can use atomic weapons tactically as well as strategically."[36]

As his advisors were debating the niceties of presenting the bomb, Eisenhower was preparing for a nuclear strike in the Korean War. Foster Dulles had
already pleaded for the Administration to discard the "false distinction"
between nuclear and other weapons; the President told consultants that,
"although there were not many good tactical targets . . . it would be worth the
cost if, through use of atomic weapons, we could (1) achieve a substantial
victory over the Communist forces and (2) get to a line at the waist of Korea".
He was restrained only by the worry about "the effects of such a move on our
allies, which be very serious, since they feel that they will be the battleground
in an atomic war between the United States and the Soviet Union".[37]

Meetings of the National Security Council in May again considered the use
of atomic weapons if hostilities resumed after an Korean armistice. Under-
secretary of State Bedell Smith assured colleagues that "a quick victory would

go far to selling our allies on even the most drastic course of action in Korea", and Eisenhower agreed that the plan for a nuclear assault was not only "most likely to achieve [US] objectives" but also "might be cheaper dollar-wise". The only real concern was Soviet reaction, "since the blow would fall so swiftly and with such force as to eliminate Chinese Communist intervention".[38] The NSC agreed "to consider the atomic bomb as simply another weapon in [the US] arsenal", a policy confirmed in the "New Look" of October.[39]

Yet the NSC, laying the foundations for the ultimate conflict, had set itself a tremendous challenge in its quest for public support: where was the hope in a story of perpetual tension and possible war? As the Secretary of the Treasury, George Humphrey, noted, "There was no use whatever in blowing hot and cold with the public on the atomic situation, frightening them one day and reassuring them the next."[40] If the US public began to ask what they were gaining through their sacrifice, vague references to "freedom" and the contest with totalitarianism might not be sufficient. Eisenhower and his advisors also had to recognize that statements for domestic consumption would be disseminated abroad as well, and foreign peoples would be loathe to endanger their lives in a US–Soviet conflict.

Eisenhower's "Chance for Peace" speech in April tried to meet this concern through its conversion into a public offer to reach agreement with the Soviets and divert military expenditure to social uses, but this was far from a long-term solution. The United States, still believing Moscow would never enter genuine negotiations, was not prepared for a summit with the Soviet Union. The shakiness of Washington's position was exposed in May to all, particularly audiences in Western Europe, when British Prime Minister Winston Churchill made a sudden call for a heads of state meeting with the Soviets and was rebuffed by Eisenhower and the State Department.

The difficulties for US strategy emerged when Robert Oppenheimer briefed the National Security Council on 27 May. All present agreed with Oppenheimer's assertion, "Our only hope in facing this situation was an informed and steady public," but there was division over the wisdom of the hard-line atomic crisis with no possibility of a negotiated resolution. Vannevar Bush argued that the time "might soon approach when, instead of being obliged to attack us with atomic weapons, the Russians would merely confront us with the necessity of agreeing to a vast Munich appeasement", but Humphrey and Charles Wilson, the Secretary of Defense, feared an approach "more likely to frighten people than to reassure them".

As usual, Eisenhower was vague and noncommittal, issuing platitudes such as "instead of trying to raise vague hopes in the minds of the American people, it should be our job to attempt to inspire some really energetic action", "[we] must do more to make people realize their own individual responsibility", and "the emphasis should be on vigilance and sobriety, not panic". The only time he tipped his hand was when Wilson tried to define the issue: "A trying part of the problem was that we would never be the first to use the atomic bomb, whereas the Russians obviously would use it when they were ready." The President responded that he was "not absolutely sure . . . [It was] possible that some action would occur which would force the Government's hand and cause us to resort to atomic bombardment." The NSC, rather than resolving such matters, simply instructed C. D. Jackson to draft a speech.[41]

The Special Assistant soon received help from an unexpected source. The Advertising Council, the institution organized by private industry for "public service" information, suggested an intensive three-month campaign "to promote understanding of the international situation". The president of the council, Theodore Repplier, would collaborate with Jackson and speechwriter Emmet Hughes on the project.[42] With the assistance of another consultant, James Lambie, the group developed Project Candor. It centered upon Jackson's warning:

> The American people do not yet grasp the importance of the President's words that we live in an age of peril. A greater effort is needed to make clear the dangers that confront us, the power of the enemy, the difficulty of reducing that power, and the probable duration of the conflict. . . . This should include information on Soviet atomic capabilities and on the rapid development of the Soviet economy.

The Advertising Council added the advice to overcome "apathy to civilian defense, blood donating, Savings Bonds, etc." The campaign would include 15-minute radio and television broadcasts, introduced and concluded by the President with contributions from Foster Dulles, Allen Dulles, J. Edgar Hoover, Henry Cabot Lodge, the US Ambassador to the United Nations, and Admiral Arthur Radford, the Chairman of the Joint Chiefs of Staff. These would cover "The Age of Peril", "Capabilities of the USSR", "The Threat to the United States", "Communism at Home", and "What Good Citizens can Do". The Advertising Council would distribute "billions of individual impressions via newspapers, magazines, radio, TV, house organs, and car cards".[43]

Over the next four months, little progress was made. Jackson later wrote that the drafts of a presidential speech "either told too much or too little and were uniformly dull",[44] but the real obstacle to the initiative was Eisenhower's hesitancy over the "Age of Peril" approach. The Jackson group's intention was to launch the campaign by early September, either at the dedication of a prototype nuclear reactor or via a national broadcast.[45] Briefed on 28 July, Eisenhower asked who would pay for the campaign and called for an explanation on US steps to counteract the Communist menace, but he set no date for a speech.[46] At the National Security Council the next day, the President called for an early pronouncement but added little beyond a suggestion to drop the tag "the Age of Peril". The NSC agreed in principle but returned the project to Jackson for further development.[47] After four weeks, Jackson returned to the NSC to report "the program was well in hand", with a speech by Eisenhower on the "atomic age" scheduled for early October, only to complain within days that Candor "showed every appearance of being loused up".[48]

The solution came only when Eisenhower came up with the positive dimension to Candor. Taking a break at the Western White House in Denver in early September, he penned a lengthy letter to Foster Dulles. He began on the same lines as Jackson, insisting "we should describe the capability now and in the near future of the H-bomb, supplemented by the A-bomb" and pointing out that the Kremlin "must be fairly assumed to be contemplating their aggressive use". Indeed the President went even further: because the cost of a lengthy commitment to military superiority over Moscow "would either drive us to war or into some form of dictatorial government . . . we would be forced to consider whether or not our duty to future generations did not require us to *initiate* war at the most propitious moment we could designate".

Yet the President also insisted that the United States had to demonstrate at home and abroad that these preparations for a military offensive "had been forced upon us because every honest peaceful gesture or offer of our own had been summarily rejected by the Communists". Thus any Presidential speech had to emphasize that "peaceful gesture" as well as psychologically arming the populace for sustained conflict.[49] Eisenhower offered the answer to his National Security Advisor, Robert Cutler: "Suppose the US and the Soviets were each to turn over to the United Nations, for peaceful use, *x* kilograms of fissionable material?"[50]

This position was clarified further throughout September. When a new draft was circulated by Admiral Radford depicting US atomic might, it was described by Jackson as "the best of any so far" but was ultimately rejected because it portrayed little more than "mortal Soviet Union attack followed by mortal US counter-attack".[51] Jackson finally caught the drift of Eisenhower's thinking. He told a high-level gathering over Saturday breakfast that the speech needed a "lift" to go beyond a description of nuclear threat. He trumpeted, "This cannot only be the most important pronouncement ever made by any President of the United States, it can also save mankind." The meeting agreed, and Candor, renamed in honour of the occasion, became Wheaties.[52]

The State Department still posed an obstacle. Foster Dulles, pushed by the director of the Department's Policy Planning Staff, Robert Bowie, fretted that any speech on atomic matters would worry Western Europeans and threaten the formation of the European Defense Community.[53] The Secretary of State suggested that any statement be deferred until the New Year. Eisenhower, however, "rather liked" the first draft of Wheaties.[54] It was agreed that the "Atoms for Peace" address would be given before the UN General Assembly in December.

While the military feared that the speech might lead to genuine disarmament talks and Foster Dulles continued to grumble, Jackson, verging on rudeness, pushed aside the objections and Eisenhower, "visibly annoyed" with his Secretary of State, settled matters.[55] After some last-minute negotiations, including discussions with British Prime Minister Winston Churchill,[56] Eisenhower delivered his message to the General Assembly on 8 December. In his eyes, he had moved from warning of the "Age of Peril" to "bringing a message of hope" with the "clear prospect of encouraging opportunity" at home and a "vastly improved" international situation.[57] Proposing "joint contributions from . . . stockpiles of normal uranium and fissionable materials to an International Atomic Energy Agency", which would devise applications "to serve the peaceful pursuits of mankind", the President concluded, "The US pledges before you – and therefore before the world – its determination to help solve the fearful atomic dilemma, to devote its entire heart and mind to find the way by which the miraculous inventiveness of man shall not be dedicated to his death, but consecrated to his life."[58]

In fact, little had changed in US policy, where the emphasis was still upon nuclear superiority. Two days after his speech, Eisenhower noted that Churchill had opposed the use of atomic weapons without advance approval by the United Nations and had expressed his concern that "no announcement of [any] proposed use" be made, since this was incompatible with Atoms for Peace. Eisenhower acknowledged the point, but Foster Dulles reiterated that the United States had "come to the conclusion that the atom bomb has to be treated just as another weapon in the arsenal". It "had not renounced its right to use atomic weapons" if hostilities resumed in Korea or "if war were forced upon us by the Soviets". The President concluded, "We, more than any other people, have accepted the atomic age in which we now live. Many European peoples are lagging far behind us and think of themselves only as the defenseless targets of atomic warfare."[59]

The President continued to insist, "If he knew any way to abolish atomic weapons which would ensure the certainty that they would be abolished, he would be the very first to endorse it,"[60] and ponder, "No one was going to be the winner in . . . a nuclear war. The destruction might be such that we might have ultimately to go back to bows and arrows."[61] Yet the National Security Council was more than prepared for atomic warfare in certain situations. Eisenhower commented in August 1954, "If the Communists tried an invasion of Formosa by a fleet of junks, this might make a good target for an atomic bomb."[62] Six months later, during the crisis over the Chinese offshore islands of Quemoy and Matsu, the Administration agreed, "The time may come when the US might have to intervene with atomic weapons," with Eisenhower also recommending napalm as the "best thing to use on land troops".[63] Foster Dulles worried to Eisenhower that US "striking power was apt to be immobilized by moral repugnance".[64] When general policy in 1957 reiterated, "The US should continue efforts to persuade its allies to recognize nuclear weapons as an integral part of the arsenal of the Free World and the need for their prompt and selective use when required," the head of the Atomic Energy Commission, Lewis Strauss, noted, "It was ... essential that public opinion come to understand that the US does possess tactical nuclear weapons and that they can be used in military operations without causing indiscriminate devastation."[65]

Atoms for Peace was no more than a ploy for US officials to avoid acknowledgement of this reality by emphasizing the non-military uses of the atom. Since few in the Administration expected the Soviets to take up Eisenhower's challenge, the speech would reap the advantages of effective propaganda without requiring concrete measures. Coverage was provided in newsreels and 19 films were shown in 79 countries, with news and commentary on the Voice of America, items in newspapers and magazines, "discussions" between Government officials and civic groups, displays at international exhibitions, and millions of leaflets with extracts from the address. To the State Department and Eisenhower's advisors it appeared the President had assumed the high ground left unoccupied after Stalin's death. "The speech captured the hopes of the common man and the imagination of the scientific and intellectual classes. ... The master stroke placed the Kremlin in the position of reacting favorably or standing condemned by their own previous propaganda pleas before the bar of world opinion."[66] US press reaction, spurred by *ad hoc* briefings of reporters on the golf course and in the press secretary's bedroom,[67] was effusive. The syndicated columnist David Lawrence called "Eisenhower's Historic Statement ... one of the craftiest and most penetrating documents flung at the Soviet government since the battle of words began".[68] A UN delegate from a neutral country, quoted in the *New York Herald-Tribune*, offered praise which fully vindicated Eisenhower's strategy: "I came to listen to a message of doom and I found myself listening to a message of hope."[69] US representatives at the United Nations claimed the "practically unanimous view" that the speech was "the most significant and important" ever made by the United States in the forum.[70]

Since, as Foster Dulles noted, "propaganda picturing us as warmongers on account of our atomic capabilities [had] done incalculable harm",[71] the exploitation of Candor and Atoms for Peace was a long-term process. The Operations Coordinating Board set up an interdepartmental working group to direct the activities.[72] Long-term projects included the establishment of an International Atomic Energy Authority, the training of foreign scientists, doctors, and engineers in US universities and laboratories, aid for technical libraries, research reactors, and limited amounts of uranium to friendly countries, and favorable publicity for US nuclear tests.[73] Atoms for Peace exhibits toured the world, for example, travelling for a year in Italy to more than 3 million people, and appeared in Helsinki to offset the World Peace Congress,[74] while $31 million was allocated to construct a nuclear-powered merchant ship for display abroad.[75] In a special exhibit for a Brazilian exposition, visitors could "irradiate a small [Atoms for Peace] souvenir medallion . . . in a large mock pile containing a radioactive source".[76] By April 1954, Jackson, the Atomic Energy Commission's Lewis Strauss, and the CIA's Tom Braden were discussing subsidies for a "private" group to promote Atoms for Peace around the world.[77]

But however impressive Candor might be, it would always be an event, not a strategy. It could always be undercut by contradictory statements, such as Foster Dulles's declaration to the Council on Foreign Relations in January 1954 that the Administration had decided "to depend primarily upon a great capacity to retaliate, instantly, by means and at places of our choosing".[78] More importantly, Candor could not provide the organization for a sustained program of psychological pressure on the Soviet Union. That would have to come through the development of the Operations Coordinating Board.

The OCB's structure resembled that of its predecessor. It was nominally headed by a board consisting of the Director of Central Intelligence, the Undersecretary of State, and the Assistant Secretary of Defence. Its permanent staff was small, consisting of only 48 officals on a $450 million budget,[79] so the bulk of the work was accomplished through a system of working groups, such as the one for the exploitation of Atoms for Peace. By March 1954, there were 23 groups on topics ranging from the projection of US economic policy abroad to operations in Korea.[80]

The essential advantage of the OCB was its placement within the Executive Branch. Because the PSB, established as an autonomous agency, was perceived by the State Department as a rival, it was constantly undermined through resistance or non-cooperation. In contrast, the OCB was sheltered from bureaucratic competition as an adjunct to the NSC, responsible for the implementation of its guidelines.[81] State Department officials accepted the OCB as merely a coordinator, rather than a creator, of operations and contributed wholeheartedly to the system of working groups. Jackson was pleasantly surprised with meetings of the OCB's Special Staff, assessing, "These are turning out to be pretty good sessions . . . [with] very bright men who enjoy a free-wheeling imagination session."[82]

Thus the OCB held out the prospect of a coherent bureaucratic system to implement the psychological offensive. Jackson and his allies, besides pursuing covert operations to weaken the Soviet bloc, were stepping up the overt pressure on Moscow in the latter part of 1953, notably the indictment before the United Nations of the Soviet Union for its reliance upon "slave labor". Western powers had exploited the issue on previous occasions. Britain's first organized propaganda campaign against the Soviets, developed in 1948, claimed 15 million political prisoners in testimony to UN committees;[83] just after the Korean War began, the American delegation focused on the topic to combat Soviet charges of racial discrimination within the United States.[84] The

Government even supervised the preparation of the film masterpiece, *I was a Prisoner in Siberia*.[85]

The forced labour issue was revived when the Eisenhower Administration entered office seeking a riposte to Moscow's "Hate America" campaign, particularly regarding Korea. The US representative at the United Nations, Henry Cabot Lodge, wrote Jackson in early March 1953, "[We must] get the idea across that the Soviets are actually behind the war in Korea, that they are the great warmongers, and therefore we will work at the General Assembly session in September to censure them as aggressors."[86] Lodge's call became urgent when the UN General Assembly, in a major *coup* for the Soviets, voted 51–5 to investigate charges of US bacteriological warfare in Korea. Jackson, disappointed that the United States did not have details "on cruel and inhuman treatment behind the Iron Curtain", called for the propaganda to pursue "communist inhumanities . . . as we go hard with our program in Korea".[87]

The United States also had to counter the skillful presentation by North Korea, China, and the Soviet Union of American prisoners of war who publicly condemned the United States and announced they would not return home after an end to hostilities. The Administration's answer was to highlight the Communist use of brainwashing. For example, Allen Dulles used a speech to his fellow alumni of Princeton University to reveal Moscow's "Brain Warfare . . . to condition the mind so that it no longer reacts on a free will or rational basis but responds to impulses implanted from outside". While Nazi Germany, Italy, and Japan had attempted with "little permanent effect" to apply the technique to their populations, the Soviets had succeeded in the mass indoctrination of hundreds of millions of people to "respond docilely to the orders of their master . . . [for] the creation of a monolithic solidarity in the Soviet state which outwardly gives it the appearance of great unity". Dulles even hinted darkly that the Communists had developed a "lie serum" to produce fabricated confessions from political prisoners and US soldiers.[88]

Privately, Allen Dulles informed the State Department that there was "little scientific evidence to support brainwashing".[89] It was the propaganda, however, that had the lasting effect. Foster Dulles told the National Security Council of an interview with a prisoner of war, belatedly returning to the United States, who "had been been thoroughly brainwashed by the Chinese Communists": "The manner in which this individual "carried on" before the press and cameras was shocking. . . . He was vitriolic in his criticism of the US to the point that it would make one's blood run cold to witness such a demonstration on the part of any American."[90] The Secretary of State may have been influenced by a concentrated effort to discredit the 21 American PoWs who had refused to return. "Recognizing that an attack should be launched based on character assassination together with labeling the 21 'zombies'," US officials "stimulated" articles by prominent journalists like John Bartlow

Martin and Hodding Carter and produced interviews with "PoW victims" of the 21 soldiers.[91]

The broader US counter-attack, including the charges about forced labor, began to take shape in April 1953. A "List of Soviet Vulnerabilities for Possible Exploitation at the United Nations" indicted Moscow for every atrocity from "police terror, purges, and political murders" to the "cultural genocide of national minorities" to "perversion, of science, art, history, and literature". Communist "banditry" included "crimes on and over the high seas, kidnappings, and brainwashing and forced confessions of free world citizens", not to mention "drug traffic, black marketeering, and illegal trade".[92]

The campaign on Soviet forced labour crystallized around an International Labor Organization report, due for release in July. Jackson noted that this was "perfect news peg" to meet claims of US responsibility for the East German uprising: "In the last analysis, what were these uprisings? Nothing but protests against slavery, that most horrible form of human bondage. Slaves will always eventually rise. It is the Communist system which has within itself the seed of its own destruction."[93] The Special Assistant arranged for Eisenhower to "answer" at a press conference that it had been "established that the work of prisoners . . . [was] of considerable significance" in the Soviet system.[94] A 138-page booklet on *A New Slavery: The Communist Betrayal of Human Rights* was prepared with the help of the National Committee for Free Europe. *Life* magazine compared "The New Slavery" with the US precedent:

> The slave owner fed, clothed, and cared for his slaves; it was against his economic interests to work them to death. In Communist-dominated countries, however, the state owns all the slaves and doesn't mind working them to death in the least.[95]

The State Department hindered the campaign, raising numerous objections to the presentations at the United Nations and offering little in the way of ideas,[96] and the military caused further problems by failing to coordinate their public statements.[97] The combination of Jackson and Lodge proved formidable, however. Lodge took on the rhetoric of his Soviet counterpart, Andrei Vyshinsky, with "great success" by comparing freedom in the United States with the lack of an alternative in the Soviet media to the regime's "hate propaganda".[98] US observers reported Vyshinsky "clearly demonstrated a feeling that he was definitely up against something new. . . . It was clear that the Lodge offensive had taken all by surprise and had disconcerted him considerably."[99]

Meanwhile, the Administration pursued its program to counter the propaganda of the defecting US soldiers in North Korea. Stories of Communist atrocities made a "very effective 1–2 punch", with the Department of Defense alone distributing 35 million copies of a booklet on Communist war crimes.[100] In fact, there had been "very few reports of atrocities after 1951", but US officials dramatized their assertions as "not just a story of 'man's inhumanity to man' – more basically a story of breakdown of human standards – more basically still, the deliberate breaking of those standards as part of a plan of world conquest".[101] This was supported by the emphasis on North Korean and Chinese prisoners of war who refused to return to their native lands, with US propaganda claiming "98 percent of the prisoners interviewed to date have refused to go through the door leading back to communism".[102]

Yet the central question remained: would the OCB risk a general offensive against the Soviets? Some officials were keen to "develop our capabilities for appropriate supporting, harassing, and diversionary actions short of precipitate overt military action",[103] but US Chiefs of Mission in Europe tried to set definite limits on any Government campaign:

> Pronouncements by important American officials about the "liberation" of Eastern Europe cause fear and anxiety in Western European capitals. It is generally believed that American impatience and implacable hostility to Communism might result in hasty and ill-considered action and that American political warfare and covert operations directed against Eastern Europe might set up a chain reaction leading to military conflict.
>
> Our psychological warfare effort should be tailored to assist in keeping this spirit [of resistance in Eastern Europe] in existence but should never incite to rebellion or revolts which could only have the effect of destroying the healthiest and best resistance elements.[104]

C. D. Jackson replied to the ambassadors in no uncertain terms. An increase in "repressive pressures" was not to be feared, since it would only bring forward the day of liberation. As for Western European opinion, Jackson was dismissive:

> Sure, we must coordinate, and get support, and reassure, and play ball, and be just as sweet and cooperative and reasonable as we can be, but every now and then we must feel free to do something in the American interest, even though it is not 100 percent acceptable in London, or Paris, or Rome, or wherever. . . .
>
> If we want peace in Europe, we'd better try it our way for a change. None of the other ways seem to have worked too well.[105]

The bureaucratic battle was destined to continue, for until the National Security Council abandoned the rhetoric of victory over Communism, irrespective of their caution about specific operations, the network for liberation would function in a vacuum of policy. Theodore Streibert, the head of the US Information Agency, summarized the effects of indecision: "We are now effectively organized to engage in psychological warfare but we have no long-term strategic plan. We have no appraisal or basis for judgement as to the enemy's cold war capabilities and whether our methods and resources as presently constituted are sufficient to win over the enemy."[106]

Notes

1 Theodore Streibert oral history, 10 December 1970, DDE, Oral History Collection
2 Jackson daily logs, 21 August and 2 October 1953, DDE, Jackson Papers, 1956, Log 1953 (2)
3 Jackson daily log, 28 October 1953, DDE, Jackson Papers, Box 56, Log 1953 (2)
4 See Eisenhower to Wilson, 2 November 1953, *Diaries*, Reel 1
5 Jackson to Cutler, 1 March 1954, DDE, Jackson Records, Box 6, Volunteer Freedom Corps
6 Kennan to Jackson, 15 September 1953, DDE, Jackson Records, Box 4, George Kennan
7 Jackson to Lodge, 20 May 1953, DDE, Jackson Records, Box 4, Henry Cabot Lodge
8 Jackson daily log, 12 November 1953, DDE, Jackson Papers, Box 56, Log 1953 (2)
9 Jackson daily log, 24 November 1953, DDE, Jackson Papers, Box 56, Log 1953 (2)
10 Obolensky to Jackson, 3 April 1953, DDE, Jackson Records, Box 5, O; Sergievsky to Stevens, 7 January 1954, DDE, Jackson Records, Box 56, Alexis A. Lodigensky
11 Scott to Smith, 20 September 1952, US DDRS, 1991 1130; CIA analysis of foreign language press, 5 January 1953, US DDRS, 1991 743
12 Thompson to Human Events, 4 April 1953, DDE, Jackson Records, Box 6, W
13 Sherer memorandum of conversation, 12 March 1954, USNA, Department of State, Lot 59 D 233, Miscellaneous Office Files of the Assistant Secretary of State for European Affairs, 1943–1957, Box 27
14 Jackson to Myers, 19 February 1953, DDE, Jackson Records, Box 6, U
15 Partridge to Allen Dulles, 3 August 1953, DDE, Jackson Records, Box 5, Radio Free Europe
16 "Who Needs Propaganda?", *New York Daily Mirror*, 5 February 1953
17 Johnson press release, 15 July 1953, *Diaries*, Reel 18
18 McCardle to Johnson, 17 March 1953, FRUS, 1952–1954, II, 1685–6
19 IIA press release and McCarthy to Johnson, 9 July 1953, *Diaries*, Reel 18
20 Jackson to Eisenhower, 3 July 1953, *Diaries*, Reel 18
21 Johnson to Eisenhower, 15 May 1955, *Diaries*, Reel 19
22 153rd NSC meeting, 9 July 1953, US DDRS, 1992 323
23 164th NSC meeting, 1 October 1953, US DDRS, 1991 1969
24 Thomas Sorenson, *The Word War: The Story of American Propaganda* (New York, 1968), 49
25 Jackson to Luce, 12 August 1953, DDE, Jackson Papers, Box 57, Henry R. Luce–Clare Boothe Luce, 1953–1954
26 Streibert to Bedell Smith, 1 March 1954, FRUS, 1952–1954, II, 1761–4
27 Thomas Powers, *The Man who Kept the Secrets: Richard Helms and the CIA* (New York, 1979), 75–7
28 Special meeting with civilian consultants, 31 March 1953, *Minutes*, 1st Supplement, Reel 1
29 Gray to Smith, 29 November 1951, US DDRS, 1991 2298; Barnes to Godel, 29 December 1951, US DDRS, 1988 1699
30 Possony memorandum, 6 October 1952, US DDRS, 1987 2333
31 "A Report of a Panel of Consultants on Disarmament of the Department of State," January 1953, *Minutes*, 1st Supplement, Reel 1
32 Briefing for 18 February 1953 National Security Council meeting, undated, *Minutes*, 1st Supplement, Reel 1; 134th NSC meeting, 25 February 1953, US DDRS, 1987 2918
33 Final report of the Jackson Committee, 30 June 1953, US DDRS, 1987 1120
34 Special meeting with civilian consultants, 31 March 1953, *Minutes*, 1st Supplement, Reel 1
35 Jackson to Dean, 3 April 1953, DDE, Jackson Records, Box 2, Gordon Dean
36 Dean speech for University of Southern California Founders' Day, 5 October 1951, DDE, Jackson Records, Box 2, Gordon Dean
37 Vojtech Mastry, *The Cold War and Soviet Insecurity: The Stalin Years* (New York, 1996),

164; Special meeting with civilian consultants, 31 March 1953, *Minutes*, 1st Supplement, Reel 1

38 144th NSC meeting, 13 May 1953, US DDRS, 1991 2013; 145th NSC meeting, 23 May 1953, *Minutes*, 1st Supplement, Reel 1

39 143rd NSC meeting, 6 May 1953, US DDRS, 1986 2027; Lay memorandum, 14 March 1955, US DDRS, 1987 2908

40 134th NSC meeting, 25 February 1953, US DDRS, 1987 2918

41 146th NSC meeting, 27 May 1953, *Minutes*, 1st Supplement

42 White House staff meeting, 26 May 1953, *Diaries*, Reel 1

43 "Project Candor," 22 July 1953, *Minutes*, 1st Supplement

44 Jackson memorandum, "Chronology Candor-Wheaties," 30 January 1954, *Office Files*, Reel 4

45 Cutler to Jackson, 20 July 1953, *Minutes*, 1st Supplement

46 Cutler to Jackson, 28 July 1953, *Minutes*, 1st Supplement

47 157th NSC meeting, 30 July 1953, *Minutes*, 1st Supplement

48 160th NSC meeting, 27 August 1953, *Minutes*, 1st Supplement; Jackson daily log, 2 September 1953, DDE, Jackson Papers, Box 56, Log 1953 (2)

49 Eisenhower to Foster Dulles, 8 September 1953, *Diaries*, Reel 1

50 Cutler memorandum, 10 September 1953, US DDRS, 1988 2352

51 Jackson daily log, 16 September 1953, DDE, Jackson Papers, Box 56, Log 1953 (2); Jackson memorandum, "Chronology Candor-Wheaties," 30 January 1954, *Office Files*, Reel 4

52 Jackson to Eisenhower, 2 October 1953, *Office Files*, Reel 8

53 Jackson daily logs, 17 and 23 October 1953, DDE, Jackson Papers, Box 56, Log 1953 (2)

54 Jackson daily log, 4 November 1953, DDE, Jackson Papers, Box 56, Log 1953 (2)

55 Jackson daily logs, 17, 27, and 30 November 1953, DDE, Jackson Papers, Box 56, Log 1953 (2)

56 Jackson summary of Bermuda 4–8 December 1953, undated, US DDRS, 1987 2943

57 Eisenhower to Harlow, 3 December 1953, *Diaries*, Reel 1. See also Dwight Eisenhower to Milton Eisenhower, 11 December 1953, *Diaries*, Reel 1

58 Quoted in Dwight Eisenhower, *The White House Years: Volume I, Mandate for Change, 1953–1956* (New York, 1963), 253

59 Eisenhower record of meeting with Foster Dulles, Churchill, and Eden, 6 December 1953, US DDRS, 1997 0517; 174th NSC meeting, 10 December 1953, *Minutes*, 1st Supplement, Reel 3

60 203rd NSC meeting, 23 June 1954, US DDRS, 1986 2815

61 272nd NSC meeting, 12 January 1956, US DDRS, 1987 427

62 209th NSC meeting, 5 August 1954, US DDRS, 1986 2883

63 Cutler memorandum of White House meeting, 11 March 1955, *Minutes*, 1st Supplement, Reel 3

64 Dulles memorandum, 28 December 1955, US DDRS, 1988 766

65 325th NSC meeting, 27 May 1957, US DDRS, 1987 1023; 326th NSC meeting, 13 June 1957, US DDRS, 1987 917

66 Summary of USIA Exploitation of Eisenhower 8 December 1953, 17 December 1953, US DDRS, 1990 420; "The Atom for Progress and Peace," undated, US DDRS, 1991 3517

67 Jackson summary of Bermuda 4–8 December 1953, undated, US DDRS, 1987 2943

68 David Lawrence, "Eisenhower's Historic Statement," undated, in DDE, Jackson Records, Box 2, C

69 Roscoe Drummond, "Some Questions the Kremlin will Ponder," 14 December 1953, in DDE, Jackson Records, Box 2, C

70 "UN Reaction to Eisenhower Speech," 9 December 1953, US DDRS, 1990 371

71 210th NSC meeting, 12 August 1954, US DDRS, 1986 2028

72 Meetings of OCB Working Group on Nuclear Energy and Information Programs, January 1955–May 1957, US DDRS, 1991 3515
73 Summary of USIA Exploitation of Eisenhower 8 December 1953, 17 December 1953, US DDRS, 1990 420; "The Atom for Progress and Peace," undated, US DDRS, 1991 3517
74 "The USIA Program," 11 August 1955, US DDRS, 1991 2022
75 244th NSC meeting, 7 April 1955, US DDRS, 1990 919
76 Outline for USIA exhibit at Sao Paulo Quadricentennial Exposition, undated [1954], US DDRS, 1991 2613
77 Jackson daily log, 14 April 1954, DDE, Jackson Papers, Box 56, Log 1954
78 For at least one official, National Security Advisor Robert Cutler, the initiative was far from a success. When a new propaganda campaign was considered in 1957, Cutler warned, "We do not wish to get involved again in anything like our ill-fated 'Operation Candor'." (312th NSC meeting, 7 February 1957, US DDRS, 1987 954)
79 Jackson to Dodge, 30 September 1953, DDE, Jackson Records, Box 1, OCB, Miscellaneous Memoranda (2); Morgan to OCB, 29 September 1953, DDE, Jackson Records, Box 1, OCB, Miscellaneous Memoranda (3)
80 See OCB progress report on International Communication of US Economic Policy, 13 September 1954, US DDRS, 1990 2369; OCB Outline Plan of Operations with Respect to Korea, 14 March 1956, US DDRS, 1990 2240
81 Technically, the OCB was not placed under the National Security Council because of a Justice Department opinion that it was not permissible under the terms of the 1947 National Security Act, but in practice the board functioned as a working "subcommittee" of the Council. (See William Jackson to Eisenhower, 1 October 1954, DDE, Jackson Papers, Box 52, William Jackson)
82 Jackson daily log, 19 October 1953, DDE, Jackson Papers, Box 56, Log 1953 (2)
83 See W. Scott Lucas and C. J. Morris, "A Very British Crusade: The Information Research Department and the Beginnings of the Cold War," in Richard Aldrich (ed.), British Intelligence, Strategy, and the Cold War (London, 1992), 85–110
84 See Helen Laville and Scott Lucas, "Edith Sampson, the NAACP, and African American Identity in the Cold War," Diplomatic History, fall 1996, 565–90
85 Report on I was a Prisoner in Siberia, 11 May 1953, DDE, Jackson Records, Box 5, Movies
86 Lodge to Jackson, 9 March 1953, DDE, Jackson Records, Box 4, Henry Cabot Lodge
87 Jackson to Lodge, 21 April 1953, Jackson Records, Box 4, Henry Cabot Lodge
88 Dulles speech to National Alumni Conference of the Graduate Council of Princeton University, 10 April 1953, DDE, Jackson Records, Box 3
89 Dulles to Under-secretary of State, undated, US DDRS, 1988 603
90 242nd NSC meeting, 24 March 1955, US DDRS, 1986 3294
91 OCB Prisoner of War Working Group, 4 February 1954, US DDRS, 1994 496
92 List of Soviet Vulnerabilities for Possible Exploitation at the United Nations, 30 April 1953, US DDRS, 1987 2111
93 Jackson to Taylor, 22 June 1953, DDE, Jackson Records, Box 6, T
94 Jackson to Hagerty, 21 July 1953, DDE, Jackson Records, Box 3, James Hagerty
95 Life, "The UN and the New Slavery," in DDE, Jackson Records, Box 2, C
96 Irwin to Craig, 19 August 1953, DDE, Jackson Records, Box 4, Henry Cabot Lodge
97 Lodge to Jackson, 29 October 1953, DDE, Jackson Records, Box 4, Henry Cabot Lodge
98 US Delegation to the United Nations press release, 23 November 1953, and Lodge to Jackson, 27 November 1953, DdE, Jackson Records, Box 4, Henry Cabot Lodge
99 OCB Prisoner of War Working Group, 8 December 1953, US DDRS, 1992 2860
100 Norberg to Acting Deputy Executive Officer, 13 September 1953, DDE, Jackson Records, Box 1, OCB, Organization, Functions, Budget, etc.
101 OCB Prisoner of War Working Group, 10 November 1953, US DDRS, 1992 2854; Norberg to CIA, 12 November 1953, US DDRS, 1992 2647

102 Craig to Jackson, 28 October 1953, US DDRS, 1992 2646
103 Hirsch to Jackson, 3 November 1953, US DDRS, 1991 3431
104 Chiefs of Mission meeting, 22–4 September 1953, "Concept and Ideas for Psychological Warfare in Europe," DDE, Jackson Records, Box 4, Luxembourg Meeting of Mission Chiefs
105 Jackson to Minnich, undated, US DDRS, 1991 2953
106 Streibert to Bedell Smith, 12 May 1954, US DDRS, 1988 437

12

A world safe for democracy

In February 1954, C. D. Jackson tried one more time to win Eisenhower's leadership of the great crusade against Moscow. He wrote the President:

> If, during 1954, we have the guts and the skill to maintain constant pressure at all points of the Soviet orbit, we will get dividends from such a policy. . . . At some time or other during 1954, the combination of external discontent and the fruits of internal unfulfilled appeasement will start working our favor in a great big way.[1]

The State Department protested, "We should like to record our strong feeling that it would be extremely dangerous to assume that the USSR, because of internal difficulties or trouble in the satellites, is so weakened that it will not any circumstances resort to war."[2] Far from rebuffing the approach, Eisenhower requested Jackson's general review of Soviet vulnerabilities. Jackson immediately consulted the CIA's Allen Dulles and Frank Wisner to draw up recommendations for action, including options within East Germany and the "detachment of Country X [Albania]".[3] (Dulles and Wisner were only curbed when, during yet another show trial of captured US agents, it became apparent that the Albanian secret police were running the supposed "resistance" within the country.[4])

This was not enough to keep Jackson in the Administration. The Special Assistant always claimed that he intended to serve the White House for only a year, instituting the grand offensive and then turning it over to other hands, but it is possible that he would have remained had he received Eisenhower's commitment to an aggressive program. In January, he had submitted his letter of resignation but recanted when Eisenhower's press secretary, James Hagerty, declared this would undercut Jackson's effectiveness at the upcoming conference of Foreign Ministers with the Soviets, the conference that Jackson had sought ever since Stalin's death. Hagerty also explained that Jackson's letter, explaining his view of the Administration's foreign policy, was "too long to release to [the] press and too corny".[5]

Jackson perceived that he had been given another opportunity to win Eisenhower over. His spirits were further lifted by his view of the conference of Foreign Ministers in Berlin. He believed the United States had triumphed on

key issues – "[the] West's position on [the] German problem [was] today unas-
sailable both intellectually and emotionally" – and had presented the better
face to global onlookers. Jackson enthused, "If Hollywood had been given the
assignment of producing the Russian delegation, they could not have done a
better job. They all look just the way we would want a Communist delegation to look."[6]

In mid-March, Jackson told the President of the conclusions reached with
Allen Dulles and Wisner and repeated the appeal to break up the Soviet bloc.[7]
When Eisenhower offered no endorsement, Jackson recognized that he would
be perpetually fighting the State Department over the campaign. He received
little consolation when the President wrote in May, "For a long time I
have been acutely conscious of the gap that has existed here ever since you
left. . . . I have a distinct sense of uneasiness."[8]

Jackson could still claim that his 14 months in the White House had produced dividends. His assertion, "The concept that there is no such thing as
'psychological warfare', separate and apart from the policies and acts of the
Government, has been accepted,"[9] was a bit disingenuous, since the out-of-
favor PSB had fought for the concept years earlier, but it did reflect the bureaucratic advances with the establishment of the Operations Coordinating Board.
Most significant was the confirmation in March 1954 by the National
Security Council, in NSC 5412, of the OCB as "the normal channel for secur-
ing coordination of support among the Departments of State and Defense
and the CIA". The National Security Council, ever cognizant "of the vicious
covert activities of the USSR and Communist China and the governments,
parties, and groups dominated by them (hereinafter collectively referred to
as 'International Communism')", again sanctioned action to "create and
exploit troublesome problems for International Communism, impairing relations between the USSR and Communist China and between them and
their satellites, complicating control within the USSR, Communist China, and
their satellites, and retarding the growth of the military and economic potential of the Soviet bloc". This would include initiatives to "develop underground resistance and facilitate covert and guerrilla operations". Significantly
the OCB would not only supervise "black" propaganda but also "gray" propaganda, "agreeing upon principles which would govern . . . unattributable
activities".[10]

An important example of the OCB's impact was its role in policy-making
on Vietnam. The conflict between France, with its colonial position in
Indochina, and Vietnamese nationalism had increasingly occupied the Truman
Administration. As early as 1949, the CIA and Voice of America were "weakening the solidarity of the Communist movement in Vietnam",[11] but it was in
April 1950, as NSC 68 was being drafted, that the National Security Council
concluded, "It is important to US security interests that all practicable
measures be taken to prevent further communist expansion in Southeast

Asia. Indochina is a key area of Southeast Asia and is under immediate threat."[12]

Time magazine led the public promotion of Indochina as "a new frontier and a new ally in the Cold War". The "former Emperor and reformed playboy" Bao Dai, now "Chief of State" of Vietnam, was honored with a cover portrait. "The job of rallying anti-Communist forces" would fall "mainly on [his] meaty shoulders", supported by US economic and military aid as well as French troops.[13] Overseas, the Administration considered propaganda themes "which appeal to legitimate nationalist aspirations of people of Associated States of Indochina without jeopardizing French efforts to stem Communist aggression".[14] Officials of the Mutual Security Agency stressed, "The US is failing to 'sell' this program to the natives. . . . We were placing too much emphasis on military aid at the expense of economic aid. . . . Our propaganda . . . was failing to bring home to the natives the connection between our military aid and their welfare."[15] This concept of "propaganda" was soon broadened to include covert action. Officials of the PSB argued:

> We can't take all the political action we'd like to because of global tie-ins. We can't take all the military action that might be desirable because we don't have all the resources. So we've got to move into the paramilitary and undercover field just to substitute for the actions that we'd like to take and can't.[16]

In one of its last reports, the PSB reiterated that US support for French military action, combined with recognition of Vietnamese national aspirations, must "be supplemented by overt, gray, and black propaganda operations".[17]

In early 1954, the situation in Vietnam became a crisis when Vietnamese forces surrounded the French garrison at Dien Bien Phu. Eisenhower established his "domino theory" with the argument that "the loss of Indochina could not be insulated and . . . would, shortly after, cost us the rest of Southeast Asia",[18] while the Operations Coordinating Board placed Vietnam within the global struggle of ideologies:

> Overall Communist ambitions in Korea was [sic] a united Korea under Communism, similarly in Indochina is a united Viet Nam (Indochina) under Communism. . . . The life blood of political culture is the Leninist dogma which flows from Moscow through Peiping to the Democratic Republic of Vietnam. The Soviets and Chinese have installed their watchdogs along the various feeder lines to ensure that party directives conform with orthodoxy.[19]

The President contributed to the ideological strategy by asking "whether it would be possible to capitalize on the religious issue . . . [with] a good Buddhist leader to whip up some real fervor". Colleagues "pointed out to the President that, unhappily, Buddha was a pacifist rather than a fighter".[20] For weeks, the Eisenhower Administration considered military intervention, notably conventional bombing and even the use of atomic weapons, but it backed away when it could not win the support of other Western powers.

Reluctantly the United States accepted the Geneva conference, where it observed – but did not sign – the agreement dividing Vietnam at the 17th parallel, but US efforts to trouble, if not topple, the Government in North Vietnam had only begun. The prescient advice of Secretary of Defence Wilson that there was "nothing but grief in store for us if we remained in this area"[21] was disregarded. In January 1954, well before the Geneva Accords, Foster Dulles argued in the National Security Council:

> If we could carry on effective guerrilla operations against this new Viet Minh government, we should be able to make as much trouble for this government as they had made for our side and against the legitimate governments of the Associated States in recent years. Moreover, the costs would be relatively low. . . . We can raise hell and the Communists will find it just as expensive to resist as we are now finding it.

Foster Dulles's specific suggestion of guerrilla activities is still classified, but the President was impressed enough to say "he wished we could have done something like this after the victory of the Communists in China". The National Security Council accordingly instructed Allen Dulles to develop plans for covert activity.[22]

The plan for "Political Warfare against the Vietminh" was produced in May. Emperor Bao Dai should be induced to hand power to a new government so the United States could implement an "intense psychological warfare program to rally popular support" and prove the "independence" of South Vietnam. Meanwhile, a campaign "to exploit fears of Chinese domination and loss of independence by states within the Communist orbit" would be waged with "all forms of unconventional guerrilla and paramilitary warfare". Within two years, a force of 20,000 in Vietnam, 5,000 in Cambodia, and 5,000 in Laos would be established.[23]

The OCB assumed the task of developing this "missing ingredient" of psychological warfare. It orchestrated the propaganda for the Geneva conference, including "material on Chinese Communist aggression, barbarism and criminal actions, [and] Chinese imperialism in Tibet and Southeast Asia" and Soviet involvement in Indochina.[24] After the conference, it established a special Working Group for Indo-China. Plans generated by the working group ranged from economic measures to cripple the North Vietnamese economy while bolstering the "free market" in the South to authorisation of new USIA radio transmitters to supervision of domestic and foreign publicity for the flow of refugees, partly induced by American covert propaganda, from North Vietnam to "Free Vietnam".[25] By January 1955, American officials could boast about the 500,000 people who had left the North: "It was quite a thrilling sight . . . to see the refugee camps. While their squalor was disheartening, one took courage from the fortitude of these people who had so prized liberty and democracy that they had fled from their homes."[26] Throughout the process, South Vietnamese Premier Ngo Dinh Diem was promoted as the savior of Vietnamese democracy, even as the United States recognized that, since Ho Chi Minh's victory was inevitable, it must sabotage the elections scheduled for July 1956 to unify Vietnam. Foster Dulles told the National Security Council, "It was altogether illusory to imagine that the US could possibly succeed in getting any agreement by the Communists for calling off these elections. . . . There were, however, . . . other techniques, many of which were very familiar to the Soviets."[27]

Those "other techniques" were spearheaded by Colonel Edward Lansdale, later the model for Graham Greene's *The Quiet American*, who was fresh from a major psychological warfare success in the Philippines.[28] In June 1954, weeks before the Geneva accords, Lansdale had organized a team of a dozen specialists to sabotage that agreement and undermine North Vietnam. In addition to stimulating the exodus of refugees from North to South through counterfeit documents, soothsayers predicting catastrophe under the Communists, and slogans like "the Virgin Mary is going south", Lansdale's unit tried to disrupt the infrastructure of the North. Foreign substances were placed in the gas tanks of buses, oil for North Vietnamese trams was treated with acid, and explosives were placed among coal for trains. Paramilitary units placed in the North gathered intelligence and tried to stimulate uprisings.[29]

This effort to "roll back" Communism in North Vietnam and maintain the regime in the South was part of a wider strategy in which China was the primary concern. A National Intelligence Estimate in October 1954 concluded, "Although the USSR possesses preponderant influence in the Sino-Soviet partnership, the main outlines of Communist policy in Asia are almost certainly determined jointly by consultation between Moscow and Peiping, not by the dictation of Moscow. Chinese Communist influence in the Sino-Soviet alliance will probably continue to grow."[30] The OCB coordinated an information and educational program for Chinese nationals who lived outside the country while the defense of Taiwan was formally incorporated into US military strategy "even at grave risk of general war". The new commitment was symbolized by the loan of 10 naval craft to the Chinese Nationalists and maneuvers of the Seventh Fleet off the coast of mainland China.[31]

Meanwhile the option of toppling Peking was kept open. Using the National Security Council's guideline to "encourage and covertly assist the Chinese Nationalist Government to develop and extend logistical support of anticommunist guerrillas on the mainland of China, for purposes of resistance and intelligence", the OCB authorized military aid to develop a Taiwanese force "capable of limited offensive operations". This would "be able to undertake more effective raids against the Communist mainland and seaborne commerce with Communist China", "continue to present a threat to Communist China and add significantly to the strategic reserves potentially available to the free world in the Far East", and "be able to initiate such large-scale amphibious operations" against the mainland with US logistic support. While the United States would not yet make the formal commitment to return the Chinese Nationalists to power in Peking, Washington would "develop Formosa [Taiwan] as an effective base for psychological operations against the main-land . . . in collaboration with the Chinese Nationalist Government when appropriate". The Voice of America supported the effort with "news from Formosa which depicted Free China as a united force".[32] CIA field operatives went so far as to propose in spring 1955 that a bomb be placed on the plane carrying Chinese Premier Chou en-Lai to a conference of non-aligned nations in Indonesia. The suggestion was supposedly vetoed by Washington; however, another aircraft carrying Chinese officials was destroyed *en route* to the conference.[33]

Other operations in Asia illustrated the comprehensive scope of the OCB's work. Plans for Thailand built upon a two-phase program designed by the PSB for Bangkok as "the logical – in fact the only possible – focus" for a US campaign "as long as the French maintain a foothold in Vietnam". Even after French withdrawal, Thailand "would continue to play a significant role in any sound U.S. strategic concept for Southeast Asia".[34] In the first phase, the United States would "stimulate, crystallize, maintain, and coordinate the active resistance in Thailand to Communist aggression, subversion, and oppression". Then the United States would "expand paramilitary and other programs beyond the borders of Thailand" into Indochina. The nature as well as the importance of the effort was symbolized by the appointment of William Donovan, the former head of the Office of Strategic Services, as US ambas-sador to Thailand.[35] By early 1954 the OCB was reporting that it had acted to "induce the Thai Government to carry out measures to reduce vulnerabil-ities to Communist subversion and combat Communist influence on former opposition leaders".[36] The Cabinet had established a board under the Prime Minister to liaise with Donovan and selected members of the US embassy. Activities were under way in the border area with Laos, the United States con-sidering a mobile transmitter under Thai control.[37]

The OCB also oversaw the culmination of a large-scale US effort to ensure a suitable government in the Philippines. Covert operations had been acceler-ated since 1950 with the dispatch of Edward Lansdale to the country. Lans-dale, backed by millions of dollars of secret funds, fought the struggle against the Hukbalahap insurgents by encouraging social development and land reform while conducting an aggressive campaign of psychological warfare. Orders, forged by Lansdale, for a Hukbalahap massacre of the citizenry were duly featured on the front page of the *Manila Times*, while, in a notorious operation, he played on fears in the Philippine countryside of vampires:

A psywar squad entered an area and planted rumors that an asuang [vampire] lived where the Communists were based. Two nights later, after giving the rumors time to circulate among Huk sympathizers, the psywar squad laid an ambush for the rebels. When a Huk patrol passed, the ambushers snatched the last man, punctured his neck vampire-fashion with two holes, hung his body until the blood drained out, and put the corpse back on the trail. As superstitious as any other Filipinos, the insurgents fled from the region.[38]

The OCB's major responsibility was the less dramatic task of detailed arrangements for the presidential elections, held in November 1953, to ensure the success of Defense Minister Ramon Magsaysay, with suitable publicity around the world.[39] Lansdale was a close advisor to Magsaysay, sleeping in the same room and, on one occasion, punching and knocking out the Minister when advice was not accepted. "I understand," reassured Magsaysay when he came to. "It is because you care so much about the Philippine people."[40]

The CIA funded the "independent" National Movement for Free Elections, which ensured the campaign arrangements favored Magsaysay. Other measures included support of propaganda units in the Filipino military for anti-Huk operations, publicity for civic programs of land reform and road building, and films like *His Honor, the Citizen*.[41] A naval task force appeared in Manila while a subtler tour was made by Anna Lord Strauss, the President of the League of Women Voters. In a country where 80 percent of the population was nominally Catholic, the Catholic Welfare Organization, the Knights of Columbus, and cooperative priests were used to spread US propaganda.[42] Magsaysay's subsequent victory was "one of the most important and favorable developments for the US in the Far East in a very long time", offering "the means of developing a much greater solidarity among the free countries of the Far East against Communism".[43] Eisenhower announced, "Now, this is the way I like to see an election run."[44]

The OCB also went further than the Psychological Strategy Board in establishing a program to "protect" Latin America from Communist infiltration. The ideology behind the policy was captured in the July 1954 progress report of the working group on the region, "The US, as the first colony of modern history to win independence for itself, instinctively shares the aspirations for liberty of all dependent and colonial peoples. It is US policy to help, not hinder, the spread of liberty. The US has in the past and will continue in the future to sponsor the development of political independence." By autumn this had been packaged as "Militant Liberty", where "the ideology of individual freedom [was] supported by self-disciplined peoples, politically and enthusiastically dedicated to freedom and the implementation of freedom on a worldwide basis".[45]

Every measure of significance – political, economic, military, "information", and cultural – was reviewed by the OCB and incorporated into regional and country plans.[46] The National Security Council sanctioned the board to "intensify appropriate [deleted] efforts to combat the activities of communist and other elements hostile to the US, through political warfare methods consistent with the proscription of [deleted] unilateral intervention". Emphasis was placed on the stimulation of indigenous propaganda.[47] In one notable case, the USIA was able to prompt a number of Catholic priests to "deliver sermons exposing communism, based on our material".[48]

This general approach influenced the centerpiece of the Eisenhower Administration's campaign to halt Communism in the western hemisphere, the overthrow of the Arbenz Government in Guatemala. The Truman Administration had been wary of the reforming policies of the regime which came to power in 1949, the State Department condemning "an excessive nationalism which has manifested itself by a hostile attitude toward private US companies operating in Guatemala, a proclivity on the part of a weak President and others in the government for fuzzy ecnomic and political philosophies and an upsurge of the influence of international communism of the Latin American variety".[49] Yet, as late as 1951, the CIA assessed that President Jacobo Arbenz Guzman was "relatively favorable to business interests, including those of the US, despite the campaign alliance which existed between Arbenz and the Communists".[50] In summer 1952, Truman did endorse development of a plan, presented by Nicaraguan dictator Anastasio Somoza, for the overthrow of Arbenz; however, as a United Fruit Company freighter loaded with weapons and ammunition moved towards the Nicaraguan base, Acheson and Bedell Smith persuaded Truman to withdraw his support.[51]

The Eisenhower Administration, spurred by the sensational reports of the press and its own officials, soon reconsidered this policy. Less than a month after the inauguration, Allen Dulles told the National Security Council, "The most serious immediate situation was in Guatemala, where the development of pro-Communist influence was such as to mark an approaching crisis. It was quite possible . . . that Guatemala's neighbors might take military action to protect themselves from the Communist infection in Guatemala."[52] C. D. Jackson called for "withdrawal of recognition from the present Guatemalan regime and a *coup* inside that country".[53] These sentiments were projected publicly via "news" like that in the *Wall Street Journal* that "Communist Minority in Guatemala Worms Way into near Control". Evidence of Communist influence included a vote in the Guatemalan Congress for 30 seconds of silence after Stalin's death and copies of the Latin American edition of the Soviet weekly *New Times* on street corners.[54]

By October, the departing US ambassador in Guatemala, Rudolf Schoenfeld, was briefing the State Department, "[The] Communist power-drive in Guatemala [had] reached an advanced state of infiltration." While Arbenz believed he could deal with Communist elements, he had "not even begun to appreciate the real purposes and techniques of communism as a power-seeking movement, not a social reform".[55] The Vice-President of the United Fruit

Company, the agricultural giant seeking Arbenz's removal because of his commitment to land reform, was shepherded around the Executive Branch by the National Security Advisor, Robert Cutler, to report on "Communist infiltration in Latin America". C. D. Jackson described the emissary as "very savvy".[56]

The OCB's role was to coordinate the campaign which followed from the conclusion that Arbenz must be removed from power. For example, it helped shape and promote the diplomatic strategy for the Caracas conference, at which the US tried to direct the Organization of American States to condemn Guatemala. The OCB framed Eisenhower's statement to US Congressmen:

> By every proper and effective means, we should demonstrate to the courageous elements within Guatemala who are trying to purge their government of its communist elements that they have the sympathy and support of all freedom-loving people both in the US and elsewhere in the hemisphere. We know that these patriotic Guatemalans represent the overwhelming majority of the people there. We wish them success.[57]

As the CIA funded a small "contra" force on the Honduras–Guatemala border and orchestrated black propaganda to undermine Arbenz, the OCB exploited the US "discovery" that Czech guns were being shipped to Guatemala. These were for the use of the militia to counter the threat of a foreign-sponsored *coup*, but Foster Dulles insisted, "Part . . . of these arms was apparently being set aside for subversive action both in Honduras and Nicaragua."[58]

US plans reached fruition in late June when the contra force moved toward Guatemala City. They were supported by US "black" propaganda via Voice of Liberation radio from Honduras and "bombing" consisting of firecrackers and even Coca-Cola bottles dropped on the Guatemalan capital. The operations almost ended in disaster when two planes crashed but the emergency "donation" of aircraft from the Somoza regime (they were actually supplied by the US Air Force via Nicaragua) and Arbenz's sudden loss of nerve saved the day. The Guatemalan President fled the country for Mexico (and, pressed to leave there, for Europe), and the contra leader, Castillo Armas, eventually took power.[59]

By the end of the year, the OCB had orchestrated $5 million in immediate economic aid for the new Government, including money for the Pacific Coastal and Inter-American Highways, and $400,000 of planes and armored cars to be paraded in December in Guatemala City. This was supported by an information policy which "intensively exploited" local radio and targeted an exchange program towards "opinion molders . . . and future leaders".[60] Beyond Guatemala, the CIA allegedly tried to depose President Jose Figueres in Costa Rica.[61] The USIA inaugurated "programs in Latin America aimed at a special effort to enroll the students on our side in the cold war", launched "a considerable sports program", and showed "how the Communists attempted to retard industrial development by inhibiting the fuel supply of Latin American countries".[62] Specific projects included covert support and creation of Latin American papers with an anti-Communist line where "newsworthy persons, in or out of government, [could] make statements which the news agencies [would] carry". Articles would also "be prepared for publication in American magazines and, if possible, the device of the letter to the *New York Times* [would] be used".[63] US efforts were tailored to key areas, such as "a vigorous campaign designed to acquaint the Brazilian people with the dangers of communism and create a hostile atmosphere toward it, to expose and render ineffectual Communist activities in all sectors of society, and to induce and assist the Brazilian government to take effective steps to destroy the party within Brazil".[64] The OCB summarized that the United States had "directed its efforts toward promoting faith in the social and economic techniques of a free society, obliterating the Communist picture of the US as an imperialist exploiter and creating appreciation, both within and outside Guatemala, of the efforts of the moderate Castillo Government to overcome the damage done by Communism".[65]

Yet the OCB could not or would not come to grips with the issue of Eastern Europe. A working group was established for general planning by NSC 174, building on the assessment that "through the skillful, judicious and full employment of current US economic, political, military, and propaganda capabilities, the US can make substantial advances toward its national objectives short of general hostilities". It further noted, "The US [could] furnish certain support to resistance activities. This current capability could be increased substantially."[66] Specific injunctions included "support or make use of refugees or exile organizations which can contribute to the attainment of US objectives, but do not recognize governments-in-exile", "keep the situation with respect to Albania under continuing surveillance with a view to the possibility of detachment of that country from the Soviet bloc", and "emphasize rights of Eastern European peoples to independent government".[67]

The problem was, as one official reminded the OCB, that NSC 174 did "not provide a clear statement of policy as to how [liberation] should be accomplished. The actions authorized in support of the basic policy set forth in NSC 174 are so hedged with restrictions and qualifications as to make dynamic application impossible."[68] For example, "the destruction of the Soviet Communist rulers from indirect aggression by . . . compounding their internal difficulties . . . [had] been checked by the fear of our allies. . . . Our allies think it too dangerous 'to prod the bear' by exploiting internal weakness."[69] The operation to detach Albania had been delayed again because negotiations over the future of Trieste were in progress; the support of both Italy and Yugoslavia, the two parties in the Trieste dispute, was needed for any liberation effort. Training of leaders and preparation of "plans for supplying weapons and equipment for use in future riots and disturbances in the satellite areas" as well as organization of resistance groups had also not progressed as quickly as desired.[70]

Allen Dulles contended that such reports were "somewhat too pessimistic in tone in view of recent successful operations".[71] The Joint Chiefs of Staff also continued to press for a "more aggressive tone" in US activity, but they were again checked by Foster Dulles, who argued in August 1954, "There should be long-range plans for a rollback in the satellites, Iran, etc., but [I wish] to emphasize that these plans would have to be very long-range indeed."[72] The NSC left the issue open: "Although the time for a significant rollback of Soviet power may appear to be in the future, the US should be prepared, by feasible current actions or future planning, to take advantage of any earlier opportunity to contract Communist-controlled areas and power."[73]

Eisenhower added to the ambiguity by circumventing or confronting the State Department to appeal for specific projects. He had diverged from Foster Dulles in August by noting, "While the time of a significant rollback was far in the future, nevertheless we should watch any opportunities and prepare plans for an earlier contracting of Soviet power."[74] Two months later, he met the Polish general Stanislaw Maczek, who appealed for $100,000 for "keeping open communications inside [the] iron curtain". The President made no promises but asked CIA Director Allen Dulles to establish contact with Maczek.[75] On a broader front, he developed Jackson's idea of stirring discontent within Communist China by asking the NSC to expand trade with that country. This was not a softening of the US position; instead "he was insisting upon some way of reaching the mass of the Chinese people".[76]

As the National Security Council revised the New Look at the end of 1954, Foster Dulles tried to close off the suggestion "in certain quarters . . . that while we continued to have atomic superiority over the enemy, we should apply strong and forceful measures to change the basic character of the Soviet system". He asserted, "The effort to implement such a course of action would involve the US in general war. If it did not, however, and we did succeed in ditching Communist China and the satellites from their alliance with the Soviet Union, this in itself would not actually touch the heart of the problem: Soviet atomic plenty." The Secretary of State could not foresake the mantra of victory, however, and in that rhetoric, he allowed the activists enough leeway for their plans:

> One could properly anticipate that there will be in the future some disintegration of the present monolithic power structure of the Soviet orbit. . . . Nationalism may quite conceivably grow apace among the satellites, and it was also logical, from the historical point of view, to expect Communist China to reveal an increased attitude of independence vis-a-vis the USSR. . . . There was already some slight evidence of such a development, and the US may itself be able to promote its further growth.[77]

So the covert State–private network continued as the locus of the US offensive in Eastern Europe. The Jackson Committee had paved the way with its recommendation that "far greater effort should be made to utilize private American organizations for the advancement of US objectives. The gain in dissemination and credibility through the use of such channels will more than offset the loss by the Government of some control over the content."[78] The National Security Council formally approved the recommendation in October 1953 with the authorization of the US Information Agency "to communicate with other peoples without attribution to the US Government on matters which could be assumed by the Government if necessary". This "gray" propaganda would complement the CIA's "black" activities, which should never be traced back to the Government.[79] As the OCB reaffirmed that "pressures should be increased against any part of the Soviet orbit where suitable opportunities appear",[80] the private practitioners of liberation gathered at an extraordinary round table in Hanover, New Hampshire.

The round table included Government officers such as Andrew Berding, the Assistant Director of the US Information Agency, Brigadier General Dale Smith of the OCB, Jesse MacKnight, the Policy Planning Staff's liaison with the CIA, and Frank Wisner. They spent three days with those who had developed the "private" offensive for liberation. Prominent were Professor Max Millikan, who had crafted Project Troy on Soviet vulnerabilities, Shepard Stone of the Ford Foundation, Vice-Admiral Leslie Stevens and Howland Sargeant of the American Committee for the Liberation of the Peoples of Russia, Richard Conlon of the Committee for Free Asia, and Lewis Galantiere of the National Committee for Free Europe. Leading psychologists and public opinion pollsters also contributed.

The conferees did not openly endorse liberation. Indeed, Galantiere noted, "For 18 months [Radio Free Europe] has taught little about keeping the hope of liberation alive," and Stevens added, "This is no time for revolution in the USSR. Radio Liberty does not incite [listeners] to revolution." There was even a hint of coexistence, albeit one that would end in US victory, in Stevens's contention, "Since the USSR has the seeds of its own decay in its system far more than is true of the West, sooner or later the continuing crisis of the USSR will culminate in a breakdown." Discussion amongst the conferees noted, "By 1953 the peoples in the Satellite countries saw somewhat new elements opening up more than two alternatives to them, including a chance of a more tolerable existence under USSR control. This meant less complete dependence on the idea of liberation, which could only come through outside US military intervention." The conference agreed that pressure must be maintained on the Soviet bloc. Galantiere noted that Radio Free Europe "demanded that the regime must keep the promises they have made", and the meeting urged plans "for a drain on Soviet strength and war potential". Yet the gathering never addressed the question: what action would be taken if the Communist regimes refused to keep their promises? Would the private outlets continue to champion the demands for freedom, risking an uprising, or would it abandon the central tenet of its propaganda?[81]

In practice, the National Committee for Free Europe expanded the broadcasts of Radio Free Europe with more powerful radio transmitters, including a one-megawatt unit in West Germany and a "saturation" campaign to Poland with the revelations of the defector Colonel Swiatlo.[82] It linked round-the-clock broadcasts to balloon operations, disseminating leaflets and false currency, inside Czechoslovakia and Hungary in Operations Veto and Focus. Czechs were urged to forge a "People's Opposition" to attain 10 specific political and economic demands, and Hungarians pressed to attain the "Twelve Demands of the National Opposition Movement", including "resoration of local autonomy and self-government, an end to persecution of the peasant and the rebirth of private agriculture, free trade unions, denationalization of retail and service trades, and a shift from heavy to light industry".[83] A typical initiative featured "Farmer Balint", who advised listeners to prevent grain deliveries to the State by ruining threshing machines.[84]

When the Hungarian Ministry of Foreign Affairs protested at the leafleting, the US legation replied that the NCFE's activities occurred "on their own initiative and responsibility. These are private organizations established and supported by private American citizens." The legation wryly noted that the leaflets were only claiming rights assured by the Hungarian Constitution and concluded, "The United States Government hopes that the day will come when balloons will no longer be necessary as a means by which the people of one country may freely communicate with peoples in other lands."[85] C. D. Jackson, having left the Government amidst pessimism, was invigorated. He wrote to Allen Dulles of émigré reports that the Hungarian Government was moving towards an independent nationalism because of the populace's passive resistance and sabotage. Jackson asserted, "[This is] all the more reason for continuing Operation Focus, wherein we have discovered (along with Veto for Czechoslovakia) how to talk about more than hope – how to get action and yet avoid bloodshed."[86]

On another front, the American Committee for the Liberation of the Peoples of Russia persisted with its mission "to conduct overt anti-Soviet activities designed to weaken the prestige and power of the Soviet dictatorship, primarily within the USSR, and thereby to reduce its threat to world security . . . [in cooperation with] moderate elements in the emigration from the USSR". It would keep alive the spirit of resistance, induce defections, and encourage dissension and strife through the "stepped-up activity" of Radio Liberty and Radio Free Russia and leaflet drops to Soviet military forces serving abroad.[87]

The problem with the committee was not a lack of clarity about its goals but the continuing lack of faith in its leadership. In May 1954 Tom Braden, the CIA officer who had supervised the International Organizations Division, asked C. D. Jackson to take over as Director of AmComLib. Jackson was wary, since "AmComLib [was] in serious trouble which is going to gather momentum". It was "all machine and little product". Braden acknowledged, "I have told the Admiral [Leslie Stevens, the Director of AmComLib] time and again . . . that he should quit fiddling with the exiles, a second priority, and get on with the job of hitting the target, either by radio, balloon, letters, or whatever."[88]

Another group which had had problems, the Committee for Free Asia, reorganized its operations to fit more closely with the Adminstration's strategy of appealing to Chinese citizens living overseas and building support for Taiwan. A "complete flop" in its initial months,[89] the CFA renamed itself the Asia Foundation and orchestrated private support "for the attainment of peace, independence, personal liberty, and social progress".[90] Radio Free Asia switched its target area from Communist China, where "results [did] not justify broadcasting", to Chinese audiences outside the country.[91]

The question of liberation might still be perplexing the Eisenhower Administration, but it was clear that, cloaked by the ideology of "freedom", the US Government was ready to sacrifice that very principle in its psychological campaigns. The Doolittle Report, reviewing American intelligence services, summarized in 1954:

> It is now clear that we are facing an implacable enemy whose avowed objective is world domination by whatever means and at whatever cost. There are no rules in such a game. Hitherto acceptable norms of human conduct do not apply. If the U.S. is to survive, long-standing American concepts of "fair play" must be reconsidered.[92]

Notes

1 Jackson to Eisenhower, 22 February 1954, *Diaries*, Reel 18
2 State Department memorandum, 2 March 1954, US DDRS, Retrospective 897A
3 Jackson to Wisner, 27 February 1954, US DDRS, 1993 3445; Jackson to Eisenhower, 8 March 1954, Diaries, Reel 18; Jackson to Smith, 15 March 1954, DDE, Jackson Papers, Box 1, OCB, Implementation of Jackson Committee Report
4 Thomas Rees, "Blunder and Betrayal in the Balkans," *Guardian Weekend*, 10 October 1998
5 Jackson draft letter, 6 January 1954, and subsequent memoranda, *Diaries*, Reel 18
6 Jackson to McCrum, 25 January 1954, and Jackson to Phillips, 9 February 1954, DDE, Jackson Papers, Box 27, Berlin, Basics and Working Papers
7 Jackson to Smith, 15 March 1954, DDE, Jackson Papers, Box 1, OCB
8 Eisenhower to Jackson, 17 May 1954, *Diaries*, Reel 18
9 Jackson to Eisenhower, 3 March 1954, *Diaries*, Reel 18
10 Lay memorandum, 15 March 1954, US DDRS, 1978 57A; OCB report, "Principles to Assure Coordination of Gray Activities," 14 May 1954, US DDRS, 1992 486
11 CIA Intelligence Memorandum 209, 20 September 1949, US DDRS, 1992 2435
12 NSC 64, 18 April 1950, *Documents*, Reel 2
13 *Time*, 10 October 1949, 27 March, 29 May 1950
14 State Department Circular 924, 7 May 1952, USNA, Department of State, Central Decimal File, 511.00/5-752

15 Leo Hochstetter, cited in Elliot to Browne, 26 September 1952, HST, Staff Memoranda and Office Files, Psychological Strategy Board Files, Box 7, 091 Indochina
16 Eleventh PSB meeting, 27 March 1952, US DDRS, 1988 1760
17 PSB D-46, "Use of American Influences in Support of US Objectives in Vietnam, Cambodia, and Laos," 6 July 1953, US DDRS, 1994 577
18 161st NSC meeting, 9 September 1953, US DDRS, 1986 2018
19 OCB report, "Sino-Soviet Direction and Nature of the Indochinese Conflict," undated, US DDRS, 1991 3104
20 185th NSC meeting, 4 February 1954, US DDRS, 1992 2739
21 219th NSC meeting, 26 October 1954, US DDRS, 1986 2157
22 180th NSC meeting, 14 January 1954, US DDRS, 1986 2868
23 "Political Warfare against the Viet Minh," 20 May 1954, US DDRS, 1989 3587
24 Jackson log, 28 August 1954, DDE, Jackson Papers, Box 56, Log 1954; OCB memorandum, "Proposed Exploitation Program for the Geneva Conference," 5 March 1954, DDE, Jackson Records, Box 3, Geneva Conference
25 OCB Special Working Group on Indo-China, 7 September 1954, US DDRS, 1991 2765
26 234th NSC meeting, 27 January 1955, US DDRS, 1986 3372
27 OCB Special Working Group on Indo-China, 12 August 1954, US DDRS, 1991 1171; OCB Special Working Group on Indo-China, 12 October 1954, US DDRS, 1991 1552; 234th NSC meeting, 27 January 1955, US DDRS, DDRS 323B
28 See the section on the Philippines later in this chapter
29 See Mike Gravel (ed.), *The Pentagon Papers* (Boston, MA, 1971); Stanley Karnow, *Vietnam: A History* (London, 1994), 236–8
30 NIE 10-7-54, "Communist Courses of Action in Asia through 1957," 7 October 1954, *Minutes*, 1st Supplement, Reel 3
31 OCB progress report on NSC 146/2, 16 July 1954, *Minutes*, 1st Supplement, Reel 3
32 OCB progress report on NSC 146/2, 16 July 1954, *Minutes*, 1st Supplement, Reel 3
33 Peter Grose, *Gentleman Spy: The Life of Allen Dulles* (Boston, MA, 1994), 411; John Ranelagh, *The Agency: The Rise and Decline of the CIA* (London, 1987), 789
34 Morgan to PSB Members, 12 June 1953, US DDRS, 1989 3566
35 PSB D-23, "US Psychological Strategy with Respect to the Thai Peoples of Southeast Asia," 2 July 1953, *Minutes*, Reel 2
36 OCB Progress Report on US Psychological Strategy Based on Thailand, 26 February 1954, US DDRS, 1991 2015
37 OCB progress report, 26 February 1954, US DDRS, 1991 2013; OCB Working Group meeting, 28 December 1953, US DDRS, 1990 2353
38 Victor Marchetti and John Marks, *The CIA and the Cult of Intelligence* (New York, 1974), 50–1; Evan Thomas, *The Very Best Men: Four who Dared in the Early Years of the CIA* (New York, 1995), 57
39 Jackson to Thompson, 18 August 1953, DDE, Jackson Records, Box 6, T; Memorandum for Jackson, 14 October 1953, DDE, Jackson Records, Box 3, G; Handwritten note on McWilliams to Bruce, 18 December 1952, USNA, Department of State, Lot 62 D 333, PSB Working File, 1951–1953, Box 8, Informal PSB Meetings
40 Thomas, *The Very Best Men*, 57–8
41 Thomas, *The Very Best Men*, 57–8; Bundy to Bishop, 27 May 1954, US DDRS, 1992 2748; OCB progress report, 21 July 1954, US DDRS, 1992 2935. See the material on Namfrel in Militant Liberty Outline Plan, 5 November 1954, US DDRS, 1997 0667
42 USIS Manila to USIA, Despatch 644, 14 December 1953, US DDRS, 1974 893A
43 170th National Security Council meeting, 12 November 1953, *Minutes*, 1st Supplement, Reel 3

44 Quoted in Thomas, *The Very Best Men*, 58. The Asian effort was given further impetus with a $3 million grant from the Mutual Security Administration. The money financed village "propaganda agents, indigenous dramatic propaganda groups, anti-communist courses, films, bulletins, pamphlets, and posters" in Indochina, anti-Communist labor organisations in Japan, paperbacks in Hong Kong and Indonesia, and atomic energy exhibits and radio programs in Pakistan. (Washburn to Stassen, 2 February 1955, US DDRS, 1992 934.) Special attention was paid "to offset unfavorable Japanese attitudes to the H-bomb" after a Japanese fishing boat was caught up in the fall-out from a US test. The OCB considered diversion of $750,000 from Mutual Security Administration funds to the affected fishermen. ("OCB Official Check List of US Actions to Offset Unfavorable Japanese Attitudes to the H-Bomb and Related Developments," 22 April 1954, US DDRS, 1992 2921; OCB Working Group on NSC 125/2, 10 June 1954, US DDRS, 1997 2877)
45 Brief of Military Liberty project, 22 October 1954, USNA, Department of State, Lot 62 D 430, Records Relating to State Department Participation in the OCB and the NSC, 1947–1963, Box 8, Miscellaneous 1953–1956
46 Woodward to Staats, 7 July 1954, *Minutes*, 1st Supplement, Reel 3
47 NSC 5432/1, 3 September 1954, US DDRS, 1992 2703; OCB progress report, "Courses of Action on Chile," US DDRS, 1991 2777
48 Walter Hixson, *Parting the Curtain: Propaganda, Culture, and the Cold War* (New York, 1997), 127
49 McWilliams memorandum, 29 May 1950, USNA, Department of State, Records of the Policy Planning Staff, Box 17
50 CIA daily digest, 21 March 1951, US DDRS, 1991 1234
51 Grose, *Gentleman Spy*, 371
52 133rd National Security Council meeting, 18 February 1953, *Minutes*, 1st Supplement
53 Jackson to Eisenhower, 2 April 1953, US DDRS, 1986 3560
54 Ray Vicker, "Communist Minority in Guatemala Worms Way into Near Control," *Wall Street Journal*, 10 April 1953
55 Hirsch memorandum, 29 October 1953, DDE, Jackson Records, Box 1, OCB, Miscellaneous Memoranda (2)
56 Jackson daily log, 28 October 1953, DDE, Jackson Papers, Box 56, Log 1953 (2)
57 OCB Working Group on Caracas Conference, 16 March 1954, US DDRS, 1992 1034; "Memorandum on Guatemalan Situation," 26 April 1954, *Diaries*, Reel 2
58 199th National Security meeting, 27 May 1954, *Minutes*, 1st Supplement
59 See Piero Gleijeses, *Shattered Hope: The Guatemalan Revolution and the United States, 1944–1954* (Princeton, NJ, 1991); Richard Immerman, *The CIA in Guatemala: The Foreign Policy of Intervention* (Austin, TX, 1982)
60 Outline Plan of Operations for Guatemala, 14 April 1955, US DDRS, 1991 2829; Summary of Armour–Mann–Holland conversation, 25 October 1954, FRUS, 1952–1954, IV, 1234. See also Foster Dulles to Stassen in FRUS, 1952–1954, IV, 1237–8
61 David Wise and Thomas B. Ross, *The Invisible Government* (New York, 1964), 127–8
62 OCB Working Group on Latin America, 9 November 1954, US DDRS, 1992 1042; OCB Working Group on Latin America, 25 January 1955, US DDRS, 1992 1051
63 Courses of Action in Chile, 3 March 1955, US DDRS, DDRS 288B
64 Outline Plan of Operations for Brazil, 1 December 1955, US DDRS, 1992 2897
65 Internal Security Plan for Guatemala, 20 May 1955, US DDRS, 1992 2691
66 Suggested Procedures for Working Group on Coordination of NSC 174, 11 February 1954, US DDRS, 1994 1785
67 OCB List of Agreed Action to Implement NSC 174, 20 August 1954, US DDRS, 1990 2383
68 O'Connor to Staats, 2 June 1954, US DDRS, 1994 1788

69 "US Foreign Policy," 16 May 1954, US DDRS, 1987 328

70 OCB Agreed Courses of Action to Implement NSC 174, 25 August 1954, USNA, Department of State, Lot 63 D 351, Records Relating to State Department Participation in the OCB and the NSC, 1947–1963, Box 76, NSC 174

71 Staats memorandum, 30 June 1954, USNA, Department of State, Lot 62 D 430, Records Relating to State Department Participation in the OCB and the NSC, 1947–1963, Box 2, OCB Minutes II

72 209th NSC meeting, 5 August 1954, US DDRS, 1986 2883

73 Staats to OCB, 20 August 1954, US DDRS, 1993 575

74 209th NSC meeting, 5 August 1954, US DDRS, 1986 2883

75 Eisenhower to Allen Dulles, 26 October 1954, *Diaries*, Reel 4. The initial request for support of a Polish exile force was made in January 1954 but was deferred while the United States considered the formation of a Volunteer Freedom Corps. (Staats memorandum, 11 January 1954, USNA, Department of State, Lot 62 D 430, Records Relating to State Department Participation in the OCB and the NSC, 1947–1963, Box 2, OCB Minutes II)

76 193rd NSC meeting, 13 April 1954, *Minutes*, 1st Supplement, Reel 2

77 229th NSC meeting, 21 December 1954, US DDRS, 1986 2212. See also Foster Dulles to Luce, 1 September 1954, US DDRS, 1987 1533

78 Lay memorandum, 1 October 1953, US DDRS, 1990 2796

79 OCB report, "Principles to Assure Coordination of Gray Activities," 14 May 1954, US DDRS, 1992 486

80 OCB memorandum, "The Situation with Respect to the Possible Detachment of a Major European Soviet Satellite," 5 January 1955, US DDRS, 1990 2168

81 "Points of Agreement Reached at the Hanover Round Table," 26–8 August 1954, HST, Sargeant Papers, Box 3

82 See Nickels to Gullion, 8 April 1960, US DDRS, 1986 3110

83 Free Europe Press pamphlet, "A New Weapon," DDE, Jackson Papers, Box 75, Radio Free Europe

84 DDE, Jackson Papers, Box 75, Radio Free Europe, "Farmer Balint Says," undated, Jackson Papers, Box 65, NCFE Operation Marshmallow; "Free Europe Committee in 'Operation Veto'," in William Daugherty and Morris Janowitz (eds), *A Psychological Warfare Casebook* (Baltimore, MD, 1958), 332–7

85 Free Europe Committee press release, 20 December 1954, DDE, Jackson Papers, Box 45, FEC Correspondence through 1956, Basic (2)

86 Jackson to Dulles, 24 November 1954, DDE, Jackson Papers, Box 40, Allen Dulles

87 ACLPR Statement of Mission, Operating Objectives, and Policy Guides, 1 September 1954, HST, Sargeant Papers, Box 11, Radio Liberty, General, 1956

88 Braden to Jackson, 6 May 1954, and subsequent letters, DDE, Jackson Papers, Box 25, Br–Bz, Miscellaneous

89 Jackson to Washburn, 3 February 1953, DDE, Jackson Papers, Box 52, Jackson Committee

90 Blum to Jackson, 10 November 1954, DDE, Jackson Papers, Box 24, Asia Foundation

91 Report of the Jackson Committee, 30 June 1953, US DDRS, 1987 1120

92 Quoted in Stephen Ambrose and Richard Immerman, *Ike's Spies* (Garden City, NY, 1981), 187

13

Stumbling towards freedom's revolution

Far from disappearing, the goal of liberation merely required a catalyst to raise it from the shadows of the bureaucracy. The opportunity almost came when Soviet leader Georgi Malenkov was ousted by the Politburo in February 1955. C. D. Jackson advised the Administration of "a milestone" that could be exploited through aggressive public statements, activation of the Volunteer Freedom Corps, increased output by the American Committee for the Liberation of the Peoples of Russia, and other measures to destabilize the Soviet bloc. The United States would make an "extra-special effort" to obtain at least one high-level Soviet defector. One possibility was the invitation of General Georgi Zhukov, the military hero and Marshal of the Soviet Union, to the United States; another was the entertainment of Soviet delegates to the United Nations by US counterparts like Henry Cabot Lodge and George Wadsworth. Jackson commented, "Wadsworth would be particularly good at this, as he has an extraordinary flair for entertaining and a marvelous voice for late-hour singing, which is frequently an 'Open Sesame' to relax a Russian." On another front, Jackson advised:

> While a new June 17th uprising might be dangerous, nevertheless the working population of East Germany should have dinned into their ears by RIAS, by agents, by leaflets, by every conceivable means, the fact that they are the ultimate victims of this new Soviet development, and that they should by their own Socialist trade union methods demand adequate food, adequate pay, adequate working conditions, and if necessary they should use the mass slowdown and sitdown as a way to get their demands.[1]

Most of his appeal for "Operation Kremlin Kracks" went unheeded, but the National Security Council did increase the number of transmitters for the "Voice of America and other US-supported international broadcast facilities".[2]

Weeks before Jackson's proposal, the National Security Council's debates of 1954 had culminated in yet another revised strategy. The working group, instructed in August to evaluate "the possibility of detaching a major European satellite of the Soviet Union", finally reported on 4 January. It concluded pessimistically that most satellites were not sufficiently vulnerable to be detached short of general war. Only East Germany offered any hope of detachment by negotiation and "concentration of political, economic, and psychological measures".[3] The new global strategy, NSC 5501, accordingly hinted that the "changes" within the Soviet system did not have to be the establishment of anti-Communist regimes, merely the assurance of "policies [in] the Soviet Communist bloc along lines more congruent with US security interests".[4] NSC 5505 on the "Exploitation of Soviet and European Satellite Vulnerabilities" added that the United States would "stress evolutionary rather than revolutionary change".[5]

The State Department seized the opportunity to curb the activities of the National Committee for Free Europe. The head of the organization, William Griffith, informed C. D. Jackson:

> Our friends [the CIA] (apparently on Department advice) are refusing to approve continuation of Veto (the Czechoslovak leaflet-balloon operation) and Focus (its Hungarian equivalent) after December 31 [1954]. They argue that leaflet-balloon operations should be specific, short-time projects aimed at single events (Czechoslovak elections, etc.) and not – as we maintain – a permanent "opposition press", implementing, jointly with opposition radio (RFE) and under the symbol of an internal opposition movement, a specific, realizable "action program" series of practical goals (e.g., the Czechoslovak Veto ten demands).

Griffith continued, "The thought of this being strangled by some third-rate epigones who burn incense daily to the God of Doing Nothing makes me really mad!" He claimed that a State Department official had recently boasted to NCFE staff, "I think we're getting back to Kennan's containment line – as if we'd ever really left it!"[6]

Griffith and the activists were saved because, as in the past, neither analysts nor policy-makers would give up all hope of future opportunities. The working group on Soviet vulnerabilities reported:

> Conditions may very possibly change . . . and it would be short-sighted not to have plans laid and possibly even a skeleton organization in being to exploit a situation of crisis if one should arise. . . .
>
> Apart from these preparatory measures, there is reason to believe that a strategy of encouraging the satellite populations to make strong but limited demands upon their leaders for improvements in their conditions of life may be even more effective in affecting choices both of the satellite and the Soviet bureaucracies.[7]

Thus "evolution" would include the spread of rumors and economic sabotage. NSC 5501 not only reiterated the need to preserve "fundamental US values and institutions . . . [by] fostering changes in the character and policies of the Soviet-Communist bloc regimes . . . by exploiting differences between such powers and their other vulnerabilities"[8]; an additional paper on the anti-Soviet émigrés, NSC 5502, asserted, "It is in the interest of the United States to give limited aid . . . to émigré or other related anti-Soviet activities," with additional support for the American Committee for the Liberation of the Peoples of Russia.[9] NSC 5505 gave activists an even greater loophole: "Covert operations (including experimentation with such anti-regime measures as might be applicable to substantially changed circumstances) [would] not necessarily have to conform to the . . . principles" elsewhere in the document.[10]

Allen Dulles kept up the pressure within Government circles for an aggressive strategy. He warned that "he for one believed that Czechoslovakia would never have been lost if someone had been there doing something about it. . . . He emphasized that the so-called completely 'soft' policy is subject to misinterpretation and we are apt to lapse into a do-nothing policy."[11] The position was reinforced in public statements such as his speech on graduation day at Columbia University: "A hard choice faces the perplexed, and probably unharmonious, group of men in the Kremlin. They lead a people who surely will come to realize the inevitability of the great precept: 'And ye shall know the truth and the truth shall make you free.' "[12]

The NSC considered the package of NSC 5501, NSC 5502, and NSC 5505 in a lengthy discussion on 27 January 1955. Eisenhower, as usual, was grandly ambiguous: "We must have prompt action. . . . The US was not in a position to state that it would promote revolution in the Soviet Union. What we must try to do is win 'these guys' over." Suddenly Vice-President Richard Nixon was pushing a renewed assault upon Moscow's grip in Eastern Europe, "[We should] not necessarily rule out resort to revolutionary methods if they seemed likely to be successful." More significantly, Allen Dulles's pressure led Foster Dulles to modify his rejection of immediate operations because of Soviet "atomic plenty": "[We do] not wish guidance for exploitation of Soviet vulnerabilities along evolutionary rather than revolutionary lines to destroy all possibility of seizing opportunites for exploiting a different type of strategy." All three papers were adopted, with the NSC agreeing that a special committee, led by the new Special Assistant for Psychological Strategy, Nelson Rockefeller, and including Allen Dulles, Undersecretary of State Herbert Hoover, Jr, and the Deputy Secretary of Defense, would develop the strategy for Eastern Europe.[13]

There was enough flexibility in the outcome for working-level officials to repeat, "Albania is still considered detachable and is to be kept under continuing surveillance for possible detachment at an appropriate time."[14] The US Information Agency ensured that "propaganda pressure on the communists was increased, their vulnerabilities were exploited, [and] their aims and policies were attacked". The agency gloated, "Information programs directed to the satellites continued to emphasize (a) that the US cannot reconcile itself to continued Soviet domination of the nations of Eastern Europe, such domination being a cause of tension; (b) that the US desires the restoration of true liberty to that area so that the captive satellite peoples may again enjoy governments and institutions of their own choosing." Operation Discord was developed for "output to the Chinese mainland . . . creating distrust of the Soviet Union and . . . encouraging a dislike for communist leadership and policies. . . . Defection of Soviet and key satellites' nationals was encouraged."[15]

Unfortunately for the activists, there were a couple of significant barriers to a renewed offensive against Moscow. The longer-term problem was the Administration's concern with nuclear weapons. In February 1955 a special committee of scientific consultants, led by James Killian of MIT, on technological capabilities reported to the President on "Meeting the Threat of Surprise Attack". The panel gloomily projected that, with Soviet advances in nuclear technology, the United States could by 1958 "be in a poor position to ward off Russian political and diplomatic moves or to make such moves of our own". Its major recommendation was the recognition of the intercontinental ballistic missile program as "highest priority", as the scientists made only a vague allusion to a non-military campaign against Moscow: "We may survive the hazards of the years ahead provided we show the courage, the firmness, and the greatness to stand steady at home and in the contest of ideologies to enlarge and strengthen the free world as a cohesive community of nations."[16]

Meanwhile, the National Security Council faced the immediate crisis of conflict with Communist China over two small islands, Quemoy and Matsu. In part, the dispute had arisen because of the US policy of keeping pressure on Peking. The Eisenhower Administration had maintained a program of political warfare directed at the Chinese military,[17] and the islands, only several miles off the mainland but claimed by Taiwan, had been used for raids and the gathering of intelligence and to help enforce an economic embargo.[18]

In September 1954, Communist shelling of the islands became a crisis issue for the NSC. Allen Dulles reported that there had been no guerrilla operations against the mainland for about a year, i.e. since the "New Look" discussions, but Admiral Arthur Radford, the Chairman of the Joint Chiefs of Staff, reiterated that the positions were a "potential jumping-off point" for an invasion. "It was precisely this threat which made the Chinese Communists so anxious to capture the islands."[19] Three days later, Eisenhower assessed, "[Chiang Kai-shek's] only hope is in a general rising in China, for which Chiang would be called back, like Napoleon from Elba." Although Foster Dulles emphasized that "there was no evidence that such an uprising would occur", the US dilemma was evident: having spoken of "liberation" for so long without clarifying the practical implications, the Administration now had to either renounce the goal publicly or risk further action from Peking.[20] George Humphrey, the Secretary of the Treasury, warned, "We had simply been temporizing, and if we continued to temporize, we would most certainly get burned."[21]

Some NSC members wanted a clean break with the Chinese Nationalists. Secretary of Defense Charles Wilson claimed, "[There was] no gain in encouraging these Formosan Nationalists to act like a gang of pirates. . . . I can't just see where we're going now except into war with China." The issue was muddled, however, amidst warnings of "an unfriendly Pacific up to our very shores. In the forward surge of a Communist victory in all Asia, the US would shortly lose all of Latin America."[22]

At the end of 1954, the Administration did arrange "not [to] agree to Chinese Nationalist offensive actions against mainland Communist China, except under circumstances approved by the President".[23] There was a further retreat the following month with the proviso that any Chinese National-ist "retaliation" against Peking must be "selected with due consideration for the undesirability of provoking further Chinese Communist reaction against Formosa and the Pescadores".[24] Yet the National Security Council still would not close the door on its covert activities in Communist China, maintaining the commitment to "encourage and covertly assist the Chinese Nationalist Government to develop and extend logistical support of anti-Communist guerrillas on the mainland of China, for purposes of resistance and intelligence".[25]

The dispute over Quemoy and Matsu continued for months before fizzling out. The Communists did not invade the islands, while the US focus, in prac-tice if not in principle, was upon the "long-term future of Formosa" rather than Chiang Kai-shek's "early return to the mainland".[26] The incident, however, had highlighted the danger of US operations within the Communist bloc leading to military escalation. The Administration had to have clear evi-dence that victory could be achieved without the possibility of a Soviet show of force before it would further operations within Eastern Europe. As a working-level report warned, "When study of Soviet vulnerabilities . . . began some five years ago, there was a thought that perhaps the Soviet system con-tained a massive weakness which might be exploited if it could be discovered. Five years of study and consideration have led to the conclusion that such a massive weakness probably does not exist."[27]

Hope was revived, however, in mid-1955 with events triggered by the replacement of Soviet leader Georgi Malenkov by Nikolai Bulganin and Nikita Khrushchev. The Department of Defense advised Nelson Rockefeller's Plan-ning Coordination Group of "the internal troubles and foreign pressures which the Soviets are finding difficult to handle and . . . offer an excellent opportunity for exploitation".[28] Rockefeller was reassured by his staff, "We would still like nothing better than to destroy the communist regimes."[29] After the signing of the Austrian Peace Treaty, which secured the withdrawal of the Soviet military from that country, Foster Dulles enthused:

> This is the first time a segment of the Red Army will have turned around and started to go back. . . . It is going to create a desire – a mounting desire – on the part of those people [in Eastern Europe] to get the same freedom from that type of occu-pation that the Austrians have got. And furthermore, this joy at their freedom which

was so manifest by the Austrian people, that is going to be contagious and it is going to spread, surely, through the neighboring countries.[30]

Two days later, Foster Dulles was predicting to the National Security Council, "The Iron Curtain is going to disappear. In the future there will be no more sharp line between the free world and the Soviet bloc. The sharp will be replaced by a fuzzy area." His normal caution over Eastern Europe was replaced by the assessment, "The satellite populations were very restless and conditions, from the Soviet point of view, anything but good. Indeed, by virtue of their action in Austria the Soviets may be loosing forces in the satellite states which they would be unable to control." In short, "[The US was] now confronting a real opportunity in the present situation for a rollback of Soviet power. Such a rollback might leave the present satellite states in a status not unlike that of Finland."[31]

Ironically, it was Allen Dulles who was now raising practical objections, "These populations know little or nothing about the Soviet concessions in Vienna. It was going to be a very big job to get this information in the hands of the satellite countries," but Eisenhower was ready to take the offensive, saying, "The US Information Agency should get to work at once" on the project.[32] A draft plan of operations, noting that developments beyond the Soviet bloc "may have a profound long-range effect" upon liberation, revived the goal of "eventual restoration of independent governments in Eastern Europe free from the control and domination of Moscow", even if progress would "probably be slow and intermittent". The United States would continue to "develop and encourage, as appropriate, increased use of passive resistance by the peoples of the [USSR and] satellites" and exploit, with publicity and operations, anticipated shortages in harvests in Eastern Europe.[33]

The Administration was still too cautious to give free rein to covert operators. It preferred to drive home a general advantage through exploitation of the Geneva Summit in July 1955, the first meeting of the heads of state of Britain, France, the United States, and the Soviet Union. Having held out for years against negotiations with Moscow, Foster Dulles now explained to a television audience, "It may possibly be the case that the Soviet Union, after this experience of trying to buck everything, may be feeling that it may be more convenient for them to conform to some of the rules and practices of a civilized community," while Eisenhower asserted, "We want to stay strong and will stay vigilant, but we are not going to extinguish the hope that a new dawn may be coming, even if . . . the sun rises very . . . slowly."[34]

On the eve of Geneva, the President pinned his hopes on the spiritual superiority of the West. "The free world is . . . not held together by force, but we are held together by this great factor, and it is this: the free world believes, under one religion or another, in a divine power. It believes in a Supreme Being."[35] The State Department translated this into a secular agenda: a united

Germany, "sovereign rights and self-government to those who have been deprived of them" in Eastern Europe, a solution to the problem of international Communism, and extension of Atoms for Peace.[36] The new National Security Advisor, Dillon Anderson, noted, "The position of the Soviet Union was weakening and . . . we should accordingly hold its feet to the fire."[37]

Meanwhile, Washington's psychological warriors were devising their secret weapon for the summit. Led by C. D. Jackson's replacement, Nelson Rockefeller, a group of advisors had gathered at Quantico, Virginia, to discuss a new strategy to defeat the Soviets. The wide-ranging talks, on topics from the arms race to Asian economic growth, led Walt Rostow to effuse, "For the first time, [I can] really see how the cold war can be won within the next ten years . . . without American initiation of major war."[38] Their most significant recommendation was for Eisenhower to make a bold and unexpected offer that held out the hope of peace while maintaining pressure on the Soviet bloc. Max Millikan of MIT provided the breakthrough with "Open Skies", the proposal that US planes could overfly the Soviet Union and Soviet planes the United States, to monitor the build-up of military forces. If accepted, Open Skies would provide the system to oversee any agreement on disarmament between the two superpowers.

Open Skies had its opponents. Pressed by State Department officials, Under-secretary of State Herbert Hoover, Jr, tried to persuade Foster Dulles to seek a presidential veto of the project, but the Secretary of State acknowledged, "The US must certainly be prepared to make some positive move in the direction of disarmament. If we did not do so . . . we would lose very important assets, such as the support of our allies and the right to use bases in the allied countries."[39] Presented with the "most striking idea of overflights" in Geneva, Foster Dulles agreed: "From the standpoints both of drama and substance, the proposal was very promising and should have a very great effect."[40] Eisenhower accordingly unveiled the plan the following day. The major powers would "give to each other a complete blueprint of our military establishments, from beginning to end, from one end of our country to the other" and "provide within our countries facilities for aerial photography".[41]

There was an immediate response: as Eisenhower finished, a thunderclap boomed and the lights went out. However, like Atoms for Peace, Open Skies had more impact as short-term publicity than as a long-term policy despite Foster Dulles's injunction "not [to] follow up on the President's plan as if it were a propaganda stunt".[42] Since the United States was developing the U-2, far more advanced than any Soviet reconnaissance plane, Washington would reap the immediate benefits of mutual overflights. Moreover, since the United States in 1955 still had a significant advantage in delivery systems for nuclear weapons, the arrangement would effectively "freeze" a position of American superiority.[43]

By the autumn, pessimism had again arisen over Eisenhower's strategy, even as officials reiterated the aspiration to "eventually . . . bring about a change in Communist policy and a retraction of Communist power".[44] Rockefeller noted that, while Eisenhower had been "brilliantly successful in sustaining American leadership and convincing the world of America's desire for peace",[45] the Soviets had achieved a "public relations success of no mean proportions by reducing substantially the unpopularity of the Soviet Union in Western European eyes. . . . The net result has been a further undermining of the Western alliance." Allen Dulles considered Moscow's line "more insidious and more difficult to combat" than the threats of Stalin's era, given the "clear and unmistakable evidence" that the West, even the United States, would not resort to war or the threat of war to liberate Eastern Europe.[46] The President could only send Foster Dulles to the follow-up to the Geneva Summit, the conference of Foreign Ministers, with the invocation, "[I want] to mention the prayers of millions everywhere, including even people from the Iron Curtain, which gives some heartening evidence that there may be some human impulses left that give ground for hope."[47] He pronounced to the National Security Council:

> At this moment in history, we cannot afford to appear, in the eyes of the world, as condemning all offers of the Soviet Union even before testing for sincerity. We should emphasize the positive aspects of US policy. We should not emphasize the direct charges and allegations against the Soviet Union, but rather we should make such points by indirection.[48]

The Operations Coordinating Board noted laconically, "Efforts to bring about a basis for a negotiated settlement and to encourage evolutionary changes in satellite regimes . . . are not always compatible with programs intended to keep alive the hopes and aspirations of the captive peoples."[49]

Outside the Government, the editors of *Life* magazine and C. D. Jackson pressed for a return to an aggressive strategy. They were not so sure that negotiation was suitable for US goals, "The danger is a growing tendency, both here and abroad, to believe that peace has already been achieved when actually the 'spirit' itself is all that has been achieved." *Life* reiterated the call for a unified Germany and disarmament with inspection. Most importantly, the occupation of Eastern Europe had to be ended: "It is probably too much to hope that we can bring about very soon an end of the local Communist dictatorships in those countries, but if the Soviets will remove the troops that keep them in power, the people themselves may be able to express their own wills."[50]

The problem was addressed by the best and brightest minds at the second Quantico conference in November 1955. Organized by Nelson Rockefeller, the gathering included C. D. Jackson, Air Force General Frederick Anderson, and prominent academics like Max Millikan, Paul Linebarger, a specialist on

Asian affairs, and a Harvard fellow named Henry Kissinger. Unsurprisingly, the group paid homage to the pre-eminence of psychological warfare in the Cold War; however, in the hundreds of pages in the conference's papers there were few ideas for a renewed US offensive. Instead, the participants were obsessed by a threat that lay not in the Soviet Union's armies but in its diplomats. Kissinger summarized, "The predominant aspect of the new diplomacy is its psychological dimension. If the US, in the process of attempting to establishing a better atmosphere, lulls its own people into a false sense of security, it may paralyze itself in the next round of negotiations. . . . If a detente is achieved in Europe, it may remove the only incentive of our European allies to support us in case of a crisis in Asia."

Scholar after scholar echoed Kissinger's warning, "The more the Soviets succeed in giving the impression that there exists a 'third alternative' in the contest between the US and the USSR, the more difficult our coalition effort becomes." Colonel George Lincoln of the US Military Academy asserted that the Soviet Union displayed "some chance of growing within a decade or two to a power center which might quickly overwhelm EurAsia and Africa, politically, economically, and psychologically, if the western world got into difficulties." Dr George Pettee of Johns Hopkins assessed, "The tactics of the third phase [of the Cold War] may be expected to follow those of the other periods in Soviet history when they talked softly, acted agreeably, and generally earned the temporary reputation of good and peaceful people," while Philip Mosely of the Council of Foreign Relations turned the "spirit of Geneva" into an ominous threat, "The 'concessions' which are being used as counters by the Soviet leadership in its present tactics are of slight or no importance to the Soviet bloc but have an impressive impact on the peoples beyond its borders."

To counter this, the experts offered little. The advice of the Air Force's Stefan Possony verged on racism: "The US should express its belief that the peoples of the world are not fundamentally unreasonable and that practically all nations, in time, can develop attitudes to political issues which characterize the commonsense behavior of the Scandinavian peoples, the Swiss, and the Anglo-Saxons." Mosely and Kissinger repeated the mantra that the United States should "negotiate actively on the really difficult policies" of a united Germany, a free Eastern Europe, and disarmament to show that the Soviet Union "remained unchanged". Even C. D. Jackson sought refuge in the undefined hope of a "coherent, convincing, compelling and, in a sense, majestic statement of American foreign policy".[51]

The contrast of the Rockefeller panel's conclusions with those of its predecessors was striking. NSC 68 had rejected any negotiations with Moscow; the only US strategy was to break up the Soviet bloc before it threatened to overwhelm the Free World. Five years later, Eisenhower's advisors had not only accepted negotiations with the enemy; they had no other recommendation for success. With the State Department opposed to liberation and the White House unwilling to give a specific endorsement to it, Washington could only cling to a recitation of "freedom" which had no substance.

Rockefeller did continue to dream. Noting the "despondent reaction" of leading emigres to the *détente* of Geneva, he called for "the skillful international exposure of true Communist purposes. The firming up of our Western allies into a sincere refusal to compromise on principle . . . should be the basis for a new hope for the captive peoples. At least the foundations for more effective actions that will be of interest to the cause of freedom in Eastern Europe have been laid."[52] A month later, however, Rockefeller had resigned, contending that he had "done all that it is possible for him to do" but the "opposition and conflict of interests [was] so great that he doubted if State will permit the Pres to decide to fill the job again".[53]

Rockefeller had not eased matters with the "technique of large staffing for no apparent worthwhile reason" and the President "was extremely disappointed at the way Nelson, for all his external sweetness, had managed to antagonize everybody".[54] Still, Eisenhower recognized the fundamental problem even if he had done little to solve it. He noted, "[Rockefeller's] was a difficult job to organize. The unfortunate thing is, every department of government is concerned a little bit in this field," and added that Foster Dulles might "have been hypersensitive" about the Special Assistant's duties.[55] The position of Rockefeller's successor, William Jackson, was strengthened by his appointment to the Operations Coordinating Board, in Eisenhower's words, "for proper coordination and timing of the execution of foreign policies",[56] but the question of US strategy against the Soviet Union was unresolved.

A progress report on exploitation of Soviet vulnerabilities concluded "that [the] effect appears to have been modest and for most part marginal".[57] This was exemplified in the continued muddle over balloon operations. At one level, the US Government maintained a puritanical detachment, rejecting any association with the program sponsored by Quaker Oats.[58] At another, it accepted the renewal of operations by the National Committee for Free Europe, even as these threatened diplomatic embarrassment. The Soviet Union issued protests not only to the US but also to Turkey, Bulgaria complained to the United Nations, and East Germany issued warnings of danger to air traffic. Eisenhower complained bitterly, in Foster Dulles's words, "that both he and I had been rather allergic to this project". He asked for a suspension of the program; Foster Dulles agreed but said, "We should handle it so it would not look as though we had been caught with jam on our fingers."[59]

C. D. Jackson was so frustrated with the Administration's indecision that, when newspapers headlined a Foster Dulles speech with "Wake to Red Peril, Ike, Dulles Pleads" and "Dulles Spurs US in Economic War with Soviet Union", he wrote the Secretary of State to urge a follow-up speech by the President.[60] The Administration would go no further, however, than considering "sending a lot of our existing surpluses to the people of West Germany and West Berlin" since "news of such delivery of US surpluses would soon trickle into East Germany". Eisenhower asked plaintively, "Could we not . . . send them three or four million pounds of pork?"[61] Jackson had to settle for small consolations such as aid to Hungary after floods swept the country and the US Information Agency's "Family of Man" exhibit: this attracted an audience of 44,000 in Berlin, one-third of them from the Eastern zone, "most of them wearing sunglasses to avoid recognition".[62]

Rather than concentrating on concrete action to achieve "freedom", the Administration occupied itself with great but vague projects to appeal to world opinion, especially in "neutral" countries, and to open up the Soviet Union. In autumn 1955, at a monthly meeting with Theodore Streibert and Abbott Washburn of the US Information Agency on "propaganda in the good sense", the President tabled the idea of developing contacts between non-governmental organisations.[63] This led to a "President's Program for Understanding", which brought together eminent representatives from 29 different areas, ranging from Foreign Affairs to Educators to Letter Writing. It was the first time that the same committee included Robert Frost, Eugene Ormandy, Conrad Hilton, and J. C. Penney.[64] Paul Hoffman, the former head of the Mutual Security Administration, went further in April 1956, requesting an advisory committee "from business, farm, labor, and women's organizations" to appeal to neutrals with "measures aimed to promote the evolution of stable, effective, and democratic societies". Hoffman concluded, "Our purpose should not be to make these nations into our own image and likeness but to help them achieve their own salvation and their own way on the free side of the Iron and Bamboo Curtains."[65]

For example, the United States could lead others to the enjoyment of "People's Capitalism". Emanating from a Yale University–Advertising Council round table for "a moralistic idea with the power to stir men's imagination", the project was adopted by the US Information Agency "to separate what we call capitalism from the skillfully exploited stereotype put out by the Communists".[66] With the centerpiece of two American homes, one from 1775 and one from 1956, and headlines like "Class Lines begin to Disappear" and "Almost Everybody became a Capitalist", the campaign emphasized a system to "fulfill man's age-old dream of a life free from want, with each individual free to develop to the fullest those talents and abilities given him by the Creator".[67]

The qualities of US culture were brought directly to the Soviet bloc with the successful tours of Isaac Stern and *Porgy and Bess*. The *New York Times* raved about the latter: "With charm and grace, members of the cast created a new perspective here for a communist-led people sensitive to reports of American race prejudice and exploitation. The contributions which such presentations make toward a better understanding of America can scarcely be exaggerated."[68] The National Security Council eventually adopted a 17-point proposal for cultural exchanges to provide "the people of the Soviet Union with accurate knowledge of the kind of opportunities that existed in the US for the ordinary run of actions".[69] Even more successful were specific economic exchanges with the Soviet Union, notably "in the fields of agriculture, medicine, mining and smelting, and general industry".[70]

The initiatives culminated in the People-to-People programme, established in September 1956 with 43 different committees, since "freer person-to-person contacts could play a major role in aiding the process of a slow evolution of the Soviet system".[71] Secretary of the Treasury Humphrey gave an even blunter assessment: "Our objectives were essentially to change the system of government and society in the Soviet Union, and even to bring down the Soviet Government. We could scarcely reveal our objectives publicly. It would be like inviting guests to tea and telling them that you were going to put poison in the food."[72] Yet, while the scheme produced a few successes such as hospital ship SS *Hope* and the Sister City Program, it was more symbol than substance.

And then, suddenly and unexpectedly, the activists were handed their best opportunity for the conquering of the Soviet bloc. It came from none other than Nikita Khrushchev.

Notes

1 "Operation Kremlin Kracks," 16 February 1955, US DDRS, 1997 3319; Jackson to Rock feller and Allen Dulles, 17 February 1955, and Brief of (*deleted*), 21 February 1955, *Diaries*, Reel 18
2 246th NSC meeting, 28 April 1955, US DDRS, 1986 2020
3 Merchant to Hoover, 4 January 1955, FRUS, 1955–1957, XXV, 4–5
4 NSC 5501, 6 January 1955, *Documents*, Reel 4
5 NSC 5505/1, undated, USNA, Department of State, Lot 63 D 351, Records Relating to State Department Participation in the OCB and the NSC, 1947–1963, Box 84, NSC 5505/1
6 Griffith to Jackson, 20 October 1954, DDE, Jackson Papers, Box 47, W. E. Griffith
7 Annex to NSC 5505/1, 18 January 1955, USNA, Department of State, Lot 63 D 351, Records Relating to State Department Participation in the OCB and the NSC, 1947–1963, Box 84, NSC 5505
8 NSC 5501, 6 January 1955, *Documents*, Reel 4
9 NSC 5502, January 1955, NSC 5502
10 NSC 5505/1, undated, USNA, Department of State, Lot 63 D 351, Records Relating to State Department Participation in the OCB and the NSC, 1947–1963, Box 84, NSC 5505/1
11 Operations Coordinating Board notes, 5 January 1955, FRUS 1955–1957 XXV 7
12 Allen Dulles speech, "Education in the Soviet Union," 1 June 1955, DDE, Jackson Papers, Box 40, Allen Dulles
13 234th NSC meeting, 27 January 1955, US DDRS, 1992 310
14 Bishop memorandum, 4 January 1955, USNA, Department of State, Lot 62 D 430, Records Relating to State Department Participation in the OCB and the NSC, 1947–1963, Box 30, Soviet Satellites 1955

15 "Part 6 – The USIA Program," 11 August 1955, US DDRS, 1991 2022

16 Killian Report, Volume 1, "Meeting the Threat of Surprise Attack," 14 February 1955, *Minutes*, Reel 2

17 See Johnson to Smith, 26 June 1953, USNA, Department of State, Lot 62 D 333, PSB Working File, 1951–1953, Box 6, PSB D-44.

18 See Joint Chiefs of Staff to Secretary of Defense, 1 October 1954, *Minutes*, 1st Supplement, Reel 3

19 213th NSC meeting, 9 September 1954, US DDRS, 1986 2829

20 214th NSC meeting, 12 September 1954, US DDRS, 1986 2832

21 216th NSC meeting, 9 October 1954, *Minutes*, 1st Supplement, Reel 4

22 216th NSC meeting, 9 October 1954, *Minutes*, 1st Supplement, Reel 4

23 232nd NSC meeting, 20 January 1955, US DDRS, 1986 3340

24 231st NSC meeting, 13 January 1955, US DDRS, 1991 362

25 Lay memorandum, 6 November 1953, US DDRS, 1988 1041

26 240th NSC meeting, 10 March 1955, US DDRS, 1986 3386

27 Planning Coordination Group minutes, 21 June 1955, USNA, Department of State, Lot 66 D 148, Records Relating to State Department Participation in the NSC, 1947–1963, Box 127, Planning Coordination Group

28 Office of the Assistant Secretary of Defense to Rockefeller, 5 April 1955, USNA, Department of State, Lot 66 D 148, Records Relating to State Department Participation in the NSC, 1947–1963, Box 127, Planning Coordination Group

29 Memorandum for Rockefeller, 5 April 1955, Department of State, Lot 66 D 148, Records Relating to State Department Participation in the NSC, 1947–1963, Box 127, Planning Coordination Group

30 Foster Dulles televised speech, 17 May 1955, *Diaries*, Reel 6

31 249th NSC meeting, 19 May 1955, US DDRS, 1986 3400

32 249th NSC meeting, 19 May 1955, US DDRS, 1986 3400

33 Outline Plan of Operations for NSC 174, 1 July 1955, US DDRS, 1993 2920

34 Foster Dulles and Eisenhower television broadcast, 17 May 1955, *Diaries*, Reel 6

35 Eisenhower television broadcast, 15 July 1955, *Diaries*, Reel 6

36 State Department press release, 18 July 1955, *Diaries*, Reel 6

37 254th NSC meeting, 7 July 1955, US DDRS, 1986 3404

38 Rostow to Rockefeller, 17 June 1955, US DDRS, 1992 3572

39 253rd NSC meeting, 30 June 1955, US DDRS, 1992 2676; Jackson log, From Quantico to Geneva, June and July 1955, DDE, Jackson Papers, Box 56, Log 1955

40 Meeting at Eisenhower villa, 20 July 1955, US DDRS, 1987 1043

41 *Public Papers of the President 1955*, 713–16

42 256th NSC meeting, 28 July 1955, US DDRS, 1992 2733

43 See the charts with the disarmament presentation of 26 May 1955 in *Minutes*, Reel 2

44 MacArthur to Murphy, 16 August 1955, USNA, Department of State, Records of the Policy Planning Staff 1955, Box 94

45 Rockefeller to Eisenhower, 26 September 1955, US DDRS, 1986 2386

46 Operations Coordinating Board report, "Psychological Implications of Geneva for US Information Programs," 31 August 1955, FRUS 1955–1957 XXV 73–4

47 Eisenhower memorandum, 19 October 1955, *Diaries*, Reel 5

48 262nd NSC meeting, 20 October 1955, US DDRS, 1990 2082

49 OCB progress report, 29 February 1956, USNA, Department of State, Lot 62 D 430, Records Relating to State Department Participation in the OCB and the NSC, 1947–1963, Box 30, Soviet Satellites 1956

50 *Life*, "Friendly Talk is Not Enough," 5 September 1955

51 "Psychological Aspect of US Strategy," November 1955, *Minutes*, Reel 2

52 Novak to Jackson, 7 November 1955, DDE, Jackson Papers, Box 45, FEC Correspondence through 1956, Basic (2); Rockefeller to Jackson, 7 November 1955, DDE, Jackson Papers, Box 75, Nelson Rockefeller

53 Jackson daily log, 19 December 1955, DDE, Jackson Papers, Box 56, Log 1955

54 Jackson to Luce, 21 December 1955, DDE, Jackson Papers, Box 56, Log 1955

55 Eisenhower diary entry, 10 October 1955, *Diaries*, Reel 5

56 Eisenhower to William Jackson, 11 April 1956, *Diaries*, Reel 8

57 Draft progress report on NSC 5505/1, 12 December 1955, Progress Report on NSC 5505/1, 14 December 1955, USNA, Lot 63 D 351, Records Relating to State Department Participation in the OCB and the NSC, 1947–1963, Box 84, NSC 5505/1

58 Unnamed memorandum on Quaker Oats Balloon Plan, 30 March 1955, USNA, Department of State, Lot 59 D 233, Miscellaneous Office Files of the Assistant Secretary of State for European Affairs, 1943–1957, Box 27, Balloons

59 Foster Dulles to Armstrong, Murphy, and Merchant, 7 February 1956, USNA, Department of State, Lot 59 D 233, Miscellaneous Office Files of the Assistant Secretary of State for European Affairs, 1943–1957, Box 28, Balloons

60 Jackson to Foster Dulles, 12 January 1956, DDE, Jackson Papers, Box 40, John Foster Dulles

61 272nd NSC meeting, 12 January 1956, US DDRS, 1987 427

62 OCB Daily Intelligence Report 591, 30 March 1956, US DDRS, 1992 2208

63 Abbott Washburn oral history, 20 April 1967, DDE, Oral History Collection

64 President's Program for Understanding, undated, *Diaries*, Reel 7

65 Hoffman to Eisenhower, 25 April 1956, *Diaries*, Reel 8

66 Walter Hixson, *Parting the Curtain: Propaganda, Culture and the Cold War, 1945–1961* (New York, 1997), 137; Jackson to Davenport, 2 November 1956, DDE, Jackson Papers, Box 37, Da Miscellaneous

67 Hixson, *Parting the Curtain*, 139

68 Hixson, *Parting the Curtain*, 137

69 289th NSC meeting, 28 June 1956, US DDRS, 1987 1632

70 Draft progress report on NSC 5505/1, 12 December 1955, USNA, Department of State, Lot 63 D 351, Records Relating to State Department Participation in the OCB and the NSC, 1947–1963, Box 84, NSC 5505/1

71 White House meeting, 31 August 1956, *Diaries*, Reel 9

72 290th NSC meeting, 5 July 1956, US DDRS, 1997 2802

14

Liberation

On the eve of Nikita Khrushchev's address to the Twentieth Congress of the Communist Party of the Soviet Union, the Eisenhower Administration had reiterated the vague policy of "taking . . . actions designed to foster changes in the character and policies of the Soviet-Communist bloc regimes".[1] The Operations Coordinating Board complained that US action "may have caused some difficulties for Moscow, but no real evidence of a schism [with the satellites] has yet made its appearance" and that "it is likely to become more and more difficult to keep hope of liberation alive in the satellite peoples". Even more striking was the report's argument that the changed international environment had jeopardized the viability of liberation: "In the absence of a cold war climate, many of the courses of action would be difficult to pursue. For example, those intended to encourage anti-communist activities and passive resistance are somewhat incompatible with a *détente*. . . . It may be that the US will have to undertake to follow simultaneously two policies with inconsistent courses of action, representing divergent approaches to the objective."[2]

On 5 February 1956, however, Khrushchev instructed his party gathering to act against "the cult of the individual and . . . its harmful consequences". In a prolonged denunciation, he told the delegates of Lenin's warning that Stalin would not "use [his] power with the required care", described and berated "mass terror against the Party cadres" from the 1930s, and criticized failure to prepare defenses against the German invasion of 1941. He concluded, in cumbrous but pointed language, "The evil caused by acts violating revolutionary socialist legality which have accumulated during a long time as a result of the negative influence of the cult of the individual has to be completely corrected."[3]

Now the United States could resolve the contradiction between anti-Communist activities and *détente*, seizing the opportunity to produce a schism in the Soviet bloc. Despite the Administration's bewilderment over the motives of the new Soviet leadership – Allen Dulles reminded the National Security Council of "the possibility . . . that Khrushchev had been drunk" – it was agreed that "these events afforded the US a great opportunity, both covertly and overtly, to exploit the situation to its advantage".[4] Events in Poland,

Bulgaria, and Czechoslovakia soon "offered the US the basis for a very effective campaign of psychological warfare", in Allen Dulles's eyes, "the greatest opportunity [the US had] had in this area for the last 10 years". Eisenhower responded with renewed enthusiasm, "No single country like Soviet Russia could really be successful in controlling indefinitely vast areas such as those comprised by the satellites unless, like ourselves, in an earlier war with the Indians, we virtually exterminated the population. . . . It was essential that we keep the hope of liberation alive in the satellites as a force on our side."[5]

A special Working Group on the Anti-Stalin Campaign was immediately established and by April was "serving a very useful purpose". In addition to "continuing followup and exploitation" of Khrushchev's secret speech, the working group gave "particular attention to what could be done by way of challenging the Soviet satellite government to remove the Iron Curtain".[6] Objectives included "expansion of the official criticism of Stalin into pressure by the people of the USSR for the diversion of effort away from military production and expansion of communism abroad toward a higher standard of living and more representative government at home" as well as "a loosening of the ties binding the satellites to Moscow and creation of conditions which will permit the satellites to evolve toward independence of Moscow". While overt US media were avoiding "an attitude of jubilation over communist embarrassment", non-attributable programs were seeking "to sow confusion and doubt in the communist world".[7]

The cornerstone of the campaign was public dissemination of the secret speech. A CIA approach to Yugoslavia to get the speech failed, but a copy was finally obtained from Polish and Israeli sources. In some areas, the CIA not only planted the text with local outlets, they altered it with a few select passages on Eastern Europe. For the most part, however, Allen Dulles was content to feed the original, unchanged transcript via the State Department to the *New York Times*.[8] Foster Dulles proclaimed the publication "the greatest feat by American Intelligence in a number of years".[9] In Budapest, the US embassy enthused, "The dominoes in Eastern Europe have begun to fall. . . . [Prime Minister Matyas Rakosi's] position is sufficiently precarious, we believe, to offer a possibility for US action to have some effect on future developments."[10]

In mid-1956, the Administration was suddenly facing the prospect of a quick triumph. Having stumbled and fumbled with liberation for more than three years, Foster Dulles was disconcerted by the apparent self-destruction of Moscow's leadership:

> Khrushchev was the most dangerous person to lead the Soviet Union since the October Revolution. He was not a coldly calculating person but rather one who reacted emotionally. He was obviously intoxicated much of the time and could be expected to commit irrational acts. The previous Soviet leaders had been for the most part the chess-playing type. Khrushchev was the first top authority in the USSR who was essentially emotional and perfectly capable of acting without a calculation

of the consequences of his action. . . . All in all . . . he would be glad indeed to see Khrushchev go, and there was evidently considerable feeling in the governing circles in the USSR that he ought to be fired.[11]

A more measured and effective response came from Radio Free Europe, which was assigning 10 transmitters exclusively to the text of Khrushchev's secret speech.[12] Its guidance emphasized, "[We] want to insure, where possible, that our audiences will demand the rights now being talked about. Fresh legitimate demands should be built upon the concessions already being made."[13]

While most of the National Security Council's subsequent decisions are still classified, the Adminstration's renewed commitment to liberation was now evident. The NSC still believed, "Soviet domination of the Eastern European satellites remains firm and there appears little immediate prospect of basic change in this regard," but it also assessed:

> This fluid situation . . . has increased the previously limited US capabilities to influence a basic change. . . . Although the Eastern European peoples continue to feel that liberation is remote, they remain responsive to our interest in their independence, provided it is expressed persistently and in terms which make it clear that this is our basic objective.[14]

Eisenhower's Special Assistant for psychological operations, William Jackson, drove home the point that the new policy "would have the effect of encouraging this Government to be more active in the satellites short of violence". Foster Dulles enthused to Eisenhower that much had been done "to revive the influences which are inherent in freedom, [and] have thereby created stresses and strains within the captive world".[15]

The National Security Council added a critical caveat, however, reflecting the persistent ambiguity in the Administration's policy. While US propaganda and covert operations would "emphasize . . . the right of the peoples of Eastern Europe to independent governments of their own choosing", the NSC reiterated its guidance of early 1955 that the United States would "stress evolutionary rather than revolutionary change".[16] For example, the United States "was not prepared to resort to war to eliminate Soviet domination of East Germany."[17] At no point did Eisenhower and his advisors address the obvious question: how could Eastern Europeans demand free elections and independence within a totalitarian system without a "revolutionary" change?

So the uncertainty continued. Policy blithely maintained, without noting the possible contradiction:

> Avoid incitements to violence or to action when the probable reprisals or other results would yield a net loss in terms of U.S. objectives. In general, however, do not discourage, by public utterances or otherwise, spontaneous manifestations of discontent and opposition to the Communist regime, despite risks to individuals, when their net results will exert pressures for release from Soviet domination.[18]

How far could the United States go? William Jackson suggested, "Actual encouragement of violence in the satellites should be the exception rather than the rule," but Foster Dulles, more and more open to aggressive action, added, "Sometimes unrest of this sort and uprisings like these [in East Germany and Poland] were an important part of the way we have to play the game in the present situation we are confronting with the Soviet Union." Vice-President Nixon concluded, "We are not saying that we are going to initiate uprisings and violence in the satellites. We are merely saying that we will not always discourage such uprisings and violence if the uprisings should occur spontaneously. The policy paper . . . should not be too 'soft' in character."[19]

Present and former members of the Administration, including C. D. Jackson, William Jackson, and Nelson Rockefeller, and academics like Walt Rostow and Max Millikan, dining at the Century Club, were distressed at a further caution from William Jackson: "I don't think I can do anything about [action within the satellites]. The idea has got to come from somewhere else, and then I can try to get something done."[20] More encouraging was the suggestion of Under-secretary of State Robert Murphy to the National Security Council to "encourage alertness to change and exploit the situation to the maximum. This [would] entail inevitable risks, but an omelet cannot be made without breaking eggs." He suggested that "voluntary sacrifices of patriotic nationalists might well stimulate a trend toward release from Soviet domination".[21]

The solution seemed to come in Poland. William Griffith, the head of the National Committee for Free Europe, wrote several months before Khrushchev's secret speech, "The opportunities for influencing developments from the outside are probably greater than at any time within the last seven years."[22] In June 1956, Griffith's associate Samuel Walker enthused, "The 'thaw', far from unsettling our staffs, . . . seems to have sparked a new vitality and level of intelligence and imagination which . . . is pretty reassuring."[23] Within days, riots in Poznan sparked general protests throughout Poland, encouraged by official, "unofficial", and covert US "information".[24]

Radio Free Europe, in more than 94 hours of broadcasts to Poland between 28 June and 3 July, tried "to carry newscasts and commentaries which would hearten but not incite, sympathize but not deplore".[25] In the aftermath of the demonstrations, US services highlighted the trials of the protest's leaders, a renewed offer of food through the Red Cross, and public statements by Foster Dulles referring "to the need for free elections in Poland".[26] They also promoted the Polish rising as only the first of many in the Soviet bloc. "International Commentary" to Bulgaria explained, "No matter how hard they try, the communists cannot hide or explain away workers' uprisings in what is supposed to be the workers' paradise." Czechs were told in similar terms, "No matter what they do, the outlook is dim for the comrades, and that goes for the other captive countries as well."[27] C. D. Jackson predicted:

Either [the Soviet Union] will have to carry their overtures to even greater extremes, which may prove a serious irreversible step for them, or they may have to revert to more Stalinist tactics. I do not think that mere continuation of Bulganin and Khrushchev smiles cum vodka and caviar is good enough anymore.[28]

Throughout the Polish crisis, Radio Free Europe maintained a delicate balance between promoting the demands for "freedom" and maintaining the fiction of US detachment by "stressing . . . that the events of Poznan developed from a wholly legitimate demand for a strike for improved living conditions and assumed revolutionary implications only when Polish Regime applied brutal Stalinist methods".[29] On the one hand, RFE's commentaries persistently reinforced the notion that any Communist system was evil and that there was no alternative for "freedom" other than the overthrow of that system: "In Poznan clear proof had been established, if any was needed, that 'liberalization' and 'communism' fundamentally are mutually exclusive and that no genuine de-Stalinization could be expected from the leaders who had helped to create, yet managed to survive, Stalin and Stalinism."[30] In the middle of the crisis, a message from Eisenhower drove home the theme of liberation:

On the fifth anniversary of Radio Free Europe, I wish to pay tribute to the people of Central and Eastern Europe for maintaining their love of freedom in the face of adversity. I congratulate RFE on its work to fortify in these peoples the spirit of liberty – a spirit that assured the ultimate achievement of their hopes and aspirations.[31]

At the same time, RFE kept a nominal distance from events by eschewing any responsibility for instigating uprisings:

It is not our function to whip up excitement or hope. We analyze events. . . . Our station is not the proper organ to try to lead anyone into action. It is not close enough to judge all the facets of the internal situation as it is constantly changing. We analyze for you, but cannot and do not issue orders or give advice. We can only say that historical forces are on the move which will, in time, sweep away the social and political reaction which is Soviet totalitarianism.

Warning its Polish audience of the failure of the 1905 revolution in Russia, it summarized, "The struggle for freedom must end in victory, for no regime based on repression can last. But in that struggle prudence is necessary. And, therefore in the name of the ardent desire, common to us all, for Poland's freedom, we must call on the people to preserve calm and refrain from acts of despair."[32]

Despite these caveats, the Administration's reserve was diminishing. Foster Dulles dropped his cautious position on liberation and told his brother Allen, "[When] they began to crack, they can crack fast. We have to keep the pressure on."[33] He spoke "eloquently" to his staff "of the need to take risks in the development of our policies, especially if we are to be 'on the offensive'. Nothing is achieved that does not have some risk to it."[34] The National Committee for Free Europe (now renamed the Free Europe Committee) was doing just that with a "third stage" of leaflet drops into Poland, Hungary, and Czechoslovakia to promote the "thaw".[35] Emigres were put in touch with the International Rescue Committee to coordinate the despatch of medical supplies and relief packages to Eastern Europe.[36] No possible line of action was excluded: a CIA representative even called on the President of the Welch Grape Juice Corporation, a long-time contact of the Agency, to discuss his letter about "strenuous efforts . . . to exploit the cracks in the Communist discipline".[37]

By October the new US strategy appeared to be vindicated throughout the Soviet bloc. In Czechoslovakia, there was an increase in worker absenteeism, demands for a Special Congress on de-Stalinisation, and organized student demonstrations. There were no thoughts of "evolution"; instead, the Free Europe Committee insisted that it was "essential that the initiative be retained by the opposition and that the opposition pressure should be intensified. . . . We [must] take care that the opposition, engaged in the piecemeal struggle with the regime, should retain a clear picture of the final aim – i.e., complete liberation."[38] In Hungary, Western propaganda was "providing the peasants with a rationale for leaving the collective farms", suggesting that the departure of Prime Minister Matyas Rakosi, succeeded by Erno Gero, opened "new avenues of hope and action", and giving proof of contacts with the Western world. The Free Europe Committee summarized concisely, "The point is not so much that Western media have created events as that they have succeeded in spreading and exploiting the impact of these events," before noting that the United States must go even further: "Western media must, in the immediate future, address themselves to the fundamental problem of depriving Communism of its power monopoly by stimulating and unifying the independent opposition forces inside Hungary."[39]

In Poland, a more liberal regime under Wladyslaw Gomulka faced down Soviet threats and took power in Warsaw on 19 October. Hungarians, following the Polish example, began to press for economic and political liberalisation from the regime; Gero himself was replaced on 24 October by Imre Nagy.[40] Radio Free Europe again played its part through "long-range programs of encouraging retention and possible extension of gains in Poland and of promoting similar liberalization in other satellites by heavy cross-reporting". The station transmitted 23 hours per day to Hungary. Even more significantly, all freedom stations' broadcasts, including demands for Hungarian withdrawal from the Warsaw Pact and "setting-up [of] Western-style democracy . . . were recorded and reported to the entire nation. At the request of freedom stations, RFE relayed several messages to the United

Nations and the White House."[41] The Free Europe Committee assessed that the treatment was "prudent, vigorous, and unquestionably effective".[42]

During the tension over Gomulka's accession, Foster Dulles was careful not to commit the US to intervention, telling an interviewer, "I do not think that we would send our own armed forces into Poland or into East Germany [if Soviet troops were involved]. I doubt if that would be a possible or desirable thing to do. It would be the last thing in the world that these people who are tyring to win their independence would want. That would [lead to] a full-scale world war and the probable result of that would be all these people would be wiped out."[43] Broadcasts to Hungary from the Voice of America walked a thin line:

> Position extremely delicate. . . . We certainly in no position to encourage revolters, especially in view of explicit statement that US would not intervene militarily under any circumstances. Conversely unless we can suggest alternatives we are in no position to discourage or describe as futile sacrifices Hungarians are making.[44]

However, the more important question was: where did Radio Free Europe draw the line in its support of a "peaceful" route to freedom? Jan Nowak, one of the key figures in the Polish service, later claimed that "protest" and "revolution" in Poland had been carefully balanced: "In the critical days of October upheaval, we used our hold over anti-Communist extremists to prevent the outbreak of a revolt."[45] As RFE pressed for more and more dramatic concessions by the Communist regimes, that balance disappeared. New guidance insisted, "Like Poland, Hungarian people will bring changes, the first of which must be the withdrawal of Soviet troops from Hungary."[46] A special commentary by "Janus" proclaimed:

> The spring of March knocked at the door of our country, although it is late in October, and it announced the determined will of a freedom-loving people. . . . The Government and its armed units are no more masters of the situation. . . . No matter what will be the outcome of this armed warfare, the Hungarian people will win in the end![47]

As fighting escalated between Soviet troops and Hungarian revolutionaries, the editor of the Hungarian service, Ladislas Farago, abandoned any pretense of avoiding armed conflict. He demanded the sabotage of railway and telephone lines and implied foreign aid would arrive if the uprising established a central military command.[48]

Far from placing clear limits on support of a Hungarian uprising, Eisenhower and Foster Dulles fueled the notion of US endorsement with several general messages. On 24 October, the President asserted, "The day of liberation may be postponed where armed forces for a time make protest suicidal, but all history testifies that the memory of freedom is not erased by fear of guns and [that] the love of freedom is more enduring than the power of tyrants."[49] Three days later, Foster Dulles told an audience in Dallas, Texas, "There is ground to believe that the trend [toward freedom] would prove to be an irreversible trend," although he did offer the sop to the Soviet Union, "We do not look upon these nations as potential military allies."[50]

On 28 October the Nagy Government arranged a cease-fire and, to the surprise of many, Soviet forces began to withdraw. Three months earlier, troop withdrawal was the most that anyone in the Administration hoped for, but now it was far from sufficient, at least for Radio Free Europe. The station piled on the rhetoric: "The Muscovite leaders, like whining dogs, did not only implore and threaten, but have cast the most wicked slanders towards those heroes who, for the great cause of Hungary's freedom, have reached out for arms in their despair," and made its aspirations clear by comparing the uprising with the 1921 Kronstadt rebellion against the Bolshevik Government.[51] "Janus" was exultant and called for free elections and further economic reforms – "The armed victory of the Hungarian people . . . must be considered a reality. . . . A political victory must follow an armed victory!" – while Balazs Balogh, in "To the Uprising Workers", insisted, "In the great chaos in Hungary, there is only one single firm point and that is the determination of the Hungarian people to adhere to the achievements of the revolution even at the cost of their lives."[52] A commentary on 2 November, at the height of the uprising, whipped up fervor:

> There is no time for any reversed "salami politics", nor for a gradual change in the composition of the government. With one single decision, all those elements must be removed from the government which by their mere presence remind [us] of the Stalinist past, as well as all those whose mere name is provocation to the nation.[53]

Radio Free Europe's advocacy of any path to freedom was now so strident that it caused a division among the staff of the Hungarian service. Three editors on the staff argued that broadcasts should concentrate on supporting Nagy and refrain from further demands for change. The majority of the personnel not only resisted this position, they labelled the trio an "anti-US political faction". Richard Condon, the European Director of RFE, finally defended the three in March 1957 when they faced dismissal from the station:

> If it was improper for RFE to have taken a negative position toward Nagy during the revolution (as audience analysis materials indicate) and in US interest that Nagy should have consolidated himself in power and established Gomulka-type system in Hungary, then this group has constantly been serving US interest more effectively than any other in the Desk and did so during revolution. . . . This very group was only one in Desk which opposed attitude of excessive questioning of Nagy towards which . . . most of Desk inclined during practically whole of revolution.[54]

Some officials in Washington did consider restricting the move towards revolution. A draft policy, NSC 5616, argued that the US and Western allies "should strive to aid and encourage forces in the satellites moving toward US objectives without provoking counter-action which would result in the suppression of 'liberalizing' influences". The Administration would "mobilize all appropriate pressures, including United Nations action, on the USSR [against repression or retaliation] ... but maintain Foster Dulles's assurance to Moscow that the United States would not pursue a military alliance with Hungary or other Soviet satellites".[55] Eisenhower supposedly rewrote a televized speech on 31 October, in part to tone down Foster Dulles's references to "irresistible" forces of "liberation".[56] Voice of America staffers were "heartbroken" at instructions not to report statements in the United Nations "extolling the heroism of the Hungarians and how the free world must come to their aid".[57]

Even these cautions were being swept away, however. The Joint Chiefs of Staff objected to any reassurance to Moscow about Hungary's military status, and the policy left open the question of further US demands for political and economic change, calling for "whatever capability we may possess to influence the new Hungarian leaders to adhere to and fulfill the commitments they have made to the Hungarian people which will advance US objectives, including the promise to seek Soviet agreement for the total withdrawal of Soviet forces from Hungary". There would also be consideration of prompting Soviet troop withdrawal from the rest of Eastern Europe. Most importantly, the policy was revised in the last days of October to advocate, "In the formative period, make potential Hungarian leaders seek to form a government as liberal and independent as possible, aware of US support of their aims; and, to the extent that their success depends on such assistance, be prepared to assist them through covert means to accomplish their purpose of forming and preserving such a government."[58]

The Administration was on the verge of embracing liberation. The new policy was to be discussed on 1 November, but Eisenhower and his colleagues set it aside to concentrate on the Suez crisis, where Britain, France, and Israel had launched an assault against Egypt. Still, with Moscow pulling its troops out of Hungary, the Administration enjoyed a moment of victory. Allen Dulles enthused, "In a sense, what had occurred there was a miracle. Events had belied all our past views that a popular revolt in the face of modern weapons was an utter impossibility. Nevertheless, the impossible had happened, and because of the power of public opinion, armed force could not effectively be used."[59] The next day, Eisenhower authorized $20 million in relief for Hungary with the proclamation, "All America pays tribute in these troubled days to the courage and sacrifices of the Hungarian people in their determination to secure freedom."[60]

Then the miracle turned to nightmare. A RFE broadcast prematurely and unwisely taunted the Soviets: "The eight days' victorious revolution have turned Hungary into a free land. .... Neither Khrushchev nor the whole of the

Soviet army have the power to oppress this new liberty. . . . What can you do against Hungary, you Soviet legions? It is in vain to pierce Hungarian souls with your bayonets. You can destroy and shoot and kill; our freedom will now forevermore defy you."[61] When Nagy announced that Hungary was to withdraw from the Warsaw Pact, effectively making the country a "neutral" in the Cold War, Moscow's hand was forced. Soviet tanks re-entered Hungary on 4 November. As those who had risen waited in vain for US aid, the appeals grew desperate:

> Do you love liberty? . . . So do we. Do you have wives and children? . . . So have we.
>   We have wounded . . . who have given their blood for the sacred cause of liberty, but we have no bandages . . . no medicine . . . And what shall we give to our children who are asking for bread? The last piece of bread has been eaten.
>   In the name of all that is dear to you . . . we ask you to help. . . . Those who have died for liberty . . . accuse you who are able to help and have not helped.[62]

Within days the demonstrators were crushed and Nagy was arrested as thousands of Hungarians fled into Austria. Some high-level CIA officials called for a US response ranging from the infiltration of emigres with paramilitary training to surgical nuclear strikes on the Hungarian frontier – all were quickly rejected by the Administration.[63] Allen Dulles confirmed in a cable to Frank Wisner, who was touring Central Europe when the uprising erupted, "Headquarters advising station that CIA tentative thinking is not to incite to action."[64] Eisenhower could only wring his hands and complain bitterly, "This was indeed a bitter pill for us to swallow. We say we are at the end of our patience, but what can we do that is really constructive? Should we break off diplomatic relations with the USSR? What would be gained by this action? The Soviets don't care. The whole business was shocking to the point of being unbelievable."[65]

One Radio Free Europe commentator was so frustrated that he broadcast, "The West could have done more for its freedom in Hungary with five divisions than with five hundred divisions which it is perhaps now preparing to set up."[66] Others in RFE clutched at straws, condemning the Soviet representative in the United Nations – "Probably no diplomat ever before has behaved so infamously, stupidly, and revoltingly. . . . [He] lied like a poultry thief before the judge." – and clinging to ultimate hopes: "The Soviet attack on Sunday could only achieve military results, but it could not break the immense longing for freedom of the population or their intention to resist further."[67] With little else to present, officials held up "Western diplomatic boycotts" against Moscow and highlighted the ransacking of the Soviet legation in Luxembourg, the burning of the Communist Party headquarters in Paris, and the refusal of Belgian and Dutch suppliers to provide food and followers to Soviet embassies.[68] A Hungarian émigré group struck by presenting invitees to a

Soviet reception at the United Nations with the telegram, "Please do not drink champagne mixed with Hungarian blood".[69] Small consolations came from the defection of Hungarian athletes at the Melbourne Olympics and the escape of Tamas Aczel, a Hungarian writer who had won the Stalin Prize, to Yugoslavia.[70]

Interestingly, within the Administration the rosiest view came from Eisenhower's Special Assistant, William Jackson:

> The opinion of the subjugated peoples of Eastern Europe and perhaps even the opinion of the Russian people themselves have not yet been conquered or mastered. When we think of the years the Soviets have had in which to impose their will and of the instruments they have had at their disposal, it is indeed heartening that these subjugated peoples still have opinions of their own, still dream of freedom, and still maintain their affinity to Western civilization.[71]

The National Security Council clung to reports of unrest among youth in the Soviet Union. Allen Dulles commented, "While these were small indications, they seemed to be signs of real discontent. There were even some signs of unrest in the field of labor."[72]

Such hopes could not hide the cruel exposure of the contradictions in US policy. The National Security Council may have clung to the illusion that it could support freedom while preventing the demonstrations from turning into "revolution", but in practice, how could the United States encourage the Hungarians to demand political and economic change without encouraging the overthrow of a Communist system that was preventing such change? Moreover, the nature of the network for propaganda and "psychological strategy" meant the Administration had little operational control. It was up to "private" organisations like Radio Free Europe to interpret the ambiguous guidelines for liberation. A Government memorandum in 1961 was still asking, "Unlike the Voice of America, is Radio Free Europe permitted to comment on, and if necessary interfere, in the internal affairs of its target countries?" since the Administration's reviews of the radio operations had been "unable to tackle the basic issues involved except in the vaguest, most general, and inconclusive terms".[73]

Given the activism of key members in these organisations, it was hardly surprising that the distinction between endorsement of reform and endorsement of revolution was blurred if not obliterated. Even after the Soviets had re-entered Hungary, Radio Free Europe broadcasts implied that, if the resistance continued until after the presidential election, Congress might approve armed intervention. Its commentaries asserted, "A practical manifestation of Western sympathy is expected at any hour."[74] A survey of 1,000 Hungarian refugees concluded that their primary motivation was the Polish rising and the reporting of it by American outlets. Almost 75 percent of the refugees had expected US military aid and half believed US broadcasts "gave the impression that the US was willing to fight, if necessary, to save Hungary".[75] A typical reaction was that of the chairman of the "revolutionary committee" in a small town north of Budapest, "The Western broadcasts have pushed and pushed us into this. Now they do nothing. They tell lies on the radio. They tell us not to work until the Russians have gone."[76] After the revolution, a Minister in the Nagy Government bitterly held that the United States "cynically and cold-bloodedly maneuvered the Hungarian people into action against the USSR".[77]

The US legation in Hungary admitted that RFE broadcasts were "in general exaggerated and often inaccurate", a sentiment echoed by Deputy Under-secretary of State Robert Murphy and Cord Meyer, the CIA official overseeing RFE. Meyer admitted in 1981, "The Polish people played it beautifully. . . . I think the Hungarian desk chief was less in control of his people."[78] While the uprisings would have occurred even if US information had been more moderate in tone, the radio policy had brought "considerable embarrassment".[79] The situation was further confused by other "black" stations urging liberation. For example, the Ukranian nationalist group NTS broadcast under the name of the Association of Hungarian Former Servicemen, and there were even reports of Communist units in East Germany falsely broadcasting as Radio Free Europe to establish US involvement in the uprising.[80]

A review by the Council of Europe's Consultative Assembly in 1957 formally cleared US services of inciting the Hungarian revolution. It concluded, "The accusation that RFE promised the Hungarian people during their revolt military aid from the West was proved to be without ground" and took time to praise Radio Free Europe's "big service to its country as well as to Europe".[81] An internal report on "Policy Guidance to Radio Free Europe" was more honest in assessing the complexities of propaganda:

> There are serious complications in attempting to give broad political guidance for any operation such as RFE. On the one hand, we say that RFE should not "incite", while on the other hand, RFE is authorized to quote from public speeches and articles by US Government officials, many of which are, in the context of the situation in Eastern Europe, provocative and can hardly be classified as other than "incitement".[82]

A leading US newspaperman wrote cogently, "The important propaganda fact is not what people hear, but rather what they think they hear. . . . From the phrasing of RFE scripts, the gap between the actual promises and implied promises was easy to bridge for people under the maximum of mental stress."[83]

The Eisenhower Administration showed brief concern over its responsibility for events. Days after the end of the uprising, Eisenhower expressed his concern to Foster Dulles, "We have excited Hungarians for all these years and now [are] turning our backs to them when they are in a jam." However, when the Secretary of State offered the fig leaf "We always have been against violent revolution," the President jumped at the chance for absolution. He claimed that he "told [US representative to the United Nations Henry Cabot] Lodge so but was amazed that he was in ignorance of this fact".[84] Under-secretary of State Herbert Hoover, Jr, in a convoluted summary, perfectly expressed the contradiction between principle and practice to Congressmen: "[The] basic US policy [was] that the satellites should be liberated not by force but by the unceasing pressure of man to be free."[85] By 14 November, Eisenhower was assuring a press conference that, while the Administration had issued state-ments to "keep freedom alive, . . . we have never in all the years that I think we have been dealing with problems of this sort urged or argued for any kind of armed revolt which could bring about disaster to our friends". When a reporter pressed the issue by noting Vice-President Nixon's statement during the Hungarian crisis on "how events proved [the] rightness of liberation", Eisenhower dissembled:

> I believe it would be the most terrible mistake for the free world ever to accept the enslavement of the Eastern European tier of nations as a part of a future world of which we approve.
>
> Now, we have said this in every possible way, and because of this we try to hold out to all the world the conviction that freedom will live, human freedom will live.
>
> Now, we have never asked, as I pointed out before, and never believed that, never asked a people to rise up against a ruthless military force and, of course, we think, on the other hand, that the employment of such force is the negation of all justice and right in the world.[86]

The activists tried in vain to recapture the fervour of late October. C. D. Jackson pressed his case at a meeting with Eisenhower and William Jackson on 7 November. C. D. Jackson's suggestions were far from radical, including an Eisenhower "call for MERCY" requesting UN Security Council members to send delegates to Budapest,[87] but the President's reply, given his previous vac-illation on liberation, was close to patronising: "I know that your whole being cries out for 'action' on the Hungarian problem. I assure you that the mea-sures taken there by the Soviets are just as distressing to me as they are to you, but to annihilate Hungary, should it become the scene of a bitter conflict, is in no way to help her." He then embarked on a homily about war which, whatever its merits, was of little consolation to C. D. Jackson and, no doubt, thousands of Hungarians:

> Partisanship has no place when such a vital question (as atomic self-destruction) confronts us. Mothers in Israel and Egypt . . . [and] in England and France, fathers and husbands in the US and in Russia are all potential victims and sufferers. After the event, all of them, regardless of nationality, will be disinterested in the petty arguments as to who was responsible – or even the niceties of procedure.[88]

When Clare Boothe Luce, the US ambassador to Italy, spoke of the "possible need for radical action", the President suggested Under-secretary of State

Hoover speak with her to put her "ideas into a little broader perspective".[89] It was left to C. D. Jackson to summarize the ultimate failure of Eisenhower's inaction over the previous three years:

> I don't seem to be able to get across to that genuinely modest man that "one indi-vidual can do a hell of a lot, particularly if he is President of the US".
>
> I know that if Eisenhower had a dramatic instinct comparable to FDR's [Franklin Roosevelt's], I would probably be the first to deplore it, but between that and the Eisenhower dramatic absolute zero lies an awful lot of legitimate theater, sorely needed right now.[90]

Notes

1 Lay memorandum, 8 February 1956, US DDRS, 1977 303A

2 Progress Report on NSC 174, 29 February 1956, US DDRS, 1987 2875. See also NIE 12–56, "Probable Developments in the European Satellites through 1960," 10 January 1956, FRUS, 1955–1957, XXV, 115–18

3 A translation of the speech is in Strobe Talbott (ed.), *Khrushchev Remembers* (New York, 1971), 608–77

4 280th NSC meeting, 22 March 1956, US DDRS, 1987 894

5 282nd NSC meeting, 26 April 1956, US DDRS, 1987 887; 284th NSC meeting, 10 May 1956, US DDRS, 1987 945; 280th NSC meeting, 22 March 1956, US DDRS, 1987 894

6 Staats memorandum, 4 April 1956, USNA, Department of State, Lot 62 D 430, Records Relat-ing to State Department Participation in the OCB and the NSC, 1947–1963, Box 2, OCB Minutes III. See RFE Special Guidance #26, 6 April 1956, US DDRS, 1991 923

7 Report of the OCB Working Group on Stalinism, 17 May 1956, USNA, Department of State, Lot 62 D 430, Records Relating to State Department Participation in the OCB and the NSC, 1947–1963, Box 43, Soviet and Related Problems

8 Thomas Powers, *The Man who Kept the Secrets: Richard Helms and the CIA* (New York, 1979), 413–14; Ray Cline, *Secrets, Spies, and Scholars* (Washington, DC, 1976), 163–4

9 289th NSC meeting, 28 June 1956, US DDRS, 1997 2802

10 Budapest to State Department, Despatch 421, 27 April 1956, FRUS, 1955–1957, XXV, 155. See also Budapest to State Department, Despatch 430, 24 May 1956, FRUS, 1955–1957, XXV, 169

11 289th NSC meeting, 28 June 1956, US DDRS, 1987 1632

12 Nickels to Gullion, 8 April 1960, US DDRS, 1986 3110

13 Radio Free Europe Special Guidance 26, 6 April 1956, US DDRS, 1991 923

14 NSC 5608/1, 18 July 1956, US DDRS, 1992 2686

15 290th NSC meeting, 5 July 1956, US DDRS, 1997 2722; Foster Dulles to Eisenhower, 9 Sep-tember 1956, cited in John Louis Gaddis, "The Unexpected John Foster Dulles," in Richard Immerman (ed.), *John Foster Dulles and the Diplomacy of the Cold War* (Princeton, NJ, 1990), 65

16 NSC 5608/1 18 July 1956, US DDRS, 1992 2686, and Appendix to NSC 5608/1, 18 July 1956, US DDRS, 1993 2271. See also Lay memorandum, 7 August 1956, US DDRS, 1990 2046

17 Briefing on NSC agenda item, "US Policy toward East Germany," 4 September 1956, US DDRS, 1986 2933

18 Appendix to NSC 5608/1, undated, USNA, Department of State, Lot 63 D 351, Records Relat-ing to State Department Participation in the OCB and the NSC, 1947–1963, Box 88, NSC 5608

19 290th NSC meeting, 5 July 1956, US DDRS, 1997 2722

20 Jackson daily log, 7 May 1956, DDE, Jackson Papers, Box 56, Log 1956

21 Murphy to Foster Dulles, 11 July 1956, USNA, Department of State, Lot 63 D 351, Records Relating to State Department Participation in the OCB and the NSC, 1947–1963, Box 88, NSC 5608

22 Griffith to Galantiere, 2 December 1955, US DDRS, 1991 724

23 Walker to Jackson, 1 June 1956, DDE, Jackson Papers, Box 45, FEC Correspondence through 1956, Basic (2)

24 Nickels to Gullion, 8 April 1960, US DDRS, 1986 3110; "Actions Taken and Planned Regarding Poznan Demonstrations," 3 August 1956, US DDRS, 1986 3553

25 Egan to Shepardson, undated, US DDRS, 1989 2970

26 "Actions Taken and Planned Regarding Poznan Demonstrations," 3 August 1956, US DDRS, 1986 3553

27 Ranft to Egan, 2 July, US DDRS, 1989 2771

28 Jackson to Dougherty, 7 September 1956, DDE, Jackson Papers, Box 39

29 Radio Free Europe, Office of the Director, Guidance 1317, 2 July 1956, US DDRS, 1989 2770

30 Egan to Shepardson, undated, US DDRS, 1989 2970

31 Cited in Nickels to Gullion, 8 April 1960, US DDRS, 1986 3110

32 Ranft to Egan, 2 July 1956, US DDRS, 1989 2771; State Department press release, 2 July 1956, USNA, Department of State, Lot 59 D 233, Miscellaneous Office Files of the Assistant Secretary of State for European Affairs, 1943–1957, Box 29, Hungary and Poland

33 Dulles to Dulles telephone call, 28 June 1956, FRUS,1955–1957, XXV, 181

34 Secretary of State's Staff Meeting, 29 June 1956, FRUS 1955–1957, XXV, 182–3

35 Free Europe Committee report, 3 October 1956, DDE, Jackson Papers, Box 44, FEC Correspondence through 1956, Basic (1)

36 "Observations on Memorandum of the International Rescue Committee," 3 August 1956, US DDRS, 1992 820

37 Kaplan to Allen Dulles, 10 August 1956, DDE, Jackson Papers, Box 52, Ka–Ki, Miscellaneous

38 "Czechoslovakia," undated (1956), DDE, Jackson Papers, Box 44, FEC Correspondence through 1956, Basic (1)

39 "Hungary," 11 October 1956, DDE, Jackson Papers, Box 44, FEC Correspondence through 1956, Basic (1)

40 See Freers to Elbrick, 31 October 1956, USNA, Department of State, Lot 59 D 233, Miscellaneous Office Files of the Assistant Secretary of State for European Affairs, 1943–1957, Box 29

41 Freers to Elbrick, 31 October 1956, USNA, Department of State, Lot 59 D 233, Miscellaneous Office Files of the Assistant Secretary of State for European Affairs, 1943–1957, Box 29, Hungary and Poland; Nickels to Gullion, 8 April 1960, US DDRS, 1986 3110

42 "Radio Free Europe and the Hungarian Uprisings," undated, DDE, Jackson Papers, Box 44, FEC Correspondence through 1956, Basic (1)

43 Foster Dulles interview, CBS Television, *Face the Nation*, 21 October 1956

44 D'Alessandro to Zorthian, 24 October 1956, FRUS, 1955–1957, XXV, 274–5. See Gary Rawnsley, *Radio Diplomacy and Propaganda: The BBC and Voice of America in International Politics, 1956–1964* (Basingstoke, 1995), 73 and 79–80, for discussion of VOA broadcasts during the crisis

45 Nowak to Hazelhoff, 27 August 1959, US DDRS, 1989 2777

46 Cited in "Radio Free Europe and the Hungarian Uprisings," undated, DDE, Jackson Papers, Box 44, Free Europe Committee through 1956 Correspondence, Basic (1)

47 Janus, "Special Commentary #3," DDE, Jackson Papers, Box 44, Free Europe Committee through 1956 Correspondence, Basic (1)

48 Burton Hersh, *The Old Boys: The American Elite and the Origins of the CIA* (New York, 1992), 399–400

49 Cited in "Radio Free Europe and the Hungarian Uprisings," undated, DDE, Jackson Papers, Box 44, Free Europe Committee through 1956 Correspondence, Basic (1). See also FRUS, 1955–1957, XXV, 265

50 Address by Foster Dulles, 27 October 1956, FRUS, 1955–1957, XXV, 317–18

51 "Calling Communists," 25 October 1956, DDE, Jackson Papers, Box 44, Free Europe Committee through 1956 Correspondence, Basic (1)

52 Janus, "Special Commentary #1," 29 October 1956, DDE, Jackson Papers, Box 44, Free Europe Committee through 1956 Correspondence, Basic (1); Balazs Balogh, "To the Uprising Workers," 24 October 1956, DDE, Jackson Papers, Box 44, Free Europe Committee through 1956 Correspondence, Basic (1)

53 Cited in Walter Ridder, "Our Propaganda in Hungary," *New Republic*, 17 December 1956

54 Condon to Egan, 1 March 1957, US DDRS, 1991 1287

55 NSC 5616, "US Policy toward Developments in Poland and Hungary," 31 October 1956, US DDRS, 1987 2177

56 Emmet Hughes, *The Ordeal of Power: A Political Memoir of the Eisenhower Years* (New York, 1963), 220

57 Rawnsley, *Radio Diplomacy and Propaganda*, 79

58 NSC 5616, "US Policy toward Developments in Poland and Hungary," 31 October 1956, USNA, Department of State, Lot 62 D 430, Records Relating to State Department Participation in the OCB and the NSC, 1947–1963, Box 89, NSC 5616

59 302nd NSC meeting, 1 November 1956, DDE, Ann Whitman Series, National Security Council, Box 8

60 Eisenhower statement, 2 November 1956, USNA, Department of State, Lot 66 D 487, PPS Office Files 1956, Box 109, Hungary

61 Quoted in David Wise and Thomas B. Ross, *The Invisible Government* (New York, 1964), 348

62 Quoted in Wise and Ross, *The Invisible Government*, 349. See also Rawnsley, *Radio Diplomacy and Propaganda*, 67

63 John Ranelagh, *The Agency: The Rise and Decline of the CIA* (New York, 1987), 305–6

64 Evan Thomas, *The Very Best Men: Four who Dared in the Early Years of the CIA* (New York, 1995), 146

65 303rd NSC meeting, 8 November 1956, DDE, Ann Whitman Series, National Security Council, Box 8

66 Cited in Ridder, "Our Propaganda in Hungary"

67 "Peter," "Hungary and the UN," 3 November 1956, and Radio Free Europe Border Reports, "Report of an Austrian Journalist," DDE, Jackson Papers, Box 44, Free Europe Committee through 1956 Correspondence, Basic (1)

68 "Special Report N-5," 8 November 1956, DDE, Jackson Papers, Box 44, Free Europe Committee through 1956 Correspondence, Basic (1)

69 "Messages from Dr Fabian," 7 November 1956, DDE, Jackson Papers, Box 42, Dr Bela Fabian

70 Intelligence Notes, 27 December 1956, US DDRS, 1992 1628

71 Jackson paper in Eisenhower to Jackson, 23 November 1956, *Office Files*, Reel 18

72 305th NSC meeting, 30 November 1956, *Minutes*, Reel 1

73 Aide-memoire on Free Europe Committee, 6 March 1961, US DDRS, 1989 2896

74 Cord Meyer, *Facing Reality: From World Federalism to the CIA* (New York, 1980), 130

75 Staff Notes #69, 30 January 1957, *Diaries*, Reel 10. One participant in the uprising, a bricklayer, recalled more than 50 years later: "Radio Free Europe said, 'Hang on three weeks, three more weeks, we come in, we help you.' So we fight for the last bullet, the last drop of blood

we was holding on to. And what happened – they was lying to us. Nobody came." (Aniko Vadja interview in BBC Television, *The Cold War*, Part 7, 7 November 1998)

76 Cited in Anthony J. Cavendish, "Rebels Bitter, Beg for Arms – Not Words," *San Francisco Chronicle*, 13 November 1956. Wisner went to the border between Austria and Hungary and had to tell refugees that the United States would provide no aid. He cabled Allen Dulles succinctly, "Discussion with refugees shows some criticism of RFE broadcasts into Hungary." Within days, Wisner would break down from the strain of developments and his belief that the CIA "had done a lot to inspire and encourage the event". (Thomas, *The Very Best Men*, 147)

77 Budapest to State Department, Cable 324, 19 November 1956, FRUS, 1955–1957, XXV, 472–3. See also 53rd Special Committee on Poland and Hungary meeting, 30 November 1956, FRUS, 1955–1957, XXV, 490–5

78 Intelligence Notes, 6 November 1956, US DDRS, 1994 1694; Robert Murphy, *Diplomat among Warriors* (London, 964), 522; Cord Meyer oral history, 13 October 1981, Hoover Institution, Sig Mickelson Collection, Audiotape 31; Meyer, *Facing Reality*, 128–30. In November 1956 Meyer wrote a post-mortem for Allen Dulles to give to Eisenhower. While defending RFE, the report made telling admissions: "A few of the scripts reviewed do indicate that RFE occasionally went beyond the authorized factual broadcasting of the demands of the patriot radio stations within Hungary to identify itself with these demands and to urge their achievement. . . . There was some evidence of auttempts by RFE to provide tactical advice to the patriots as to the course the rebellion should take and the individuals best qualified to lead it." (Quoted in John Prados, *Presidents' Secret Wars: CIA and Pentagon Covert Operations from World War II to Iranscam* (New York, 1986), 125)

79 Intelligence Notes, 20 November 1956, US DDRS, 1994 1695

80 Note to Editor of Radio Free Europe, 29 November 1956, DDE, Jackson Papers, Box 44, Free Europe Committee through 1956 Correspondence, Basic (1)

81 Cited in Nickels to Gullion, 8 April 1960, US DDRS, 1986 3110

82 "Policy Guidance to Radio Free Europe," 4 December 1956, USNA, Department of State, Lot 62 D 430, Records Relating to State Department Participation in the OCB and the NSC, 1947–1963, Box 10, OCB Luncheon Items 1956

83 Ridder, "Our Propaganda in Hungary." In 1960 C. D. Jackson acknowledged to another committee investigating information services, "While the charge of inciting to revolt was largely disproven, the mere fact that we were broadcasting to the Hungarian people was considered an 'implicit' promise to help them." (Staff meeting of President's Committee on Information Activities Abroad, 25 April 1960, US DDRS, 1991 1065)

84 Eisenhower–Foster Dulles phone call, 9 November 1956, *Diaries*, Reel 10

85 White House meeting with Congressional leaders, 9 November 1956, *Diaries*, Reel 10

86 Cited in Annex to NSC 5616/2, 19 November 1956, US DDRS, 1987 2178. See also MacArthur–Goodpaster briefing of Eisenhower, 13 November 1956, FRUS, 1955–1957, XXV, 435, and forty-sixth Special Committee on Poland and Hungary meeting, 13 November 1956, FRUS, 1955–1957, XXV, 436

87 Sarrazac-Soulage to Jackson, 9 November 1956, *Office Files*, Reel 18

88 Eisenhower to Jackson, 19 November 1956, *Diaries*, Reel 10

89 Eisenhower–Hoover meeting, 19 November 1956, *Diaries*, Reel 10

90 Jackson to Luce, 26 November 1956, DDE, Jackson Papers, Box 41, Eisenhower, Correspondence through 1956 (1)

15

Freedom's legacy

The aftermath of Hungary lingered within the Administration. The activists had accepted the quelling of the revolution, but they sought any measure to show "the Kremlin has been rocked to its foundations, its mystique shattered, and its omnipotence revealed as brute force".[1] Proposals included dropping food from balloons,[2] but little more was done than taking up Darryl Zanuck's offer to make a film about the Hungarian refugees.[3]

C. D. Jackson took up the cudgels in February 1957 with a letter to the National Security Advisor, Robert Cutler. He chided, "I think it is pretty dreadful that the whole Free World, led by the US, seems to have only one slogan for the people behind the Iron Curtain – 'Don't be Courageous'," and then insisted on a "positive rather than a negative approach" with an initiative similar to the 60-day programme in the aftermath of the East German uprising of 1953.[4] Cutler's reply, crafted after consultation with Allen Dulles and the new Under-secretary of State, Christian Herter, was devastating: "There are obvious differences in today's world from the world of several years ago, in terms of risk and weapons and power positions, to mention some, and we ourselves may not be as electric as once we were."[5] Jackson wrote another psychological warrior in desperation:

> What I find . . . fascinating is that, with so much evidence of sullen unhappiness, with the startling evidence of economic bankruptcy presented by the bond repudiation, with the satellite situation in the most precarious balance, with confused disillusionment evident in the communist organizations around the world – all adding up to the unmistakable fact that the current management does not seem to be on top of the situation – we appear once again to be ready to fall for the soft talk. Will we ever learn?[6]

The story played out to anticlimax in late 1957 with the submission of a UN subcommittee's report on Hungary and debates over the accreditation of the "official" Hungarian delegation. The labelling of the report as "interim" diluted its impact, and the official delegation was eventually seated.[7] Ironically, Eisenhower was writing C. D. Jackson at the same time:

How much I miss you – your imagination, your energy, and your refreshing point of view. In these days, when seemingly the problems have been multiplied a million-fold, I often wish that I had someone around, like yourself, who is willing to tackle a large problem, eager to think it through, and to come up with a concrete suggestion for a coordinated plan of attack (and not merely another speech by me!).[8]

When Imre Nagy and his former Defense Minister were executed in July 1958, US exploitation was limited to distributing news of the event, along with copies of books like Nagy's *On Communism* and documentaries on the revolution.[9]

The issue of liberation had been resolved, not by the National Security Council but by the Soviet tanks rumbling through Budapest. Foster Dulles explained to the President, "A 'showdown' with Russia would not have more than one chance in three of working and two chances out of three in making global war inevitable. . . . We must rely on the basic soundness of our position and the growth of internal difficulties within the Soviet orbit."[10] Addressing the National Security Council in February 1957, Eisenhower issued the ritual disclaimer, "In the recent case of Hungary, we were accused by large sections of the world press of having actually inspired the Hungarian revolt, which was of course wholly untrue," before resolving, "It would be wise to make our policy with respect to such revolts clear in the present paper."[11] Foster Dulles confirmed to the British Foreign Secretary, "The best course is to promote peaceful evolution among the satellites away from the USSR," even though "he did not feel . . . that we could condemn those who have died for their freedom in Hungary as they were martyrs for a great cause".[12]

The shift in US policy was evident by the autumn of 1957. Official broadcasts to the Soviet orbit were governed by the edict that "evolution, not revolution, [was] the only programming policy now justified by political realities and audience temper". The message would be shaped by the audience's desire for "realism" rather than "hope". Not only would US services avoid a "strongly anti-communist line", they would remember that some populations took pride in the accomplishments of their countries since 1945.[13] A report for the National Security Council on Eastern European leaders in exile damned the CIA for an "unwarrantably optimistic picture of the present and future role of the Russian anti-Communist emigration. It fails to mention the relatively low calibre of the post-World War II emigration, and the fact that defections often have occurred through sordid rather than ideological motivation."[14] The NSC resolved in May 1958 that "flexible US courses of action, involving inducements as well as probing actions and pressures, [were] required". US officials would not work as closely with the "national committees" that had been central to "private" efforts like those of the Free Europe Committee (FEC), since "there [was] no evidence that émigré politicians [had] any significant following in their homelands". Even "the use of US Government broadcast facilities to convey message of exiled leaders" would be discouraged.[15] In short, "dominated peoples should seek their goals gradually".[16]

The Administration put its hope instead in the development of economic links and cultural contacts with Eastern European countries. Eisenhower told the Foreign Minister of West Germany that "the 'law of gravity' in politics would draw the Eastern countries toward the West and . . . the liberation of the Satellites".[17] The National Security Council's Planning Board called for "a more positive initiative by increasing its efforts . . . to influence changes in the Soviet Bloc through expanded exchanges and cotacts, liberalized multilateral trade controls, etc."[18]

The effort focused on the "liberal" Government that had taken power in Poland after the protests of 1956. The Operations Coordinating Board concluded that US economic aid "should facilitate Polish trade with the West, promote industrial decentralization, freedom of labor, and agricultural decollectivization, and reduce Soviet Union power to manipulate Poland". Information programmes would "influence the new Polish leaders to continue . . . reforms that are conducive to the attainment of US objectives" while "avoiding any material that (1) invites, or treats as desirable, resort to violence; (2) appears to justify changes in Poland as being inspired from without or that the US seeks military, economic, or political advantage for itself or its allies in an independent Poland".[19] By early 1958, the US Government had provided $55 million in loans and $138 million in agricultural commodities to Poland, liberalized export controls, and encouraged voluntary agencies to start distribution programmes. Polish jamming of US broadcasts had been stopped and Warsaw gave tacit consent to the dissemination of "information" material provided it was not attributed to the US Information Agency. The move towards political liberalisation had slowed as popular enthusiasm for further reforms waned; however, it was agreed that "US interests [were] best served by a semi-independent Poland with a potential for evolving toward full independence by gradual means".[20]

A subsequent review of "US Policy toward the Soviet-dominated Nations in Eastern Europe" reiterated the hope of evolution. It concluded that, "despite Soviet efforts to enforce rigid ideological conformity", changes in Poland, the influence of Yugoslavia's "independent" Communism, and Soviet failure to establish a broad base of support "continued to afford moderate opportunities over a long term for the US".[21] Liberation had been replaced by the gradual approach, since "any meaningful assessment of the effectiveness of US policy may be possible only after the efforts and experience of several years".[22]

Not everyone in the "private" network sponsored by the Government had given up on the break-up of the Soviet bloc in the near future. A 1960 presidential committee noted that the "issues between State Department and CIA" over "private" radio operations "were still very much alive".[23] The Free Europe Committee clung to the tenet "that the great historical trends of our time favor the triumph of freedom over communism" to sustain the general aim of "fortifying in all audiences a sense of national identity and purpose, stimulating thereby pressures toward national independence and government with the consent of the governed".[24] It even established a subsidary, Assembly of Captive European Nations, to "help keep frustrated East European exiles busy".[25] The Free Europe Committee's work was paralleled by groups like the American Friends of the Captive Nations, whose executive committee included Leo Cherne, the head of the International Rescue Committee, Angier Biddle Duke, *Reader's Digest* editor Eugene Lyons, the scholar Moshe Decter, and Mrs Kim Roosevelt, the wife of one of the CIA's most famous operatives.[26] Donors like Time Inc. made contributions to cover cuts in the FEC's covert budget.[27]

Yet these "private" efforts would inevitably be restricted by the ebbing support from Washington's policy-makers. Activists like C. D. Jackson continued to press their former colleagues in the Government to "subtly revive, via RFE and Radio Liberation, the concept of liberation for the satellite countries",[28] but their voices were increasingly isolated. On occasion, Jackson's correspondents would sound a conciliatory note – Allen Dulles, for example, wrote, "I fully agree that we should move from the defensive to the offensive, and not let K[hrushchev] and Company feel that they can push us around without stirring up some trouble in their own backyard"[29] – but they always retreated from action. Shortly before his death in 1964, Jackson wrote bitterly, "I consider it shockingly gullible of the sentimental and emotional and generous American people to keep on making ... talk about keeping hope alive behind the Iron Curtain while actually preparing to abandon these people in return for some phony deal on Berlin or some other friction point."[30]

The future of psychological strategy did not lie in liberation. The decade-long crusade for freedom did have a significant legacy but, ironically, it lay in US policy towards the areas that were already "free". Both the organization and the nature of American operations, molded by the ideological imperative, would be devoted to the maintenance of the "free world", even if in practice this meant associating the US with repression and dictatorship rather than individual progress and democracy.

Eisenhower told the National Security Council in November 1954 that it "must think of our policy in Latin America as chiefly designed to play a part in the cold war against our enemies. Russia would shortly step into any vacuum if we allowed one to develop in Latin America."[31] After the *coup* in Guatemala, the US began to implement "Militant Liberty" throughout the region, with a working group of the Operations Coordinating Board supervising the implementation of the strategy through economic, diplomatic, military, and propaganda measures. Through "all appropriate attributable and non-attributable action", the United States obtained the understanding by "political parties, church, armed forces, labour, students and youth, intellectuals and educators, businessmen, women, agrarian elements, and key local groups . . . of the subversive, conspiratorial, fraudulent, and brutal nature of communist action, and of its overriding ulterior purpose to service Soviet Bloc intervention at the sacrifice of the welfare of the people of the country". This was contrasted with "the intellectual, technological, and social dynamism of the US".[32]

In practice, this pursuit of freedom came not from economic and political reforms, but from alliances with anti-Communist dictatorships. Secretary of the Treasury George Humphrey cut through the veneer of ideology to state, "Wherever a dictator was replaced, Communists gained. In [his] opinion, the US should back strong men in Latin American governments." His honest assessment merely brought platitudes from Nelson Rockefeller that "in the long run, the US must encourage the growth of democracies in Latin America if communism is to be defeated in the area" and from Eisenhower that "if power lies with the people, then there will be no aggressive war".[33] Richard Nixon's tale to the National Security Council after his Latin American trip of March 1955 was revealing: while "Guatemala had endured ten years of virtual Communist government", the new President of Guatemala, Castillo Armas, was "a good man with good intentions. . . . He had said to [me], in effect, 'Tell me what you want me to do and I will do it'." Similarly, Nicaraguan strongman Luis Somoza "really desires to do what the US wants him to do".[34]

The Operations Coordinating Board feigned ignorance of the realities of US policy, claiming "increased unfounded charges . . . that the US was supporting dictatorships".[35] The President found a different way to reconcile the ideology of "freedom" and the undemocratic side of anti-Communism. He cited "the odd character of the Somoza dictatorship in Nicaragua – a dictatorship which seems to permit a great many freedoms to flourish".[36] Meanwhile the Administration could complain that democracy was hindered because "many Latin Americans could not distinguish between people's capitalism in the American style and old-fashioned capitalist imperialism".[37] Foster Dulles noted "in recent years a tremendous surge in the direction of popular government by peoples who have practically no capacity for self-government and indeed are like children in facing this problem"; the situation was ripe for Communist exploitation.[38] The National Security Council was warned that the freely elected government in Venezuela contained "as many as six actual Communists or fellow-travellers" and that there "were no plans to face up to the Communist menace".[39]

Venezuela eventually mended its fences with Washington and was allowed to continue its path to freedom; Fidel Castro in Cuba became the new threat to US principles. Cuba might not be "Communist-dominated" but Communists had penetrated trade unions and the armed forces. Moreover, Castro had shown "singularly bad behavior" in accepting an invitation to speak to US newspaper editors without informing the State Department and had "behaved badly enough ... [by] holding up so-called US imperialism as the greatest enemy of Cuba and as the great obstacle to all the reforms".[40]

Allen Dulles's solution was to treat "the new Cuban officials ... more or less like children. They had to be led rather than rebuffed. If they were rebuffed, like children, they were capable of doing almost anything."[41] By the end of 1959, however, even he was acknowledging "a number of things in the covert field [that] could be done which might help the situation in Cuba".[42] Within three months, that number of things would include plans for the assassination of Castro and an uprising within Cuba.[43]

These visions of freedom and Communism also affected US policy in the Middle East. Ironically, US plans to overthrow the Egyptian government in 1956 were not motivated by the belief that President Gamal Abdel Nasser was tied to Moscow; they were linked instead with Arab–Israeli disputes, Anglo-Egyptian friction, and tensions within the Arab world. The Eisenhower Doctrine of 1957 asserted, however, that the United States had to defend Middle Eastern States "from any country controlled by international Communism".[44] Allen Dulles and Foster Dulles revived the programme to topple the Syrian regime by assuring Eisenhower "of a dangerous and classic pattern" in which "the country [would] fall under the control of International Communism and become a Soviet satellite, whose destinies are directed from Moscow".[45] The Iraqi revolution of 1958 led to Foster Dulles's conclusion that "the real authority behind the Government of Iraq was being exercised by Nasser and behind Nasser by the USSR".[46] Persistent warnings followed from the CIA, supported by Vice-President Nixon and Secretary of Defense McElroy, that "the Communists [were] today the only dynamic and well-organized element in Baghdad"[47]; the US embassy in Baghdad recorded in horror that "things had reached a point where the Communist Party actually signed statements and manifestos openly".[48] The NSC's Special Group for covert operations accordingly studied proposals "to avoid a Communist takeover". While the situation was never quite right for a US-backed *coup*, "contingency plans" were constantly "updated and coordinated with [Britain] in deep secrecy".[49]

Africa, long neglected by both the Truman and Eisenhower Administrations except for the North African rim, was brought on to the agenda with Vice-President Richard Nixon's visit to the continent in early 1957 and his conclusion, "We must look most carefully at our information output which, I suspect, is by no means as effective as that being disseminated by the Communists."[50] Washington's grappling with new notions of "freedom" was epitomized by Eisenhower's confession to the National Security Council that "he would like to be on the side of the natives" and put his hope in "a recent movie which had stressed the theme that the black man, under the influence of religion, was taking a more realistic view of the situation".[51] The problem, according to a Government report, was that "the Spirit of 1776 was running wild throughout the area. The various states and colonies want independence now, whether they are ready for it or not. In some respects, this phenomenon was rather terrifying."[52] The Secretary of Commerce, Maurice Stans, added tactfully, "Many Africans still belonged in the trees."[53] Once again Allen Dulles resolved matters by telling the National Security Council, "In Africa ... the Communists will clothe themselves in Islamic, racist, anti-racist, or nationalist clothing." When Eisenhower raised the potential objection that the tenets of Islam were anti-Communist, he was assured by Allen Dulles's deputy, Charles Cabell, that Islamic influence "could be manipulated in favor of Communism as, for example, in Egypt today".[54]

It was in Asia that the US campaign for "hearts and minds" would have its most lasting effect. Even after the crises of 1956, the United States clung to the illusion of a liberated China. Rejecting a call from the Bureau of the Budget to "make clear to the Government of the Republic of China that ... our future military and economic assistance programs will not be premised on the assumption of the GRC's return to power on the mainland", Foster Dulles told the National Security Council, "It was indeed only this hope of a return to mainland China that sustained morale on Taiwan, even if the hope was remote." This remote hope was not only for appearances; it was central to the ideological battle: "The reason these small island and peninsular countries [in Asia] maintain their will to freedom is because of their hope that Communist China will one day blow up. Nor was this to be thought altogether a forlorn hope. ... What had happened in Hungary and Poland could conceivably happen in Communist China." The President agreed with Foster Dulles's judgement that, "if all hope of a Nationalist return to the mainland were to be destroyed, the US would lose the whole show in the Far East".[55]

The US position contributed to a second crisis over the offshore islands in 1958. Communist shelling led to "firm and forceful steps" by the United States, including the rapid deployment of military forces and an increase in aid to Taiwan. Washington balked at overt support for a Chinese Nationalist attack on the mainland and tried to "ensure that the [Nationalists] continued to eschew use of the islands for provocative actions" but left the issue open with an ambiguous communiqué, agreed between Foster Dulles and Chiang Kai-shek, that the overthrow of Peking would be achieved "principally by political means".[56]

Gordon Gray, now the National Security Advisor, persisted with the aggressive line, complaining, "Our basic national security policy now calls for efforts to exploit differences between the Soviet Union and Communist China. ... I believe that we are doing virtually nothing to implement this policy." He asked for guidance on "whether we would be prepared to give support to the rebelling forces and to what extent and under what conditions".[57] The Eisenhower Administration continued to vacillate until the end of its term, but officials assessed in mid-1960, "Given the dictatorial nature of the Communist regime, the harsh domestic policies it is following, and the serious economic problems with which it must deal, the possibility that a large-scale revolt against Communist rule may break out with little warning cannot be ruled out."[58] The President, visiting Taiwan, was briefed to check Chiang Kai-shek's desire for paratroop drops into the mainland but to restate the position, "We are convinced that the day will come when all China will again be free."[59]

The fear of a Communist take-over, under the influence of Moscow and/or Peking, of any other Asian country led to a black comedy in Indonesia, where the nationalist government of Sukarno had emerged in the early 1950s. Ironically Richard Nixon, the committed foe of Communism, had told the National Security Council up to January 1954 that Sukarno was "the greatest and most able leader" in the Far East. Although Sukarno was "naive about Communism", he would "attempt as long as he lives to prevent Indonesia from going Communist".[60] For Nixon, he was "our main card, and it is a good card, it is a strong card, because he is a strong man".[61] Within a year, however, Allen Dulles was reporting that "the [Indonesian] government was losing its grip"[62] and Eisenhower was asking, "Why the hell did we ever urge the Dutch to get out of Indonesia?"[63] Quick approval was supposedly given to a CIA program to provide $4 million to a "progressive" Muslim party in elections in autumn 1955.[64]

There was a partial reconciliation in spring 1956, with Sukarno's visit to the United States publicized to "practically every village" for "enhanced US prestige",[65] but as the Indonesian leader maintained a "neutralist" position and, according to Allen Dulles, "instituted 'guided democracy' along Soviet lines"[66], the Administration inevitably supported a rebellion. Frank Wisner told his staff, "If some plan to do this were not forthcoming, Santa might fill our stockings with assignments for far worse jobs."[67] The effort ended in ignominy in 1958 when a US pilot, Allen Pope, was shot down and captured by Indonesian forces. Embarrassed by revelations of their backing of the insurrection, the Eisenhower Administration immediately suspended operations. Troops loyal to Sukarno took control within weeks.

Failure in Indonesia did not deter the United States from increasing its role in the Asian theater; to the contrary, the Eisenhower Administration redoubled its resolve to demonstrate the strength of a "free" Asia in Indochina. Economic and military aid to South Vietnam was increased and the covert programme to destabilize the North Vietnamese Government was maintained. Project Action was devised "to strengthen the Central Government of Premier Diem by teaching the Vietnamese the concepts of the Free World Way".[68] But as evidence emerged that Diem's leadership did not follow the model set by US values, the Eisenhower Administration developed more and more convoluted explanations of its defence of freedom:

While [Diem] has been criticized for his concept of a benevolently authoritarian form of government, his insistence on absolute loyalty to himself as head of the government, his egoism and intransigence, he is also widely respected for his dedication, his unquestioned integrity, and his personal courage.

He feels that Vietnam, in its present situation and given its own heritage, is not yet ready for a democratic government as it is known in the West. His concept is one of a benevolent authoritarianism and many of the more reprehensible aspects of that philosophy he views as essential means to an ultimate good end. The President feels that more important than individual and political freedom as such, as never to be interfered with by them, are economic security, justice, and an opportunity for the individual to develop his true worth to society. At present he believes that the Vietnamese people are not the best judges of what is good for them and that, although the government should work for and elicit their support, it should direct them and not be directed by them.[69]

Only in 1971, as freedom's war was ending in domestic division and defeat overseas, could the State Department's Lucius Battle reflect: "The policy of opposing communism around the globe was an oversold, overfollowed policy. It should have been tested a little more carefully earlier, and the American public prepared for it. But the same sorts of speeches were still being made, the same kind of arguments were still being made advanced in the early 1960s that were advanced in the late 1940s."[70]

Notes

1 Jackson to Hadley, 30 November 1956, DDE, Jackson Papers, Box 48, Arthur Hadley
2 Jackson to Braden, 7 January 1957, DDE, Jackson Papers, Box 25, Bm–Bo, Miscellaneous
3 Voorhees to Adams, 5 January 1957, *Office Files*, Reel 1
4 Jackson to Cutler, 26 February 1957, DDE, Jackson Papers, Box 37, General Robert Cutler
5 Cutler to Jackson, 27 February 1957, DDE, Jackson Papers, Box 37, General Robert Cutler
6 Jackson to Dougherty, 24 April 1957, DDE, Jackson Papers, Box 39, W. H. Dougherty
7 Jackson to Allen Dulles, 11 December 1957, *Office Files*, Reel 18; OCB Committee on Reconvened UN General Assembly on Hungary, 19 July 1957, US DDRS, 1992 1603
8 Eisenhower to Jackson, 21 October 1957, *Office Files*, Reel 18
9 Report on Exploitation of Hungarian Situation, 23 July 1958, US DDRS, 1990 1103
10 Cited in Hanes to Bowie, 5 December 1956, USNA, Department of State, Policy Planning Staff Office Files, Box 106, Foreign Policy
11 313th National Security Council meeting, 21 February 1957, *Minutes*, Frame 860
12 Foster Dulles–Lloyd meeting, 22 March 1957, US DDRS, 1992 163
13 Report of Chairman of fourth Annual Conference on US Broadcasting to the Soviet Orbit, 9 September 1957, US DDRS, 1986 2369
14 Richards to Egner, 28 February 1957, USNA, Department of State, Records Relating to State Department Participation in the OCB and the NSC, 1947–1963, Box 48, Miscellaneous
15 NSC 5811/1, "US Policy toward the Soviet-dominated Nations in Eastern Europe," 24 May 1958, US DDRS, 1990 2041
16 Briefing on Policy toward Soviet-dominated Nations of Eastern Europe, 21 May 1958, US DDRS, 1990 317
17 Eisenhower–Von Brentano meeting, 7 March 1957, US DDRS, 1994 176

18 Draft NSC Planning Board summary of NSC 5810, 29 April 1958, US DDRS, 1991 1471
19 OCB memorandum, "Operation Guidance with Respect to Poland," 2 April 1957, US DDRS, 1992 536. See also Rewey to Trivers, 7 March 1957, US DDRS, 1989 1124
20 NSC 5808/1, "US Policy toward Poland," US DDRS, 1989 970
21 OCB report on NSC 5811/1, 7 January 1959, US DDRS, 1989 954
22 OCB report on NSC 5811/1, 15 July 1959, US DDRS, 1989 955
23 Staff meeting of President's Committee on International Information Activities, 25 April 1960, US DDRS, 1991 1065
24 Richardson to Board of Directors, 2 December 1963, DDE, Jackson Papers, Box 43, Free Europe Committee 1963
25 "The ACEN," 1 July 1963, DDE, Jackson Papers, Box 43, Free Europe Committee 1963
26 Emmet to Jackson, 9 March 1961, DDE, Jackson Papers, Box 42, Chris Emmet
27 Jackson to Streibert, 18 December 1963, DDE, Jackson Papers, Box 43, Free Europe Committee 1963
28 Jackson to Allen Dulles, 25 March 1959, DDE, Jackson Papers, Box 40, Allen Dulles
29 Allen Dulles to Jackson, 31 March 1959, DDE, Jackson Papers, Box 40, Allen Dulles
30 Jackson to Steele, 17 June 1963, DDE, Jackson Papers, Box 43, Free Europe Committee 1963
31 224th NSC meeting, 15 November 1954, *Minutes*, 1st Supplement, Reel 3
32 Melbourne to Board Assistants, 5 April 1956, US DDRS, 1991 2172. The first "field test" in Ecuador "demonstrated that State and Defense do have materials of great value in the psychological phase of cold war – if we could just use them with a purpose". (Cutler to Foster Dulles, 16 October 1954, US DDRS, 1979 416B)
33 237th NSC meeting, 17 February 1955, US DDRS, 1986 3432
34 240th NSC meeting, 10 March 1955, US DDRS, 1986 3386
35 OCB report on US Policy toward Latin America, 21 May 1958, US DDRS, 1987 2185
36 409th NSC meeting, 4 June 1959, US DDRS, 1990 971
37 366th NSC meeting, 22 May 1958, US DDRS, 1990 325
38 369th NSC meeting, 19 June 1958, US DDRS, 1990 327
39 358th NSC meeting, 13 March 1958, US DDRS, 1990 358
40 400th NSC meeting, 26 March 1959, US DDRS, 1990 950
41 396th NSC meeting, 12 February 1959, US DDRS, 1990 930
42 429th NSC meeting, 16 December 1959, US DDRS, 1990 884
43 "A Program of Covert Action against the Covert Regime," 16 March 1960, US DDRS, 1990 3004
44 *Public Papers of the President 1957*, 6–16
45 Foster Dulles to Eisenhower, 20 August 1957, US DDRS, 1987 2094
46 373rd NSC meeting, 24 July 1958, US DDRS, 1990 330
47 399th NSC meeting, 12 March 1959, US DDRS, 1990 1018
48 405th NSC meeting, 7 May 1959, US DDRS, 1990 910
49 432nd NSC meeting, 14 January 1960, US DDRS, 1991 1946. For a more complex reading of ideology and US foreign policy in the Middle East, see Scott Lucas, "The Limits of Ideology: US Foreign Policy and Arab Nationalism in the Early Cold War," in D. Ryan (ed.), *The United States and Decolonisation* (London, 1999)
50 Report on Richard Nixon visit to Africa 28 February–21 March 1957, 5 April 1957, *Minutes*, Reel 2. The State Department finally established a Bureau of African Affairs later in 1957. See Hoskins memorandum, 20 August 1957, US DDRS, 1997 678
51 375th NSC meeting, 7 August 1958, US DDRS, 1992 315
52 365th NSC meeting, 8 May 1958, US DDRS, 1990 298
53 432nd NSC meeting, 14 January 1960, US DDRS, 1991 1946
54 335th NSC meeting, 22 August 1957, US DDRS, 1987 964
55 338th NSC meeting, 3 October 1957, US DDRS, 1997 3375

56 OCB report on US Policy toward Taiwan, 15 April 1959, US DDRS, 1987 865
57 Gray to Under-secretary of State, 14 January 1959, US DDRS, 1987 1065
58 Briefing for Eisenhower's Far East trip, 6 June 1960, US DDRS, 1987 489
59 Briefing for Eisenhower's Far East trip, 8 June 1960, US DDRS, 1987 488
60 177th NSC meeting, 23 December 1953, *Minutes*, 1st Supplement, Reel 3
61 Nixon report, 8 January 1954, US DDRS, 1992 137
62 220th NSC meeting, 28 October 1954, US DDRS, 1986 2061
63 226th NSC meeting, 1 December 1954, US DDRS, 1986 2077
64 John Prados, *Presidents' Secret Wars: CIA and Pentagon Covert Operations from World War II to Iranscam* (New York, 1986), 132
65 Walter Hixson, *Parting the Curtain: Propaganda, Culture, and the Cold War, 1945–1961* (New York, 1997), 127
66 322nd NSC meeting, 10 May 1957, US DDRS, 1987 846
67 Prados, *Presidents' Secret Wars*, 132
68 "Guidance for Appropriate Agencies Participating in the Application of Project Action with Respect to Vietnam," undated, US DDRS, 1990 2586
69 Briefing book for May 1957 visit of Diem, undated, US DDRS, 1987 2950
70 Lucius Battle oral history, 23 June 1971, HST, Oral History Collection

CONCLUSION

Ensuring We're Number One

Superficially, Dwight Eisenhower would give way in 1961 to a younger President with a different background, a different style, and a different political party. The Kennedy Administration also restructured the organisation for policy-making, abolishing the Operations Coordinating Board and preferring informal meetings of an "inner circle" of advisors to the formal mechanism of the National Security Council. Yet, in the words of Kennedy's first inaugural address, there was an important continuity: "Let every nation know, whether it wishes us well or ill, that we shall pay any price, bear any burden, meet any hardship, support any friend, oppose any foe, in order to assure the survival and the success of liberty."[1]

The national security of the United States was never produced solely by geopolitical strategy or by the search for economic hegemony. As Deborah Welch Larson noted in her study of the Truman Administration:

> Vital interests are usually defined as those values for which a nation is willing to go to war. There are no geographic factors or commonly understood objective criteria for determining whether an interest is vital; it is a matter of human judgement. In the post-war period, until the disillusioning experience of Vietnam, the United States adopted an expansive conception of its security requirements to include a world substantially made over in its own image.[2]

In his more telling comments to the National Security Council, Eisenhower came close to acknowledging the abstract nature of "interest": "Of course he was willing to go to any lengths to defend the vital interests of the US, but as soon as you attempted to define what these vital interests were, you got into an argument."[3]

The value of the ideological approach was that it overcame any troublesome ambiguities in the definition of these interests. It wasn't a question of "American" values but of the United States exalting and defending "universal" values. A 1956 planning guide for the Operations Coordinating Board emphasized, "Caution must be exercised to avoid any appearance of a line that freedom is uniquely American. These values are . . . epitomized by the preamble to the Charter of the United Nations, and to the Constitutions of the

Philippines, Burma, and India."[4] Five years after Harry Truman's speech before
the American Society of Newspaper Editors, Eisenhower told the same body:

> Our forefathers did not claim to have discovered novel principles. They looked on
> their findings as universal values, the common property of all mankind. . . .
>   These ideas of freedom are still the truly revolutionary political principles abroad
> in the world. They appeal to the timeless aspirations of mankind. In some regions
> they flourish; in some they are officially outlawed. But everywhere, to some degree,
> they stir and inspire humanity.[5]

So the United States could be seen as the positive force in the world, addressing Henry Cabot Lodge's concern that "the world knows we are against colo-
nialism but often it wonders what specific things we are for".[6] Exalting
"freedom", it could castigate the Soviet promotion of "peace", with annoy-
ing consequences such as calls for US disarmament or for high-level negotiations, as "a cover whereby evil men can perpetrate diabolical wrongs".[7] Even
after the collapse of hopes of liberation, the National Security Council sustained this notion of US values. For example, the revision of national security
policy in 1958 reiterated:

> The spiritual, moral, and material posture of the US rests upon established princi-
> ples which have been asserted and defended throughout the history of the Repub-
> lic. The genius, strength, and promise of America are founded in the dedication of
> its people and government to the dignity, equality, and freedom of the human being
> under God. These concepts and our institutions which nourish and maintain them
> with justice are the bulwark of our free society and the basis of the respect and lead-
> ership which have been accorded our nation by the peoples of the world.
>   Our constant aim at home is to preserve the liberties, expand the individual
> opportunities, and enrich the lives of our people. Our goal abroad must be to strive
> unceasingly, in concert with other nations, for peace and security and to establish
> our nation firmly as the pioneer in breaking through to new levels of human achieve-
> ments and well-being.[8]

The United States must continue to combat "the determination and ability of
the hostile Soviet and Chinese Communist regimes to direct their political and
ideological influence and their rapidly growing military and economic strength
toward shifting the power balance away from the West and, ultimately, toward
achieving world domination".[9]

Of course, the notion of "freedom" was highly elastic in application. The
Truman Doctrine had no difficulties in labeling the Greek and Turkish
Governments as free, a tenuous conclusion to draw in 1947. After 1948, successive Administrations would always cope with "the difficult task of supporting the continued independence of Yugoslavia but in doing so treat Tito
for what he is, that is a communist dictator".[10] Years later US officials tried
to maintain that Nicaraguan President Luis Somoza had started a "trend
toward a more democratic type of government" while complaining that

Somoza was "still viewed by many liberal Latin Americans with disfavor" and that US liberals were claiming "that the US favors dictatorships".[11] Only George Humphrey, the Secretary of the Treasury, was honest enough to accept, "We should . . . stop talking so much about democracy, and make it clear that we are quite willing to support dictatorships of the right if their policies are pro-American." Eisenhower added, "You mean they're OK if they're our SOBs."[12]

This relativism would be overcome, however, by recourse to an American guardianship of universal values, as Louis Hartz put it, "an impulse to impose Locke everywhere".[13] The Jackson Committee concluded in 1953:

[US] peoples share fundamental beliefs and basic values with millions of the men and women [that] the US is attempting to win to its side: belief in God, belief in individual and national freedom and the right to ownership of property, belief in a peaceful world and in the common humanity of men and nations compromising their differences and cooperating in the United Nations. Sharing such beliefs, the US has partners and allies abroad, not subservient satellites held by force.[14]

Thus the United States had the inherent advantage of being able to provide political and moral instruction to others. Eisenhower explained, "If we had not trained the Filipinos in democracy for some 40 years, the Philippines would now have become a military dictatorship," suggesting that this training become a model for US programmes in countries like Japan.[15] There might be limits on the ideological campaign – in the President's opinion, "If you go and live with . . . Arabs, you will find that they simply cannot understand our ideas of freedom or human dignity"[16] – but in the end US "information" would prevail. Eisenhower noted that "we could use a little more money for [US Information Agency] much more effectively than we could use a lot more money on our foreign aid programs".[17] A decade later, he was advising Lyndon Johnson about Vietnam, "The US could take a half-billion dollars out of other governmental programs and put it into [the information service] with greater advantage. There is too little understanding around the world of the record of the US through recent years, e.g., from 1920 onward."[18]

There were occasions when US leaders recognized that the battle for hearts and minds might not be as simple as trumpeting America's moral qualities. Eisenhower worried in 1955, "It was very alarming to observe how the Communists had managed to identify themselves and their purposes with . . . emergent nationalism. The US, on the other hand, had failed to utilize this new spirit of nationalism in its own interest."[19] In the later years of his presidency, he would note the role of economics in choices of political systems: "We were constantly hearing stories of Communist penetration and domination in countries all over the world. He wondered how many Communists had been won over to communism by bad living conditions and how many by the hope of power. We apparently did not have the secret of appealing to people in the same way."[20] Even as his Administration was plotting the demise of Fidel Castro and increasing aid to the Shah of Iran, the President pondered:

> The US has been working since 1947 and very intensively since 1953 to achieve stability throughout the world but instead seems to have been faced with unrest and unhappiness. . . . Could we continue to support governments which would not carry out land reform and which would not lay out any constructive program for the betterment of the situation?[21]

These concerns might lead to economic aid and eventually programmes like the Alliance for Progress but, in the end, US officials always returned to a fundamental conception of freedom's fight with Communism. As Foster Dulles told British Prime Minister Harold Macmillan in 1957:

> These days may well be decisive for the next few centuries. For several hundred years the Christian West had dominated the world. Now it faced the question of whether that kind of society would be submerged for several centuries by "Christian Socialism". . . .
> We must go on the offensive, not by copying the force, terror and fraud of the Soviets but by showing the fruits which freedom can produce.[22]

Eisenhower was even blunter with British officials, "He would rather be atomized than communized. . . . The only justifiable cause for war is the maintenance of freedom and rights."[23]

In this linkage of ideology and economics, pursuit of land reform was always secondary to support of an anti-Communist regime and understanding of nationalism would await the removal of Governments perceived as hostile to the Free World. A 1960 presidential committee offered a tangled justification for denying self-determination in the name of "freedom":

> Today we are facing a revolt of the have-nots, particularly in Asia, Africa, and Latin America. We have to deal with the Lumumbas, the Castros, and the Sukarnos. They are largely immune to persuasion: they basically prefer a governmental system based on the dictatorship of the proletariat with themselves as dictators, rather than any democratic, representative type of free government.
> In parts of Asia, Africa, and Latin America . . . anything resembling free government has broken down. . . . If . . . military or personal dictatorships collapse, the people, left without strong leadership, are highly vulnerable to the appeals, both economic and political, of Moscow and Peiping.[24]

So the 1951 exposition of a domino theory in which the loss of Indochina would lead to the fall of Burma, Thailand, and Malaya to Chinese Communism[25] would remain the paradigm for the US Government for more than 20 years. Walt Rostow, the MIT academic turned Deputy National Security Advisor, told President Johnson in 1964:

> Unless we can find a way to make our enormous military and political power effective soon . . . the US will suffer a major defeat as a world power, we shall lose

our leverage in the Western Pacific, the Indian subcontinent will become vulnerable ..., the Communists will extend the technique of Wars of National Liberation into other continents, and these will be consequences, hard to define precisely, which will weaken our position in Western Europe.[26]

Similarly, in Latin America, the rigid division between Free and Communist led not only to the US campaign against Castro but also to the intervention of troops in the Dominican Republic in 1965, a step which ensured that a military junta prevented the restoration of the freely elected Government of Juan Antonio Bosch,[27] and the protracted program to topple Salvador Allende in Chile. The same ideological prism could transform initial assessments of the Sandinista Government in Nicaragua as a movement to remedy "an economy beset with disparities" into a junta "putting Nicaragua well on the road to becoming the first authoritarian Marxist state in Latin America" in which Cuba would have a "major influence".[28]

"Freedom" had shaped official policy in the Cold War but it also had a far more significant effect. The forging of the State–private network from the 1940s would reinforce the pursuit of ideology, not because the Government was imposing a strategy which had to be accepted by the populace but because the interests of officials and those of private organizations coincided in the crusade against Soviet Communism. As the OCB framed it, the Government would "stimulate private support from foundations, citizen groups, and other non-governmental organizations" and "provide such groups with assurances of governmental interest and moral support".[29]

Even after the trauma of Vietnam, the shock of domestic division, and the exposure in 1967 of the CIA's role in "private" operations, the network would be sustained. A Council on Foreign Relations discussion in 1968 paid lip service to the warning of "grave dangers in such activities for our society because of the importance of private institutions" but then emphasized that it supported the Government's conclusion that "situations involving national security interests might arise when such subsidies would become necessary". The problem was not the contradiction between "freedom" and secret Government involvement in private activity; "the basic task [was] to improve the secrecy of covert operations".

A glance at the make-up of the discussion group explains why networks were so resilient. After 20 years of Cold War, the line between State and private had worn very thin. Former high-level CIA officials Robert Amory, Richard Bissell, Frank Lindsay, and Allen Dulles were involved, as was Frank Altschul, the driving force behind Radio Free Europe in its initial years. Two current employees of the State Department were involved and another participant was a former ambassador who had just left department service. Yet there were also "autonomous" individuals from key sectors. Journalist Joseph Kraft, IBM vice-president Eugen Fobini, trade union activist Meyer Bernstein, and academics William Harris, David Truman, Adam Yarmolinsky, and Harry Howe Ransom were all involved. Fittingly the conclusions of the study would be passed to Walt Rostow, the scholar who made his name working with Project Troy and C. D. Jackson before joining the National Security Council staff in the 1960s.[30]

The controversy over covert funding had damaged State–private links in some areas. Continued support for the National Student Association, the focus of the 1967 press revelations, was out of the question with the organization badly damaged by the affair. The women's group, the Committee of Correspondence, dissolved amidst the bitterness of those members "unwitting" of CIA involvement and the inability to find another source of income. US support of the cultural network in Europe, notably through the Congress for Cultural Freedom and journals like *Encounter*, was sharply reduced.

However, the Government's links with key groups like the Free Europe Committee and the Asia Foundation continued. Soon after the 1967 controversy, the State Department's Charles Bohlen and William Bundy assured that they would "write in some dough for the Asia Foundation in their own budget",[31] and funding for the radio services and foundations moved on to an "open" basis in the early 1970s. For example, in 1975 Secretary of State Henry Kissinger made a vigorous appeal to President Gerald Ford to raise the annual grant to the Asia Foundation from $5 million to $7 million.[32] Meanwhile President Ford, while backing the overt funding of Radio Free Europe and Radio Liberty, stubbornly refused to release documents on the two organizations to Congressional investigators.[33]

The prosecution of "freedom's war" would be carried out through these tangible State–private intersections. *Détente* would be undone in part in the 1970s by the challenge of the consultants of 'Team B' to the official CIA estimates on the Soviet threat and the lobbying of the resurrected Committee on the Present Danger.[34] The National Endowment for Democracy would battle the global Communist menace and promote the US vision through projects such as the "establishment of an intellectual review for Chinese students abroad, small grants to the Afghan resistance and Polish Solidarity union for food and clothing, and other grants to democratic-minded groups in Argentina and Guatemala". One journalist made the historical link: "In the 1950s and 1960s the CIA, to a similar end, funnelled secret subsidies to foreign political groups, but the new project's supporters say their campaign will be more successful because all financing will be done in public."[35]

Yet, after a half-century, it can be argued that the lasting significance of "freedom's war" lay not in any specific effort but in the more abstract drive for ideological consensus. Eastern Europe may not have been liberated in the 1950s but there were always other peoples to be defended against the enemy or freed from their captive existence. The crusade could be re-launched through Ronald Reagan's call for "a plan and a hope for the long term – the march of freedom and democracy which will leave Marxism–Leninism on the ash heap of history,"[36] a plan and hope translated into US operations to vanquish Cuban construction workers in Grenada, factions in the Lebanon, Libyan 'madmen', or Nicaraguan Marxists. Even when operations unravelled, as in the Iran-Contra episode, those implicated could escape retribution by invoking the higher authority of freedom's crusade. Colonel Oliver North stood down Congressional inquisitors with the declaration, "I am going to walk from here with my head high . . . because I am proud of what we accomplished. I am proud of the efforts that we made and I am proud of the fight that we fought."[37]

And, even though the Cold War stuttered to a halt and receded into the past, US foreign policy moved to other venues with freedom repackaged as the "New World Order". Strongmen who had previously been on the CIA's payroll to stand firm against Communists or Islamic fundamentalists were transformed into the new threats. Crisis in Panama was succeeded by the Gulf War, which was followed by interventions in Somalia and Haiti, which faded into memory as new dramas arose over evil in Baghdad. The clarion call of the Truman Doctrine of 1947 could always be sounded again, be it through Reagan's denunciation of "the aggressive impulses of an evil empire" or Bill Clinton's State of the Union message in February 1997:

> Fifty years ago, a farsighted America led in creating the institutions that secured victory in the Cold War and built a growing world economy. As a result, today more people than ever embrace our ideals and share our interests. . . . For the first time ever, more people live under democracy than dictatorship, including every nation in our own hemisphere but one – and its day, too, will come. (Applause)[38]

Despite this relentless re-presentation of the American ideology, there is no reason to accept the inevitability of freedom's war.[39] Dissent can seize upon the contradictions in the presentation of "freedom" to challenge policy, as in the case of the protests against US intervention in Vietnam or efforts to curb the "contra" campaign in Nicaragua in the 1980s. Yet this dissent has been limited, not because the populace are coerced into acceptance of Government policy or because they cannot get access to information needed to make an informed judgement, but because they share or acquiesce in notions put forward by the network of State and private organizations. It may not quite be a case of "we have met the enemy and he is us"; however, as long as the consensus of an American supremacy of values goes unchallenged, the United States will march into new battles against new enemies. Louis Hartz's troubling questions about a "fixed, dogmatic liberalism", asked in 1955 as others were proclaiming the American "end of ideology", still await a reply:

> Can a people "born equal" ever understand peoples elsewhere that have to become so? Can it ever understand itself?[40]

Notes

1 A copy of the speech is at http://www.byu.edu/ipt/vlibrary/curriculum
2 Deborah Welch Larson, *Origins of Containment: A Psychological Explanation* (Princeton, NJ, 1985), 348–9
3 221st NSC meeting, 2 November 1954, US DDRS, 1986 2073. Speaking in a public forum in 1974, Director of Central Intelligence William Colby solved the problem with an expansive definition of "national security". Asked, "Do you see any national security threat that would justify any covert operations at this time in a third world country, . . . with no conceivable capacity to endanger the American people here in the United States?" Colby replied, "There are some, yes. . . . By security of the US, I do not mean that the capital will fall tomorrow as a result. I mean the position of the US in the world today and in the world ahead. . . . There are certain things which today are not an immediate danger to the US but if allowed to grow can become a serious problem and consequently a problem to the security of the US." (Colby testimony, 13 September 1974, US DDRS, 1989 7)
4 OCB Ideological Planning Guide, 16 April 1956, US DDRS, 1993 2961
5 Eisenhower to American Society of Newspaper Editors, 21 April 1956, USNA, Department of State, Lot 66 D 487, Policy Planning Staff Office Files, 1956, Box 106, Foreign Policy
6 Lodge memorandum, 3 November 1953, US DDRS, 1994 306
7 Foster Dulles speech to the All-Jesuit Alumni Dinner, 11 April 1955, USNA, Department of State, Lot 66 D 70, Records of the Policy Planning Staff, 1955, Box 94, Foreign Policy. See also E. P. Thompson, *Beyond the Cold War* (London, 1982), 6
8 Lay memorandum on NSC 5810, 5 May 1958, US DDRS, 1980 379A
9 411th NSC meeting, 25 June 1959, US DDRS, 1990 926
10 Taylor memorandum, 11 July 1952, US 1991 598
11 Calhoun to Goodpaster, 30 January 1959, US DDRS, 1987 2808. In 1955, less than a year after the *coup* in Guatemala by US-supported forces based in Honduras, Foster Dulles could tell the National Security Council without irony about another *coup* in Costa Rica that the United States should cooperate with the Organization of American States "to prevent one country as a base of military operations against another". (231st NSC meeting, 13 January 1955, US DDRS, 1991 362.) This self-delusion would continue beyond the Eisenhower Administration. In 1965 the US embassy in Guatemala was upset that "the *New York Times* referred just the other day to 'reactionary military dictatorship . . . denying social justice'. This [is] utter nonsense." (Guatemala City to State Department, Cable 965, US DDRS, 1991 1391)
12 229th NSC meeting, 21 December 1954, US DDRS, 1986 2212. See also the exchange between Humphrey and Eisenhower over Indonesia, culminating in Humphrey's assertion, "He very much preferred dictatorship over the socialist system because at least, in his opinion, dictatorships got things done." Eisenhower assented, "In countries such as Indonesia, some kind of strong leadership was required." (281st NSC meeting, 5 April 1956, US DDRS, 1997 2227)
13 Louis Hartz, *The Liberal Tradition in America* (New York, 1955), 13
14 Jackson Committee report (abridged), undated, US DDRS, 1988 1163
15 410th NSC meeting, 18 June 1959, US DDRS, 1990 832. See also Eisenhower's comments on the Philippines at 244th NSC meeting, 7 April 1955, US DDRS, 1986 3354
16 410th NSC meeting, 18 June 1959, US DDRS, 1990 832
17 267th NSC meeting, 21 November 1955, US DDRS, 1990 2090
18 Eisenhower–Johnson meeting, 17 February 1965, US DDRS, 1990 673. See also White House meeting, 16 May 1965, US DDRS, 1991 1781
19 244th NSC meeting, 7 April 1955, US DDRS, 1986 3354
20 437th NSC meeting, 17 March 1960, US DDRS, 1991 2044
21 449th NSC meeting, 30 June 1960, US DDRS, 1991 2029
22 Dulles–Macmillan meeting, 23 October 1957, US DDRS, 1992 458

23 Eisenhower–Caccia meeting, 16 June 1959, US DDRS, 1992 469

24 Conclusions and Recommendations of the President's Committee on Information Activities Abroad, December 1960, US DDRS, 1990 2211

25 NIE-20, "Resistance of Thailand, Burma, and Malaya to Communist Pressures in the Event of a Communist Victory in Indochina in 1951," 15 March 1951, US DDRS, 1986 3007. See also NSC 124/2 on Southeast Asia, 25 June 1952, US DDRS, 1989 995

26 Rostow to Johnson, 6 June 1964, US DDRS, 1988 3558

27 By 1960 US agencies were pursuing the assassination of Castro and considering, if not implementing, plans to "liquidate" Bosch's predecessor, the military leader Rafael Trujillo. See "Dominican Republic," April 1960, US DDRS, 1989 148, and Eisenhower diary entry, 25 April 1960, US DDRS, 1991 1037

28 National Foreign Assessment Center, "Nicaragua: Slow Rebuilding of a Shattered Economy," 1 January 1981, US DDRS, 1988 1399

29 OCB interdepartmental meeting, 10 July 1957, US DDRS, 1990 582

30 Dillon to Rostow, 22 November 1968, US DDRS, 1989 2326

31 Jessop to Rostow, 27 June 1968, US DDRS, 1990 1074

32 Kissinger to Ford, August 1975, US DDRS, 1990 2837

33 Duval memorandum, 20 November 1975, US DDRS, 1992 1773

34 See John Ranelagh, *The Agency: The Rise and Decline of the CIA* (London, 1986), 622–4; Jerry Sanders, *Peddlers of Crisis: The Committee on the Present Danger and the Politics of Containment* (Boston, MA, 1983)

35 Mark Hosenball, "Party Time for Democratic Crusade," *Sunday Times* (London), 9 December 1984

36 Reagan address to British House of Commons, 8 August 1982, transcript at http://reagan.webteamone.com/speeches/ empires.html

37 "Plain and Simple, Congress is to Blame," *The Times* (London), 10 July 1987

38 "Reagan Calls Soviet Union an Evil Empire," *Guardian*, 9 March 1983; Clinton address at http://www.usis.usemb.se/speeches/stateoft.html

39 See, for example, E. P. Thompson's comment: "The US is the leader of the 'Free World', and the Communists are the Other. They need this Other to establish their own identity, not as blacks or Poles or Irish, but as free Americans"

40 Hartz, *The Liberal Tradition in America*, 9 and 309

Bibliography

Archives

Dwight D. Eisenhower Library, Abilene, Kansas (DDE)
Franklin D. Roosevelt Library, Hyde Park, New York (FDR)
Harry S. Truman Library, Independence, Missouri (HST)
Hoover Institution, Stanford, California
National Security Archives, Washington, DC (NSA)
Public Record Office, Kew, Surrey, Britain (PRO)
Schlesinger Library, Radcliffe College, Cambridge, Massachusetts
Sophia Smith Collection, Smith College, Northampton, Massachusetts
United States National Archives, Washington, DC (USNA)

Primary documents (published)

Documents of the National Security Council 1947–1977 (Frederick, MD: University Publications of America) (*Documents*)
Final Report of the Select Committee to Study Governmental Operations with Respect to Intelligence Activities, *Foreign and Military Intelligence*, Book I, 26 April 1976
Foreign Relations of the United States (FRUS)
Minutes of Meetings of the National Security Council with Special Advisory Reports (Frederick, MD: University Publications of America) (*Minutes*)
National Security Archive, *The US Intelligence Community: Organization, Operations, and Management, 1947–1989* (Alexandria, VA: Chadwyck-Healey)
Office Files of President Dwight D. Eisenhower (Frederick, MD: University Publications of America) (*Office Files*)
Public Papers of the President
The State Department Policy Planning Staff Papers
United States Declassified Document Reference System (Woodbridge, CT, Primary Source) (US DDRS)
United States National Archives, Washington, DC (USNA)
Warner, Michael (ed.). *The CIA under Harry Truman* (Washington, DC: CIA Historical Staff)

Diaries

Ferrell, Robert (ed.). *Eisenhower's Diaries* (London, 1982)
Ferrell, Robert (ed.). *The Diary of James C. Hagerty* (Bloomington, IN, 1983)
Millis, Walter (ed.). *The Forrestal Diaries* (New York, 1951)
Vandenberg (ed.) Arthur H. *The Private Papers of Senator Vandenberg* (Boston, MA, 1952)

Memoirs and biographies

Acheson, Dean. *Present at the Creation* (New York, 1969)

Adams, Sherman. *First-Hand Report* (London, 1961)

Ambrose, Stephen. *Eisenhower the President* (London, 1982)

Beal, J. R. *John Foster Dulles* (New York, 1959)

Bohlen, Charles. *Witness to History* (New York, 1973)

Callahan, David. *Dangerous Capabilities: Paul Nitze and the Cold War* (New York, 1990)

Childs, Marquis. *Eisenhower, Captive Hero* (New York, 1958)

Colby, William. *Honourable Men: My Life in the CIA* (London, 1978)

Crozier, Brian. *Free Agent: The Unseen War, 1941–1991* (London, 1993)

Donovan, Robert. *Eisenhower: The Inside Story* (New York, 1956)

Donovan, Robert. *Conflict and Crisis: The Presidency of Harry S. Truman, 1945–1948* (New York, 1977)

Donovan, Robert. *Tumultuous Years: The Presidency of Harry S. Truman, 1949–1953* (New York, 1982)

Drummond, Roscoe and Coblentz, Gaston. *Duel at the Brink* (London, 1961)

Duberman, Martin B. *Paul Robeson* (New York, 1988)

Eisenhower, Dwight. *The White House Years, Volume 1: Mandate for Change, 1953–1956* (London, 1963)

Eisenhower, Dwight. *The White House Years, Volume 2: Waging Peace, 1956–1961* (London, 1966)

Gelderman, Carol. *Mary McCarthy* (London, 1989)

Gerson, Louis. *John Foster Dulles* (New York, 1967)

Grose, Peter. *Gentleman Spy: The Life of Allen Dulles* (Boston, MA, 1994)

Guhin, Michael. *John Foster Dulles: A Statesman and his Times* (New York, 1972)

Hook, Sidney. *Out of Step: An Unquiet Life in the Twentieth Century* (New York, 1987)

Hughes, Emmet. *The Ordeal of Power: A Political Memoir of the Eisenhower Years* (New York, 1963)

Jones, Joseph. *The Fifteen Weeks* (New York, 1955)

Kennan, George. *Memoirs, 1925–1950* (Boston, MA, 1967)

Kennan, George. *Memoirs, 1950–1963* (London, 1973)

Krock, Arthur. *In the Nation, 1932–1966* (New York, 1966)

Krock, Arthur. *Memoirs* (New York, 1968)

Krupnick, Mark. *Lionel Trilling and the Fate of Cultural Criticism* (Evanston, IL, 1986)

Lyon, Peter. *Eisenhower: Portrait of a Hero* (Boston, MA, 1974)

McCullough, David. *Truman* (New York, 1992)

McGehee, Ralph. *Deadly Deceits: My Twenty-five Years in the CIA* (New York, 1983)

Meyer, Cord. *Facing Reality: From World Federalism to the CIA* (New York, 1980)

Miller, Arthur. *Timebends: A Life* (London, 1987)

Miller, Merle. *Plain Speaking: An Oral Biography of Harry S. Truman* (London, 1976)

Miscamble, Wilson. *George Kennan and the Making of American Foreign Policy, 1945–1950* (Princeton, NJ, 1992)

Mosley, Leonard. *Dulles* (New York, 1978)

Murphy, Robert. *Diplomat among Warriors* (London, 1964)

Nitze, Paul. *From Hiroshima to Glasnost: At the Center of Decision* (New York, 1989)

Oshinsky, David. *A Conspiracy so Immense: The World of Joe McCarthy* (New York, 1983)

Parmet, Herbert. *Eisenhower and the American Crusade* (London, 1972)

Philby, Kim. *My Silent War* (St Albans, 1976)

Phillips, David A. *The Night Watch: Twenty-five Years inside the CIA* (London, 1977)

Powers, Thomas. *The Man who Kept the Secrets: Richard Helms and the CIA* (London, 1979)

Rovere, Richard. *Affairs of State: The Eisenhower Years* (London, 1956)

Schoenbaum, Thomas J. *Waging Peace and War: Dean Rusk in the Truman, Kennedy, and Johnson Years* (New York, 1988)

Smith, Gaddis. *Dean Acheson* (New York, 1972)

Smith, Sally B. *In All his Glory: The Life and Times of William S. Paley and the Birth of Modern Broadcasting* (New York, 1990)

Smith, Walter B. *Moscow Mission, 1946–1949* (London, 1950)

Steel, Ronald. *Walter Lippmann and the American Century* (New York, 1980)

Stephanson, Anders. *Kennan and the Art of Foreign Policy* (Cambridge, MA, 1989)

Swanberg, W. A. *Luce and his Empire* (New York, 1973)

Talbott, Strobe (ed.). *Khrushchev Remembers* (New York, 1971)

Talbott, Strobe. *The Master of the Game: Paul Nitze and the Nuclear Peace* (New York, 1988)

Thomas, Evan. *The Very Best Men: Four who Dared in the Early Years of the CIA* (New York, 1995)

Truman, Harry. *Memoirs: Year of Decisions* (Garden City, NY, 1956)

Wedemeyer, Albert. *Wedemeyer Reports!* (New York, 1958)

Wreszin, Michael. *A Rebel in Defense of Tradition: The Life and Politics of Dwight Macdonald* (New York, 1994)

Books

Agee, Philip. *Inside the Company: CIA Diary* (Harmondsworth, 1975)

Agee, Philip and Wolf, Louis (eds). *Dirty Work: The CIA in Western Europe* (New York, 1983)

Alexander, Charles. *Holding the Line: The Eisenhower Era, 1952–1961* (Bloomington, IN, 1975)

Alexandre, Lauren. *The Voice of America: From Detente to the Reagan Doctrine* (Norwood, NJ, 1988)

Althusser, Louis. *Lenin and Philosophy and Other Essays* (London, 1971)

Ambrose, Stephen and Immerman, Richard. *Ike's Spies* (Garden City, NY, 1981)

Apter, David (ed.). *Ideology and Discontent* (London, 1964)

Aronson, James. *The Press and the Cold War* (Ithaca, NY, 1970)

Bell, Daniel. *The End of Ideology* (New York, 1962)

Bernstein, Barton (ed.). *Politics and Policies of the Truman Administration* (Chicago, 1970)

Bloom, Alexander. *Prodigal Sons: The New York Intellectuals and their World* (New York, 1986)

Bogart, Leo. *Premises for Propaganda: The USIA's Operating Assumptions in the Cold War* (New York, 1976)

Borosage, Robert and Marks, John. *The CIA File* (New York, 1976)

Bower, Tom. *The Red Web: MI6 and the KGB Master Coup* (London, 1993)

Boyer, Paul. *By the Bomb's Early Light: American Thought and Culture at the Dawn of the Atomic Age* (New York, 1985)

Brands, H. W., Jr. *Cold Warriors: Eisenhower's Generation and American Foreign Policy* (New York, 1988)

Brenner, Robert and Reichard, Gary (eds). *Reshaping America: Society and Institutions, 1945–1960* (Columbus, OH, 1982)

Brown, Seyom. *The Faces of Power: Constancy and Change in US Foreign Policy from Truman to Johnson* (New York, 1968)

Browne, Donald. *International Radio Broadcasting: The Limits of the Limitless Medium* (New York, 1982)

Bryson, Lyman *et al. Foundations of World Organization: A Political and Cultural Appraisal* (New York, 1952)

Buckley, William. *Up from Liberalism* (New York, 1959)

Bundy, McGeorge. *Danger and Survival: Choices about the Bomb in the first Fifty Years* (New York, 1988)

Campbell, David. *Writing Security: US Foreign Policy and the Politics of Identity* (Minneapolis, MN, 1992)

Carter, Dale. *The Final Frontier* (London, 1988)

Carter, Dale (ed.). *Cracking the Eisenhower Age: Aspects of Fifties America* (Aarhus, 1992)

Chen, J. *Ideology in United States Foreign Policy: Case Studies in US China Policy* (Westport, CT, 1992)

Chomsky, Noam. *American Power and the New Mandarins* (Harmondsworth, 1969)

Chomsky, Noam. *The Culture of Terrorism* (London, 1988)

Chomsky, Noam and Herman, Edward. *After the Cataclysm: Post-war Indochina and the Reconstruction of Imperial Ideology* (Boston, MA, 1979)

Chomsky, Noam et al. *The Cold War and the University* (New York, 1997)

Clarfield, Gerard and Wiecek, William. *Nuclear America: Military and Civilian Nuclear Power in the United States, 1940–1980* (New York, 1984)

Cline, Ray. *Secrets, Spies, and Scholars* (Washington, DC, 1976)

Coleman, Peter. *The Liberal Conspiracy: The Congress for Cultural Freedom and the Struggle for the Mind of Post-war Europe* (New York, 1989)

Constantine, Alex. *Virtual Government: CIA Mind Control Operations in America* (Venice, CA, 1997)

Cook, Blanche W. *The Declassified Eisenhower: A Divided Legacy* (New York, 1984)

Copeland, Miles. *The Real Spy World* (London, 1978)

Copeland, Miles. *The Game Player: Confessions of the CIA's Original Political Operative* (London, 1989)

Corson, William. *The Armies of Ignorance: The Rise of the American Intelligence Empire* (New York, 1977)

Costigliola, Frank. *France and the United States: The Cold Alliance since World War II* (New York, 1992)

Crossman, Richard (ed.). *The God that Failed* (New York, 1964)

Cumings, Bruce. *The Origins of the Korean War*, Volume 2: *The Roaring of the Cataract, 1947–1950* (Princeton, NJ, 1990)

Dallek, Robert. *The American Style of Foreign Policy: Cultural Politics and Foreign Affairs* (New York, 1983)

Darling, Arthur. *The Central Intelligence Agency: An Instrument of Government, to 1950* (University Park, PA, 1990)

Daugherty, William and Janowitz, Morris (eds), *A Psychological Warfare Casebook* (Baltimore, MD, 1958)

de Santis, Hugh. *The Diplomacy of Silence: The American Foreign Service, the Soviet Union, and the Cold War, 1933–1947* (Chicago, 1980)

Diamond, Sigmund. *Compromised Campus: The Collaboration of Universities with the Intelligence Community, 1945–1955* (New York, 1992)

Divine, Robert. *Eisenhower and the Cold War* (Oxford, 1981)

Dockrill, Saki. *Eisenhower's New-Look National Security Policy, 1953–1961* (London, 1996)

Dulles, Allen. *The Marshall Plan* (Oxford, 1993)

Eagleton, Terry. *Ideology* (London, 1991)

Ellul, Jacques. *Propaganda: The Formation of Men's Attitudes* (New York, 1973)

Faligot, Roger and Krop, Pascal. *La Piscine* (London, 1989)

Fisher, Harold (ed.). *American Research on Russia* (Bloomington, IN, 1959)

Foot, Rosemary. *A Substitute for Victory: The Politics of Peacemaking at the Korean Armistice Talks* (Ithaca, NY, 1990)

Forgacs, David (ed.). *A Gramsci Reader* (London, 1988)

Fortune editors with Davenport, Russell. *USA: The Permanent Revolution* (New York, 1951)

Fossedal, Gregory. *The Democratic Imperative: Exporting the American Revolution* (New York, 1989)

Fowler, Robert Booth. *Believing Skeptics: American Political Intellectuals, 1945–1964* (Westport, CT, 1978)

Freeland, Richard. *The Truman Doctrine and the Origins of McCarthyism* (New York, 1972)

Gaddis, John L. *The United States and the Origins of the Cold War* (New York, 1972)

Gaddis, John L. *Strategies of Containment: A Critical Appraisal of Post-war American National Security Policy* (New York, 1982)

Gaddis, John L. *The Long Peace: Inquiries into the History of the Cold War* (New York, 1987)

Gaddis, John L. *The United States and the End of the Cold War: Implications, Reconsiderations, Provocations* (New York, 1992)

Gaddis, John L. *We Now Know: Rethinking Cold War History* (New York, 1997)

Gellman, Barton. *Contending with Kennan: Toward a Philosophy of American Power* (New York, 1984)

Gleijeses, Piero. *Shattered Hope: The Guatemalan Revolution and the United States, 1944–1954* (Princeton, NJ, 1991)

Graebner, Norman (ed.). *Ideas and Diplomacy: Readings in the Intellectual Tradition of American Foreign Policy* (New York, 1964)

Gravel, Mike (ed.). *The Pentagon Papers* (Boston, MA, 1971)

Greenstein, Fred. *The Hidden-Hand Presidency* (New York, 1982)

Gremion, Pierre. *Intelligence de l'anti-communisme: le Congrès pour la liberté de la culture à Paris* (Paris, 1995)

Guilbaut, Serge. *How New York stole the Idea of Modern Art: Abstract Expressionism, Freedom, and the Cold War* (Chicago, 1983)

Halberstam, David. *The Powers that Be* (New York, 1979)

Halle, Louis. *The Cold War as History* (London, 1967)

Harbutt, Fraser. *The Iron Curtain: Churchill, America, and the Origins of the Cold War* (New York, 1986)

Harriman, Averell. *Peace with Russia* (London, 1960)

Hartz, Louis. *The Liberal Tradition in America* (New York, 1955)

Heald, Morrell and Kaplan, Lawrence. *Culture and Diplomacy: The American Experience* (Westport, CT, 1979)

Hersh, Burton. *The Old Boys: The American Elite and the Origins of the CIA* (New York, 1992)

Hinds, Lynn Boyd and Windt, Theodore Otto. *The Cold War as Rhetoric: The Beginnings, 1945–1950* (New York, 1991)

Hixson, Walter. *Parting the Curtain: Propaganda, Culture, and the Cold War, 1945–1961* (New York, 1997)

Hogan, Michael and Paterson, Thomas (eds). *Explaining the History of American Foreign Relations* (Cambridge, UK, 1991)

Hogan, Michael. *The Marshall Plan: America, Britain, and the Reconstruction of Western Europe 1947–1952* (Cambridge, UK, 1987)

Hogan, Michael (ed.). *The End of the Cold War: Its Meaning and Implications* (Cambridge, UK, 1992)

Holt, Robert. *Radio Free Europe* (Minneapolis, MN, 1958)

Hoopes, Townsend. *The Devil and John Foster Dulles* (Boston, MA, 1973)

Horne, Gerald. *Black and Red: W. E. B. DuBois and the Afro-American Response to the Cold War, 1944–1963* (Albany, NY, 1986)

Horowitz, David (ed.). *Corporations and the Cold War* (New York, 1969)

Hunt, Michael. *Ideology and US Foreign Policy* (New Haven, CT, 1987)

Immerman, Richard. *The CIA in Guatemala: The Foreign Policy of Intervention* (Austin, TX, 1982)

Immerman, Richard (ed.), *John Foster Dulles and the Diplomacy of the Cold War* (Princeton, NJ, 1990)

Jeffreys-Jones, Rhodri. *The CIA and American Democracy* (New Haven, CT, 1989)

Jones, Howard. *A New Kind of War* (New York, 1980)

Kahin, Audrey and Kahin, George. *Subversion as Foreign Policy: The Secret Eisenhower and Dulles Debacle in Indonesia* (New York, 1995)

Kammen, Michael. *Spheres of Liberty: Changing Perceptions of Liberty in American Culture* (Madison, WI, 1986)

Kaplan, Amy and Pease, Donald (eds). *Cultures of US Imperialism* (Durham, NC, 1993)

Karnow, Stanley. *Vietnam: A History* (London, 1994)

Kennan, George. *American Diplomacy 1900–1950* (Chicago, 1951)

Kennedy-Pipes, Caroline. *Stalin's Cold War: Soviet Strategies in Europe, 1943 to 1956* (Manchester, 1995)

Koen, Ross. *The China Lobby in American Politics* (New York, 1960)

Kolko, Gabriel and Kolko, Joyce. *The Limits of Power* (New York, 1972)

Kuniholm, Bruce. *The Origins of the Cold War in the Near East: Great Power Conflict and Diplomacy in Iran, Turkey, and Greece* (Princeton, NJ, 1980)

Lafever, Ernest. *Ethics and US Foreign Policy* (Cleveland, OH, 1957)

Larson, Deborah Welch. *Origins of Containment: A Psychological Explanation* (Princeton, NJ, 1985)

Lasch, Christopher. *The Agony of the American Left* (London, 1968)

Leary, William. (ed.), *The Central Intelligence Agency: History and Documents* (University, AL, 1984)

Leffler, Melvyn. *A Preponderance of Power: National Security, the Truman Administration, and the Cold War* (Stanford, CA, 1992)

Leffler, Melvyn. *The Specter of Communism: The United States and the Origins of the Cold War, 1917–1953* (New York, 1994)

Liebovich, Louis. *The Press and the Cold War, 1944–1947* (New York, 1988)

Leibowitz, Nathan. *Daniel Bell and the Agony of Modern Liberalism* (Westport, CT, 1985)

Levering, Ralph. *The Public and American Foreign Policy, 1918–1978* (New York, 1978)

Lipsitz, George. *Time Passages: Collective Memory and American Popular Culture* (Minneapolis, MN, 1990)

Lipsitz, George. *Rainbow at Midnight: Labor and Culture in the 1940s* (Urbana, IL, 1994)

Lundestad, Geir. *The American "Empire"* (Oxford, 1990)

McCormick, Thomas. *America's Half-Century: United States Foreign Policy in the Cold War* (Baltimore, MD, 1989)

Macdonald, J. Fred. *Television and the Red Menace: The Video Road to Vietnam* (New York, 1985)

Marchetti, Victor and Marks, John. *The CIA and the Cult of Intelligence* (New York, 1974)

Mastny, Vojtech. *The Cold War and Soviet Insecurity: The Stalin Years* (New York, 1996)

May, Ernest and Neustadt, Richard. *Thinking in Time: The Uses of History for Decision-makers* (New York, 1986)

May, Ernest (ed.). *American Cold War Strategy: Interpreting NSC 68* (Boston, MA, 1993)

May, Lary (ed.). *Recasting America: Culture and Politics in the Age of Cold War* (Chicago, 1989)

Melanson, Richard and Thompson, Kenneth (eds.). *Foreign Policy and Domestic Consensus* (Lanham, MD, 1985)

Mickelson, Sig. *America's Other Voices: The Story of Radio Free Europe and Radio Liberation* (New York, 1983)

Miller, James. *The United States and Italy, 1940–1950: The Politics and Diplomacy of Stabilization* (Chapel Hill, NC, 1986)

Nadel, Alan. *Containment Culture* (Durham, NC, 1995)

Navasky, Victor. *Naming Names* (New York, 1980)

Ninkovich, Frank. *The Diplomacy of Ideas: US Foreign Policy and Cultural Relations, 1938–1950* (Cambridge, UK, 1981)

Novick, Peter. *That Noble Dream: The Objectivity Question and the American Historical Profession* (New York, 1988)

Panfilov, A. F. and Karchevsky, Yuri. *Subversion by Radio: Radio Free Europe and Radio Liberty* (Moscow, 1974)

Parenti, Michael. *The Anti-Communist Impulse* (New York, 1969)

Paterson, Thomas. *Meeting the Communist Threat from Truman to Reagan* (New York, 1988)

Peck, James (ed.). *The Chomsky Reader* (New York, 1987)

Pells, Richard. *The Liberal Mind in a Conservative Age: American Intellectuals in the 1940s and 1950s* (New York, 1985)

Pells, Richard. *Not Like Us: How Europeans Have Loved, Hated, and Transformed American Culture* (New York, 1997)

Peterson, H. C. *Propaganda for War: The Campaign against American Neutrality, 1914–1917* (Norman, OK, 1938)

Pirsein, Robert. *The Voice of America* (New York, 1979)

Pisani, Sallie. *The CIA and the Marshall Plan* (Edinburgh, 1991)

Prados, John. *Presidents' Secret Wars: CIA and Pentagon Covert Operations from World War II to Iranscam* (New York, 1986)

Ranelagh, John. *The Agency: The Rise and Decline of the CIA* (New York, 1987)

Rawnsley, Gary. *Radio Diplomacy and Propaganda: The BBC and Voice of America in International Politics, 1956–1964* (Basingstoke, 1995)

Robbins, Christopher. *Air America* (New York, 1979)

Rorty, James and Decter, Moshe. *McCarthy and the Communists* (Boston, MA, 1954)

Rositzke, Harry. *The CIA's Secret Operations: Espionage, Counter-espionage and Covert Action* (New York, 1977)

Ross, Andrew. *No Respect: Intellectuals and Popular Culture* (New York, 1989)

Ross, Irwin. *The Loneliest Campaign* (New York, 1968)

Rostow, W. W. *Europe after Stalin: Eisenhower's Three Decisions of March 11, 1953* (Austin, TX, 1982)

Roszak, Theodore (ed.). *The Dissenting Academy* (Harmondsworth, 1969)

Sanders, Jerry. *Peddlers of Crisis: The Committee on the Present Danger and the Politics of Containment* (Boston, MA, 1983)

Schlesinger, Arthur, Jr. *The Crisis of Confidence* (London, 1969)

Schlesinger, Arthur, Jr. *The Cycles of American History* (Boston, MA, 1986)

Schlesinger, Arthur, Jr. *The Vital Center* (New York, 1988 [1949])

Schrecker, Ellen. *No Ivory Tower: McCarthyism and the Universities* (Oxford, 1986)

Schuman, Frederick. *The Cold War: Retrospect and Prospect* (Baton Rouge, LA, 1967)

Short, K. R. M. (ed.). *Western Broadcasting over the Iron Curtain* (London, 1986)

Shulman, Holly C. *The Voice of America: Propaganda and Democracy, 1941–1945* (Madison, WI, 1990)

Simpson, Christopher. *Blowback: America's Recruitment of Nazis and its Effects on the Cold War* (New York, 1988)

Sobchack, Vivian (ed.). *The Persistence of History: Cinema, TV, and the Historical Event* (New York, 1996)

Soley, Lawrence C. *Radio Warfare: OSS and CIA Subversive Propaganda* (New York, 1989)

Sorenson, Thomas. *The Word War: The Story of American Propaganda* (New York, 1968)

Stone, I. F. *The Truman Era* (London, 1953)

Stone, I. F. *The Haunted Fifties, 1953–1963* (Boston, MA, 1989 [1964])

Suid, Lawrence (ed.). *Film and Propaganda in America: A Documentary History, Volume III, 1945 and After* (New York, 1991)

Theoharis, Athan. *Seeds of Repression: Harry S. Truman and the Origins of McCarthyism* (Chicago, 1971)

Thompson, E. P. *The Poverty of Theory and Other Essays* (London, 1978)

Thompson, E. P. *Beyond the Cold War* (London, 1982)

Treverton, Gregory *Covert Action: The CIA and the Limits of American Intervention in the Post-war World* (London, 1989)

Wagnleitner, Reinhold. *Coca-Colonization and the Cold War: The American Cultural Mission in Austria after World War II* (Chapel Hill, NC, 1994)

Wala, Michael. *The Committee on Foreign Relations and American Foreign Policy in the Early Cold War* (Oxford, 1994)

Wald, Alan. *The New York Intellectuals: The Rise and Decline of the Anti-Stalinist Left from the 1930s to the 1980s* (Chapel Hill, NC, 1987)

Wall, Irwin. *The U.S. and the Making of Post-war France, 1945–1954* (Cambridge, UK, 1991)

Whitfield, Stephen. *The Culture of the Cold War* (Baltimore, MD, 1991)

Whitton, John and Larson, Arthur. *Propaganda: Towards Disarmament in the War of Words* (Dobbs Ferry, NY, 1964)

Wilford, Hugh. *The New York Intellectuals: From Vanguard to Institution* (Manchester, 1995)

Williams, William A. *The Tragedy of American Diplomacy* (New York, 1991 [1959])

Winks, Robin. *Cloak and Gown: Scholars in the Secret War, 1939–1961* (New York, 1987)

Wise, David and Ross, Thomas B. *The Invisible Government* (New York, 1964)

Yergin, Daniel. *Shattered Peace: The Origins of the Cold War and the National Security State* (Boston, MA, 1977)

Young, John. *Winston Churchill's Last Campaign: Britain and the Cold War, 1951–1955* (Oxford, 1996)

Zubok, Vadislav and Pleshakov, Constantine. *Inside the Kremlin's Cold War* (Cambridge, MA, 1996)

Articles

Adler, Les K. and Paterson, Thomas G. "Red Fascism: The Merger of Nazi Germany and Soviet Russia in the American Image of Totalitarianism, 1930's–1950's," *American Historical Review* (April 1970)

Aldrich, Richard. "OSS, CIA and European Unity: The American Committee on United Europe, 1948–60," *Diplomacy and Statecraft* (March 1997)

Barrett, Edward. "American Values and the Ideological Struggle: Truth is our Weapon," in Kenneth Thompson (ed.), *Institutions for Projecting American Values Abroad*: Volume III (Lanham, MD, 1983)

Bekes, Csaba. "New Findings of the 1956 Hungarian Revolution," *Cold War International History Project Bulletin* (fall 1992)

Biddle, Tami D. "Handling the Soviet Threat: 'Project Control' and the Debate on American Strategy in the Early Cold War Years," *Journal of Strategic Studies* (September 1989)

Braden, Thomas. "I'm Glad the CIA is Immoral," *Saturday Evening Post*, 20 May 1967

Carew, Anthony. "Labour and the Marshall Plan," in Charles Maier (ed.), *The Cold War in Europe* (New York, 1991)

Cook, Blanche W. "First Comes the Lie: C. D. Jackson and Political Warfare," *Radical History Review* (spring 1984)

Cumings, Bruce. " 'Revising Postrevisionism', or, The Poverty of Theory in Diplomatic History," *Diplomatic History* (fall 1993)

Dravis, Michael. "Storming Fortress Albania: American Covert Operations in Microcosm, 1949–1954," *Intelligence and National Security* (October 1992)

Dudziak, Mary. "Desegregation as a Cold War Imperative," *Stanford Law Review*, November 1988

Ellwood, David W. "The 1948 Elections in Italy: A Cold War Propaganda Battle," *Historical Journal of Film, Radio, and Television* (1993)

Filippelli, "Luigi Antonini, the Italian-American Labor Council, and Cold War Politics in Italy," *Labour History* (winter 1992)

Gaddis, John Louis. "The Unexpected John Foster Dulles," in Richard Immerman (ed.), *John Foster Dulles and the Diplomacy of the Cold War* (Princeton, NJ, 1990)

Gaddis, John L. and Nitze, Paul. "NSC 68 and the Soviet Threat Reconsidered," *International Security* (spring 1980)

Garson, Robert. "American Foreign Policy and the Limits of Power: Eastern Europe 1946–1950," *Journal of Contemporary History* (1986)

Gluchowski, L. W. "Poland, 1956: Khrushchev, Gomulka, and the 'Polish October'," *Cold War International History Project Bulletin* (spring 1995)

Griffith, Robert. "Dwight D. Eisenhower and the Corporate Commonwealth," *American Historical Review* (February 1982)

Griffith, Robert. "The Selling of America: The Advertising Council and American Politics, 1942–1960," *Business History Review* (autumn 1983)

Heuser, Beatrice. "Covert Action within British and American Concepts of Containment, 1948–1951," in Richard Aldrich (ed.), *British Intelligence, Strategy and the Cold War, 1945–1951* (London, 1992)

Higashi, Sumiko. "Anti-modernism as Historical Representation in a Consumer Culture: Cecil B. DeMille's *The Ten Commandments*, 1923, 1956, 1993," in Vivian Sobchack (ed.), *The Persistence of History: Cinema, Television, and the Historical Event* (New York, 1996)

Ingimundarson, Valur. "Cold War Misperceptions: The Communist and Western Responses to the East German Refugee Crisis in 1953," *Journal of Contemporary History* (July 1994)

Jones, Howard and Woods, Randall. "Origins of the Cold War in Europe and the Near East" (commentaries by Emily Rosenberg, Anders Stephanson, and Barton J. Bernstein), *Diplomatic History* (spring 1993)

Larres, Klaus. "Eisenhower and the First Forty Days after Stalin's Death: The Incompatibility of *Détente* and Political Warfare," *Diplomacy and Statecraft* (July 1995)

Lashmar, Paul. "Killer on the Edge," *New Statesman and Society* (15 September 1995)

Laville, Helen. "The Committee of Correspondence: The CIA and the Funding of Women's Groups, 1952–1967," *Intelligence and National Security* (January 1997)

Laville, Helen and Lucas, Scott. "The American Way: Edith Sampson, the NAACP, and African American Identity in the Cold War," *Diplomatic History* (fall 1996)

Lears, T. Jackson. "The Concept of Cultural Hegemony: Problems and Possibilities," *American Historical Review* (June 1985)

Leffler, Melvyn. "The American Conception of National Security" (commentaries by John L. Gaddis and Bruce Kuniholm), *American Historical Review* (April 1984)

Lieberman, Robbie. "Communism, Peace Activism, and Civil Liberties: From the Waldorf Conference to the Peekskill Riot," *Journal of American Culture* (fall 1995)

Liebich, Andre. "Mensheviks Wage the Cold War," *Journal of Contemporary History* (1995)

Little, Stuart. "The Freedom Train: Citizenship and Post-war Political Culture, 1946–1949," *American Studies* (spring 1993)

Lucas, Scott. "Campaigns of Truth: The Psychological Strategy Board and American Ideology, 1951–1953," *International History Review* (May 1996)

Lucas, Scott. "The Myth of Leadership: Dwight Eisenhower and the Quest for Liberation," in Constantine Pagedas and Thomas Otte (eds), *Personalities, War, and Diplomacy* (Basingstoke, 1997)

Lucas, Scott. "Beyond Diplomatic History: Propaganda, Ideology, and US Foreign Policy," in Gary Rawnsley (ed.), *Cold War Propaganda in the 1950s* (London, 1998)

Lucas, Scott. "The Limits of Ideology: US Foreign Policy and Arab Nationalism in the Early Cold War," in David Ryan (ed.), *The United States and Decolonisation* (London, 1999)

Lucas, Scott. "Appealing the Verdict of Cold War 'History'," *Over Here: Reviews in American Studies* (1999)

Lucas, W. Scott and Morris, C. J. "A Very British Crusade: The Information Research Department and the Beginnings of the Cold War," in Richard Aldrich (ed.), *British Intelligence, Strategy, and the Cold War* (London, 1992)

McCarthy, Kathleen D. "From Cold War to Cultural Development: The International Cultural Activities of the Ford Foundation, 1950–1980," *Daedalus* (winter 1987)

McCauley, Brian. "Hungary and Suez, 1956: The Limits of Soviet and American Power," *Journal of Contemporary History* (October 1981)

McLean, David. "American Nationalism, the China Myth, and the Truman Doctrine: The Question of Accommodation with Peking, 1949–1950," *Diplomatic History* (winter 1986)

Mark, Eduard. "American Policy toward Eastern Europe and the Origins of the Cold War, 1941–1946: An Alternative Explanation," *Journal of American History* (September 1981)

Mathews, Jane de Hart. "Art and Politics in Cold War America," *American Historical Review* (1976)

Matray, James. "Truman's Plan for Victory: National Self-determination and the 38th Parallel Decision in Korea," *Journal of American History* (September 1979)

May, Ernest. "The Cold War," in C. Vann Woodward (ed.), *The Comparative Approach to American History* (New York, 1968)

Mr. X [George Kennan]. "The Sources of Soviet Conduct," *Foreign Affairs* (July 1947)

Nader, Laura. "The Phantom Factor," in Noam Chomsky *et al.*, *The Cold War and the University* (New York, 1997)

Nechell, Allan. "'Truth is our Weapon': Project Troy, Political Warfare, and Government–Academic Relations in the National Security State," *Diplomatic History* (summer 1993)

Ostermann, Christian. "Implementing 'Roll-back': NSC 158," *SHAFR Newsletter* (September 1996)

Parry-Giles, Shawn. "'Camouflaged' Propaganda: The Truman and Eisenhower Administrations' Covert Manipulation of News," *Western Journal of Communication* (April 1996)

Rabe, Stephen. "Eisenhower Revisionism: A Decade of Scholarship," *Diplomatic History* (winter 1993)

Rees, Thomas. "Blunder and Betrayal in the Balkans," *Guardian Weekend*, 10 October 1998

Rollins, Peter. "*Nightmare in Red*: A Cold War View of the Communist Revolution," in John O'Connor (ed.), *American History/American Television: Interpreting the Video Past* (New York, 1983)

Rosenberg, Emily. "'Foreign Affairs' after World War II: Connecting Sexual and International Politics," *Diplomatic History* (winter 1994)

Slotkin, Richard. "Myth and the Production of History," in Sacvan Bercovitch and Myra Jehlen (eds), *Ideology and Classic American Literature* (Cambridge, UK, 1986)

Smith, Geoffrey. "National Security and Personal Isolation: Sex, Gender, and Disease in the Cold War United States," *International History Review* (May 1992)

Stueck, William. "The March to the Yalu: The Perspective from Washington," in Bruce Cumings (ed.), *Child of Conflict: The Korean–American Relationship, 1943–1953* (Seattle, WA, 1983)

Sutton, Francis X. "The Ford Foundation: The Early Years," *Daedalus* (winter 1987)

Thorne, Christopher. "American Political Culture and the End of the Cold War," *Journal of American Studies* (December 1992)

Trout, B. Thomas. "Rhetoric Revisited: Political Legitimation and the Cold War," *International Studies Quarterly* (September 1979)

Van Pelt, Mark. "The Cold War on the Air," *Journal of Popular Culture* (fall 1984)

Wala, Michael. "Selling the Marshall Plan at Home: The Committee for the Marshall Plan to Aid European Recovery," *Diplomatic History* (summer 1986)

Warner, Michael. "The Origins of the Congress of Cultural Freedom, 1949–1950," *Studies in Intelligence* (1995)

Wells, Samuel F., Jr. "Sounding the Tocsin: NSC 68 and the Soviet Threat," *International Security* (fall 1979)

Windmiller, Marshall. "The New American Mandarins," in Theodore Roszak (ed.), *The Dissenting Academy* (Harmondsworth, 1969)

Yoder, Jon. "The United World Federalists: Liberals for Law and Order," in Charles Chatfield (ed.), *Peace Movements in America* (New York, 1973)

Unpublished papers

Belmonte, Laura. "Almost Everyone is a Capitalist: The USIA presents the American Capitalist, 1953–1959," Annual Conference of Society for Historians of American Foreign Relations, 24 June 1994

Belmonte, Laura. "Defining Democracy: Images of Politics in US Propaganda, 1945–1959," Annual Conference of Society for Historians of American Foreign Relations, June 1997

Bernhard, Nancy. "Clearer than Truth: The State Department's Domestic Information Campaigns, 1948–1952," typescript in author's possession

Burstow, Robert. "Sculpture and the Cold War," Aston University, 21 March 1996

Corke, Sarah-Jane. "Bridging the Gap: Containment, Covert Action and the Search for the Missing Link in American Cold War Policy in Eastern Europe, 1948–1953," Annual Conference of Society for Historians of American Foreign Relations, June 1996

Edwards, Jill. "The Cold War and Religion in Truman's Presidency," Annual Conference of Society for Historians of American Foreign Relations, 24 June 1994

Gienow, Jessica. "Bringing Faith to the Pagans: The Awkward Invention of U.S. Journalism and other Cultural Values in Post-war Germany, 1945–1948," paper presented before the Society of Historians of American Foreign Relations, 26 June 1994

Johnstone, Andrew. "Private Interest Groups and the Lend-Lease Debates, 1940–1941," M.Phil. dissertation, University of Birmingham, 1998

Lambert, Emma. "Cultural Cold Warriors? Time Inc. and the Eisenhower Administration," University of Birmingham American and Canadian Studies research seminar, 18 November 1998

Marchio, Jim. "Resistance Potential and Rollback: U.S. Intelligence and the Eisenhower Administration's Policies toward Eastern Europe," Annual Conference of Society for Historians of American Foreign Relations, 24 June 1994

Ostermann, Christian. "The Eisenhower Administration: Psychological Warfare and the East German Uprising of 1953," Annual Conference of Society for Historians of American Foreign Relations, 22 June 1997

Stanley, John P. "The Politics of Persuasion: Radio Free Europe/Radio Liberty and the Limits of American Propaganda," Seniors Honors thesis, Harvard University, 1990

Young, John. "Britain and Liberation," University of Birmingham Modern History Seminar, 7 May 1997

Index